Everyday Spelling

Authors

James Beers • Ronald L. Cramer • W. Dorsey Hammond

Scott Foresman
Addison Wesley

Editorial Offices: Glenview, Illinois • Menlo Park, California
Sales Offices: Reading, Massachusetts • Atlanta, Georgia • Glenview, Illinois
Carrollton, Texas • Menlo Park, California

1-800-552-2259
http://www.sf.aw.com

■ ACKNOWLEDGMENTS

ILLUSTRATIONS

pp. 12, 13, 15, 19, 23, 27, 31, 147, 167Top: Roger Chandler; pp. 12Center, 13C, 13Bottom Right, 38C, 39C, 84, 116, 124: Jared D. Lee; pp. 14, 18, 26, 44, 52, 70, 78, 96, 104, 122, 130, 148, 156: Thomas Kovacs; pp. 16Top Left, 16Center Left: John Holm; p. 17: Gwen Connelly; pp. 21, 29, 30, 56, 66, 82, 90, 91, 93, 97, 101, 105, 108, 109, 129: Randy Chewning; pp. 22, 48, 74, 100, 102, 126, 152: C. K. Poedtke; pp. 24TL, 24CL, 136, 139: Barbara Samanich; pp. 28, 72: Randy Verougstraete; pp. 30, 56, 82, 108, 134, 160: Donna Ingemanson; pp. 32, 106, 132, 165T: Corasue Nicholas; pp. 34, 60, 86, 112TL, 138, 164: Maria Stroster; pp. 38T, 39T: Harry Roolaart; pp. 40, 66, 92, 118, 144: Lloyd Brooks; pp. 42TL, 42CL: Thomas Penna; pp. 43, 133, 160: Margaret Sanfilippo; pp. 46, 142, 143, 145, 149, 153, 157, 161: Susan Keeter; pp. 47, 51, 59, 137, 163: Shelley Dietrichs; pp. 54, 80, 140, 141B, 158, 162: Mary Jones; p. 58: Eldon Doty; pp. 61, 63, 115T, 115B, 155: Paul G. Somers; pp. 62, 73, 81, 103, 150: Joe Rogers; pp. 64, 65, 67, 71, 75, 79, 83: John Stephen Henry; pp. 68, 125, 154: Yoshi Miyake; pp. 60, 69C, 69Bottom, 134, 159: Marianne D. Wallace; p. 76: Melinda Levine; pp. 77, 87, 88, 165B: Richard Syska; pp. 89T, 89B, 94, 166T, 166B: Rebecca D. Brown; pp. 95, 99, 111, 191C: Steven Mach; pp. 98, 112BR, 114, 116, 117, 119, 123, 127, 131, 135: Kathy Petrauskas; p. 113: Paul Sharp; pp. 120, 141T, 323: Terry J. Sirrell; pp. 121, 151: Patti Green; p. 128: Marcy Ramsey; pp. 146, 167B: Larry Frederick; pp. 170, 171T, 171B, 178C, 182C, 182BL, 183Right, 184B, 196C, 203R, 209C, 222C, 223C: Precision Graphics; pp. 171B, 192B, 193TR, 193CB, 199C, 217: Ray Vella; pp. 172C, 173, 223B: Chris Costello; pp. 174T, 186, 194, 206, 207, 226B, 227T, 227C, 227B: Dale Glasgow; pp. 177R, 179C: Stephanie Peterson; pp. 183C, 205: Randy Royter; pp. 184, 185T, 191BR, 210, 211: Greg Harris; pp. 188, 189: Marc Yankus; pp. 200, 201, 202, 203, 204, 224, 225: Alexander & Turner; pp. 208, 209R: Joe De Cerchio; pp. 218, 219: Cary Austin; p. 316: Gil Ashby; p. 318: Walter Stuart; p. 321: Liz Conrad

PHOTOGRAPHS

p. 110: Library of Congress; p. 174Center: Barry Iverson; p. 174Bottom Left: Ray Ellis/Photo Researchers; p. 174Bottom Right: Jane Lewis/Tony Stone Images; p. 175Top: Carole Salman/Superstock; p. 175Center Right: Massimo Borchi/Bruce Coleman, Inc.; p. 175Center Left: Steve Vidler/Superstock; p. 175BR: Rich LaSalle/Tony Stone Images; p. 175BL: A. J. Hewerdine/Bruce Coleman, Inc.; p. 176BL: The Nelson-Atkins Museum of Art, Kansas City, Missouri (Acquired through the generosity of Donald J. and Adele C. Hall, Mr. and Mrs. Herman Robert Sutherland, an anonymous donor, The Nelson Gallery Foundation and the William Rockhill Nelson Trust (by exchange) 87-7.); p. 176BR: Art Resource; p. 177: Lee Boltin; p. 179: Anthony Cassidy/Tony Stone Images; p. 180CL: Eastcott/Mamatiuk/Woodfin Camp & Associates; pp. 180BL, 181C, 185, 220CR: Superstock; p. 180C: The Granger Collection; p. 181TL: John Christiansen from the book *Science & Civilization in China* by Joseph Needham; p. 181TR: Adler Planetarium; p. 181BL: Anthony Cassidy/Tony Stone Images; p. 181BR: Giraudon/Art Resource; p. 185: Penny Tweedie/Woodfin Camp & Associates; p. 186Right: Hugh Sitton/Tony Stone Images; p. 186BL: David Hiser/Tony Stone Images; p. 187TL: Kal Muller/Woodfin Camp & Associates; p. 187BL: Charles Marden Fitch/Superstock; p. 187BR: Bernard Pierre Wolff/Photo Researchers; p. 220CL: NY Morgan Library; p. 220C: The Museum of London, London Wall; p. 221T: Bibliotheque National, Paris; pp. 221C, 258T, 281, 283, 288, 304Bottom: Courtesy NASA; p. 221BL: Art Resource; pp. 254, 256, 257T, 257B, 263, 270, 272, 274T, 275, 279, 282T, 282B, 285T, 285B, 287T, 287B, 291, 300, 301, 302, 311T, 311B: Cynthia Clampitt; 255T: Smithsonian Institution; pp. 259, 310: E. G. Stout; p. 271: Arnold Genthe/Library of Congress; p. 274B: U. S. G. S.; p. 315: The Museum of Modern Art/Film Stills Archive; p. 325: Dale E. Boyer/Photo Researchers; p. 326: The Kobal Collection

All photographs not specifically credited are Scott Foresman - Addison Wesley photographs.

UNIT 1

■ CONTENTS

UNIT 3

■ CONTENTS

UNIT 5

■ CONTENTS

UNIT 6

STRATEGY WORKSHOP................................142
Choosing the Best Strategy

31 MULTISYLLABIC WORDS................................144
Think and Practice Making Connections, Pronunciations
Strategic Spelling Choosing the Best Strategy
Proofreading and Writing An Advertisement
Vocabulary Building Review: Definitions,
  Multicultural Connection: Environment

32 RELATED WORDS 3................................148
Think and Practice Rhymes, Definitions
Strategic Spelling Seeing Meaning Connections
Proofreading and Writing A Description
Vocabulary Building Review: They Said It,
  Word Study: Latin Root

33 LATIN ROOTS 3................................152
Think and Practice Word Association, Syllables
Strategic Spelling Seeing Meaning Connections
Proofreading and Writing A Letter
Vocabulary Building Review: Crossword Puzzle,
  Dictionary: Synonym Studies

34 PREFIXES de-, dis-, non-, un-................................156
Think and Practice Hidden Words, Context Clues
Strategic Spelling Building New Words
Proofreading and Writing A News Article
Vocabulary Building Review: Analogies,
  Word Study: Figurative Language

35 UNUSUAL SPELLINGS................................160
Think and Practice Classifying, Making Inferences
Strategic Spelling Choosing the Best Strategy
Proofreading and Writing A Story
Vocabulary Building Review: Context Clues,
  Word Study: Idioms

36 REVIEW................................164
List Words in Context

8

Cross-Curricular Lessons

■ CONTENTS

✳ FREQUENTLY MISSPELLED WORDS!

Lots of words on your spelling lists are marked with green asterisks ✳. These are the words that are misspelled the most by students your age.*

Pay special attention to these frequently misspelled words as you read, write, and practice your spelling words.

there	they	let's	heard	everyone
a lot	you're	really	different	friends
too	finally	then	everything	everywhere
their	our	usually	again	around
that's	Christmas	we're	believe	everybody
it's	off	went	except	maybe
because	where	sometimes	something	no
don't	Halloween	through	were	restaurant
probably	didn't	which	always	Saturday
they're	until	doesn't	anything	someone
Easter	buy	favorite	especially	there's

* **Research in Action** is a research project conducted in 1990–1993. This list of frequently misspelled words is one result of an analysis of 18,599 unedited compositions. Words are listed in the order of their frequency of misspelling.

strategy Workshop

Developing Spelling Consciousness

DISCOVER THE STRATEGY Sometimes the worst kinds of spelling mistakes you can make are the most obvious.

Your invited to by somthing special at Harold's Finer Foods.

 In this book they're called **frequently misspelled words** because students your age misspell them again and again in their writing.

no	there's	anything	friends
too	buy	until	they
off	our	everywhere	they're
a lot	always	didn't	you're
don't	it's	because	maybe
went	which	where	everything
then	were	everybody	
around	let's	something	
we're	that's	again	

> Which of these words are misspelled on the billboard above? Find them and write them, correctly spelled.

1. _____

2. _____

3. _____

We know most of these words, but we just don't "see" them when we write. We need to make ourselves aware of these words. We need to develop our **spelling consciousness**.

TRY IT OUT Proofread each billboard for six misspellings of short, simple words, and write each word correctly. *Hint:* A word that looks right may actually be the wrong word, so proofread carefully for meaning.

DELROE'S

You see are pizzas all aroun the town because we deliver everwhere.

Wich pie all ways stands tallest? Thats us way up there. Reach up, up, up for Peak's.

4. _____   6. _____   8. _____

5. _____   7. _____   9. _____

LOOK AHEAD You'll find more frequently misspelled words in the spelling lessons that follow. Each one is marked by the asterisk symbol you see in this lesson. You'll find them in proofreading exercises as well. Look through the lists for the next five lessons and write down any frequently misspelled words that are spelling problems for you.

1. _____   4. _____

2. _____   5. _____

3. _____

Getting Letters in Correct Order

Watch for letter combinations that are hard to keep in order and pay special attention to those parts: **believe**, **perfume**.

■ **STUDY** Say each word and pay attention to the underlined letters. Then read the meaning phrase.

1. **completely** — **completely** covered with mud
2. **believe** ✽ — didn't **believe** their lies
3. **weirdest** — **weirdest** looking new haircut
4. **beige** — dull, boring **beige** walls
5. **through** ✽ — water flowing **through** a pipe
6. **thirtieth** — **thirtieth** day of June
7. **experiment** — an **experiment** in science class
8. **perfume** — smell of **perfume** in the air
9. **doesn't** ✽ — **doesn't** live here anymore
10. **decision** — your **decision** to join the club

11. **politely** — asked **politely** for a pencil
12. **fierce** — a **fierce,** snarling tiger
13. **briefcase** — business papers in the **briefcase**
14. **sleigh** — horse pulling a **sleigh**
15. **lieutenant** — **lieutenant** in the army
16. **maneuver** — tried to **maneuver** into a good position
17. **recruit** — will **recruit** football players
18. **biscuit** — **biscuit** with jelly and butter
19. **gauge** — a **gauge** for measuring rainfall
20. **preserve** — will **preserve** our forests

■ **PRACTICE** Look over the list of words and write those that are hardest for you to spell. Be careful as you write each word. Then write the rest of the words.

■ **WRITE** Choose three phrases to include in a paragraph.

1.
2.
3.
4.
5.
6.
7.
8.
9.
10.
11.
12.
13.
14.
15.
16.
17.
18.
19.
20.

CHALLENGE!

unyielding
beguiling
beauteous
precipitation
preferably

✽ **WATCH OUT FOR FREQUENTLY MISSPELLED WORDS!**

CONTEXT CLUES Use the context in each sentence to help you write the correct list word.

1. A total eclipse will occur on the ____ of October.
2. The horses pulled the ____ through the snow.
3. The soldiers stood at attention as a ____ entered the room.
4. The attorney put the important papers into her ____.
5. With those dark brown pants you shoud wear ____ socks.
6. Arguing with the umpire just ____ do any good.
7. Letting you drive is strictly your parents' ____.
8. The blowfish puffs itself up to make it look more ____.

WORD ASSOCIATION Write the list words suggested by each group of words.

9. sweet-smelling, cologne
10. bread, baked, roll
11. keep, save, protect
12. strangest, oddest
13. laboratory, trial, test
14. think, accept, suppose
15. courteously, nicely, elegantly
16. scale, measure, instrument
17. newly enlisted soldier, new member
18. plan, clever trick, movement
19. done with, over, finished
20. thoroughly, totally

Strategic Spelling

Developing Spelling Consciousness

We sometimes misspell familiar words that we shouldn't miss. Proofread the paragraph. Write four misspelled words correctly.

   My forgetful dad went to the car wash aroud the corner again, and guess what happened this time? He did'nt roll up his back windows. As he whent thourgh the wash, the back seat got soaped, rinsed, and blown dry!

1. _____
2. _____
3. _____
4. _____
5. _____
6. _____
7. _____
8. _____
9. _____
10. _____
11. _____
12. _____
13. _____
14. _____
15. _____
16. _____
17. _____
18. _____
19. _____
20. _____

21. _____   23. _____

22. _____   24. _____

FREQUENTLY MISSPELLED WORDS ✳ FREQUENTLY MISSPELLED WORDS ✳

Are you confused about spelling **believe?**
Just remember: Don't be**lie**ve a **lie.**

≡	Make a capital.
/	Make a small letter.
∧	Add something.
ℓ	Take out something.
⊙	Add a period.
¶	New paragraph

PROOFREAD FOR PUNCTUATION

Put quotation marks around the exact words a speaker says. Remember to always use quotation marks in pairs. For example:

"I didn't see the other car coming," said the dazed passenger.

Check Quotation Marks Correct the five errors by writing the quotation mark and the word that comes before or after it.

I was taken completely by surprise," said the driver of the beige van that was hit. That was the weirdest thing I ever saw, chimed in an eyewitness. "You know, the witness continued, "that van could have ended up smashing into me.

1. _____

2. _____

3. _____

4. _____

5. _____

PROOFREAD A NEWSPAPER ARTICLE Find the five misspelled words in the article and write them correctly. These errors may be list words or words you learned before. Fix four errors with quotation marks too.

> "He tried to manuver around the briefcase in the highway, but he compleatly lost control of the van, another witness said. A police luitenant reported that she did'nt believe any of the injuries were serious. Our desicion was to take three people to the hospital, she said," "but only as a precaution."

WRITE A NEWSPAPER ARTICLE Plan and write a brief newspaper article about an event you witnessed. Use three spelling words and a personal word.

Word List

briefcase	preserve
fierce	recruit
believe	biscuit
sleigh	lieutenant
weirdest	thirtieth
beige	doesn't
experiment	through
completely	maneuver
politely	gauge
perfume	decision

Personal Words

1. _____

2. _____

Review

DRAWING CONCLUSIONS
Write the word from the box that fits each clue.

completely	thirtieth
believe	experiment
weirdest	perfume
beige	doesn't
through	decision

1. A scientist would conduct this.
2. This color is neutral, not bright.
3. This is a contraction for *does not.*
4. You should not do this for some advertisements.
5. This adverb is a synonym for *totally.*
6. After a discussion, a group tries to reach this.
7. A woman wanting to smell nice might use this.
8. You would go this way if you come to a tunnel.
9. This is a synonym for *strangest.*
10. This is an ordinal number.

1. _____
2. _____
3. _____
4. _____
5. _____
6. _____
7. _____
8. _____
9. _____
10. _____

Word *Study*

ANALOGIES
A word analogy compares the relationship of a pair of words. For example, read this **part/whole analogy:**

> lieutenant : army : : supervisor : business

This may be read "*Lieutenant* is to *army* as *supervisor* is to *business.*" A lieutenant is part of an army in the same way a supervisor is part of a business. Other analogies include **cause/effect analogies** (virus : flu : : fire : heat) and **worker/product analogies** (baker : pie : : writer : book). Use the list of words in the box to complete the analogies that follow.

birds	sadness	week	picture	forest	light

Part/Whole Analogies
1. March : year : : Monday : ___
2. house : city : : tree : ___

Cause/Effect Analogies
3. happiness : smiles : : ___ : tears
4. clouds : rain : : sun : ___

Worker/Product Analogies
5. writer : story : : painter : ___
6. bees : hive : : ___ : nest

1. _____
2. _____
3. _____
4. _____
5. _____
6. _____

Unexpected Consonant Spellings

SPELLING FOCUS

Some words have unexpected consonant spellings:
penguin, parachute, examination, exhibit, meanwhile.

■ **STUDY** Say each word. Look carefully at its spelling as you say it. Then read the phrase.

1.	**penguin**	black and white **penguin**
2.	**language**	speaks another **language**
3.	**parachute**	a white, billowing **parachute**
4.	**Michigan**	moving to **Michigan**
5.	**examination**	an eye **examination** for glasses
6.	**executive**	an **executive** in a large corporation
7.	**exhibit**	an **exhibit** of artwork at a museum
8.	**exhausted**	**exhausted** firefighters
9.	**whirlpool**	water bubbling in a **whirlpool**
10.	**meanwhile**	**meanwhile** waited their turn

11.	**distinguished**	well dressed and **distinguished**
12.	**guacamole**	**guacamole** made from ripe avocados
13.	**extinguish**	water to **extinguish** the fire
14.	**brochure**	**brochure** about a music camp
15.	**chauffeur**	**chauffeur** who drove a big car
16.	**chandelier**	the glowing lights of a **chandelier**
17.	**exempt**	not **exempt** from the history test
18.	**exotic**	**exotic** South American birds
19.	**exertion**	tired from so much **exertion**
20.	**overwhelming**	**overwhelming** problems

■ **PRACTICE** Write the following list words:
- five words in which /gw/ is spelled **gu**
- five words in which /sh/ is spelled **ch**
- seven words in which /gz/ is spelled **x** or **xh**
- three words in which /hw/ is spelled **wh**

■ **WRITE** Choose ten phrases to rewrite as sentences.

1. _____
2. _____
3. _____
4. _____
5. _____
6. _____
7. _____
8. _____
9. _____
10. _____
11. _____
12. _____
13. _____
14. _____
15. _____
16. _____
17. _____
18. _____
19. _____
20. _____

CHALLENGE!

bilingual
nonchalant
exhilaration
exasperate
whimsically

CLASSIFYING   Write the list word that belongs in each group.

1. manager, supervisor, ___
2. leaflet, pamphlet, ____
3. rare, unusual, ____
4. candle holder, lamp, ____
5. Illinois, Iowa, ____
6. at the same time, in the time between, ____

ANALOGIES   Write the list word that completes each analogy.

7. Cab driver is to taxicab as ____ is to limousine.
8. Life jacket is to swimmer as ____ is to sky diver.
9. Jaguar is to cat as ____ is to bird.
10. Soccer is to sport as Russian is to ____.

SENTENCE COMPLETION   Write the list word that best completes each sentence.

11. Freddy must pass this ____ in order to graduate.
12. We went to an ____ featuring the works of Picasso.
13. Senior citizens are ____ from paying the admission fee.
14. After running in the marathon, Roberto felt ____.
15. My problem seemed ____ until I got help.
16. Please ____ all the candles before leaving the room.
17. Ripe avocados make the best ____.
18. Selena was tired after all her ____.
19. The leaves twirled round and round in the ____.
20. Our next speaker is a ____ federal judge.

1. _____
2. _____
3. _____
4. _____
5. _____
6. _____
7. _____
8. _____
9. _____
10. _____
11. _____
12. _____
13. _____
14. _____
15. _____
16. _____
17. _____
18. _____
19. _____
20. _____

Strategic Spelling

Using the Problem Parts Strategy

Write two list words that you sometimes misspell. Mark the part or parts of each word that give you problems. Then picture the words and focus on the problem parts.

21. _____   22. _____

Did You Know?
The largest penguin, the emperor, can stand four feet tall and can weigh one hundred pounds!

	Make a capital.
/	Make a small letter.
∧	Add something.
ℯ	Take out something.
⊙	Add a period.
⁋	New paragraph

PROOFREAD FOR PUNCTUATION

Use commas to separate a series of items. A comma must always separate a city and state. For example:

Pack a lunch‿rent a bicycle‿and ride a few miles to discover beauty‿history‿and adventure in Dearborn‿Michigan.

Check for Commas Correct five errors with commas by writing each word and the comma that should come after it.

A chauffeur will meet you at the airport in Detroit Michigan, and drive you to historic Greenfield Village Michigan. There you will go sight-seeing hiking dining and dancing.

PROOFREAD A TRAVEL BROCHURE

Find the five misspelled words in the brochure and write them correctly. Some may be words you learned before. Also correct three mistakes with commas.

1. _____
2. _____
3. _____
4. _____
5. _____

Spend the day visiting Thomas Edison's completly restored laboratory the courthouse where Abe Lincoln practiced law and a chandalier shop. If you're exausted from all this exsertion, unwind in a whirlpool bath in your room. Then you're of to Battle Creek Michigan, breakfast capital of the United States.

Word List

whirlpool	language
overwhelming	extinguish
brochure	guacamole
penguin	meanwhile
examination	exotic
distinguished	chauffeur
executive	exertion
parachute	Michigan
exhibit	exhausted
exempt	chandelier

Personal Words

1. _____
2. _____

WRITE A TRAVEL BROCHURE

Write a travel brochure that would encourage people to visit your community. Use three list words and a personal word.

Review

DEFINITIONS Write the word from the box for each meaning.

penguin	executive
language	exhibit
parachute	exhausted
Michigan	whirlpool
examination	meanwhile

1. an important manager in a company
2. very tired
3. spoken or written speech
4. a current of water that goes rapidly in a circle
5. a state made up of two large peninsulas
6. one kind of flightless bird
7. at the same time
8. an inspection or test
9. an umbrellalike apparatus used for floating downward
10. show or display

1. _____
2. _____
3. _____
4. _____
5. _____
6. _____
7. _____
8. _____
9. _____
10. _____

Using a *Thesaurus*

PARTS OF AN ENTRY A thesaurus is a helpful resource for finding precise words. Study the following part of a thesaurus page and the labels. Then answer the questions.

Entry Word   Definition   Part of Speech

Language means the speech or writing of a group of people who understand each other. It includes vocabulary and grammar. *The airport announcer repeats messages in several languages.* (noun)

Tongue can mean a language. It is used mostly in books. *The armies of Islam carried the Arabic tongue to many countries.*

Example Sentence — **Speech** can mean spoken language. *Words often become common in speech before they are accepted in writing.*

Synonym — **Dialect** means a local form of a language. *Spanish is a language with a number of different dialects that are spoken in different countries or in different areas of the same country.*

Lingo is an informal word that means speech containing unknown words and therefore not understood by the listener. *When I try to teach my dad about computers, he complains about my lingo.*

Jargon can mean the language, especially the vocabulary, of some special group. *TV shows about doctors and police are full of jargon.*

1. What part of speech is *language*?
2. What is the following sentence called? *The airport announcer repeats messages in several languages.*
3. How many synonyms for *language* are defined?
4. Which word in parentheses is the best one in this sentence? *The slow drawl of southern Georgia is an interesting ___ to hear.* (dialect, language, lingo, tongue)
5. Which two synonyms for *language* are appropriate in this sentence? *Teenagers seem to have a ___ that only they understand.*

1. _____
2. _____
3. _____
4. _____
5. _____

One Consonant or Two?

SPELLING FOCUS

Sometimes double consonants stand for one sound. For example, you hear the sound /f/ one time in **diff**erent and the sound /m/ one time in reco**mm**end.

■ **STUDY** Notice the double consonants. Then read the phrase.

1. | 1. **recommend** | will **recommend** a movie
2. | 2. **different** ✳ | two **different** jackets
3. | 3. **graffiti** | vandalized the wall with **graffiti**
4. | 4. **successfully** | **successfully** finished the job
5. | 5. **embarrass** | mistakes that **embarrass** me
6. | 6. **necessary** | **necessary** for life
7. | 7. **parallel** | **parallel** lines of the parking lot
8. | 8. **Halloween** ✳ | made a costume for **Halloween**
9. | 9. **Connecticut** | governor of **Connecticut**
10. | 10. **approximately** | **approximately** twenty students

11. | 11. **commitment** | **commitment** to playing their best
12. | 12. **accommodate** | big enough to **accommodate** us all
13. | 13. **accomplishment** | an **accomplishment** to be proud of
14. | 14. **possession** | the **possession** you value most
15. | 15. **harass** | shouldn't **harass** zoo animals
16. | 16. **confetti** | threw **confetti** during the parade
17. | 17. **abbreviation** | the **abbreviation** for our state
18. | 18. **interruption** | rude **interruption** of the speaker
19. | 19. **cinnamon** | **cinnamon** and sugar on toast
20. | 20. **mayonnaise** | **mayonnaise** on my chicken sandwich

■ **PRACTICE** Sort the list by writing
- four words with two or more sets of double consonants
- five other words with double **m**, **r**, or **s**
- five other words with double **f**, **l**, or **t**
- six other words with double **b**, **c**, **n**, or **p**

■ **WRITE** Choose three phrases to include in a paragraph.

CHALLENGE!

commemoration
questionnaire
penicillin
recollection
interrogation

✳ **WATCH OUT FOR FREQUENTLY MISSPELLED WORDS!**

RIDDLES Use the clues in the riddles to write the correct list word.

1. Spread me on bread.
2. Scare me today with your costume!
3. For Sale! 2 bkes., 1 rd., 1 blck. TL 555-7809 in P.M.
4. Toss me during a party or parade!
5. I'm great sprinkled on toast or baked apples.
6. I look ugly spray-painted on buildings.
7. I'm one of the original thirteen states.
8. We lines are always together but never meet.

SYNONYMS Write the list word that means the same as each pair of synonyms. Use your Spelling Dictionary if necessary.

9. achievement, fulfillment
10. ownership, property
11. advise, suggest
12. disturb, torment
13. intermission, break
14. essential, required

15. prosperously, fortunately
16. almost, nearly
17. pledge, promise
18. shame, humiliate
19. contain, hold
20. distinct, separate

Seeing Meaning Connections

| unsuccessful |
| successor |
| successive |
| succession |
| succeed |

21. Write the list word that is related in spelling and meaning to the words in the box. Use the words in the box to complete the paragraph. Check your Spelling Dictionary if you need to.

Have you been (22) at building all those muscles you've wanted? We at Atlas Dumbbells can help you (23) with ease! You will be able to perform our simple (24) of exercises at home, at school, even at the playground. By exercising on (25) Fridays, you might even become the latest (26) to the title *World Class Body Builder*.

21. _____
22. _____
23. _____

24. _____
25. _____
26. _____

1. _____
2. _____
3. _____
4. _____
5. _____
6. _____
7. _____
8. _____
9. _____
10. _____
11. _____
12. _____
13. _____
14. _____
15. _____
16. _____
17. _____
18. _____
19. _____
20. _____

FREQUENTLY MISSPELLED WORDS * **FREQUENTLY MISSPELLED WORDS** * **FREQUENTLY MISSPELLED WORDS**

Hint: Do you spell *different* differently every time you write it? Try saying it to yourself like this: dif•fer•ent.

=	Make a capital.
/	Make a small letter.
∧	Add something.
ℯ	Take out something.
⊙	Add a period.
¶	New paragraph

PROOFREAD FOR USAGE Some verbs are formed in an unusual way. Be careful when using verbs such as *bring, come, put, is,* and *take*. Check a dictionary to find the correct forms of these verbs. For example:

    You should have ~~bringed~~ ^brought^ all ingredients to room temperature.

Check Irregular Verbs Correct the five errors with irregular verbs in these sentences. If a sentence is correct, write "Correct."

  1. Here's how I maked those Halloween cookies.
  2. It was so easy that I doed it all in a half hour.
  3. First, I taked butter and mixed it with sugar.
  4. Then I getted two cookie sheets and greased them.
  5. Now here's how you complete the rest of the recipe.

1. _____

2. _____

3. _____

4. _____

5. _____

PROOFREAD A RECIPE Find five misspelled words in the recipe and write them correctly. These errors may be list words or words you learned before. Fix three errors with verbs.

Add the cinammon. Next, use the tablespoon you have took from the drawer. Make parralel rows of dough. You should have putted three rows across and five rows down on each sheet when you'r through. This next step are absolutely neccesary: Try a cookie and enjoy your acomplishment!

Word List

different	cinnamon
abbreviation	graffiti
parallel	confetti
recommend	Halloween
accommodate	interruption
harass	mayonnaise
accomplishment	possession
Connecticut	successfully
embarrass	necessary
approximately	commitment

Personal Words

1. _____

2. _____

WRITE A RECIPE Make a list of ingredients and tell how to make a food you like. Use three list words.

Review

MAKING CONNECTIONS Write the word from the box that fits each clue.

recommend	necessary
different	parallel
graffiti	Halloween
successfully	Connecticut
embarrass	approximately

1. This is a math term relating to lines.
2. This adverb is used when you can't be exact.
3. This adverb means you've done something well.
4. This is one of the smaller states of the United States.
5. When things are not the same, they are this.
6. This is what your four-year-old sister would do to you if she threw a temper tantrum in a store with you.
7. This is a form of vandalism.
8. This is the relationship of water to life as we know it.
9. This is what you hope a teacher will do for you so that you can get a part-time job.
10. This happens just before November starts.

1. _____

2. _____

3. _____

4. _____

5. _____

6. _____

7. _____

8. _____

9. _____

10. _____

Multicultural Connection

COSTUMES Costumes play a big part of Halloween in some parts of the United States. In fact, people all over the world throughout history have worn costumes to mark special occasions.

- Samurai warriors, warlords in feudal Japan, wore a **warrior's costume** as a sign of rank.
- Hindus in India wear a white **funeral costume,** because Hindus consider white a color of mourning.
- The **celebratory costume** worn by a Mexican girl at a *quince años* (kēn′se ä′nyōs), honoring her fifteenth birthday, is often very formal.

Look at the pictures and name the kind of costume being worn.

1. _____   2. _____   3. _____

Homophones

SPELLING FOCUS

A homophone is a word that sounds exactly like another word but has a different spelling and meaning: **herd, heard.**

■ **STUDY** Say each word and phrase. Pay special attention to which spellings go with which meanings.

1.	herd	a large **herd** of elephants
2.	heard ✲	**heard** what I whispered in her ear
3.	capital	Jackson, the **capital** of Mississippi
4.	capitol	the gold dome of the **capitol** building
5.	principle	the **principle** of one person, one vote
6.	principal	visited the **principal** of our school
7.	there ✲	asked me to put it over **there**
8.	their ✲	left **their** books at our house
9.	straight	the **straight** and narrow road
10.	strait	ships in a dangerous, rocky **strait**
11.	compliment	a nice **compliment** on my new shirt
12.	complement	shoes that **complement** his suit
13.	stationery	writing with pen and **stationery**
14.	stationary	**stationary** table but movable chairs
15.	idle	sat around **idle** all day
16.	idol	the **idol** of all the younger musicians
17.	hostel	stayed overnight at a youth **hostel**
18.	hostile	safe from **hostile** troops
19.	sheer	curtains made of a **sheer** material
20.	shear	**shear** sheep for their wool

■ **PRACTICE** First write the homophone pairs that are the most confusing for you to spell. As you write each word, think of its meaning. Then write the rest of the homophones.

■ **WRITE** Choose four phrases to rewrite as questions and answers.

1.
2.
3.
4.
5.
6.
7.
8.
9.
10.
11.
12.
13.
14.
15.
16.
17.
18.
19.
20.

CHALLENGE!

guerrilla	gorilla
adolescents	adolescence
oral	aural

✲ **WATCH OUT FOR FREQUENTLY MISSPELLED WORDS!**

WORD PAIRS   Use the context to help you write the correct homophone pair for each sentence.

The (1) of buffalo stampeded because they (2) the blast of the hunters' rifles.
Lionel said he never met anyone at a youth (3) in Europe who was (4) to him.
We wanted them to park (5) car over (6) under the shade of that tree.
The (7) of our school insists that students wear long pants as a matter of (8).
Ships must steer a (9) course when they navigate through the narrow (10).
Though she had been the (11) of movie fans everywhere, she has been (12) for more than a decade.

WORD ASSOCIATION   Write the list words suggested by each group of words. Use the Spelling Dictionary for help.

13. letter; A, B, or C
14. writing paper, envelopes
15. cut, trim
16. praise, congratulate

17. building, dome
18. transparent, thin
19. immovable, still
20. supplement, complete

Strategic Spelling

Seeing Meaning Connections

| straight-faced |
| straightforward |
| straighten |
| straightedge |

21. Write the list word that is related to the words

in the box. _____

Write the words in the box that fit the definitions.

22. showing no emotion _____

23. strip of wood or metal used to make

straight lines_____

24. honest, direct _____

25. put in the proper order _____

1. _____
2. _____
3. _____
4. _____
5. _____
6. _____
7. _____
8. _____
9. _____
10. _____
11. _____
12. _____
13. _____
14. _____
15. _____
16. _____
17. _____
18. _____
19. _____
20. _____

FREQUENTLY MISSPELLED WORDS ✳ FREQUENTLY MISSPELLED WORDS ✳ FREQUENTLY

Do you have trouble keeping *there* and *their* straight? Remember: Start **here** to get t**here.**

===	Make a capital.
/	Make a small letter.
∧	Add something.
ℓ	Take out something.
⊙	Add a period.
¶	New paragraph

PROOFREAD FOR USAGE When using adjectives and adverbs to compare, add -er or -est to short words or use more, most, less, or least with long words and words that end in **-ly.** NEVER do both.

We are planning a tasty new menu with ~~more~~ healthier food.

Check Adjectives and Adverbs Read each sentence. Correct the adjective and adverb errors. Write "Correct" if there is no error.

1. We had the most largest response to our questionnaire.
2. The results should be healthier, more cheaper, and tastier food.
3. You spoke more loudlier than ever—and we heard you!
4. We are now ready to begin the hardest part.
5. Help our committee find the menu that will serve us most best.

1. _____

2. _____

3. _____

4. _____

5. _____

PROOFREAD A MESSAGE Find the six misspelled words in this message and write them correctly. Some may be words you learned before. Fix three errors with adjectives or adverbs.

> Your comments were not hostel, but thay went strait to the heart of the issue. You voted the salads the most blandest and the pretzels the least crispiest. Our principle agrees that their is a solution. A more leaner hamburger will appear, are eggs will not be "the greasiest on the planet."

Word List

heard	there
herd	their
capital	straight
capitol	strait
compliment	idle
complement	idol
stationery	hostel
stationary	hostile
principle	sheer
principal	shear

Personal Words

1. _____

2. _____

WRITE A MESSAGE What might you like to tell your classmates? Plan and write a message about it. Use three list words and a personal word.

Review

WORDS IN CONTEXT Write the word from the box that completes each sentence.

herd	principal
heard	there
capital	their
capitol	straight
principle	strait

1. Juan and Graciela said that ___ mother was coming.
2. My ___ is that I will always be honest.
3. The ___ between the cliffs was dangerously narrow.
4. The state legislature is in session in the ___ building.
5. Are you going ___ for lunch?
6. The ___ gave an inspiring speech at school.
7. With these scissors you can really cut a ___ line.
8. In the meadow, we spied a ___ of antelope.
9. The class learned much in the ___ city of the state.
10. We just ___ a marvelous piece of music!

1. _____
2. _____
3. _____
4. _____
5. _____
6. _____
7. _____
8. _____
9. _____
10. _____

Using a *Dictionary*

PARTS OF AN ENTRY A dictionary has the facts you need to help you use words correctly. Study the parts of a dictionary page and an entry. Then write the answer to each question.

preferable | projection ——— guide words

——— pronunciation key

a	hat	ėr	term	ô	order	ch	child	ə stands for	
ā	age	i	it	oi	oil	ng	long	a	in about
ä	far, calm	ī	ice	ou	out	sh	she	e	in taken
âr	care	o	hot	u	cup	th	thin	i	in pencil
e	let	ō	open	ů	put	ŦH	then	o	in lemon
ē	equal	ȯ	saw	ü	rule	zh	measure	u	in circus

entry word ——— pronunciation ——— definition

prin•ci•pal (prin′sə pəl), *adj.* **1** most important; main; chief: *Chicago is the principal city of Illinois.* —*n.* **1** a chief person; one who gives orders. **2** the head, or one of the heads, of an elementary or secondary school.

illustrative sentence

1. What is the word **prin•ci•pal** called?
2. What is the sentence *Chicago is the principal city of Illinois* called?
3. Which definition for *principal* is being used in this sentence? *The principal was known for being fair to all students.*
4. The **i** and the **a** in *principal* are pronounced like the **o** in another word. Where do you look to find this out?
5. Where do you look to find where the accent is in *principal?*

1. _____
2. _____
3. _____
4. _____
5. _____

Adding -ed **and** -ing

Five things to remember when adding **-ed** and **-ing** are:
- Some base words are not changed: **travel, traveled, traveling.**
- In words that end with **e**, drop the **e**: **receive, received, receiving.**
- In words that end with **c**, add **k** before adding **-ed** or **-ing**: **panic, panicked, panicking.**
- In words that end with **y**, change the **y** to **i** when adding **-ed**: **qualified**, but keep the **y** when adding **-ing**: **qualifying.**
- If words accented on the last syllable end with **consonant-vowel-consonant**, the final consonant is doubled: **control, controlled, controlling.**

■ **STUDY**   Study the words in each column. Notice if the base word changes when different endings are added.

travel	1. **traveled**	2. **traveling**
receive	3. **received**	4. **receiving**
panic	5. **panicked**	6. **panicking**
qualify	7. **qualified**	8. **qualifying**
control	9. **controlled**	10. **controlling**

research	11. **researched**	12. **researching**
argue	13. **argued**	14. **arguing**
mimic	15. **mimicked**	16. **mimicking**
horrify	17. **horrified**	18. **horrifying**
commit	19. **committed**	20. **committing**

■ **PRACTICE**   Sort the words by writing
- four words in which final **e** is dropped before **-ed** or **-ing** is added
- four words in which the final consonant is doubled
- two words in which **y** is changed to **i**
- four words in which **k** is added
- six words in which the base word doesn't change

■ **WRITE**   Choose ten words to write in sentences.

1. _____
2. _____
3. _____
4. _____
5. _____
6. _____
7. _____
8. _____
9. _____
10. _____
11. _____
12. _____
13. _____
14. _____
15. _____
16. _____
17. _____
18. _____
19. _____
20. _____

CHALLENGE!

benefited	benefiting
prophesied	prophesying
transferred	transferring

SENTENCE COMPLETION Write the form of the base word in parentheses that completes each sentence.

1. (argue) You two are always ____ about who gets to sit by the window.
2. (research) The graduate student published her findings after she thoroughly ____ the subject of hurricanes.
3. (horrify) The scream was absolutely ___ to hear.
4. (qualify) After taking guitar lessons for ten years, Connie felt ____ for the job with the band.
5. (panic) Many lives were saved because no one ____ during the fire.
6. (mimic) Is that bird ____ what I just said?
7. (control) We saw an exhibition of remote-____ aircraft.
8. (horrify) Gary was ____ when he heard the grim news.
9. (commit) They ___ the robbery, didn't they?
10. (commit) They're through ___ crimes.

SYNONYMS Write the list word that means the same as each pair of synonyms. Use the Spelling Dictionary for help.

11. imitated, copied
12. journeying, moving
13. losing control, not thinking
14. disputed, debated
15. journeyed, moved
16. getting, taking
17. inquiring, investigating
18. succeeding, achieving
19. got, took
20. regulating, directing

Strategic Spelling

Building New Words

Add the endings **-ed** and **-ing** to each of these words to make new words: *frolic, believe, prefer, magnify.* Remember what you learned.

Add -ed

21. _____
22. _____
23. _____
24. _____

Add -ing

_____
_____
_____
_____

1. _____
2. _____
3. _____
4. _____
5. _____
6. _____
7. _____
8. _____
9. _____
10. _____
11. _____
12. _____
13. _____
14. _____
15. _____
16. _____
17. _____
18. _____
19. _____
20. _____

Take a Hint
Don't *panic* when you have to spell *panicked.* Remember help will arrive in the **NICK** of time.

≡	Make a capital.
/	Make a small letter.
∧	Add something.
ℓ	Take out something.
⊙	Add a period.
¶	New paragraph

PROOFREAD FOR CAPITALIZATION

Use capitals correctly in the heading, inside address, greeting, and closing of a business letter. For example:

100 south street
Hampton, VA 23360
may 12, 19—

Check Capitalization Fix the capitalization errors in these parts of an inside address and greeting. Write the words correctly.

1. _____
2. _____
3. _____
4. _____

1. mr Miguel Lopez
2. 134 elm Street
3. valdosta, GA 31603
4. Dear Mr. lopez:

PROOFREAD A BUSINESS LETTER
Find five misspelled words in the body of the letter and write them correctly. Some may be words you learned before. Fix two errors in capitalization.

> We at Acme Travel hope you received our
> newsletters about travling in Asia. We remain
> commited to bringing you bargains. You can
> become qualifyed to win a trip to Tokyo,
> Japan! Please dont hesitate to call.
>
>   sincerely,
>
>   *Agnes acme*

Word List

researched	panicked
researching	panicking
traveled	controlled
traveling	controlling
argued	committed
arguing	committing
received	qualified
receiving	qualifying
mimicked	horrified
mimicking	horrifying

Personal Words

1. _____
2. _____

WRITE A BUSINESS LETTER
Write to a travel agency for information about a place you want to visit. Use three list words.

Review

DRAWING CONCLUSIONS   Write the word from the box that fits each clue.

traveled	panicking
traveling	qualified
received	qualifying
receiving	controlled
panicked	controlling

1. the adjective for a preliminary contest in which people who do well get into the finals
2. what the referees in yesterday's game did to restore order
3. what the ballplayers are doing to get to the next city
4. what the player did to the quarterback's pass
5. what the children did who thought they saw a monster
6. what the president of the company is doing with its future
7. what the couple did who went around the world
8. what the unprepared student with a report due tomorrow is doing
9. what the runner did who is in the final race
10. in many companies, the name of the department that accepts shipments and packages

1. _____

2. _____

3. _____

4. _____

5. _____

6. _____

7. _____

8. _____

9. _____

10. _____

Word *Study*

LATIN ROOTS: *mit, miss*   The list word *committed* comes from the root **mit,** which means "send." The root **miss** also means "send." The words in the box all come from these roots.

Write the **mit** and **miss** words that complete the word web below. Use your Spelling Dictionary if you need help.

emissary
emitted
permission
omitted
submit

"permitting, consent"
1. _____

"person sent on a mission"
2. _____

mit, miss—"send"

"left out, neglected"
5. _____

"give in"
3. _____

"sent out, gave off"
4. _____

Complete each sentence with a word from the web.

6. We didn't know it, but the ___ was actually a spy.
7. My father gave me ___ to stay up late Saturday night.
8. After it was scolded, the dog decided to ___ and obey.
9. The play ran short because the second act was ___.
10. In the movie, the alien's weapon ___ rays that shrank people.

6. _____

7. _____

8. _____

9. _____

10. _____

Review

Lesson 1: Getting Letters in Correct Order
Lesson 2: Unexpected Consonant Spellings
Lesson 3: One Consonant or Two?

Lesson 4: Homophones
Lesson 5: Adding -ed and -ing

REVIEW WORD LIST

1. beige
2. believe
3. biscuit
4. briefcase
5. completely
6. decision
7. doesn't
8. experiment
9. fierce
10. gauge
11. perfume
12. sleigh
13. thirtieth
14. through
15. weirdest
16. brochure
17. chauffeur
18. distinguished
19. examination
20. exhibit
21. exotic
22. guacamole
23. meanwhile
24. Michigan
25. penguin
26. accomplishment
27. approximately
28. cinnamon
29. Connecticut
30. different
31. Halloween
32. harass
33. interruption
34. necessary
35. possession
36. recommend
37. capital
38. heard
39. principal
40. sheer
41. stationery
42. straight
43. strait
44. there
45. panicked
46. qualified
47. received
48. researching
49. traveled
50. traveling

■ PROOFREADING

Find the spelling errors in each passage and write the words correctly. All passages have seven errors except the last one, which has eight.

1. _____
2. _____
3. _____
4. _____
5. _____
6. _____
7. _____

PROOFREAD A RECIPE

Jamie's French Toast

4 eggs
1/2 teaspoon salt
1 cup milk

1/2 teaspoon vanilla
8 slices of bread
cooking oil

In a large bowl, beat the eggs. Add the salt, milk, and vanilla. The bread can be cut into rounds with a bisciut cutter. Dip the bread completly into the mixture. Brown the bread in a small amount of cooking oil in a skillet for approximatley 3-5 minutes on each side. Guage the time carefully so the toast isn't too dark. Serve sprinkled with cinnoman or exsperiment with other toppings. I also recomend serving with maple syrup or honey.

PROOFREAD A FABLE

A feirce dog stole some meat from a butcher one day, and as he was travaling home thru a field, he came to a stream. There he saw his shadow reflected. "I beleive that is another dog with another piece of meat," he thought to himself. Deciding to take posession of that meat, he opened his mouth to snap at it—bad desicion! The meat he was carrying fell strait into the water.

Moral: We often lose what we have when we reach for imagined riches.

1. _____
2. _____
3. _____
4. _____
5. _____
6. _____
7. _____

PROOFREAD AN INVITATION

To: The Seventh Grade Class

From: Marla

What: a Haloween party

Where: 47 W. Thirtyeth Street, the biege house

When: October 28, 19—, at 7 o'clock

Please come to my party. Their will be refreshments. Prizes will be given for the wierdest and the most exotick costumes. Wearing a costume is not nesassary, however.

1. _____
2. _____
3. _____
4. _____
5. _____
6. _____
7. _____

PROOFREAD A FRIENDLY LETTER

1. _____
2. _____
3. _____
4. _____
5. _____
6. _____
7. _____

September, 19—

Dear Uncle Clyde,

Have you herd that we are moving to Conneticut? Are you paniced that we will now be close enough to your farm to harrass you on weekends? Seriously, Dad recieved notice that he has been transferred. Ben is reserching places to visit on our trip east. Meanhwile, Mom is packing. We hope to see you soon.

Sincerely,

Lou

PROOFREAD A NEWSPAPER FEATURE STORY

1. _____
2. _____
3. _____
4. _____
5. _____
6. _____
7. _____

Date   Page 5

Davis School Doings

Last week the Davis School had a distingwished visitor from Mishigan. Governor Smith travled from the state capitol in a car with a chauffuer. The principle introduced him to all the classes, and then he visited the science exibit in 221B.

PROOFREAD A TELEPHONE MESSAGE

Dad,

    Mr. Alvarez called. He thinks he left his brief case in your office, but he does'nt know for sure. In it are a travel broshure, an examunation booklet, some stationary, and a gift-wrapped bottle of prefume for his wife's birthday. He is sorry for the interuption, but call him if you find it. He's at 555-7310.

                        Hector

1. _____
2. _____
3. _____
4. _____
5. _____
6. _____
7. _____

PROOFREAD A POEM

Food for Thought

Last night I had the strangest dream:
A penquin in a slay
slid up to me and said he'd heard
that I was on my way
to swim across a polar straight
without my shear inner tube!
I knew it would be differnt,
becoming an ice cube,
but I shook my head and said that I'd
supposed I wasn't kwalified
for this acomplishment.
Was it the three-cheese pizza I ate before I slept?
Not wholly—
I think it was the guacamoley.

1. _____
2. _____
3. _____
4. _____
5. _____
6. _____
7. _____
8. _____

STRATEGY WORKSHOP

Pronouncing for Spelling

"Man-aise." It sounds fine when I say it, but it doesn't look right at all. What's the problem?

The egg acts as a binder keeping the oil and vinegar separate in manaise.

DISCOVER THE STRATEGY 1 Chris misspells the middle part of *mayonnaise* because she mispronounces it. She should try this correct pronunciation strategy:

1. Read the word aloud carefully and correctly. Listen to the sound of each letter.

2. Pronounce the word again as you write it.

TRY IT OUT Now practice this strategy.

- Pronounce the words in dark type slowly and correctly. As you do, listen carefully to the sounds of the underlined letters.
- Pronounce each word again as you write it.

1. **diff<u>e</u>rent** (not "dif-rent") _____

2. **usu<u>a</u>lly** (not "usally") _____

3. **<u>a</u>thletic** (not "athaletic") _____

4. **<u>e</u>specially** (not "expecially") _____

5. **mac<u>a</u>roni** (not "macroni") _____

"May-on-naise." That's better. But what about "Connecticut"? I miss that second c because it's silent. So how would pronouncing the word correctly help me?

DISCOVER THE STRATEGY 2 Sometimes making up a secret pronunciation may help you spell a word.

- Pronounce the silent letters in the word to yourself. For example, say the second **c** in *Connecticut:* "Con-ne**c**t-i-cut."
- Exaggerate or change the way you say a tricky sound in the word. To remember the **o** in *attorney*, for example, say the second syllable like the word *torn*: at-**torn**-ey. To remember the second **i** in *citizen*, say it like the letter **i**: cit-**i**-zen.

TRY IT OUT Now practice this strategy.

- Make up secret pronunciations for the words below.
- Concentrate on the underlined letters.
- Write each word as you say its secret pronunciation to yourself.

6. su<u>b</u>tle
7. difficult
8. s<u>w</u>ord
9. sax<u>o</u>phone
10. accomm<u>o</u>date
11. ex<u>h</u>ibit

LOOK AHEAD Look ahead at the next five lessons. Write four list words that you could use these strategies with. Mark the part of each word that you'll pay special attention to when you pronounce it.

6. _____

7. _____

8. _____

9. _____

10. _____

11. _____

1. _____

2. _____

3. _____

4. _____

Words with No Sound Clues

1. _____
2. _____
3. _____
4. _____
5. _____
6. _____
7. _____
8. _____
9. _____
10. _____
11. _____
12. _____
13. _____
14. _____
15. _____
16. _____
17. _____
18. _____
19. _____
20. _____

SPELLING FOCUS

Some words have more letters than you might expect. To spell these words, pronounce each syllable carefully: **real_ly.** In many words the vowel sound you hear gives no clue to its spelling: **fav_o_rite.**

■ **STUDY**   Say each word slowly and carefully. Then read the meaning phrase.

1.	**mathematics**	likes story problems in **mathematics**
2.	**really** ✳	**really** want to go
3.	**audience**	the cheering, clapping **audience**
4.	**usually** ✳	**usually** can run faster than that
5.	**diamond**	ball **diamond** behind the school
6.	**favorite** ✳	visited my **favorite** cousin
7.	**memory**	good **memory** for batting averages
8.	**restaurant** ✳	**restaurant** with tablecloths
9.	**recognize**	didn't **recognize** a friend
10.	**disgusted**	felt **disgusted** at such meanness

11.	**secretary**	talked to the principal's **secretary**
12.	**miniature**	**miniature** model of the White House
13.	**tournament**	second in the bowling **tournament**
14.	**vacuum**	unable to breathe in a **vacuum**
15.	**Delaware**	clams and oysters from **Delaware**
16.	**gratitude**	flood victims' **gratitude** for help
17.	**elementary**	teachers at the **elementary** school
18.	**juvenile**	threw a **juvenile** temper tantrum
19.	**victim**	**victim** of the robbers
20.	**category**	foods in the healthy **category**

CHALLENGE!

luxurious
auxiliary
penitentiary
badminton
boulevard

■ **PRACTICE**   Look over the list words. First write those that you find easy to spell. Then write the words that are harder for you to spell. Underline the letters that you find troublesome.

■ **WRITE**   Choose ten phrases to rewrite as sentences.

✳ **WATCH OUT FOR FREQUENTLY MISSPELLED WORDS!**

BEFORE AND AFTER Write the list word that begins and ends with the same letters as each word below.

1. celebrity
2. rainy
3. unlikely
4. gasoline

5. monopolize
6. tenement
7. eventually
8. ridicule

DRAWING CONCLUSIONS Write the list word that matches each clue.

9. It's something that you like more than all others.
10. This occurs in an empty space when no air is present, as in outer space.
11. This is a subject you are required to take in school.
12. You might call a younger person this.
13. If you attend a concert, you are part of this gathering.
14. This person might type a report for the boss.
15. You might feel this way if you smell a very bad odor or see something you hate.
16. This is a place where you order from a menu.
17. Tricks to help you remember things should improve this.
18. You might find one of these in an engagement ring.
19. Dover is the capital of this state.
20. We might refer to a person in an accident as this.

Pronouncing for Spelling

Write five list words that are not spelled the way they're pronounced. Make up a secret pronunciation for each one. Circle the letters you want to exaggerate.

21. _____
22. _____
23. _____
24. _____
25. _____

1. _____
2. _____
3. _____
4. _____
5. _____
6. _____
7. _____
8. _____
9. _____
10. _____
11. _____
12. _____
13. _____
14. _____
15. _____
16. _____
17. _____
18. _____
19. _____
20. _____

Did You Know?
The word *secretary* is from a Latin word meaning "secret." That's because a secretary is expected to keep the boss's secrets.

	Make a capital.
/	Make a small letter.
∧	Add something.
℮	Take out something.
⊙	Add a period.
¶	New paragraph

PROOFREAD FOR CARELESS ERRORS

Proofread carefully in order to catch words you may have left out. For example:

Our team is probably *the* best one this school has seen in years.

Check for Careless Errors Read the beginning of this report below and write the five words that have been carelessly omitted.

The championship game was one of most exciting in recent memory. The score tied 4-4 for the first six innings. Adamji, Plotsky, and Lee all struck out in seventh inning and no runs were scored the eighth. The score was 5-4 in the top the ninth.

1. _____

2. _____

3. _____

4. _____

5. _____

PROOFREAD A REPORT

Find six misspelled words in the rest of the report and write them correctly. They may be list words or words you learned before. Write three words that were left out.

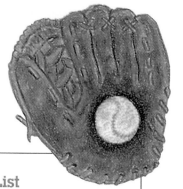

There was great excitement on the dimond as we took the field. Our pitcher fell victum to a dislocated shoulder and had to be pulled from tournement. We where able to hold them at 5-4, however. Then we took the field and Prado hit a homer with the bases loaded. The thrill of that day will be favrite memorie for the fans. We won championship 8-5.

Word List

secretary	elementary
really	favorite
memory	audience
mathematics	disgusted
diamond	juvenile
Delaware	victim
usually	category
miniature	recognize
tournament	restaurant
gratitude	vacuum

Personal Words

1. _____

2. _____

WRITE A REPORT

Write a report of a game you have played in or watched. Use three list words and a personal word.

Review

CLASSIFYING   Write the word from the box that belongs in each group.

mathematics	favorite
really	memory
audience	restaurant
usually	recognize
diamond	disgusted

 1. thought, recollection, ___
 2. stage, actors, ___
 3. know, identify, ___
 4. emerald, ruby, ___
 5. history, science, ___
 6. truly, actually, ___
 7. offended, sickened, ___
 8. eatery, inn, ___
 9. generally, frequently, ___
10. best-loved, preferred, ___

1. _____
2. _____
3. _____
4. _____
5. _____
6. _____
7. _____
8. _____
9. _____
10. _____

Word *Study*

ANALOGIES   Analogies are used in writing to make comparisons between two ideas. Often an unfamiliar or complex idea will be compared to a familiar or simpler one in order to explain the first. Read the analogy below.

> I approach writing as a swimmer. Some days I float and wait for the warmth of inspiration. It peeks through the clouds, and I easily gather my thoughts ray by ray. Other days I work hard—stroking and kicking—fighting waves of unworkable prose. I reach shore exhausted, but pleased with my effort.

Here are two ways the analogy above might be stated:

> a writer is to a thought as a swimmer is to water

or

> writer : thought : : swimmer : water

Complete each analogy below using a word from the box.

conductor	trial
water	zoologist
secretary	heartbeat

 1. student : school : : ___ : office
 2. examination : passing or failing : : ___ : innocence or guilt
 3. accountant : computer : : ___ : baton
 4. thermometer : temperature : : stethoscope : ___
 5. golfer : grass : : swimmer : ___
 6. astronomer : stars : : ___ : animals

1. _____
2. _____
3. _____
4. _____
5. _____
6. _____

Related Words 1

Related words often have parts that are spelled the same but pronounced differently: **crime, criminal; except, exception.**

■ **STUDY** Read each pair of related words and notice the differences in the two. Then read the meaning phrases.

1.	**crime**	on trial for a **crime**
2.	**criminal**	a **criminal** in prison
3.	**except** ✻	everyone **except** you
4.	**exception**	an **exception** to the rule
5.	**combine**	if you **combine** yellow and blue
6.	**combination**	your locker **combination**
7.	**imitate**	can **imitate** the singer's voice
8.	**imitation**	laughed at her **imitation**
9.	**operate**	will **operate** to remove his tonsils
10.	**operation**	was sore after the **operation**
11.	**academy**	applied for entrance to the **academy**
12.	**academic**	gym class and five **academic** courses
13.	**depart**	will **depart** at 10:41 A.M.
14.	**departure**	delayed their **departure**
15.	**inspire**	will **inspire** you with her courage
16.	**inspiration**	**inspiration** for the other students
17.	**participate**	will **participate** in the game
18.	**participation**	**participation** in the discussion
19.	**regulate**	rules to **regulate** their behavior
20.	**regulation**	**regulation** of the temperature

■ **PRACTICE** Sort the related words by writing
• four pairs of words in which a vowel sound is changed
• six pairs of words in which the sound of a **t** is changed

■ **WRITE** Choose two phrases to write in a rhyme, riddle, or dialogue.

1. _____
2. _____
3. _____
4. _____
5. _____
6. _____
7. _____
8. _____
9. _____
10. _____
11. _____
12. _____
13. _____
14. _____
15. _____
16. _____
17. _____
18. _____
19. _____
20. _____

CHALLENGE!

indicate	indicative
deprive	deprivation
implicate	implication

✻ **WATCH OUT FOR FREQUENTLY MISSPELLED WORDS!**

WORDS IN CONTEXT Write the list word that is missing from each person's statement.

1. Flight attendant: "The plane will ___ in one hour."
2. Jeweler: "Don't buy an ___ diamond. Buy the real thing."
3. Chef: "I often ___ garlic and rosemary in spaghetti sauce."
4. General: "I attended the military ___ for four years."
5. Teacher: "I'd like all students to ___ in this discussion."
6. Surgeon: "You will need an ___ to correct this condition."
7. Poet: "A poem is one tenth ___ and nine tenths perspiration."
8. Traffic Officer: "Speeding is a violation of a traffic ___."
9. Store Owner: "Shoplifting is a very serious ___."
10. Child (to parent): "All the kids are allowed to go ___ me!"

WORD MATH Complete each equation to make a list word.

11. regular - r + te =
12. instead - stead + spire =
13. participant - nt + tion =
14. academy - y + ic =
15. imitative - ive + e =
16. excepting - ing + ion =
17. departing - ing + ure =
18. crimp - p + inal =
19. operator - or + e =
20. combining - ing + ation =

STRATEGIC SPELLING

Seeing Meaning Connections

Complete each sentence with a word from the box.

Words with *operate*

operational
operator
postoperative

21. If you can't find the phone number, call the

_____.

22. After an operation, a patient may have

_____ therapy.

23. When the television breaks down it is no

longer _____.

1. _____
2. _____
3. _____
4. _____
5. _____
6. _____
7. _____
8. _____
9. _____
10. _____
11. _____
12. _____
13. _____
14. _____
15. _____
16. _____
17. _____
18. _____
19. _____
20. _____

Did You Know?
Crime comes from the Latin word
crimen, meaning "accusation, offense."

Make a capital.	
Make a small letter.	
Add something.	
Take out something.	
Add a period.	
New paragraph	

PROOFREAD FOR USAGE A run-on **sentence** results when one sentence runs into another without **a)** the proper punctuation or **b)** the necessary conjunction. For example:

The surgeon is handed a scalpel, the operation begins.

The surgeon is handed a scalpel, and the operation begins.

Check for Run-on Sentences Read the sentences below. If a sentence is a run-on, write "RO." If it is correct, write "Correct."

1. My uncle Luis is the surgeon, his speciality is the eye.
2. My uncle's dedication may inspire others, he is tireless.
3. As a surgeon, he must stand for hours, he must be alert.
4. An operating room can be a cold, frightening place.
5. My uncle always reassures his patients they adore him.

1. _____

2. _____

3. _____

4. _____

5. _____

PROOFREAD A CHARACTER STUDY Write five misspelled words in this passage correctly. Fix two run-on sentences.

> The hands of a surgeon like Uncle Luis combin science and humanity. He may perform an operashen for ten hours, he may then have to partisapat in a consultation. Without excipton, Uncle Luis will then rush to reassure a nervous family they need his advice and insparation.

Word List

combine	crime
combination	criminal
depart	academy
departure	academic
except	participate
exception	participation
imitate	inspire
imitation	inspiration
operate	regulate
operation	regulation

Personal Words

1. _____

2. _____

WRITE A CHARACTER STUDY Write about someone whom you admire. Use three list words and a personal word.

Review

MAKING INFERENCES   Write the word from the box that fits each clue.

crime	combination
criminal	imitate
except	imitation
exception	operate
combine	operation

1. person who can be found in prison
2. what a young child will often do to learn
3. what you need to know in order to open some locks
4. what the removal of a person's appendix is called
5. the opposite of *as well as*
6. what the police will arrest you for
7. how a doctor might treat an internal injury
8. a counterfeit or copy
9. what you do to some ingredients of a recipe
10. what you make by not following a rule one time

1. _____
2. _____
3. _____
4. _____
5. _____
6. _____
7. _____
8. _____
9. _____
10. _____

Word *Study*

SYNONYMS   Synonyms are words with the same general meaning. "She likes to *mimic* me" could just as well be stated "She likes to *imitate* me." *Mimic* and *imitate* are **synonyms.** Synonyms are seldom interchangeable in all usages, however. In the phrase "a painting that seemed to *imitate* Picasso," *mimic* could not be substituted for *imitate*. In this context, *imitate* means "resemble."

inspire	gratitude
operate	offense
architecture	

Read each sentence below. Substitute a synonym from the box for each underlined word.

1. Their only <u>crime</u> was ignoring their friend's warning.
2. I love to study the <u>structure</u> of old buildings.
3. I don't know how to <u>run</u> this machine.
4. I gave the man who saved my life my sincere <u>thankfulness</u>.
5. The teacher was able to <u>influence</u> her students to learn.

Choose the synonym in parentheses that you think would best fit in each sentence. Use the Spelling Dictionary if you need help.

6. The Rolls-Royce is a (distinguished, well-known) car.
7. This ground is too (hard, difficult) to dig.
8. The lawyer found a (suitable, fit) office.
9. We saw the (noiseless, still) and sad swans.
10. They like to be (lazy, idle) on weekends.

1. _____
2. _____
3. _____
4. _____
5. _____
6. _____
7. _____
8. _____
9. _____
10. _____

Endings -ty, -ity, -tion

SPELLING FOCUS

When **-ty**, **-ity**, and **-tion** are added to some words, one or more letters may change: **secure, security; recognize, recognition.**

■ **STUDY** Read each word and notice its ending. Then read the meaning phrase.

1.	**safety**	**safety** tips for bicycle riders
2.	**loyalty**	constant **loyalty** to the team
3.	**society**	laws for the good of **society**
4.	**security**	**security** guards at the bank
5.	**personality**	her friendly **personality**
6.	**university**	students at the **university**
7.	**authority**	was given the **authority** to rule
8.	**recognition**	wore a mask to escape **recognition**
9.	**description**	an accurate **description** of the room
10.	**introduction**	**introduction** of new students

11.	**certainty**	a 100% **certainty** for thundershowers
12.	**specialty**	the restaurant's **specialty**
13.	**cruelty**	no **cruelty** to animals
14.	**publicity**	**publicity** to get people to attend
15.	**electricity**	wires for **electricity**
16.	**reality**	wasn't a story about **reality**
17.	**subscription**	renew a magazine **subscription**
18.	**retention**	good memory for the **retention** of facts
19.	**intention**	had no **intention** of leaving
20.	**reduction**	**reduction** of the price for the sale

■ **PRACTICE** Sort the words by writing
- seven words that end in **-tion**
- seven words that end in **-ity**
- six words that end in **-ty**

■ **WRITE** Choose three phrases to include in a paragraph.

1.
2.
3.
4.
5.
6.
7.
8.
9.
10.
11.
12.
13.
14.
15.
16.
17.
18.
19.
20.

CHALLENGE!

subtlety
technicality
hospitality
deception
acquisition

ANTONYMS Write the list word that means the opposite of each word below. Use the Spelling Dictionary for help.

1. kindness
2. conclusion
3. danger
4. fantasy
5. insecurity
6. disloyalty
7. enlargement
8. uncertainty

CONTEXT CLUES Write the list word that completes each sentence.

9. If you have a good ___ people probably like you.
10. Their work for peace will benefit all of ___.
11. During storms, a ___ pond holds water to prevent flooding.
12. She received the award in ___ for her volunteer work.
13. When a restaurant has a ___, many people order it.
14. There should be a person in ___ in any organization.
15. If you want people to know about your product, use ___.
16. Without ___ we couldn't turn on the lights.
17. If you lose your dog, post a ___ in the paper.
18. Never make it your ___ to deliberately hurt someone.
19. If you have a hobby, order a ___ to a hobby magazine.
20. People who want a higher education may go to a ___.

STRATEGIC SPELLING
Building New Words

Add the ending to each word to make a new word. Remember: one or more letters may change when the ending is added.

Add -tion

21. inscribe _____

22. reduce _____

Add -ity

23. real _____

24. hostile _____

1. _____
2. _____
3. _____
4. _____
5. _____
6. _____
7. _____
8. _____
9. _____
10. _____
11. _____
12. _____
13. _____
14. _____
15. _____
16. _____
17. _____
18. _____
19. _____
20. _____

Take a Hint
Publicity and **electricity** are very important to any **city!**

PROOFREAD FOR USAGE Using more than one negative word in a sentence is called a **double negative**. For example:

> For years, Barbara McClintock didn't receive ~~no~~ scientific recognition.

Check for Double Negatives Read each sentence. Write the word you would take out to correct any double negatives. If a sentence is correct, write "Correct."

1. McClintock believed that DNA was not never fixed in place.
2. Her fellow scientists didn't have no respect for her work.
3. Experiments in the 1970s proved that DNA jumped around.
4. She received the 1983 Nobel Prize for her research on corn.
5. She wasn't at ease with the fame the prize brought.

1. _____

2. _____

3. _____

4. _____

5. _____

PROOFREAD A REPORT Find five misspelled words and write them correctly. Fix two double negatives.

> Barbara McClintock didn't never think a career in science was a sertainty. However, socity didn't have any intenshen of encouraging women in such pursuits. For years, she couldn't get no support for her research at a major universty, but she never gave up. Science owes alot to McClintock.

Word List

certainty	authority
specialty	security
cruelty	reality
safety	subscription
loyalty	introduction
society	retention
personality	intention
university	description
electricity	reduction
publicity	recognition

Personal Words

1. _____

2. _____

WRITE A REPORT Write about a person you think made a difference. Use two list words and one personal word.

Review

DEFINITIONS Write the boxed word that matches each clue.

safety	university
loyalty	authority
society	recognition
security	description
personality	introduction

1. a picture in words
2. a knowing again or being identified
3. an institution of learning beyond high school
4. the first part of a book or speech
5. a showing of faithfulness
6. a guard responsible for the safety of people or property
7. the person or group that has the right to control or command
8. freedom from harm or danger
9. the qualities that make someone different from another
10. a group of people joined together for a common purpose or by a common interest

1. _____
2. _____
3. _____
4. _____
5. _____
6. _____
7. _____
8. _____
9. _____
10. _____

Word *Study*

LATIN ROOTS: *scrib, script* The words *describe* and *subscription* come from the Latin **scrib** (sometimes written **script**), meaning "write." The words in the box all come from this root.

Write the words from the box to complete the word web. Use the Spelling Dictionary if you need help.

scribble
script
subscribe
transcribe

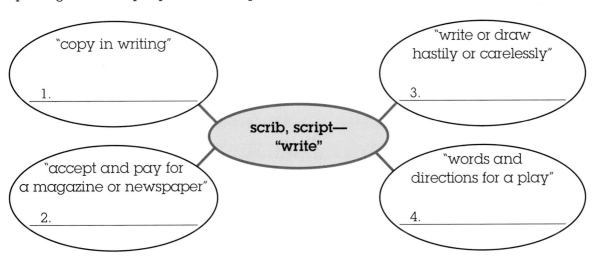

"copy in writing"

1. _____

"write or draw hastily or carelessly"

3. _____

scrib, script— "write"

"accept and pay for a magazine or newspaper"

2. _____

"words and directions for a play"

4. _____

Use one of the words from the web to complete each sentence.

5. The court reporter will ___ your description.
6. I always ___ drawings on a pad while talking on the phone.
7. She wrote the director's suggestions on her ___.
8. The new library will ___ to hundreds of different magazines.

5. _____
6. _____
7. _____
8. _____

Irregular Plurals

Most plurals are formed by adding **-s** or **-es.** However, usually change **f** or **fe** to **v** before adding **es: yourselves.** Make the main word plural in hyphenated compounds: **brothers-in-law.** Some plurals are the same as the singular: **series.** Some have a new form: **bacterium, bacteria.**

■ **STUDY**   Notice whether the plural differs from the base word.

handcuff	1.	**handcuffs**
chef	2.	**chefs**
zero	3.	**zeros**
torpedo	4.	**torpedoes**
yourself	5.	**yourselves**
bookshelf	6.	**bookshelves**
brother-in-law	7.	**brothers-in-law**
series	8.	**series**
bacterium	9.	**bacteria**
medium	10.	**media**

portfolio	11.	**portfolios**
avocado	12.	**avocados**
cargo	13.	**cargoes**
motto	14.	**mottoes**
calf	15.	**calves**
great-uncle	16.	**great-uncles**
aircraft	17.	**aircraft**
alumnus	18.	**alumni**
datum	19.	**data**
oasis	20.	**oases**

1. _____
2. _____
3. _____
4. _____
5. _____
6. _____
7. _____
8. _____
9. _____
10. _____
11. _____
12. _____
13. _____
14. _____
15. _____
16. _____
17. _____
18. _____
19. _____
20. _____

CHALLENGE!

dynamos
innuendoes
curricula
nuclei
fungi

■ **PRACTICE**   Sort by writing three plurals in which **f** changed to **v**, ten in which just **-s** or **-es** was added, two that match their singular form, and five other plurals not formed with **-s** or **-es.**

■ **WRITE**   Choose ten words to write in sentences.

DRAWING CONCLUSIONS   Write the list word that matches each clue. Use the Spelling Dictionary for help.

1. Add a million of these together and you'll still have nothing.
2. These are welcome sights to desert travelers.
3. A police officer uses these to restrain criminals.
4. Smash these up to make a delicious guacamole.
5. These people know what herbs and spices are all about.
6. When these grow up, they moo a lot.
7. When these travel, they travel underwater.
8. "Think before you speak" and "Be prepared" are these.
9. Your favorite reading material can be stored on these.

WORD FORMS   Write the plural forms of the words in parentheses.

10. Television, radio, and newspapers make up the (medium).
11. Be sure to use commas to separate items in a (series).
12. All of you need to take better care of (yourself).
13. Two of my (great-uncle) will be at the family reunion.
14. Collect more (datum) before you draw conclusions.
15. Hand in your writing (portfolio) on Monday.
16. Those geese flying in V-formation look like (aircraft).
17. Certain species of (bacterium) cause diseases.
18. Supertankers with (cargo) of petroleum have docked.
19. My sisters' husbands are my (brother-in-law).
20. Some (alumnus) donate money to their colleges.

STRATEGIC SPELLING
Building New Words

Form the plurals of *crisis, radius, headquarters,* and *sister-in-law*. Remember what you learned. Use the Spelling Dictionary if you need help.

21. _____

22. _____

23. _____

24. _____

1. _____
2. _____
3. _____
4. _____
5. _____
6. _____
7. _____
8. _____
9. _____
10. _____
11. _____
12. _____
13. _____
14. _____
15. _____
16. _____
17. _____
18. _____
19. _____
20. _____

Did You Know?
Avocados have the highest number of calories of any fruit!

PROOFREAD FOR USAGE Notice how the writer corrected this mistake in a diary.

First we lost our map. Then we ~~run~~ ^{ran} out of water.

Since the event took place in the past, both verbs should be in the past tense. Don't change verb tense without a good reason.

Check Verb Tense If the underlined verb is correct, write "Correct." If it's not, write it correctly.

1. After that, a hot wind <u>comes</u> and blew sand at us.
2. Then a series of truly unfortunate events <u>happened</u>.
3. One camel went lame and another <u>stops</u> for a rest.
4. I got sand in my eyes. Then it <u>gets</u> in my ears.
5. I couldn't see or hear, and my throat <u>aches</u>.

PROOFREAD A TRAVEL DIARY Correct the five misspelled words. Also fix two mistakes with verb tense.

1. _____
2. _____
3. _____
4. _____
5. _____

> We knew there were two oasises nearby, but we look everwhere and all we saw was sand. "You must help yourselfs now," our guide said. Suddenly we spot two aircrafts overhead. My brother-in-laws had found us!

WRITE A TRAVEL DIARY Write a diary entry about a trip you took. Use three list words and two personal words.

Word List

yourselves	torpedoes
bookshelves	cargoes
calves	mottoes
handcuffs	data
chefs	bacteria
zeros	alumni
portfolios	oases
brothers-in-law	media
great-uncles	series
avocados	aircraft

Personal Words

1. _____
2. _____

Proofreading Marks

☰	Make a capital.
/	Make a small letter.
∧	Add something.
ℓ	Take out something.
⊙	Add a period.
¶	New paragraph

Review

CONTEXT CLUES   Use the context in each sentence to help you write the correct word from the box.

handcuffs	bookshelves
chefs	brothers-in-law
zeros	series
torpedoes	bacteria
yourselves	media

1. A powerful microscope is needed to see dangerous ___.
2. I have found that ___ are useful for storing many things besides books.
3. It took several ___ of numbers before we saw the pattern.
4. The submarine carried many ___ to sink enemy ships.
5. Both large numbers and small numbers may include many ___.
6. The fire chief yelled to the men, "Get out and save ___!"
7. The police used ___ to keep the prisoners from escaping.
8. All my uncles, my mom's ___, came to the family party.
9. The ___ falsely say that they merely report the news but are not responsible for making news.
10. The cooking contest attracted many great ___.

1. _____
2. _____
3. _____
4. _____
5. _____
6. _____
7. _____
8. _____
9. _____
10. _____

Multicultural Connection

LANGUAGES   Many English words come from **Spanish,** the official language of Spain, Mexico, and most of Central and South America. In the box are six words derived from Spanish.

avocado	hammock
cargo	maize
hurricane	savanna

Words that come into another language usually change spelling but often resemble the original word. Write the English word from the box that comes from each Spanish word below.

1. *sabana*
2. *huracán*
3. *cargar*
4. *hamaca*
5. *aguacate*
6. *maíz*

Write the word from the box that each sentence refers to. You may need to use your Spelling Dictionary.

7. This word names the corn grown by Indians in Mexico and Central America at the time of Spanish colonization.
8. This word originated on Haiti, an island where the tropical storm this word names can cause death and destruction.
9. This word names a treeless plain found in parts of tropical North, South, and Central America.
10. This word names a lightweight hanging bed made of cord or rope, often found in tropical countries.

1. _____
2. _____
3. _____
4. _____
5. _____
6. _____
7. _____
8. _____
9. _____
10. _____

Plural or Possessive?

1. _____

2. _____

3. _____

4. _____

5. _____

6. _____

7. _____

8. _____

9. _____

10. _____

11. _____

12. _____

13. _____

14. _____

15. _____

16. _____

17. _____

18. _____

19. _____

20. _____

SPELLING FOCUS

Form possessives in these ways: singular nouns—add an apostrophe (') and **s: niece's;** plural nouns ending with **s**—add an apostrophe: **countries';** plural nouns *not* ending with **s**—add **'s: salesmen's.** Don't add an apostrophe to form a possessive pronoun or a plural noun: **its, nieces.**

■ **STUDY** Notice which words are plural and which possessive.

1.	**niece's**	his **niece's** birthday party
2.	**nieces'**	their **nieces'** matching dresses
3.	**nieces**	took her two **nieces** to the movie
4.	**country's**	our **country's** leaders in Washington
5.	**countries'**	several **countries'** different languages
6.	**countries**	traveled through several **countries**
7.	**salesman's**	a **salesman's** heavy sample case
8.	**salesmen's**	competing **salesmen's** products
9.	**its**	fastened **its** flea collar
10.	**ours**	**ours** to keep or give away

11.	**Mr. Murphy's**	**Mr. Murphy's** bushy red beard
12.	**Murphys**	the **Murphys** on Oak Street
13.	**witness's**	one **witness's** testimony
14.	**witnesses'**	four **witnesses'** different stories
15.	**witnesses**	four **witnesses** to the crime
16.	**secretary's**	this **secretary's** smart decision
17.	**secretaries'**	all the **secretaries'** desks
18.	**secretaries**	new computers for the **secretaries**
19.	**theirs**	better than **theirs** is
20.	**hers**	keeps **hers** locked in a drawer

CHALLENGE!

congress's
congresses
communities'
communities
April Fools' Day

■ **PRACTICE** Sort the words by writing five plural nouns, then four possessive pronouns, then six singular possessive nouns, and finally five plural possessive nouns.

■ **WRITE** Choose ten phrases to rewrite as sentences.

CONTEXT Write the correct form of the word in parentheses to complete each sentence.

1. Both of my (niece) birthdays are in August.
2. Is this your coat or is it (her)?
3. Several (country) ambassadors met at the opening of the peace conference.
4. The four (witnesses) testimony helped convict the defendant of the robbery charge.
5. The cabin was (our) for the entire week!
6. The (secretary) notebook was in the lost-and-found.
7. Aunt Loretta made her (niece) wedding dress.
8. How did this (salesman) order book get so wet?
9. The mare helped (it) foal cross the river.
10. That bat is (their), not yours.

FORMING PLURALS AND POSSESSIVES Follow the directions at the top of each list to write the correct list word.

Form the Plural
11. Murphy
12. country
13. niece
14. witness
15. secretary

Form the Possessive
16. Mr. Murphy
17. secretaries
18. witness
19. country
20. salesmen

STRATEGIC SPELLING

Building New Words

Write the correct forms of each of these words to complete the chart: *calf, library, avocado.*

Singular Possessive	Plural Possessive
21.	24.
22.	25.
23.	26.

1. _____
2. _____
3. _____
4. _____
5. _____
6. _____
7. _____
8. _____
9. _____
10. _____
11. _____
12. _____
13. _____
14. _____
15. _____
16. _____
17. _____
18. _____
19. _____
20. _____

Take a Hint
Confused whether to write "The dog ate its bone" or "The dog ate it's bone"? Read the sentence using "it is" and if that sounds right, you need the apostrophe.

☰	Make a capital.
/	Make a small letter.
∧	Add something.
ℓ	Take out something.
⊙	Add a period.
¶	New paragraph

PROOFREAD FOR PUNCTUATION

Abbreviations that are titles, dates, addresses, and initials need periods. For example:

To: Ms L Uchida, Ph D.

1402 Dodge St

Check Abbreviations Find the five mistakes with abbreviations below. Write the abbreviations correctly.

From: Dr Dan R Tynan
Subject: Our secretaries' time off
Date: Aug 20

As you know, Mr Val Halsted and Ms Doris Gaines were witnesses to an accident. As a result, they must spend this week testifying in court.

1. _____

2. _____

3. _____

4. _____

5. _____

PROOFREAD A MEMO
Correct the five misspelled words. Also fix one error with abbreviations.

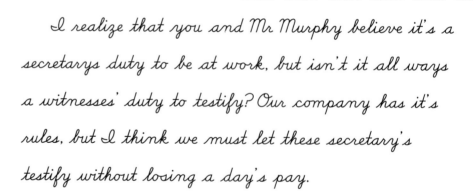

I realize that you and Mr. Murphy believe it's a secretarys duty to be at work, but isn't it all ways a witnesses' duty to testify? Our company has it's rules, but I think we must let these secretary's testify without losing a day's pay.

Word List

its	salesmen's
ours	secretaries
theirs	secretary's
hers	secretaries'
Murphys	witnesses
Mr. Murphy's	witness's
nieces	witnesses'
niece's	countries
nieces'	country's
salesman's	countries'

Personal Words

_____

_____

WRITE A REPLY
Pretend you are Mr. Murphy or Ms. Uchida. Write a memo telling Dr. Tynan what you think of his suggestion. Use three list words and a personal word.

Review

DEFINITIONS   Write the word from the box that means the same as each phrase below.

niece's	countries
nieces'	salesman's
nieces	salesmen's
country's	its
countries'	ours

1. belonging to a sister's daughters
2. of two or more sellers
3. more than one nation
4. belonging to us
5. a brother's daughters
6. of a nation
7. of a seller
8. belonging to a thing
9. belonging to several nations
10. belonging to a sister's daughter

1. _____
2. _____
3. _____
4. _____
5. _____
6. _____
7. _____
8. _____
9. _____
10. _____

Word *Study*

CLIPPED WORDS   One of a secretary's duties is to type memos. *Memo* is a shortened form of *memorandum,* just as *piano* and *bus* are shortened forms of *pianoforte* and *omnibus.* We call these short forms **clipped words.**

You'll find more clipped words in the box. The longer words they came from are the numbered words in the silly story below. Replace these longer words with their clipped forms.

gas	tend	van	scram	flu	pants
wig	fortnight	phone	cab	mum	

My doorbell rang at 3 A.M. a (1) <u>fourteen nights</u> ago. Zip, I pulled on my pleated (2) <u>pantaloons</u> and rushed to answer the door while adjusting my pesky (3) <u>periwig</u>, which had slid over my eyes. It was Murphy. He stopped by to tell me about his bossy niece. She had a case of (4) <u>influenza</u>, so he'd caught a (5) <u>cabriolet</u> and rushed over to (6) <u>attend</u> to her needs. "Water my (7) <u>chrysanthemum</u>," she'd ordered. "Answer the (8) <u>telephone</u>. Put (9) <u>gasoline</u> in the (10) <u>caravan</u>—" "Wait a minute, Murphy," I said. "I must get some sleep, so (11) <u>scramble</u>. I'll see you tomorrow."

1. _____
2. _____
3. _____
4. _____
5. _____
6. _____
7. _____
8. _____
9. _____
10. _____
11. _____

Review

Lesson 7: Words with No Sound Clues
Lesson 8: Related Words 1
Lesson 9: Endings -ty, -ity, -tion
Lesson 10: Irregular Plurals
Lesson 11: Plural or Possessive?

REVIEW WORD LIST

1. audience
2. Delaware
3. diamond
4. disgusted
5. elementary
6. juvenile
7. mathematics
8. memory
9. miniature
10. really
11. recognize
12. restaurant
13. tournament
14. usually
15. victim
16. academy
17. combination
18. combine
19. crime
20. criminal
21. depart
22. departure
23. except
24. imitate
25. inspiration
26. participate
27. regulate
28. authority
29. introduction
30. personality
31. publicity
32. safety
33. society
34. subscription
35. university
36. aircraft
37. alumni
38. avocados
39. chefs
40. data
41. great-uncles
42. media
43. series
44. countries
45. country's
46. its
47. nieces
48. ours
49. theirs
50. witness's

■ PROOFREADING

Find the spelling errors in each passage and write the words correctly. All passages have seven errors except the last one, which has eight.

1. _____

2. _____

3. _____

4. _____

5. _____

6. _____

7. _____

PROOFREAD A SCHEDULE

Schedule for Class Trip

9 A.M.   diparchur from lot behind ball dimond

10 A.M.   arrival at Art Institute and tour of miniture rooms

Noon   lunch at restrant in Art Institute

1 P.M.   Bus A will dipart for zoo.

Bus B will return to school. All students who will partisapat in the soccer tournament should be on Bus B!

3 P.M.   Bus A returns to school.

Students will not be allowed on buses without parental approval slips.

PROOFREAD A BOOK REVIEW

Great Sports Stories

Kim Nakimura

My favorite book is <u>Great Sports Stories</u> by Clyde Hanson. One story was about a player who was discusted with the medea publisity he usally received about his private life and quit baseball. Another one was about a universty player injured in a football game. His efforts to recover from that injury were realy inspiring. The funniest story was about one countrys swimming team in the Olympics. Anyone who likes sports should read this.

1. _____
2. _____
3. _____
4. _____
5. _____
6. _____
7. _____

PROOFREAD A FRIENDLY LETTER

August 19, 19—

Dear Tracey,

As you know, we are visiting in delaware. Our trip has been great exept for the weather. At our family reunion, I met my grandmother, two grate uncles (her brothers), and some of Mom's neices—my cousins. I met my cousins before, but this time I didn't reconize them. They go to a science acadamy. At the airport, we picked up some luggage that we thought was our's, but it wasn't! I wound up with some pretty strange outfits, but we got it all straightened out.

Love,
Jennifer

1. _____
2. _____
3. _____
4. _____
5. _____
6. _____
7. _____

PROOFREAD A NEWS STORY

1. _____
2. _____
3. _____
4. _____
5. _____
6. _____
7. _____

August 16, 19__

The Clarion

Page 5

Robbery on Redwood Drive

Students heard the first in a series of talks last week on how to help prevent crim and regulate behavior around the school. Two police officers told the adience that so far there has been some crimanal activity, including one robbery on Redwood Drive. The victdom, according to one witnesses' story, was an elementry school student. who had been showing friends money he had gotten as birthday gifts. Students were warned "Don't become juvinile statistics!"

PROOFREAD A MYTH

1. _____
2. _____
3. _____
4. _____
5. _____
6. _____
7. _____

Daedalus and Icarus

A wise man named Daedalus was put into prison by King Minos. His son Icarus was in prison with him. One day Daedalus had an insperation. He gathered hundreds of feathers, sewed them together, covered them with wax, and made wings for himself and his son. "We will imitat the birds," he said to Icarus, and off they flew over the prison walls. Then Daedalus told Icarus to regyulate his flight so that he flew neither too high nor too low. Icarus knew that his father was worried about his safty, and he respected his father's athority, but nevertheless he flew higher and higher. Soon he could see many countries'. "Surely my father won't mind if I fly a little higher," he said to himself. "Birds fly high, and my wings are better than theres." Icarus had forgotten one thing, however. His wings were covered with wax. When he flew too close to the sun, the wax melted and the wings fell apart.

PROOFREAD A SURVEY

We are gathering datas for some possible changes next year.

1. What is your favorite school subject?

English   social studies   mathmatics

science   health   other _____

2. Would you be interested in a course that would combin science and math?

Yes   No   Maybe

3. Would you be interested in a seres of music appreciation classes in combanation with concerts?

Yes   No   Maybe

4. Would you be interested in joining a drama club or sociaty if it's meetings were held after school?

Yes   No   Maybe

1. _____
2. _____
3. _____
4. _____
5. _____
6. _____
7. _____

PROOFREAD AN ADVERTISEMENT

Students! Take advantage of a discount subscripshun now!

For a limited time, this can be your interduction to an exciting new magazine. Features in upcoming issues that we know you will want to read include these:

quiz on determining your personalty type

easy recipes from famous chef's

directions for building model air craft

tips on improving your memorie

profiles of famous university alumnuses

how to grow the seeds of avocadoes

There's much more. Act now!

1. _____
2. _____
3. _____
4. _____
5. _____
6. _____
7. _____
8. _____

Divide and Conquer

DISCOVER THE STRATEGY Here's a strategy for studying extra-long words that give you trouble. Cut them down to size by dividing them up. Then study them piece by piece. How do you divide them? That depends on the kind of word you're dealing with.

Compounds: divide between base words	Words with Affixes: divide between affix and base word	Other Words: divide between syllables
your/selves brief/case hand/cuffs	weight/less pre/histor/ic loyal/ty	tour/na/ment Con/nect/i/cut graf/fi/ti

TRY IT OUT Now try this divide and conquer strategy.

Compounds Write these compounds.

> **whirlpool aircraft bookshelves everywhere cheerleader**

Work with a partner. Draw a line between the two base words that make up each compound. *Note:* This will show you that two words have been put together with no letters lost.

1. _____
2. _____
3. _____
4. _____
5. _____

Affixes Write these words.

| fortunate usually improper activate certainty |

Work with a partner. Draw lines between each base word and any prefixes or suffixes. *Note:* This will show you whether adding a suffix changes the spelling of the base word.

Now look back at the words you wrote. Two base words changed spelling when the suffix was added. Underline these base words that changed spelling.

Syllables Write these words.

| chandelier audience principal accommodate portfolios |

Work with a partner. Say each word. Listen carefully for the syllables and draw lines between them. Check a dictionary for any words that you're not sure of.

LOOK AHEAD Look ahead at the next five lessons. Write six list words that you could use these strategies with. Say each word to yourself and divide it into smaller pieces. For each word, choose the way that works best for you.

6. _____

7. _____

8. _____

9. _____

10. _____

11. _____

12. _____

13. _____

14. _____

15. _____

1. _____   4. _____

2. _____   5. _____

3. _____   6. _____

Vowels in Final Syllables

SPELLING FOCUS

Vowels in final syllables often sound alike even when they are spelled differently, because they have the **schwa** sound (/ə/): **hospital, acceptable; abandon, cardigan; murmur, interior.**

■ **STUDY**   Read each word and meaning phrase. Notice how the final vowel sound is spelled in each word.

1.	**hospital**	rode in an ambulance to the **hospital**
2.	**vertical**	a sweater with **vertical** stripes
3.	**acceptable**	an **acceptable** excuse
4.	**multiple**	**multiple** bruises from the fall
5.	**abandon**	can **abandon** a plan that won't work
6.	**comparison**	a **comparison** of the two cities
7.	**cardigan**	button a **cardigan** sweater
8.	**murmur**	**murmur** of voices in the next room
9.	**interior**	cool **interior** of the shaded house
10.	**ancestor**	an old picture of an **ancestor**

11.	**identical**	picked up a coat **identical** to mine
12.	**logical**	answered with **logical** reasoning
13.	**impartial**	an **impartial** umpire for the game
14.	**rectangle**	the **rectangle** next to the circle
15.	**companion**	good **companion** for the bus trip
16.	**suburban**	sprawling **suburban** towns
17.	**metropolitan**	the daily **metropolitan** newspaper
18.	**sulfur**	the smell of **sulfur** from a lit match
19.	**sponsor**	wore team shirts from our **sponsor**
20.	**superior**	was praised for **superior** work

■ **PRACTICE**   Sort the words by writing eight words that end in **al** or **le**, then six words that end in **an** or **on**, and, finally, six words that end in **ur** or **or**.

■ **WRITE**   Choose three phrases to include in a paragraph.

1. _____

2. _____

3. _____

4. _____

5. _____

6. _____

7. _____

8. _____

9. _____

10. _____

11. _____

12. _____

13. _____

14. _____

15. _____

16. _____

17. _____

18. _____

19. _____

20. _____

CHALLENGE!

acquittal
quadruple
chameleon
amphibian
endeavor

ANALOGIES   Write the list word that completes each analogy.

1. Guest is to motel as patient is to ___.
2. A nickel's shape is to circle as a dollar bill's shape is to ___.
3. Inside is to outside as ___ is to exterior.
4. Up is to down as horizontal is to ___.
5. Parka is to jacket as ___ is to sweater.
6. Shout is to yell as whisper is to ___.
7. Excellent is to poor as ___ is to inferior.
8. Advertiser is to billboard as ___ is to TV commercial.
9. Towns and villages are to rural areas as cities and suburbs are to ___ areas.

WORD ASSOCIATION   Write the list word suggested by each group of words.

10. earlier generation, forefather, long ago
11. friend, comrade, sidekick
12. mineral, flammable, yellow
13. fair, just, not prejudiced
14. a lot, several, many
15. leave, desert, give up
16. sensible, reasonable, rational
17. agreeable, satisfactory, alright
18. not urban, not rural
19. mirror image, exactly alike, same
20. likeness, similarity, difference

1. _____
2. _____
3. _____
4. _____
5. _____
6. _____
7. _____
8. _____
9. _____
10. _____
11. _____
12. _____
13. _____
14. _____
15. _____
16. _____
17. _____
18. _____
19. _____
20. _____

STRATEGIC SPELLING

The Divide and Conquer Strategy

Sometimes it helps to study longer words piece by piece. Write *metropolitan, interior, companion,* and *comparison.* Draw lines to break them into smaller parts. Study the parts.

21. _____
22. _____
23. _____
24. _____

Did You Know?
The word *cardigan* comes from the seventh Earl of *Cardigan,* a British officer in the Crimean War in 1855, supposedly because he wore one.

	Make a capital.
/	Make a small letter.
∧	Add something.
ℓ	Take out something.
⊙	Add a period.
⌓	New paragraph

PROOFREAD FOR PUNCTUATION Use a colon to introduce three or more items.

The Grace High Action Council is now recruiting volunteers for these projects: hospital work, food distribution, and child care.

Check Colons Correct the sentences below by writing the colon and the word it follows.

1. Volunteers will be accepted in these numbers ten in child care, ten at local hospitals, and six to do food distribution.
2. Qualifications are as follows sincere commitment, parental consent, acceptable grades, and teacher recommendation,
3. Volunteers do three things commit to one year's service, work three hours per week, and help with recruitment.

1. _____

2. _____

3. _____

PROOFREAD A PARAGRAPH Find the four misspelled words in the paragraph and write them correctly. The errors may be words you learned before. Find two errors involving colons.

After looking into many projects, were certain that these are the most lojical. The metropoliten food program includes the following urban relief, subrban food drives, and combined programs. Hospital work involves: serving food and being a companion to the homebound.

Word List

acceptable	comparison
ancestor	logical
abandon	interior
hospital	vertical
multiple	metropolitan
sulfur	impartial
rectangle	companion
suburban	cardigan
sponsor	murmur
identical	superior

Personal Words

1. _____

2. _____

WRITE A PARAGRAPH Which of the projects would you volunteer for? Write a paragraph about it. Include your reasons.

Review

DRAWING CONCLUSIONS

Write the word from the box that fits each clue.

hospital	comparison
vertical	cardigan
acceptable	murmur
multiple	interior
abandon	ancestor

1. This would annoy a teacher who wants a silent room.
2. You could wear this if you were cold.
3. This is what you should do to a burning building.
4. You would go here if you were very ill.
5. Clothes with this kind of stripes make you look taller.
6. Your great-grandmother is one.
7. You make this before deciding which of two radios to buy.
8. This is the part of a box where you store things.
9. Twins or triplets are this kind of birth.
10. If you have a taste for an orange, a banana might not be this.

1. _____
2. _____
3. _____
4. _____
5. _____
6. _____
7. _____
8. _____
9. _____
10. _____

Multicultural Connection

FAMILY TREES Throughout history, people have kept track of their ancestors through **family trees.** A family tree is a chart that shows how all members of a family—going back to great-great-grandparents and before—are related. Some families keep carefully written records, while others rely on elders to tell stories.

Answer the questions about the family tree below.

1. When was Angela's grandfather Bernardo born?

   _____

2. What is the name of Angela's grandmother on her mother's side?

   _____

3. How old was Angela's mother when Angela was born?

   _____

Bernardo Morales born Sept. 3, 1930

Juanna Torres born April 12, 1935

Patrick Sullivan born Dec. 24, 1936

Moira Donahue born June 8, 1941

Geraldo Benito Morales born Aug. 6, 1958

Kathleen Sullivan born Aug. 6, 1962

Angela Morales born Nov. 28, 1985

Vowels in Unstressed Syllables

SPELLING FOCUS

In many unstressed syllables, the vowel sound you hear is a schwa /ə/. It gives no clue to its spelling: **vit_a_min.**

■ **STUDY** Read each word and meaning phrase. Notice that the underlined vowels have the same sound—that of the **schwa.**

1. **vitamin** — a **vitamin** found in orange juice
2. **medicine** — **medicine** for an earache
3. **continent** — **continent** of North America
4. **material** — a walkway made of sturdy **material**
5. **probably** ✳ — **probably** will meet you at the mall
6. **opinion** — your **opinion** of the new gym floor
7. **Saturday** ✳ — slept late on **Saturday**
8. **treasure** — pirate **treasure** in an old chest
9. **finally** ✳ — **finally** saved enough money
10. **popular** — used to be a **popular** song

11. **bulletin** — a letter on the **bulletin** board
12. **competition** — **competition** in the poster contest
13. **invitation** — received an **invitation** to the party
14. **literal** — **literal** meaning of the saying
15. **binoculars** — used **binoculars** to spot the eagle
16. **senator** — wrote to a **senator** in Washington
17. **cemetery** — the **cemetery** next to the church
18. **ingredients** — the **ingredients** for fudge cake
19. **episode** — gloomy **episode** in our hero's life
20. **substitute** — no **substitute** for peanut butter

■ **PRACTICE** Sort the words by writing
- twelve words that have two or three schwa sounds
- eight words that have one schwa sound

Underline the schwa sounds in each word.

■ **WRITE** Choose two phrases to write in an advertisement, slogan, or saying.

1. _____
2. _____
3. _____
4. _____
5. _____
6. _____
7. _____
8. _____
9. _____
10. _____
11. _____
12. _____
13. _____
14. _____
15. _____
16. _____
17. _____
18. _____
19. _____
20. _____

CHALLENGE!

indecision
meticulous
despondent
misdemeanor
paralysis

✳ **WATCH OUT FOR FREQUENTLY MISSPELLED WORDS!**

MAKING INFERENCES   Write the list word that fits each clue.

1. Recipes contain lists of these.
2. Your parents may vote for this person.
3. A country is located on one of these.
4. You'll see this on TV if a severe storm is coming.
5. You might receive this if someone is having a party.
6. Legends say you'll find this at the end of a rainbow.
7. This person teaches you when your own teacher is sick.
8. Bird watchers and spies use these.
9. This is the day you can spend time with friends.
10. A doctor prescribes this to cure a particular illness.
11. Some people take one of these each day to be healthy.

DEFINITIONS   Write the list word that means the same as the underlined word or phrase in each sentence.

12. She described the most important <u>incident</u> in the novel.
13. The plane came out of the fog and <u>at last</u> touched down.
14. In my <u>judgment</u>, that jacket looks terrific on you.
15. Some people understand only the <u>exact</u> meaning of words.
16. We <u>almost certainly</u> will go to the game this weekend.
17. The soldier's family visited the <u>graveyard</u> on Memorial Day.
18. The countertop is made of a <u>substance</u> that resists stains.
19. The soccer match was marked by fierce <u>rivalry</u>.
20. His sense of humor makes him <u>liked</u> at school.

STRATEGIC SPELLING

Seeing Meaning Connections

| 1. |
| 2. |
| 3. |
| 4. |
| 5. |
| 6. |
| 7. |
| 8. |
| 9. |
| 10. |
| 11. |
| 12. |
| 13. |
| 14. |
| 15. |
| 16. |
| 17. |
| 18. |
| 19. |
| 20. |

medicate
medicinal
medic

21. Write the list word that is related to the words in the box. Then write the word that fits each definition.
22. a doctor or medical student
23. having use or value as medicine
24. to treat with medicine

21. _____ 23. _____
22. _____ 24. _____

FREQUENTLY MISSPELLED WORDS

Students often misspell **Saturday.** It may help to remember that *Saturday* means "day of Saturn," the Roman god for whom the planet was also named.

71

PROOFREAD FOR USAGE Adjectives modify ONLY nouns or pronouns. Adverbs modify ONLY verbs. For example:

Do supervisors expect you to perform ~~good~~ *well*?
[*Well*, an adverb, modifies the verb *perform*.]
Do you feel ~~badly~~ *bad* when you are criticized?
[*Bad*, an adjective, modifies the noun *you*.]

Check Adjectives and Adverbs Correct errors using adjectives and adverbs.

1. _____

2. _____

3. _____

4. _____

5. _____

1. Do you like to do your job good and get a bonus?
2. Does your manager listen good when you give opinions?
3. Would you stay home or come to work if you felt badly?
4. Do you feel well that you can work after school?
5. Does it bother you when fellow workers perform bad?

PROOFREAD A QUESTIONNAIRE Correct five misspelled words. Also fix two mistakes with adverbs or adjectives.

✓ What is your opinon on after-school jobs?

✓ Are jobs at fast-food places populer?

✓ Do employees their get paid good?

✓ Are part-time employees treated bad?

✓ Would you probaly like to work on a Saterday?

Word List

probably	ingredients
Saturday	episode
treasure	invitation
binoculars	medicine
finally	literal
senator	continent
vitamin	material
bulletin	opinion
cemetery	popular
competition	substitute

Personal Words

1. _____

2. _____

WRITE A QUESTIONNAIRE Write a questionnaire on an issue that interests you. Ask classmates to answer it. Then compare results. Use two list words and a personal word.

Review

ANALOGIES   Write the word from the box that best completes each analogy.

vitamin	opinion
medicine	Saturday
continent	treasure
material	finally
probably	popular

1. Well-known is to famous as well-liked is to ___ .
2. Gold is to garbage as ___ is to trash.
3. Zinc is to mineral as C is to ___ .
4. Perhaps is to ___ as definitely is to yes.
5. "Rocks are dense" is to fact as "Rocks are pretty" is to ___ .
6. Optical shop is to glasses as drugstore is to ___ .
7. Words are to writing as ___ is to construction.
8. Beginning is to ending as first is to ___ .
9. December is to year as ___ is to week.
10. Island is to lake as ___ is to ocean.

1. _____
2. _____
3. _____
4. _____
5. _____
6. _____
7. _____
8. _____
9. _____
10. _____

Word *Study*

FORMAL AND INFORMAL ENGLISH   A senator uses formal English when addressing the members of Congress, but a student talking to friends uses **informal English**—for example, "It's really important that you come to this meeting, guys." That same student running for student council president might say, "It is with great concern that I urge you to attend this function."

The words you choose in writing as well as in speaking should suit your audience and purpose. Read each pair of sentences and write "F" if the wording is "Formal" or "I" if the wording is "Informal."

1. a. I cannot honor your invitation because my vehicle is unusable.
   b. I can't come over because my bike has a flat.
2. a. Lousy weather kept the plane from leaving.
   b. Inclement weather postponed the plane's departure.

Read these two sentences. First, write whether the sentence is "Formal" (F) or "Informal" (I). Then write the formal sentence using informal English and the informal sentence using formal English.

3. Please, allow me to assist you in your time of need.
4. Don't bother me!

1a. _____
1b. _____
2a. _____
2b. _____

3. _____

4. _____

Greek Word Parts

1. _____
2. _____
3. _____
4. _____
5. _____
6. _____
7. _____
8. _____
9. _____
10. _____
11. _____
12. _____
13. _____
14. _____
15. _____
16. _____
17. _____
18. _____
19. _____
20. _____

SPELLING FOCUS

Many words are formed from the Greek word parts **micro-**, meaning "small"; **-logy**, meaning "study of"; and **astro-** or **aster-**, meaning "star": <u>micro</u>scope, eco<u>logy</u>, <u>astro</u>naut.

■ **STUDY**   Read each word and meaning phrase.

1.	**microscope**	studied bacteria using a **microscope**
2.	**microchip**	the tiny **microchip** in a computer
3.	**microwave**	**microwave** radiation in an oven
4.	**ecology**	learned about the **ecology** of a swamp
5.	**biology**	studied worms and leeches in **biology**
6.	**mythology**	Norse or Greek **mythology**
7.	**technology**	the **technology** of weather reporting
8.	**astronaut**	an **astronaut** who walked in space
9.	**astronomy**	studied planets in **astronomy** class
10.	**disaster**	rebuilt their homes after the **disaster**

11.	**microcosm**	classroom as a **microcosm** of society
12.	**microbe**	the **microbe** that turns milk into yogurt
13.	**microfilm**	newspaper article stored on **microfilm**
14.	**sociology**	the **sociology** of a rural society
15.	**geology**	searched for rocks on a **geology** trip
16.	**etymology**	knew the **etymology** of _microscope_
17.	**astrology**	horoscopes based on **astrology**
18.	**astronomer**	an **astronomer** photographing sunspots
19.	**asteroid**	an **asteroid** with an unusual orbit
20.	**asterisk**	main points marked with an **asterisk**

■ **PRACTICE**   Sort the words by writing
- one word with both **astro-** and **-logy**
- seven other words with **-logy**
- six other words with **astro-** or **aster-**
- six words with **micro-**

■ **WRITE**   Choose ten phrases to rewrite as sentences.

CHALLENGE!

microbiology
microminiature
meteorology
anthropology
astronomical

WORD HISTORIES   Write the list word that answers each question.

1. What word means "great misfortune"?
2. What word names a scientist who studies stars and planets?
3. What word names a part in a computer?
4. What word is from *asteroeides* meaning "minor planet"?
5. What word names a short radio wave?
6. What word names a crew member in a spacecraft?
7. What word names a film used to make tiny photographs?
8. What word (from *asterikos*) means a star-shaped mark?
9. What word (from *mikros* and *bios*) means "germ"?
10. What word names a magnifying instrument?
11. What word names the science studied by astronomers?
12. What word (from *mikros* and *kosmos)* means "little world"?

CLASSIFYING   Use the clues in the first column with the word histories in the second column to write the correct list word.

13. environment, natural resources   *oikos + -logia*
14. plants, animals   *bios + -logia*
15. families, communities   *socius + -logia*
16. stars, predictions   *astron + -logia*
17. word origins, word histories   *etymon + -logia*
18. stories about gods, Greek stories   *mythos + -logia*
19. tools, inventions   *technē + -logia*
20. Earth's history, rock formations   *gē + -logia*

STRATEGIC SPELLING

Seeing Meaning Connections

Write the word with **-logy** that fits each clue.

Words with *-logy*
zoology
criminology
psychology

21. This science's name comes from *psyche*.
22. This subject studies lawbreakers.
23. This branch of biology concentrates on animals.

1. _____
2. _____
3. _____
4. _____
5. _____
6. _____
7. _____
8. _____
9. _____
10. _____
11. _____
12. _____
13. _____
14. _____
15. _____
16. _____
17. _____
18. _____
19. _____
20. _____

21. _____   23. _____

22. _____

Did You Know?
The great **astronomer** Copernicus was the first to demonstrate that the the planets revolve around the sun.

≡	Make a capital.
/	Make a small letter.
∧	Add something.
ℯ	Take out something.
⊙	Add a period.
¶	New paragraph

PROOFREAD FOR CARELESS ERRORS

Do not use capitals in words that don't need them. Capitalize the first word in a sentence, proper nouns and adjectives, and the pronoun *I*.

My Friend Shawna and I gather mushrooms in the Summer. While She makes Spore Prints, I chart the Stars.

Check Capitalization   Read the sentences below and correct words that should not be capitalized.

1. Shawna and I are good Friends with different interests.
2. I like to study the Stars and planets and mythology.
3. Shawna is interested in plant Life and geology.
4. She enjoys investigating life on the Forest floor.
5. I prefer looking up to the Sky through my telescope.

1. _____

2. _____

3. _____

4. _____

5. _____

PROOFREAD A COMPARISON   Correct five misspelled words. Fix five words that should not be capitalized.

> I want to be an astronomer and Shawna prefers peering at a microb. That's know reason We can't be Best Friends. I gaze through my telescop with the dreams of an astronot, while She peers at Life's microcosm under a micrascop.

WRITE A COMPARISON   Create a list comparing your interests to those of a friend. Write a paragraph based on your list. Use two list words and a personal word.

Word List

microscope	geology
sociology	microwave
microbe	etymology
asteroid	disaster
biology	technology
microcosm	asterisk
astronaut	astronomer
mythology	ecology
microchip	microfilm
astronomy	astrology

Personal Words

1. _____

2. _____

Review

MAKING CONNECTIONS   Write the word from the box that best completes each unfinished sentence.

microscope	mythology
microchip	technology
microwave	astronaut
ecology	astronomy
biology	disaster

1. The tiny life in pond water becomes visible through a ___.
2. Advances in ___ in the 1990s made the Internet possible.
3. If fire follows an earthquake, the combination is a terrible ___.
4. A study of ___ provides people with insights about the stars.
5. Many homes now have ___ ovens.
6. An emphasis on Earth's ___ has caused people to recycle more.
7. Almost every early society had a ___ of gods and goddesses.
8. With a new memory ___, a computer can operate faster.
9. The internal systems of animals is studied in ___ class.
10. On July 20, 1969, Neil Armstrong because the first ___ to step onto the moon.

1. _____
2. _____
3. _____
4. _____
5. _____
6. _____
7. _____
8. _____
9. _____
10. _____

Word Study

CONTEXT: DEFINITIONS AND EXAMPLES   You can often understand an unfamiliar word from its **context**—the words around it. Read the sentences below to understand how definitions and examples give you context clues to words.

The **etymology,** or word history, of *dandelion* is very interesting. (The word *etymology* may be unfamiliar, but the definition "word history" tells you that this is what it means.)

We studied **parasites** such as mites and lice using a microscope. (*Mites* and *lice,* the examples used in the context, tell you that these are kinds of parasites.)

Write the words that give the definition of each underlined word.

1. Try using a metronome to keep musical time.
2. Down from an eider is softer than down from other ducks.
3. Exercise is not a panacea—it is not a cure-all.

1. _____
2. _____
3. _____

The underlined words below are examples that give you clues to the meaning of other words in each sentence. Write the word or words being explained through examples.

4. Cows and horses are domestic ungulates. Another hoofed animal is the wild rhinoceros.
5. Percussion instruments, such as the kettle drum and cymbals, are important to an orchestra's rhythm.
6. Roses come in many hues, from red to pink to yellow.

4. _____
5. _____
6. _____

77

Words with -ice, -ise, -ize

The sound /īz/ can be spelled **ize** or **ise**: **memorize**, **advertise**. The sound /īs/ can be spelled **ice** or **ise**: **sacrifice**, **paradise**. The sound /is/ is spelled **ice**: **notice**.

■ **STUDY** Say each word and meaning phrase. Take special notice of the last three letters of each word.

1. **memorize**   will **memorize** the whole poem
2. **organize**   did **organize** my desk
3. **specialize**   will **specialize** in heart surgery
4. **advertise**   will **advertise** the popcorn on TV
5. **compromise**   will **compromise** to avoid a fight
6. **supervise**   can **supervise** the computer club
7. **paradise**   an island said to be a tropical **paradise**
8. **sacrifice**   **sacrifice** some things to reach a goal
9. **notice**   didn't **notice** the warning sign
10. **justice**   the **justice** of the punishment

11. **sympathize**   can **sympathize** with a hurt child
12. **civilize**   tried to **civilize** the nomadic barbarians
13. **socialize**   usually **socialize** in the lunchroom
14. **legalize**   may **legalize** owning pigs in the city
15. **enterprise**   a new business **enterprise**
16. **improvise**   can **improvise** lyrics to any tune
17. **merchandise** **merchandise** on the racks and tables
18. **prejudice**   **prejudice** against unemployed people
19. **apprentice**   became an **apprentice** to a carpenter
20. **cowardice**   showed **cowardice** in not speaking out

■ **PRACTICE** Sort the words by writing
- six words that end in **-ice**
- seven words that end in **-ise**
- seven words that end in **-ize**

■ **WRITE** Choose three phrases to include in a paragraph.

1. _____
2. _____
3. _____
4. _____
5. _____
6. _____
7. _____
8. _____
9. _____
10. _____
11. _____
12. _____
13. _____
14. _____
15. _____
16. _____
17. _____
18. _____
19. _____
20. _____

CHALLENGE!

characterize
individualize
enfranchise
accomplice
solstice

WORD BUILDING Write a list word by adding either **-ice,** **-ise,** or **-ize** to the base words below.

1. sympathy
2. prejudge
3. legal
4. note
5. civil
6. social
7. just
8. special
9. memory
10. coward
11. improve

CONTEXT CLUES Write the list word that completes each sentence.

12. They feel they are in ____ since they retired to Hawaii.
13. Starting a tutoring service was a great business ____ for Tim.
14. Try to ____ your fiction and nonfiction writing into folders.
15. She had to ____ many things to put three of her children through college.
16. We need a trustworthy person to ____ the playground.
17. The store displayed a wide array of holiday ____.
18. You need to ____ to let people know about your new gourmet restaurant.
19. The two countries did agree to ____ on the issues in order to avoid war.
20. After graduation, he worked as an ____ to an architect.

1. _____
2. _____
3. _____
4. _____
5. _____
6. _____
7. _____
8. _____
9. _____
10. _____
11. _____
12. _____
13. _____
14. _____
15. _____
16. _____
17. _____
18. _____
19. _____
20. _____

STRATEGIC SPELLING

Building New Words

Add **-ize** to each base word to make a new word. Remember: when an ending that begins with a vowel is added to a word that ends with a consonant and **y,** the **y** is dropped.

21. apology _____

22. italic _____

23. critic _____

24. energy _____

Take a Hint
Why should you think of frozen water when you spell **justice?** Because it's **just ice!**

=	Make a capital.
/	Make a small letter.
∧	Add something.
ℓ	Take out something.
⊙	Add a period.
¶	New paragraph

PROOFREAD FOR CAPITALIZATION

In business letters, capitalize words in the heading, inside address, and in the greeting and closing. For example:

1638 east park place

bend, or 97701

Check Capitalization Correct the five errors in capitalization in the passage below by writing the words correctly.

Dear sir or madam:

I am writing to tell you how delighted I am with your product. I tried out clock mart, timeland, and Techno City, without success.

PROOFREAD A BUSINESS LETTER   Correct five misspelled words in this letter. Also fix three errors in capitalization.

1. _____

2. _____

3. _____

4. _____

5. _____

I had to sacrafice toys and movies to by the

Upinattum clock, but I wouldn't comprimise. It does

what you advertize. I wake up to the sounds of a

Caribbean paridice one day and a ball game the next.

yours truly,

don marley

Word List

merchandise	socialize
sympathize	compromise
prejudice	cowardice
sacrifice	supervise
legalize	specialize
notice	improvise
civilize	justice
advertise	organize
apprentice	paradise
enterprise	memorize

Personal Words

1. _____

2. _____

WRITE A BUSINESS LETTER   Write a letter complaining to or praising the makers of a product. Use proper business-letter form, as described on page 245 of your Writer's Handbook.

Review

MEANING CONNECTIONS Write the word in the box that means the same as the words in each of the following.

1. a place of great beauty or happiness
2. come to an agreement in which each side gives up something
3. learn by heart, commit to the mind
4. pursue a special branch of study or knowledge
5. give up
6. make known, publicize
7. watch over, manage
8. observe, see
9. arrange, put together
10. fairness

memorize	supervise
organize	paradise
specialize	sacrifice
advertise	notice
compromise	justice

1. ___
2. ___
3. ___
4. ___
5. ___
6. ___
7. ___
8. ___
9. ___
10. ___

Word *Study*

LATIN AND GREEK ROOTS: GOVERNMENT WORDS
Most of our ideas about democracy and government come to us from the Greeks and Romans, and so do many of the words we use about politics. The list word *civilize* comes from the Latin word *civis*, meaning "citizen." Most words with *civ* in them have something to do with "*citizen.*"

Write a word from the box to answer each question below. Use your Spelling Dictionary if you need help.

civilize	autocrat
civilian	legislate
democracy	legal

1. Which word contains *dēmos*, meaning "people," and *crat*, meaning "rule"?
2. Which word contains *civ* and means "improve in manners"?
3. Which word is made up of *auto*, meaning "self," and *crat*?
4. Which word contains *leg* and means "propose a law"?

Now use the words in the box to complete each sentence.

5. It's ___ to drive if you have a license.
6. You can ___ yourself by studying art and music.
7. Congress can ___ a bill into law.
8. The ___ thought he alone knew best.
9. A person who is not in the army is a ___.
10. In a ___, the people make the laws.

1. ___
2. ___
3. ___
4. ___
5. ___
6. ___
7. ___
8. ___
9. ___
10. ___

Compound Words

SPELLING FOCUS

Some compound words are closed: **homemade.** Some compound words are hyphenated: **runner-up.** Still other compound words are open: **field trip.**

■ **STUDY** Read each compound word. Notice how it is formed. Then read each meaning phrase.

1.	**homemade**	my grandmother's **homemade** quilt
2.	**roommate**	**roommate** at soccer camp
3.	**everyone** ✳	told **everyone** the news
4.	**sometimes** ✳	**sometimes** went bowling
5.	**runner-up**	**runner-up** in the spelling contest
6.	**all-around**	the best **all-around** athlete
7.	**twenty-one**	won by **twenty-one** points
8.	**field trip**	a **field trip** to a history museum
9.	**French fries**	ate a hamburger and **French fries**
10.	**free throw**	won the game with a **free throw**

11.	**stomachache**	bent over with a **stomachache**
12.	**racquetball**	strong arm of a **racquetball** player
13.	**snowmobile**	delivered medicine on a **snowmobile**
14.	**someone** ✳	**someone** in this class
15.	**newsstand**	a **newsstand** on the windy corner
16.	**make-believe**	little child's **make-believe** friends
17.	**full-length**	**full-length** picture of the celebrity
18.	**son-in-law**	her daughter and **son-in-law**
19.	**rain forest**	humid, shadowy **rain forest**
20.	**end zone**	leaped wildly into the **end zone**

■ **PRACTICE** Sort the words by writing
- nine closed compounds
- five open compounds
- six hyphenated compounds

■ **WRITE** Choose ten phrases to rewrite as sentences.

CHALLENGE!

straightedge
cross-examination
wash-and-wear
chain reaction
blood pressure

1.
2.
3.
4.
5.
6.
7.
8.
9.
10.
11.
12.
13.
14.
15.
16.
17.
18.
19.
20.

✳ **WATCH OUT FOR FREQUENTLY MISSPELLED WORDS!**

COMPOUNDS Find the two words in each sentence that together make a list word. Write the compound word.

1. There is more rain in the forest than in the grasslands.
2. She bought a new racquet; now all she needs is a ball.
3. He decided to make up a story that they would believe.
4. When you race through the field that way, I fear you'll trip.
5. The costume had a full skirt with stripes along its length.
6. Because of all the snow, we were not mobile for six days.
7. The baby's sun-burned stomach made my heart ache.
8. Park Street marks the end of the commercial zone in town.
9. We all agree that the Cougars are the best team around.

PARAGRAPH COMPLETION Complete the diary entry.

Sports camp is great! I feel homesick (10) even though (11) here is friendly. The food isn't too bad—the (12) are crispy and the pies are (13). Jerina, my (14), is (15) Mom would like. Her basketball team was the (16) in the state tournament last year. She scored (17) points in one game! She promised to give me tips on doing a perfect (18). I bought a paper at the (19) and read that Ms. Hunt's (20) is going to be Lincoln School's new basketball coach. I'm anxious to show her my awesome lay-ups!

STRATEGIC SPELLING

Seeing Meaning Connections

1. ___
2. ___
3. ___
4. ___
5. ___
6. ___
7. ___
8. ___
9. ___
10. ___
11. ___
12. ___
13. ___
14. ___
15. ___
16. ___
17. ___
18. ___
19. ___
20. ___

Words with *up*
uproar
up-to-date
runner-up
uprising

Write the words from the box that fit the clues.

21. loud or confused noise
22. second-place team
23. revolt or rebellion
24. keeping up; modern

21. ___
22. ___

23. ___
24. ___

FREQUENTLY MISSPELLED WORDS

Students often misspell *someone* and *sometimes.* This rule may help: NEVER drop the **e** in **some** when you use it to form a compound word.

=	Make a capital.
/	Make a small letter.
∧	Add something.
ℯ	Take out something.
⊙	Add a period.
¶	New paragraph

PROOFREAD FOR USAGE   Join compound sentences by using a comma and a combining word. You can also join compound sentences with a semicolon only.

You hunger for souffle, but you can't get one to rise.
Your guests are due for dinner; the oven's in demise.

Check Run–on Sentences   Read each sentence. Correct any errors by writing either a comma and the combining word that follows it or a semicolon and the word that follows it. Write "Correct" if the sentence has no error.

1. You're tired of cooking and you want a special treat.
2. You're having a party and, gazpacho would be neat.
3. You've run out of time but guests are due at eight.
4. Call our number, and we'll never make you wait.
5. Call CATERMATES today you'll have a party tonight!

1. _____
2. _____
3. _____
4. _____
5. _____

PROOFREAD A LEAFLET   Find six misspelled words and write them correctly. Some may be words you learned before. Fix two errors in punctuating compound sentences.

> We at CATERMATES believe that every one needs our services now and agin. Do you long for a quiet, home made meal or would you like to surprise your roomate with a special dinner? Call us. We offer your all round favorites we use only fresh ingrediants.

Word List

everyone	French fries
free throw	runner-up
make-believe	snowmobile
newsstand	field trip
rain forest	homemade
sometimes	son-in-law
twenty-one	roommate
stomachache	someone
full-length	end zone
racquetball	all-around

Personal Words

1. _____
2. _____

WRITE A LEAFLET   Is there something you do well that you would like to tell others about? Write a leaflet about it. Use rhyme, if you wish. Use two list words and one personal word.

Review

CONTEXT   Use the context in each sentence to help you write the best word from the box.

homemade	all-around
roommate	twenty-one
everyone	field trip
sometimes	French fries
runner-up	free throw

1. The woman who won the gold medal as the best ___ gymnast had amazingly difficult routines.
2. The children were awed by what they saw on the ___ .
3. It seems as if ___ is humming that new tune.
4. With so many contestants, she was glad to be even the ___ .
5. You can ___ see a rainbow after a storm.
6. We lost the game when our best player missed a ___ .
7. The room was packed because ___ guests came to the party.
8. My sister gets along well with her college ___ .
9. I'd rather have a baked potato than ___ .
10. Clothes made by machine don't seem to outlast ___ clothes.

1. _____
2. _____
3. _____
4. _____
5. _____
6. _____
7. _____
8. _____
9. _____
10. _____

Word *Study*

CONNOTATION   Most words have meanings beyond the definitions in a dictionary. A word's **connotation,** the feelings it brings to your mind, is important too. For example, we know that a *rain forest* is a "very dense forest," but to some people, *rain forest* has a positive connotation—perhaps "beautiful," "life-giving," and "exotic." For others, *rain forest* has a negative connotation—perhaps "humid," "buggy," and "dangerous."

Choose words from the box to describe the feelings that come to your mind when you think of each word below.

boring
relaxing
comforting
fun-filled
togetherness
scary
quiet
expensive
exotic
hectic

nighttime

1. _____
2. _____
3. _____

vacation

4. _____
5. _____
6. _____

Many connotations are based on positive or negative feelings the words suggest. Read the pairs in the second box. For each pair, write one word under "Positive" and one under "Negative."

bookworm
scholar
arrogant
confident
inquisitive
nosy

Positive

7. _____
8. _____
9. _____

Negative

10. _____
11. _____
12. _____

Review

Lesson 13: Vowels in Final Syllables
Lesson 14: Vowels in Unstressed Syllables
Lesson 15: Greek Word Parts
Lesson 16: Words with -ice, -ise, -ize
Lesson 17: Compound Words

REVIEW WORD LIST

1. abandon
2. ancestor
3. companion
4. comparison
5. hospital
6. identical
7. interior
8. logical
9. metropolitan
10. multiple
11. sponsor
12. vertical
13. cemetery
14. competition
15. episode
16. finally
17. ingredients
18. invitation
19. medicine
20. opinion
21. popular
22. probably
23. Saturday
24. substitute
25. treasure
26. asteroid
27. astronomer
28. astronomy
29. disaster
30. geology
31. microbe
32. microscope
33. mythology
34. apprentice
35. improvise
36. notice
37. organize
38. paradise
39. sacrifice
40. supervise
41. sympathize
42. everyone
43. field trip
44. homemade
45. roommate
46. runner-up
47. someone
48. sometimes
49. stomachache
50. twenty-one

■ PROOFREADING

Find the spelling errors in each passage and write the words correctly. All passages have seven errors except the last one, which has eight.

PROOFREAD A JOURNAL ENTRY

1. _____
2. _____
3. _____
4. _____
5. _____
6. _____
7. _____

Today we went on a feildtrip to the planetarium. We heard an astomoner give a talk on astromony. When the enterior of the planetarium was dark, we saw a chart of the sky. We saw the Big Dipper and the constellation of Orion. (Orion was a giant hunter in Greek mitholigey.) We also learned the difference between a meteor and an astaroid. Then we got to see a moon rock and hear about the geologee of the moon.

PROOFREAD A SCIENCE REPORT

Anton van Leeuwenhoek (lā'vən hŭk),
who lived from 1632–1723 in the
Netherlands, looked at a drop of water
through his microscop one day and saw
not one microb but hundreds of these tiny
creatures. Eventually he found microscopic
organisms in practically everything he
looked at. The populaur opinon of the time
was that such findings were impossible.
Until he was near death, however,
Leeuwenhoek sent regular reports to the
Royal Society in London about everything
he discovered and measured through his
home made lens. The Royal Society
encouraged this amateur scientist, who
had left school at sixteen to become an
apprentence in a dry-goods store. Nobody,
including Leeuwenhoek, knew that some of
these organisms could cause disease, for
medicen had not advanced that far.

1. _____
2. _____
3. _____
4. _____
5. _____
6. _____
7. _____

PROOFREAD AN INVITATION

To: Every one in the seventh grade

From: Sylvia Hernandez

What: A tresure hunt

When: Saterday, October 30

Where: My house at 23 North Willow

Please come to my party. There will be a compotition to see
who can use the multaple clues to find a prize in the shortest
time. A prize will be awarded to the runnerup too. We will
organise the hunt at 3:00 P.M. and have supper at 5:00 P.M.

1. _____
2. _____
3. _____
4. _____
5. _____
6. _____
7. _____

1. _____
2. _____
3. _____
4. _____
5. _____
6. _____
7. _____

PROOFREAD CLUES FOR A TREASURE HUNT

Start at Sylvia's and go to where
a weeping willow some times sighs.
You'll probly find an ansestor there,
and your first clue if you are wise.
Take the old cemetary road.
(You may have to impravize.)
It's not a scary epasode.
Clue two is quite near paridice.

1. _____
2. _____
3. _____
4. _____
5. _____
6. _____
7. _____

PROOFREAD AN EXPLANATORY PARAGRAPH

Look below and notess the two nearly idenacul figures. Which horizontal line is longer? Most people think it's logicle that the line in Figure A is longer, but when you make a compairson of the two figures, you see that the horizontal lines are exactly the same length. This experiment was developed by some one to show how our eyes can play tricks. The illusion also works if you subsitute vertacle lines for horizontal ones.

Fig. A

Fig. B

PROOFREAD A NOTICE

The metropoletan park district is looking for responsible students to help supervize at twenty one day-care centers after school. The park district will sponser ice-skating classes for preschoolers if you can help. If you can be a companiun to a small child and can sacrafice two hours after school, this is your invatation to join us.
Call 555-1345 or stop by the office to pick up an application.

1. _____
2. _____
3. _____
4. _____
5. _____
6. _____
7. _____

PROOFREAD A THANK-YOU NOTE

November 9, 19_

Dear Amy,

Thanks for sending me a card while I was in the hospitle. I had a bad stomach ache, but everything turned out OK. The doctor said it could have been caused by one of the ingrediants in some food I ate, so it wasn't a desaster. My rommate turned out to be someone I knew from camp, and we could sympathise with each other! I finly had to abanden plans to go to the ice show. Maybe I'll make it next year.

Sincerely,

Sara

GET WELL

1. _____
2. _____
3. _____
4. _____
5. _____
6. _____
7. _____
8. _____

Using Meaning Helpers

DISCOVER THE STRATEGY   Word pairs like *special* and *specialize* are related in spelling and meaning. The shorter word can be a meaning helper—a reminder of how to spell the longer word. For example:

Longer Word	Helper	Clue
specialize	special	special + ize
comparison	compare	compare - e + ison

TRY IT OUT   Now try this meaning helpers strategy. Tell how the helper reminds you of how to spell the longer word. Be sure to note any spelling changes that take place between the two words.

Longer Word	Helper	Clue
1. hostility	hostile	_____
2. memorize	memory	_____
3. secretary	secret	_____
4. authority	author	_____

Some meaning helpers are extra-helpful. They remind you of how a tricky sound is spelled in the longer word. For example:

Longer Word	Helper	Clue
invitation	invite	invitation = invite - e + ation The long **i** in *invite* reminds me that the second syllable of *invitation* is spelled with an **i**.
departure	depart	departure = depart + ure The sound of **t** in *depart* reminds me that there's a **t** in the last syllable of *departure.*

Work with a partner. Tell how the helper gives a sound clue for the longer word. Be sure to show any spelling changes.

Longer Word	Helper	Clue
5. exception	except	_____
6. possession	possess	_____
7. inspiration	inspire	_____

LOOK AHEAD   Look ahead at the next five lessons for list words that you might use this strategy with. Find two and write them down. Under each one, write a meaning helper. Use this strategy when you study those words.

1. _____

_____

2. _____

Suffixes -ary, -ery, -ory

SPELLING FOCUS

When adding the suffixes **-ary**, **-ery**, and **-ory**, there are often no sound clues to help you decide whether to use an **a**, an **e**, or an **o**. Sometimes these two clues might help.

■ Use the base word as a clue: **brav̱e, brav̱ery**.
■ Use a related word as a clue: **imagiṉation, imagiṉary**.

■ **STUDY** Look at each word carefully. Then read the phrase.

1.	**bravery**	showed **bravery** by saving lives
2.	**scenery**	painted **scenery** for the play
3.	**surgery**	had **surgery** to remove his appendix
4.	**imaginary**	not real, but **imaginary**
5.	**vocabulary**	improved our **vocabulary** by reading
6.	**ordinary**	just my **ordinary**, everyday clothes
7.	**temporary**	a **temporary** classroom for one year
8.	**satisfactory**	a **satisfactory** score on the test
9.	**advisory**	an **advisory** committee of students
10.	**directory**	a **directory** listing phone numbers

11.	**bribery**	an officer convicted of **bribery**
12.	**nursery**	a **nursery** full of babies
13.	**machinery**	dust raised by the road **machinery**
14.	**secondary**	not primary, but **secondary**
15.	**solitary**	one **solitary** tree in the yard
16.	**anniversary**	fiftieth **anniversary** of their marriage
17.	**explanatory**	wrote an **explanatory** paragraph
18.	**migratory**	**migratory** birds flying south in the fall
19.	**exploratory**	an **exploratory** trip into the jungle
20.	**mandatory**	**mandatory** courses that I must take

■ **PRACTICE** Sort the list words by writing seven words with the suffix **-ary**, then six words with the suffix **-ery**, and, finally, seven words with the suffix **-ory**.

■ **WRITE** Choose three phrases to include in a paragraph.

1.

2.

3.

4.

5.

6.

7.

8.

9.

10.

11.

12.

13.

14.

15.

16.

17.

18.

19.

20.

CHALLENGE!

complimentary
itinerary
confectionery
discriminatory
inflammatory

ANTONYMS   Write the list word that means the opposite of the underlined word in each sentence.

1. The hero of this novel is <u>real</u>.
2. Those <u>stationary</u> animals travel south each winter.
3. You'll fail the class if you don't do the <u>optional</u> assignments.
4. This job is <u>permanent</u>, so we'll be here only six months.
5. It was a routine, <u>extraordinary</u> day.
6. She showed great <u>cowardice</u> in confronting that bully.

MAKING INFERENCES   Write the list word that is missing from each person's statement.

7. Nurse: "Plan to spend a few days resting after your ___."
8. Student: "I learn a new word every day to add to my ___."
9. Lawyer: "She is charged with ___ of a police officer."
10. Mayor: "I agree with the advice of my ___ committee."
11. Hermit: "I enjoy my ___ life."
12. Factory worker: "This improved ___ speeds up the job."
13. Teacher: "The ___ paragraph will tell you what to do first."
14. Adventurer: "I made an ___ trip to Antarctica."
15. Train passenger: "I like to sit back and watch the ___."
16. Married couple: "Our children sent us cards on our ___."
17. Builder: "This carpenter's work is ___, so I'll hire her again."
18. Firefighter: "Saving a building is ___ to the primary task of saving lives."
19. Shopper: "I'll find where coats are by reading the store ___."
20. Grandparent: "We visited our infant grandson in the ___."

STRATEGIC SPELLING
Using the Meaning Helper Strategy

Use meaning helpers to help you spell. Write *machinery* and *bravery*. Write a meaning helper below each one. Mark the matching letters.

21. _____   22. _____

1. _____
2. _____
3. _____
4. _____
5. _____
6. _____
7. _____
8. _____
9. _____
10. _____
11. _____
12. _____
13. _____
14. _____
15. _____
16. _____
17. _____
18. _____
19. _____
20. _____

Did You Know?
Bravery is not limited to adults. Young people have also courageously saved others from injury and death. The U.S. Department of Justice has honored many of these heroic youngsters by awarding them the Young American Medal for Bravery.

93

Make a capital.	═
Make a small letter.	/
Add something.	∧
Take out something.	ℯ
Add a period.	⊙
New paragraph	¶

PROOFREAD FOR USAGE   Make sure that your subjects and verbs are either both singular or both plural, even when other words separate them. For example:

The scenery in the mountains ~~were~~ was beautiful.

Check Subjects and Verbs   Correct five verbs in this passage that don't agree with their subjects.

By early June, the drought have become a battle. At first, the temporary freedom from classes energize you, and the scorching winds of June feels overwhelming. You're out all day in the steamy woods and the shallow river. In July, temperatures over a hundred forces you inside. Two months of heat has exhausted you.

1. _____

2. _____

3. _____

4. _____

5. _____

PROOFREAD A DESCRIPTION   Correct five misspelled words in this description. Some may be words you learned before. Fix three verbs that don't agree with their subjects.

When lightning and thunder bursts outside, my ordenary classroom become an imaginery zone. To me, it is the dim workshop of a solatary inventor who create futuristic mashinery, or its the drenched deck of a ship in a wild storm. The scenery is great, but only for me.

Word List

satisfactory	directory
bribery	vocabulary
advisory	surgery
explanatory	ordinary
bravery	nursery
migratory	imaginary
secondary	machinery
solitary	temporary
exploratory	scenery
anniversary	mandatory

Personal Words

1. _____

2. _____

WRITE A DESCRIPTION   Describe a real or imaginary scene that involves weather or some aspect of nature. Use three list words and a personal word.

Review

DEFINITIONS Write the word from the box that matches each clue.

bravery	ordinary
scenery	temporary
surgery	satisfactory
imaginary	advisory
vocabulary	directory

1. acceptable, good enough
2. usual, normal
3. the stock of words used by a person or group
4. natural features of a landscape
5. a list of names with their addresses or locations
6. make-believe, not real
7. fearlessness, courage
8. operation
9. having the power to recommend
10. lasting for a short time only

1. _____
2. _____
3. _____
4. _____
5. _____
6. _____
7. _____
8. _____
9. _____
10. _____

Word *Study*

WORDS OF TIME Words like *anniversary* and *temporary* refer to time. Use the meanings of the word parts below to help you answer the riddles with words of time. Use the Spelling Dictionary if you need help.

Root	Meaning	Root	Meaning	Root	Meaning
anni, enni	year	*dur*	long-lasting	*simul*	at the same time
temp	time	*chron*	time	*bi*	two
cent	hundred	*pre*	before	*semi*	half

1. Is a sleeping bag a durable bed or a temporary one?
2. Would you rather have an annual or semiannual vacation?
3. Would a yearling or a centenarian live in a senior-citizen residence?
4. Are calendar dates in alphabetical or chronological order?
5. In 1876 did the United States celebrate its centennial or bicentennial?
6. Does your birthday occur annually or bimonthly?
7. When you are listening to the same program on TV and on radio, is it a preview or a simulcast?
8. Is a stopwatch a chronograph or a tempest?
9. If you saw the end of a movie, did you leave after the duration or the preview?

1. _____
2. _____
3. _____
4. _____
5. _____
6. _____
7. _____
8. _____
9. _____

Latin Roots 1

SPELLING FOCUS

Many words are made up of the Latin roots **ject,** meaning "to throw"; **rupt,** meaning "to break"; **pend,** meaning "to hang"; and **duct,** meaning "to lead": **projector, disruptive, suspended, conductor.**

■ **STUDY**   Say each word. Then read the meaning phrase.

1.	**projector**	found the **projector** and screen
2.	**objective**	the **objective,** or aim, of the game
3.	**injection**	sore arm from the nurse's **injection**
4.	**disruptive**	noisy, **disruptive** party next door
5.	**eruption**	**eruption** of the volcano
6.	**bankrupt**	final sale at the **bankrupt** store
7.	**suspended**	**suspended** by a single silky thread
8.	**appendix**	a painful **appendix** that might rupture
9.	**conductor**	an orchestra led by its **conductor**
10.	**productivity**	high **productivity** of the busy factory

11.	**conjecture**	a **conjecture** that turned out to be right
12.	**dejected**	felt **dejected** at coming in last
13.	**rupture**	the **rupture** in the leaky pipe
14.	**corruption**	a speech about government **corruption**
15.	**pendant**	**pendant** hanging from a gold chain
16.	**pendulum**	regular swing of the clock's **pendulum**
17.	**impending**	warned of tonight's **impending** storm
18.	**deductive**	**deductive** reasoning to solve a crime
19.	**induction**	**induction** as a way of thinking
20.	**abduction**	**abduction** of the man by kidnappers

1. _____
2. _____
3. _____
4. _____
5. _____
6. _____
7. _____
8. _____
9. _____
10. _____
11. _____
12. _____
13. _____
14. _____
15. _____
16. _____
17. _____
18. _____
19. _____
20. _____

CHALLENGE!

trajectory
interjection
perpendicular
expenditure
aqueduct

■ **PRACTICE**   Sort the words by writing
- five words with **duct**
- five words with **ject**
- five words with **rupt**
- five words with **pend**

■ **WRITE**   Choose ten phrases to rewrite as sentences.

WORD ASSOCIATION   Write the list word suggested by each pair of words. Check the answers in the Spelling Dictionary.

1. guess, opinion
2. break, tear
3. in debt, penniless
4. sad, discouraged
5. disorderly, destructive
6. leader, director
7. aim, goal
8. dishonesty, wickedness
9. hanging, locket
10. outburst, explosion
11. coming, threatening

MAKING CONNECTIONS   Write the list word that answers each question. Use the Spelling Dictionary to check your answers.

12. What is one device you can use to show a film?
13. If you deduce a conclusion, what kind of reasoning do you use?
14. What swings back and forth in a pattern?
15. What would a kidnapper be accused of?
16. What is one quality of a successful factory or farm?
17. What might you get when you visit the doctor?
18. If you induce a conclusion, what kind of reasoning do you use?
19. What is something that surgeons often remove?
20. What is the condition of a lamp that is hung from a ceiling?

Seeing Meaning Connections

product
productive
producer

21. Write the list word that is related in spelling and meaning to the words in the box.

Then use the words to complete the paragraph.

The B. Warm Company is a (22) of sportswear. Recently this company's sweat suits have become a very popular (23). To meet the demand, the company will have to be more (24).

1. _____
2. _____
3. _____
4. _____
5. _____
6. _____
7. _____
8. _____
9. _____
10. _____
11. _____
12. _____
13. _____
14. _____
15. _____
16. _____
17. _____
18. _____
19. _____
20. _____

21. _____
22. _____
23. _____
24. _____

Did You Know?
Append means "to add to a larger thing." The human appendix certainly seems like an add-on. It was added to the large intestine, but it has no known function!

≡	Make a capital.
/	Make a small letter.
∧	Add something.
ℓ	Take out something.
⊙	Add a period.
⁋	New paragraph.

PROOFREAD FOR CARELESS ERRORS

One-syllable words should not be divided at the end of a line.

By using deduction, detectives could ~~pro-~~ *prove* v̶e̶ that Lonnie committed the crime.

Check for Incorrectly Divided Words Write four words that are divided incorrectly.

Induction allows you to make general statements bas-ed on examples. For instance, if you see a fire truck racing down the street nearly every night, but not at other times, you mi-ght say most fires where you live occur at night. Deduction go-es from the general to the particular: *All fires are destructive. The hospital caught fire. The hospital suffered some destruction.*

1. _____

2. _____

3. _____

4. _____

PROOFREAD A PROBLEM AND SOLUTION

Find the four misspelled words in the passage. Some may be words you learned before. Fix three words that are divided incorrectly.

My mom was dejeted because she had lo-st her pendent, an anniversery gift. She said it had to be in her room. Thin I was sure it was by the sofa. She had go-ne to sleep there last night! Wasn't that a brilliant deduction?

Word List

objective	disruptive
deductive	abduction
appendix	projector
conjecture	induction
dejected	conductor
rupture	injection
pendant	pendulum
impending	eruption
corruption	bankrupt
suspended	productivity

Personal Words

1. _____

2. _____

WRITE A PROBLEM AND SOLUTION

Imagine that the pendant was not found by the sofa. Write a paragraph giving another solution. Create statements that support your solution.

Review

DRAWING CONCLUSIONS   Write the word from the box that goes best with each clue.

projector	bankrupt
objective	suspended
injection	appendix
disruptive	conductor
eruption	productivity

1. This happens when a volcano "blows its top."
2. This is why some people don't like to visit the nurse.
3. You hope this never happens to your bank!
4. This person stands up and leads an orchestra.
5. This is said of people in the audience who stand up, move around, and talk during an orchestra concert.
6. You would be amazed if a magician actually did this to the assistant.
7. At a factory, if the absentee rate is low, this is probably high.
8. This is what the goal line is for a football team.
9. Every movie theater has at least one of these.
10. If your stomachache isn't because of your stomach, it may be because of this.

1. _____
2. _____
3. _____
4. _____
5. _____
6. _____
7. _____
8. _____
9. _____
10. _____

Using a *Dictionary*

MULTIPLE MEANINGS   The word *appendix* means "an addition at the end of a book." It also means "a slender tube attached to the large intestine." You probably wouldn't confuse those meanings—but you might need to study other words with more than one meaning.

suspend (sə spend′) *v.t.* **1** hang down by attaching to something above: *The lamp was suspended from the ceiling.* **2** hold in place as if by hanging: *We saw the smoke suspended in the still air.* **3** stop for a while: *suspend work.* **4** remove or exclude for a while from some privilege or job: *suspend a student for infraction of rules.*

Notice that each meaning of **suspend** is numbered in the dictionary entry. Write the number of the definition that fits each sentence below.

1. Class was **suspended** because of a fire drill.
2. The sailor **suspended** the anchor from a line of rope.
3. He wasn't **suspended,** but he had to serve some detentions.
4. The dancer looked as if she were **suspended** in air.
5. The people saw a hot-air balloon **suspended** above them.
6. I **suspended** activity on the project until the weather cooled.

1. _____
2. _____
3. _____
4. _____
5. _____
6. _____

People Suffixes

SPELLING FOCUS

Words with the suffixes **-ian, -ant, -ent,** or **-ist** often refer to people.

■ **STUDY**   Look at each word and read the meaning phrase. Notice that each word ends in **-ian, -ant, -ent,** or **-ist.**

1.	**comedian**	laughed at the **comedian** on stage
2.	**musician**	the **musician** with her flute
3.	**custodian**	floors polished by the **custodian**
4.	**physician**	sore throat checked by a **physician**
5.	**accountant**	taxes figured by the **accountant**
6.	**defendant**	testified against the **defendant**
7.	**dependent**	my daughter, and thus my **dependent**
8.	**novelist**	a book of fiction by a **novelist**
9.	**specialist**	a **specialist** in skin diseases
10.	**soloist**	a spotlight on the **soloist**

11.	**pedestrian**	a **pedestrian** waiting to cross the street
12.	**technician**	**technician** in the TV repair shop
13.	**politician**	the **politician** running for office
14.	**attendant**	an **attendant** to help at the store
15.	**participant**	a **participant** in the contest
16.	**superintendent**	the **superintendent** of the factory
17.	**incumbent**	the **incumbent** who was re-elected
18.	**pharmacist**	a prescription filled by the **pharmacist**
19.	**motorist**	the **motorist** with a flat tire
20.	**chemist**	substance analyzed by a **chemist**

■ **PRACTICE**   Sort the words by writing
- seven words with the suffix **-ian**
- four words with the suffix **-ant**
- three words with the suffix **-ent**
- six words with the suffix **-ist**

■ **WRITE**   Choose four phrases to write in a paragraph.

1. _____
2. _____
3. _____
4. _____
5. _____
6. _____
7. _____
8. _____
9. _____
10. _____
11. _____
12. _____
13. _____
14. _____
15. _____
16. _____
17. _____
18. _____
19. _____
20. _____

CHALLENGE!

pediatrician
descendant
adherent
medalist
accompanist

WORDS IN CONTEXT   Complete the sentence with a list word that makes sense. The suffix in parentheses is a clue.

1. (-ist) A famous ___ sang with the chorus.
2. (-ant) He asked the flight ___ for a glass of juice.
3. (-ent) A son is usually a ___ of his parents until adulthood.
4. (-ist) The stranded ___ waited for the police to come.
5. (-ian) The skilled ___ played three instruments.
6. (-ant) My new ___ asked for my financial records.
7. (-ist) My favorite ___ is a science-fiction writer.
8. (-ent) The candidate set up a debate with the ___ mayor.
9. (-ist) The professor is a ___ in the history of the Civil War.
10. (-ant) The jury found the ___ not guilty of theft.

SEEING RELATIONSHIPS   Write the list word that names the person who might make each statement.

11. "I go to different companies to fix their computers."
12. "Doctors send me prescriptions to fill for their sick patients."
13. "I need to write twenty new jokes for a performance."
14. "I've treated patients with flu and measles today."
15. "I'll run tests to identify the substances in this powder."
16. "I am head of all the schools in the city."
17. "Elect me and I will spend a lot of time in the state capital."
18. "I want to take part in the variety show."
19. "I always obey the Walk and Don't Walk signals."
20. "My crew and I will clean up after the school's open house."

STRATEGIC SPELLING

Seeing Meaning Connections

accountable
account
on any account

21. Write the list word that is related in spelling and meaning to the words in the box.

_____

Then complete each phrase with a word or phrase from the box.

22. wouldn't quit _____

23. held _____ for the mistake

24. gave an _____ of their journey

1. _____
2. _____
3. _____
4. _____
5. _____
6. _____
7. _____
8. _____
9. _____
10. _____
11. _____
12. _____
13. _____
14. _____
15. _____
16. _____
17. _____
18. _____
19. _____
20. _____

Take a Hint
Remember this when you need to spell *attendant* and *defendant*: In an ant colony, workers **attend** and **defend** the queen **ant.**

═	Make a capital.
/	Make a small letter.
∧	Add something.
ℓ	Take out something.
⊙	Add a period.
⁋	New paragraph

PROOFREAD FOR PUNCTUATION

Apostrophes are used with possessive nouns and contractions.
For example:

> Brenda coaches women's basketball at a college. She says that it isnt just a job to her. It's a profession.

Check Possessives and Contractions   Find five mistakes with possessive nouns or contractions. Write the words correctly.

1. The announcer reports whats happening in a game.
2. A companys accountant suggests ways to save money.
3. Tom enjoys chemistry, and hed like to be a pharmacist.
4. Many novelists first books may not sell many copies.
5. Wendy's job as a journalist isnt dull.

1. _____

2. _____

3. _____

4. _____

5. _____

PROOFREAD A CAREER DESCRIPTION   Correct five misspelled words in the career description. Also fix three errors with possessive nouns or contractions.

> Jason wants to be a computer musican.
> He works with a partner who is a speshialist.
> They've created software to control a computers
> activity. Jasons hope is that everbody will use thier
> software to become a participent in making music.

Word List

superintendent	defendant
novelist	musician
comedian	specialist
pharmacist	participant
attendant	motorist
technician	custodian
accountant	soloist
pedestrian	incumbent
dependent	chemist
politician	physician

Personal Words

1. _____

2. _____

WRITE A CAREER DESCRIPTION   Write a description of a career you would like. Tell why it fits with your interests and talents. Try to use two list words and a personal word.

 Review

WHO ARE THEY? Write the person word from the box that fits each clue.

comedian	defendant
musician	dependent
custodian	novelist
physician	specialist
accountant	soloist

1. a person who sings or plays a musical instrument
2. a medical doctor
3. a writer of fictional books
4. the person being accused or sued in a court of law
5. a person who performs without a partner
6. a person who makes a study of one particular branch of business, law, medicine, or the like
7. someone who relies on another for help and support
8. someone who tells jokes and makes people laugh
9. a person who works with and interprets business records and financial affairs
10. a person whose job is to clean up after people

1. _____
2. _____
3. _____
4. _____
5. _____
6. _____
7. _____
8. _____
9. _____
10. _____

Multicultural *Connection*

LANGUAGES All of your list words, such as *musician* and *motorist,* describe people and who they are or the things that they do. The words in the box, which also describe people, have come into English from Asian languages.

Word	Meaning	Word	Meaning
samurai	warrior in feudal Japan	**tycoon**	wealthy, powerful businessperson
thug	criminal	**nabob**	a rich or important person
pundit	expert		

Read the descriptions for these characters from a play. Write the missing words using the best word from the box.

LENORA HUMFY, *owner of an international chain of newspapers and soft-drink companies, and a ruthless (1) who stops at nothing*

RIP JONES, *Humfy's bodyguard, a petty thief and (2)*

MILTON SMITH, *a (3) on Japanese culture who is writing an encyclopedia article on the powerful Japanese (4) of the 1300s*

I. M. WELLTY, *a fun-loving (5) who inherited billions*

1. _____
2. _____
3. _____
4. _____
5. _____

Easily Confused Words

SPELLING FOCUS

Some words are easily confused because they have similar pronunciations and spellings: **advice, advise.**

■ **STUDY** Say each pair of words carefully. Notice the difference in the way each word sounds. Then read the phrase.

1.	**advice**	**advice** on how to earn money
2.	**advise**	did **advise** me to take an umbrella
3.	**proceed**	removed a barrier so cars can **proceed**
4.	**precede**	a first step to **precede** the others
5.	**affect**	pollution that can **affect** our breathing
6.	**effect**	saw the **effect** of rain on the dry plants
7.	**continual**	the **continual** flow of the river
8.	**continuous**	made a **continuous** line across the field
9.	**adapt**	can **adapt** to the new system
10.	**adopt**	will **adopt** the orphan child

11.	**respectively**	two who drew and sang **respectively**
12.	**respectfully**	**respectfully** opened a door for the king
13.	**formerly**	**formerly** lived in another state
14.	**formally**	dressed **formally** for the wedding
15.	**moral**	learned a **moral** from the story
16.	**morale**	the low **morale** of the team that lost
17.	**disinterested**	a fair, **disinterested** person as a judge
18.	**uninterested**	**uninterested** in everything but clothes
19.	**descent**	their **descent** down the steep trail
20.	**dissent**	a tax that caused people to **dissent**

■ **PRACTICE** Some word pairs are more confusing than others. Write the word pairs that you know how to spell and use correctly. Then write the pairs that you need to check.

■ **WRITE** Choose four phrases to rewrite as questions and answers.

1. _____
2. _____
3. _____
4. _____
5. _____
6. _____
7. _____
8. _____
9. _____
10. _____
11. _____
12. _____
13. _____
14. _____
15. _____
16. _____
17. _____
18. _____
19. _____
20. _____

CHALLENGE!

preposition	proposition
persecution	prosecution
adverse	averse

SIMILAR MEANINGS   Write the list word that has nearly the same meaning as each word below.

1. adjust
2. advance
3. unbroken
4. previously
5. impartial
6. politely
7. result
8. disagreement
9. lesson
10. recommendation

WORD CHOICE   Write the correct list word to complete each sentence.

11. The (continual, continuous) heat made us thirsty.
12. I (advice, advise) you to plan your project before you start.
13. We saw the climbers' (descent, dissent) from the mountain.
14. Exercise can (affect, effect) your muscle tone and weight.
15. Judy and Bill are my sister and cousin (respectively, respectfully).
16. He seems (disinterested, uninterested) in the TV program.
17. To improve the soldier's (moral, morale), send him a letter.
18. We plan to (adapt, adopt) a child from another country.
19. The flag bearers will (precede, proceed) the band.
20. The ambassador (formally, formerly) introduced the officers by stating their full names and ranks.

Building New Words

Add the suffix to the base word to make a new word. If the base word ends with a **consonant-vowel,** drop the vowel before adding the suffix. Use the Spelling Dictionary if you need help.

Base Word	Suffix	New Word
21. precede	-ence	_____
22. advise	-able	_____
23. adapt	-able	_____
24. adopt	-ive	_____

1. _____
2. _____
3. _____
4. _____
5. _____
6. _____
7. _____
8. _____
9. _____
10. _____
11. _____
12. _____
13. _____
14. _____
15. _____
16. _____
17. _____
18. _____
19. _____
20. _____

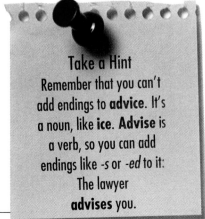

Take a Hint
Remember that you can't add endings to **advice.** It's a noun, like **ice. Advise** is a verb, so you can add endings like *-s* or *-ed* to it: The lawyer **advises** you.

≡	Make a capital.
/	Make a small letter.
∧	Add something.
ℓ	Take out something.
⊙	Add a period.
⁋	New paragraph

PROOFREAD FOR CAPITALIZATION

Capitalize proper nouns and the pronoun *I*. Look for them when you proofread.

After the game, i heard the warren warriors shout a victory cheer.

Check Proper Nouns and *I* Write correctly the words that should be capitalized. If a sentence is correct, write "Correct."

1. The Smith children watched their cousin play quarterback.
2. We picked up aunt linda, who always is late.
3. The owner of barry's Hobby Shop never misses a game.
4. Dr. osgood treats injured players at Pritchard Hospital.
5. I'm always nervous that i'll let the Warriors down.

1. _____

2. _____

3. _____

4. _____

5. _____

PROOFREAD A CHARACTER SKETCH Correct five

misspelled words in this character sketch. Some may be words you learned before. Also fix three capitalization errors.

> When I met B. j. Huff, I thought she was unintrested in sports. The easy-going texan had formerlly lived in Austin; that's were she learned to play her guitar. Later i saw her talent as a runner. She had a continuse flow of energy, and her humor had a good effect on team moral.

Word List

precede	moral
proceed	morale
advice	disinterested
advise	uninterested
adapt	descent
adopt	dissent
affect	continual
effect	continuous
formally	respectively
formerly	respectfully

Personal Words

1. _____

2. _____

WRITE A CHARACTER SKETCH Write a character sketch of

someone you know. Describe how the person looks, acts, or reacts. Try to use two list words and a personal word.

Review

advice	effect
advise	continual
proceed	continuous
precede	adapt
affect	adopt

MEANING MATCH   Write the word from the box that means about the same as the underlined word or words.

1. Frequently repeated practice will make you a good pianist.
2. You are to follow in the footsteps of those who go before you.
3. I urge you to follow this course of action.
4. Cloudy skies influence some people by making them feel sad.
5. Some workers will have to change themselves slightly to the new boss's ways.
6. The line for tickets for the popular concert was unbroken.
7. Many employees take on the style of a new boss to try to make a good impression.
8. Studies show smoking can have a deadly result on your health.
9. Only a fool would ignore wise and beneficial suggestions.
10. You must fulfill these requirements before you can continue.

1. _____
2. _____
3. _____
4. _____
5. _____
6. _____
7. _____
8. _____
9. _____
10. _____

Word *Study*

SYNONYMS   **Synonyms** are words that have similar, but not necessarily identical, meanings. When you write, choose the best synonym for the situation. For numbers 1 through 9, write these six synonyms where they best fit in the chart below: *fanciful, caution, everyday, usual, warn, fantastic.* Then add three synonyms of your own.

imaginary	ordinary	advise
1. _____	4. _____	7. _____
2. _____	5. _____	8. _____
3. _____	6. _____	9. _____

Now replace each numbered word in the following paragraph with a synonym from the chart. Choose the word that you think best fits the sentence.

I daydream when I do **(10) ordinary** chores. Once when I was raking leaves, I could almost see this **(11) imaginary** creature. It had golden eyes and a tall, shimmery, silver body. The being was more **(12) imaginary** than characters in science-fiction books. It said, "I **(13) advise** you to stay away from Green Hill tonight." That hill was where I take my dog for its **(14) ordinary** evening walk. Then the image vanished. I rushed to **(15) advise** everyone to avoid Green Hill, but I didn't take that advice.

10. _____
11. _____
12. _____
13. _____
14. _____
15. _____

Including All the Letters

SPELLING FOCUS

Some words have more letters than you might expect: **laboratory, candidate.** Sometimes these "extra" letters are silent, but often they are not. To spell these words, it may help to pronounce each syllable carefully.

■ **STUDY** Say each word and concentrate on how many letters it has. Then read the meaning phrase.

1. **laboratory**   used a microscope in the **laboratory**
2. **candidate**   a **candidate** to run for governor
3. **accidentally**   **accidentally** spilled the lemonade
4. **practically**   **practically** finished with the book
5. **Christmas** ✳   gave presents on **Christmas**
6. **specific**   had a **specific** reason to stay home
7. **extremely**   live in **extremely** cold temperatures
8. **sincerely**   am **sincerely** sorry for hurting you
9. **eighth**   next year in **eighth** grade
10. **frightened**   **frightened** by the shadow in the fog

11. **quantity**   a large **quantity** of paper
12. **boundary**   back **boundary** of the volleyball court
13. **funeral**   attend the **funeral** of our grandfather
14. **identity**   learned the **identity** of the stranger
15. **definitely**   **definitely** will go to the skating party
16. **Easter** ✳   to church and an egg hunt on **Easter**
17. **errands**   ran three **errands** for a sick neighbor
18. **threatening**   the dark, **threatening** sky
19. **supposedly**   **supposedly**, but not really, an expert
20. **headache**   had a **headache**, chills, and a fever

■ **PRACTICE** Choose ten words that you are most likely to misspell in writing. Write them first. Then write the remaining ten words.

■ **WRITE** Choose two phrases to write in a rhyme, riddle, or dialogue.

1. _____
2. _____
3. _____
4. _____
5. _____
6. _____
7. _____
8. _____
9. _____
10. _____
11. _____
12. _____
13. _____
14. _____
15. _____
16. _____
17. _____
18. _____
19. _____
20. _____

CHALLENGE!

incidentally
correlation
indictment
meringue
rapport

✳ **WATCH OUT FOR FREQUENTLY MISSPELLED WORDS!**

ANALOGIES   Write the list word that completes each analogy.

1. Stomach is to stomachache as head is to ___.
2. Independence Day is to July as ___ is to December.
3. Large is to small as general is to ___.
4. Fourth is to fifth as seventh is to ___.
5. "How good" is to quality as "how much" is to ___.
6. "By chance" is to "on purpose" as ___ is to intentionally.
7. Athlete is to gymnasium as scientist is to ___.
8. Normally is to unusually as moderately is to ___.
9. Pleased is to smile as ___ is to scream.
10. Thursday is to Thanksgiving as Sunday is to ___.
11. Happily is to gladly as ___ is to honestly.

DEFINITIONS   Write the list word that answers each question.

12. What word refers to short trips you do for someone else?
13. What word means "certainly"?
14. What word means "nearly"?
15. What word refers to a person's name?
16. What means "a ceremony that may include a burial"?
17. What word means "a line between two states or countries"?
18. What word means "possibly" or "probably"?
19. What word names a person who is running for office?
20. What word is a synonym for "menacing"?

STRATEGIC SPELLING
Using the Meaning Helper Strategy

Use meaning helpers to help you spell. Write *threatening, practically, supposedly,* and *eighth*. Write a meaning helper below each one. Underline the matching letters.

21. _____   23. _____

_____   _____

22. _____   24. _____

_____   _____

1. _____
2. _____
3. _____
4. _____
5. _____
6. _____
7. _____
8. _____
9. _____
10. _____
11. _____
12. _____
13. _____
14. _____
15. _____
16. _____
17. _____
18. _____
19. _____
20. _____

Hint
Christmas and *Easter* are frequently misspelled because students often forget to capitalize them. Spell those special days in a special way. Capitalize them!

FREQUENTLY MISSPELLED WORDS ✳ FREQUENTLY MISSPELLED WORDS ✳

=	Make a capital.
/	Make a small letter.
∧	Add something.
ℓ	Take out something.
⊙	Add a period.
¶	New paragraph

PROOFREAD FOR CAPITALIZATION

When you're proofreading, be sure that names of cities, states, countries, and titles are capitalized. For example:

Charles Lindbergh flew the *Spirit of St. Louis.* I read about him in the *Daily Herald,* a newspaper, and *Into the Unknown,* a book.

Check Proper Names   Read each sentence. Write the words correctly that should be capitalized.

1. William Herschel first identified the planet uranus in 1781.
2. In 1930, Amy Johnson flew alone from england to Australia.
3. Huge crowds cheered her during a parade in london.
4. In world war II, women were pilots of passenger airplanes.
5. We saw a shuttle at the Kennedy Space Center in florida.

1. _____
2. _____
3. _____
4. _____
5. _____

PROOFREAD AN INTERVIEW   Find the five misspelled

words in this interview and write them correctly. Some may be words you learned before. Also fix three capitalization mistakes.

> Reporter: I'm with the <u>Daily star,</u> in utica.
>
> Do you like your job as a mission speicalist on the
>
> jupiter I Space Shuttle?
>
> Dr. Cerk: I sincerly do. I repair machianry, and
>
> in a laboratory on board I perform scientific
>
> experiments wich are extremly interesting.

Word List

Christmas	errands
Easter	extremely
sincerely	threatening
quantity	definitely
boundary	practically
laboratory	supposedly
accidentally	identity
specific	eighth
candidate	frightened
funeral	headache

Personal Words

1. _____
2. _____

WRITE AN INTERVIEW   Imagine that you are a reporter

interviewing a student about his or her plans for the future. Write the interview. Use two list words and a personal word.

Review

CONTEXT   Use the context to complete each sentence with a word from the box.

laboratory	specific
candidate	extremely
accidentally	sincerely
practically	eighth
Christmas	frightened

1. Though he didn't mean to, he ___ scraped his car on the wall.
2. Children can hardly wait for ___ to arrive.
3. A person who wants to be believed will speak very ___.
4. August is the ___ month of the year.
5. You need to fill in this blank with a ___ word.
6. The continents of Africa and Antarctica are ___ different from each other.
7. Many scientific discoveries have been made in the ___.
8. A ___ for political office will sometimes make wild promises.
9. Small children can be ___ by the sights and sounds of Halloween.
10. Those two are only slightly different—they are ___ the same.

1. _____
2. _____
3. _____
4. _____
5. _____
6. _____
7. _____
8. _____
9. _____
10. _____

Word *Study*

JARGON   Technical language, or **jargon,** uses words that are specific to a certain profession, sport, or other subject. For instance, the word *interface* is part of the jargon used by people who work with computers and in business. It means "connect two things so they will interact." As you read these sentences, notice that jargon can be confusing in ordinary speech.

Jargon at work: "This computer interfaces with the new printer."

Jargon in ordinary speech: "We'll interface at the game today."

writing	use
secretary	gather
send	ideas
responses	mistake

The school principal uses a lot of jargon in the message below. Make the message easier to understand by substituting words from the box for the numbered jargon words.

Dear Students:
      We need your **(1) input** about this year's activities. Please **(2) utilize** the attached form for **(3) recording** your **(4) feedback.** After we **(5) compile** your choices, we will **(6) transmit** them to each class. Students can vote for their favorite activities. If you notice a **(7) bug** in this document, please tell the **(8) processor** in the front office. Have a good year!

                              Mr. Otto Mation
                              Principal

1. _____
2. _____
3. _____
4. _____
5. _____
6. _____
7. _____
8. _____

Review

Lesson 19: Suffixes -ary, -ery, -ory
Lesson 20: Latin Roots 1
Lesson 21: People Suffixes

Lesson 22: Easily Confused Words
Lesson 23: Including All the Letters

REVIEW WORD LIST

1. anniversary
2. bribery
3. directory
4. ordinary
5. satisfactory
6. scenery
7. surgery
8. temporary
9. vocabulary
10. appendix
11. bankrupt
12. conductor
13. conjecture
14. corruption
15. pendant
16. suspended
17. accountant
18. attendant
19. chemist
20. comedian
21. custodian
22. dependent
23. incumbent
24. motorist
25. musician
26. novelist
27. pedestrian
28. pharmacist
29. physician
30. soloist
31. technician
32. advice
33. advise
34. affect
35. formerly
36. proceed
37. respectfully
38. uninterested
39. accidentally
40. candidate
41. Christmas
42. definitely
43. eighth
44. extremely
45. identity
46. practically
47. quantity
48. sincerely
49. specific
50. supposedly

■ PROOFREADING

Find the spelling errors in each passage and write the words
correctly. All passages have seven errors except the last one,
which has eight.

PROOFREAD A LOST-AND-FOUND NOTICE

1. _____
2. _____
3. _____
4. _____
5. _____
6. _____
7. _____

Found on chrismas Eve, an extremely
old pendent sespended from a gold
chain. Contact Jim, custodien at Briar
School. Owner must give spesific
description of lost item and prove
idenity. Phone 555-1079 days.

PROOFREAD A FEATURE STORY

New Exhibit

Are you planning a trip abroad one day? There's an exhibit of foreign money in the school library that may be useful. If you're bankrup in Kenya, for example, you'll need some shillings. If you have an accountent in Brazil, you'll probably have to spend a cruzeiro or two. If you're traveling in India, take our advise and carry a few rupees. In the Netherlands, you'll be dependant on the guilder. In Japan you'll need a large quanity of yen, and in France you'll definitly need francs. Money from practicaly every major country in the world will be on display.

1. _____
2. _____
3. _____
4. _____
5. _____
6. _____
7. _____

PROOFREAD A REPORT

People from the United States who travel in England have to learn new meanings for ordanary English vocabalery. If they need to go to the office of a dentist or phisician, they have to find a surgury. If they need a pharmecis, they must look for the chemest. When taking a road trip, U.S. travelers find that a British moterist fills up the car with petrol instead of gas. Of course, the car runs just as well since both words mean the same thing in England.

1. _____
2. _____
3. _____
4. _____
5. _____
6. _____
7. _____

PROOFREAD A POSTCARD

1. _____
2. _____
3. _____
4. _____
5. _____
6. _____
7. _____

December 14, 19--

Dear Luis,

Right now, I'm on the train feeling bored. Since it's night, I can't watch the senery so I'm trying to guess what the people in the seats around me do for a living. I think the woman with the clarinet case is a musicien, and the guy who is using a computer is a novalist. The character who keeps telling jokes to everyone including the cunducter said he formally was a comedan. I can understand why he changed jobs—this audience is totally unintrested in him. I'll bet you wish you were here!

See you soon,
Paul

Luis Ruiz

1759 N. Talman

Chicago, IL 60614

PROOFREAD A SIGN

1. _____
2. _____
3. _____
4. _____
5. _____
6. _____
7. _____

Notice

During construction of our temperary walk, please follow the pedestrien tunnel and preceed to the main floor of the store. Consult the store directery or ask an attendent if you need further directions. The Snack Bar is now on the eigth floor. Renovations do not effect any departments above the first floor.

PROOFREAD A TELEPHONE MESSAGE

1. _____
2. _____
3. _____
4. _____
5. _____
6. _____
7. _____

Mom,

You got three calls. Mrs. Henderson phoned to say that the soloest for the aniversery party just had her appendex removed. She wants you to substitute. Also, the TV technition called. He would arise us to buy a new TV

and pick up the old one. Mr. Nagy's message was that he accidently sideswiped your car. It's not too bad, suposedly. What's for dinner?

Marty

PROOFREAD AN INTERVIEW

1. _____
2. _____
3. _____
4. _____
5. _____
6. _____
7. _____
8. _____

Reporter: As a canidate for mayor, you have made several charges about coruption in city hall. Can you support those charges?

J.T.: Of course! Read this report! Now the public will know that bribary in our government is not a matter of conjecshure, but the sad truth.

Reporter: The incumbant mayor has denied these charges.

J.T.: Then I respecfuly submit that the mayor is not aware of what is right under his nose.

Reporter: Do you sincerly believe that you can win this election?

J.T.: Absolutely! The results of my polls have been more than satisfactery—they've been very encouraging.

STRATEGY WORKSHOP

Creating Memory Tricks

DISCOVER THE STRATEGY Use memory tricks to outwit words that are tricky for you to spell.

1. Begin by marking the letters that give you problems.

   diamond
   ~~dimond~~

2. Then think of memory helpers—words or phrases you already can spell—with the same tricky letters.

   dial   I am
   diagram

3. Now create your memory trick. Link your word with a memory helper that helps you remember it.

I am a diamond!

Tips: Can your trick be pictured? Then **visualize** the scene as you say the trick to yourself. Don't think your trick has to be serious or even make sense, as long as it helps you remember how to spell the word.

More tips: Your helper could be one word or more. Your trick could be a phrase **(the elo<u>qu</u>ent <u>qu</u>estion)** or a sentence **(<u>Al</u> <u>al</u>ways <u>a</u>cts).**

TRY IT OUT   Now try this strategy.

Write a helper from the box to complete each memory trick. Underline the matching letters.

your	Conrad felt tiny	Rachel	them

1. ___ confetti.
2. ___ has a he<u>ada</u>che.
3. Give ___ mathematics.
4. ___ tou<u>rna</u>ment

1. _____

2. _____

3. _____

4. _____

With a partner, pick a helper from the box and create a memory trick for each word below. Underline the matching letters in the word and helper. Draw any tricks you can visualize.

guard	up and under	eight	kicked

5. panicked _____

6. sleigh _____

7. vacuum _____

8. guacamole _____

LOOK AHEAD   Look ahead at the next five lessons for list words that might give you problems. Create memory tricks for two of them. Share your results with the class.

1. _____

2. _____

Words from Many Cultures

SPELLING FOCUS

Many words in English come from other languages and may have unexpected spellings: **chimpanzee.**

STUDY Say each word and pay attention to any unusual spellings. Then read the meaning phrase.

1. **chimpanzee**   the **chimpanzee** clinging to its mother
2. **bagel**   golden, chewy **bagel** for breakfast
3. **coffee**   pot of **coffee** without caffeine
4. **tornado**   twisting **tornado** moving over the plain
5. **mosquito**   an annoying itch from a **mosquito** bite
6. **iceberg**   an **iceberg** floating in frigid waters
7. **hurricane**   roofs blown off by a **hurricane**
8. **cocoa**   drank hot **cocoa** after sledding
9. **volcano**   lava pouring out of the **volcano**
10. **lagoon**   quiet, protected water of the **lagoon**

11. **pretzel**   ate a **pretzel** as a low-fat snack
12. **caribou**   the antlers on the **caribou**
13. **bayou**   alligators swimming in the **bayou**
14. **yogurt**   thick **yogurt** made from milk
15. **opossum**   the scared **opossum** playing dead
16. **reservoir**   water held in a **reservoir** for public use
17. **monsoon**   wind and rain of the **monsoon** season
18. **jaguar**   a leopard, a tiger, and a **jaguar**
19. **tundra**   the treeless landscape of a **tundra**
20. **typhoon**   flood caused by a raging **typhoon**

PRACTICE Sort the words by writing
- five words that name things we eat or drink
- five words that name animals
- four words that describe types of weather
- six words that name landforms or structures

WRITE Choose two phrases to write in an advertisement, slogan, or saying.

1.
2.
3.
4.
5.
6.
7.
8.
9.
10.
11.
12.
13.
14.
15.
16.
17.
18.
19.
20.

CHALLENGE!

gazelle
orangutan
terrapin
ptarmigan
wildebeest

RIDDLES   Write the list word that answers each riddle. Use your Spelling Dictionary if you need help.

1. From a Bantu word, I am a kind of ape.
2. I am from a Dutch word meaning "ice mountain."
3. I am a wild cat named by the Tupi of South America.
4. I am a dark brown drink whose Italian name is *caffè.*
5. I take my name from *mosca,* the Spanish word for "fly."
6. I am from a Russian word meaning "frozen, treeless plain."
7. From an Algonquian word, I can fake being dead.
8. I am a Turkish word for a thick liquid food made from milk.
9. I am a large reindeer with an Algonquian name.
10. From the Yiddish *beigel,* I am a hard roll shaped like a ring.

DEFINITIONS   Write the list word that fits each definition. Use your Spelling Dictionary if you need help.

11. a rainy season, from the Arabic word *mausim*
12. a hard, salty biscuit, from the German word *brezel*
13. a tropical storm, called a *hurakán* by the Taino people
14. a water-storage place, from the French word *réservoir*
15. an opening in the earth's crust, from an Italian word based on the ancient Roman god Vulcan
16. a destructive whirlwind, from the Spanish word *tronada*
17. a sluggish body of water, from the Choctaw word *bayuk*
18. a powder made from beans called *cacao* by the Spanish
19. a tropical storm, from the Chinese words *tai fung*
20. a pond or small lake connected with a larger body of water, from the Italian word *laguna*

Using the Memory Tricks Strategy

Use memory tricks to help you spell. Create memory tricks for two list words that are hard for you. Underline the matching letters in the list words and helpers.

21. _____

_____

22. _____

_____

1. _____
2. _____
3. _____
4. _____
5. _____
6. _____
7. _____
8. _____
9. _____
10. _____
11. _____
12. _____
13. _____
14. _____
15. _____
16. _____
17. _____
18. _____
19. _____
20. _____

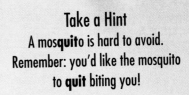

Take a Hint
A mos**qui**to is hard to avoid.
Remember: you'd like the mosquito
to **quit** biting you!

≡	Make a capital.
/	Make a small letter.
∧	Add something.
℮	Take out something.
⊙	Add a period.
⌐F	New paragraph

PROOFREAD FOR CAPITALIZATION
Capitalize the first word in every sentence and all proper nouns. For example:

When Hurricane andrew hit florida, it caused extensive damage.

Check for Capital Letters Read each sentence. Write correctly the five words that need capitalization.

However, that doesn't mean we're canceling our trip to whitman park. once there you can take a quiet ride on a blue lagoon. also, take a ride on the bayou on the Crocodile coaster.

1. _____
2. _____
3. _____
4. _____
5. _____

PROOFREAD A TRAVEL BROCHURE
Find the six misspelled words and write them correctly. Some may be words you learned before. Also fix three capitalization errors.

We also offer trips to visit Mt. St. helen's, a volcano in washington. May be you'll canoe on the nearby resivore or lagune. a walk in the forest might bring you face to face with a caribo or opossum to. Finally, from your cabin you can watch the sun set while sipping a cup of hot coffee or coco.

Word List

hurricane	bagel
chimpanzee	mosquito
typhoon	cocoa
jaguar	pretzel
volcano	bayou
iceberg	tornado
monsoon	opossum
reservoir	lagoon
caribou	yogurt
tundra	coffee

Personal Words

1. _____
2. _____

WRITE A TRAVEL BROCHURE
Write a travel brochure telling about a fantasy vacation place you want to visit. Use three list words and a personal word.

Review

WHO AM I? Use the clues and the words in the box to decide who is speaking.

chimpanzee	iceberg
bagel	hurricane
coffee	cocoa
tornado	volcano
mosquito	lagoon

1. All I am is a big ice cube floating in the ocean.
2. I don't care if I look like one—I am *not* a doughnut!
3. People who like chocolate love me.
4. I am a huge circular storm that was born in the Atlantic Ocean, and you don't want me to grow up and reach land!
5. Many people think of me as a "wake-up call" in the morning.
6. I am a pain in the neck—or arm, or face, or leg, or . . . .
7. I may look somewhat like a gorilla, but I think I'm *much* cuter.
8. I may be just a little body of water, but I have connections.
9. Everyone thinks of me as a terrifying cloud.
10. I may look like a mountain, but don't get near me when I let off steam!

1. _____
2. _____
3. _____
4. _____
5. _____
6. _____
7. _____
8. _____
9. _____
10. _____

Word *Study*

SIMILES When you compare two unlike things using the word *like* or *as,* you are creating a **simile** (sim′ ə lē). For instance, if your little sister were bothering you while you're trying to read, you could say:

My sister is as pesky as a mosquito.

Similes are useful tools you can use in your writing to help create images in your readers' minds. Can't you just see your little sister as a mosquito, buzzing around your head?

You might also use the words in the box to create similes. Complete each simile with one of those words.

hurricane
lagoon
chimpanzee
jaguar
iceberg
pretzel
coffee

1. "Come in and sit by the fire," Grandma said. "You look as cold as an ___."
2. The runner looks like a ___ as she gracefully leaps over the hurdles.
3. While stretching in yoga class, we each looked like a ___.
4. His eyes were as blue as the water in a ___.
5. The cave was as black as a cup of ___.
6. He smiled like a ___ eating a bunch of bananas.
7. The four-year-old stormed into the room like a ___.

1. _____
2. _____
3. _____
4. _____
5. _____
6. _____
7. _____

Related Words 2

Related words often have parts that are spelled the same but pronounced differently: **elastic**, **elasticity**; **detect**, **detection**.

■ **STUDY** Say each pair of related words and notice how the pronunciation changes. Then read each meaning phrase.

1. **elastic**   the loose **elastic** in the waistband
2. **elasticity**   a stiff swimsuit without **elasticity**
3. **detect**   can **detect** a gas leak by smell
4. **detection**   **detection** through using fingerprints
5. **alternate**   a longer but easier **alternate** route
6. **alternative**   had no **alternative** but to run
7. **economy**   an **economy** based on making steel
8. **economics**   study **economics** and finance in college
9. **normal**   **normal** amount of noise in the hallway
10. **normality**   the **normality** in a daily schedule

11. **concentrate**   can **concentrate** in a quiet room
12. **concentration**   **concentration** broken by the noise
13. **initiate**   will **initiate** a new business
14. **initiative**   took **initiative** to form a new team
15. **restore**   must **restore** order in this room
16. **restoration**   began **restoration** of the old cabin
17. **evaluate**   will **evaluate** your basketball skills
18. **evaluation**   an **evaluation** of your hearing ability
19. **office**   waited in the principal's **office**
20. **official**   an **official** invitation from the mayor

■ **PRACTICE** Which pairs of related words do you already know how to spell? Write these words first. Then write the word pairs that you don't know as well.

■ **WRITE** Choose four phrases to rewrite as questions and answers.

1. _____
2. _____
3. _____
4. _____
5. _____
6. _____
7. _____
8. _____
9. _____
10. _____
11. _____
12. _____
13. _____
14. _____
15. _____
16. _____
17. _____
18. _____
19. _____
20. _____

CHALLENGE!

distinct	distinction
confiscate	confiscation
contaminate	contaminatio

SENTENCE COMPLETION   Complete each unfinished sentence in this diary entry with a pair of related words.

Dear Diary,

     Today was the first day at my new school, and it really got off to a bad start. As I walked through the school door, I somehow tore the (1) in the waistband of my pants, and without (2), my pants were Droop City! I had no (3) but to pin them, since I don't exactly keep an (4) set of clothes in my backpack. I tried to put on an air of (5), as if it was perfectly (6) to walk around with my pants pinned together. I couldn't (7) in class and missed an easy answer, which caused one boy to say I must have left my (8) at home. So during lunch, I went to the principal's (9), where a lady who looked very (10) let me call home to ask Dad to bring me another pair of pants. What a relief that was!

WORD RELATIONSHIPS   Write the list word that matches each definition. Then write the list word that is related to it.

11–12. to bring back
13–14. to find the value or amount of
15–16. a country's system of making and distributing goods
17–18. to discover
19–20. to begin

STRATEGIC SPELLING
Seeing Meaning Connections

21. Write the list word that is part of each word in the box. _____

Then write the word in the box that fits each definition.

> normalize
> abnormal
> normalcy

22. opposite of *normal* _____

23. condition of being normal _____

24. make normal _____

1. _____
2. _____
3. _____
4. _____
5. _____
6. _____
7. _____
8. _____
9. _____
10. _____
11. _____
12. _____
13. _____
14. _____
15. _____
16. _____
17. _____
18. _____
19. _____
20. _____

> **Did You Know?**
> Both **ecology** and **economy** are based on the same Greek word meaning "house." **Ecology** is the study of our "house," which is Earth. **Economics** is the study of how we manage the finances in our house.

≡	Make a capital.
/	Make a small letter.
∧	Add something.
ℓ	Take out something.
⊙	Add a period.
¶	New paragraph.

PROOFREAD FOR CARELESS ERRORS

Sometimes we write too quickly or we write carelessly and drop or add letters to words.

A worsening ~~economy~~ *economy* indicates that ~~alernate~~ *alternate* health care coverage is needed, a White House press release stated.

Check for Added or Dropped Letters Read each sentence. Correct the seven words that are misspelled because of added or dropped letters.

> The Presiden will initiate steps to pass a health bil. Meanwhile, many senator opose the idea. "Who will pay for all the exspencses?" Sen. Kole demaded. "Are the taxpayers once again going to get stuck restoing our economy?"

1. _____

2. _____

3. _____

4. _____

5. _____

6. _____

7. _____

PROOFREAD A NEWS STORY

Correct six misspelled words. Four misspellings are careless errors. Some may be words you learned before.

> In the Oval Office, the President promised the restoration of health benefits or at least a return to normallity. "We must consintrate on an evalation of health care that will help everbody," the President said. Later, a White House offical said, "That's the President's first initative on this issue."

Word List

concentrate	economy
concentration	economics
elastic	normal
elasticity	normality
initiate	evaluate
initiative	evaluation
alternate	office
alternative	official
restore	detect
restoration	detection

Personal Words

1. _____

2. _____

WRITE A NEWS STORY

Write a brief news story about an event in your neighborhood. Present details from most to least important. Use three list words and a personal word.

elastic	alternative
elasticity	economy
detect	economics
detection	normal
alternate	normality

Review

DEFINITIONS   Write the word from the box that means the same as the underlined word or phrase in each sentence.

1. There was an appearance of <u>usualness</u> about the busy house.
2. Her degree in <u>the science of goods and services</u> allowed her to work for the government.
3. The <u>rubberized tape</u> in my jacket's waistband no longer holds it comfortably tight.
4. The road sign said we would have to use the <u>different</u> road for six months.
5. The police officer received an award for his abilities at the <u>discovery</u> of the habits of criminals.
6. That rubber band is too old to have much <u>flexibility</u>.
7. When the tire went flat, we felt we had no <u>other choice</u> than to walk.
8. This is not the <u>regular</u> way I like to do things.
9. The <u>system of goods and services management</u> of the United States was in serious trouble in the 1930s.
10. By putting blue coloring into the water, the plumber could <u>find</u> the leak.

1. _____
2. _____
3. _____
4. _____
5. _____
6. _____
7. _____
8. _____
9. _____
10. _____

Word *Study*

CONTEXT: SYNONYMS   Imagine that you read this in an article in your reading book: "Maria took the lead and started a neighborhood baby-sitting service. Her *initiative* is beginning to pay off for her." If *initiative* were an unfamiliar word, you could still get its meaning from the **context,** or words around it. Here, the word *lead* is a **synonym** for *initiative* and provides a clue to its meaning.

Write the synonym or synonym phrase in each sentence below that gives you a clue to the underlined word's meaning.

1. Her <u>entrepreneurialism</u> is rare these days. It takes courage to show such risky effort.
2. State <u>licensing</u> at first was difficult, but once she received that permission, Maria was off and running.
3. Services of a <u>pediatrician</u> were needed, but few children's doctors would offer their services.
4. Their <u>expertise</u> was needed in case a child became suddenly ill and their knowledge could help save a life.
5. Food <u>purveyors</u> were hired as suppliers of milk and snacks.
6. Maria's <u>dogged</u> determination won recognition from the mayor, who said, "Being stubborn can be good."

1. _____
2. _____
3. _____
4. _____
5. _____
6. _____

Number Prefixes

Some prefixes show an amount or number. The prefix **bi-** means "two" or "twice," **tri-** means "having three" or "three," **semi-** means "half" or "partly," and **uni-** means "one."

■ **STUDY**   Read each word and meaning phrase. Notice that each word begins with **bi-**, **tri-**, **semi-**, or **uni-**.

1.	**biweekly**	**biweekly** on the 5th and 19th
2.	**bicycle**	pumped up the tires on my **bicycle**
3.	**triangle**	three sides to a **triangle**
4.	**triple**	**triple** in price to thirty-six cents
5.	**triplets**	**triplets** in their three-seated stroller
6.	**semicircle**	sat in a **semicircle** around the TV
7.	**semisweet**	ate **semisweet** chocolate chips
8.	**semifinals**	five contests in the **semifinals**
9.	**unison**	called out in **unison,** "Good-by!"
10.	**universal**	**universal** hope of all people

11.	**bifocals**	read the newspaper using **bifocals**
12.	**bicentennial**	United States **bicentennial** in 1976
13.	**biceps**	bulging **biceps** in the athlete's arm
14.	**tripod**	steadied the camera on a **tripod**
15.	**trillion**	million, billion, **trillion**
16.	**semiprivate**	a **semiprivate** room for our banquet
17.	**semicolon**	a **semicolon** between the sentences
18.	**unicycle**	rode a **unicycle** in the circus
19.	**unify**	will **unify** the members of the team
20.	**unique**	a **unique** idea for an electric car

■ **PRACTICE**   Sort the words by writing
- five words with **uni-**
- five words with **bi-**
- five words with **semi-**
- five words with **tri-**

■ **WRITE**   Choose three phrases to include in a paragraph.

1. _____
2. _____
3. _____
4. _____
5. _____
6. _____
7. _____
8. _____
9. _____
10. _____
11. _____
12. _____
13. _____
14. _____
15. _____
16. _____
17. _____
18. _____
19. _____
20. _____

CHALLENGE!

bicultural
trigonometry
semiprofessional
semiprecious
uniformity

DEFINITIONS   Write the list word that means the same as the underlined word or phrase in each sentence.

1. Food and shelter are needs that are <u>common to all</u>.
2. Ever since they had <u>three children born at the same time</u>, our neighbors are very busy.
3. When she arrives, shout "Surprise!" in <u>perfect agreement</u>.
4. She developed her <u>large frontal upper-arm muscles</u>.
5. For his <u>three-part</u>-scoop cone, he ordered chocolate, strawberry, and vanilla ice cream.
6. It's difficult to keep upright on a <u>vehicle with one wheel</u>.
7. My father has <u>eyeglasses with two lenses for each eye</u>.
8. The new leader wants to <u>unite</u> the regions into one country.
9. It's so clear out, you can see a <u>thousand billion</u> stars.
10. I'm hoping to get a <u>two-wheeled vehicle</u> for my birthday.
11. That scarf is unusual, but it's not <u>one of a kind</u>.

WORD FORMS   Write the list word that contains each base word.

12. private
13. angle
14. sweet
15. weekly
16. finals

17. centennial
18. colon
19. pod
20. circle

Building New Words

Add the prefix **semi-** to each base word to make a new word. Remember that adding a prefix does <u>not</u> change the spelling of the base word.

21. conscious   _____

22. monthly   _____

23. official   _____

24. skilled   _____

25. soft   _____

1. _____
2. _____
3. _____
4. _____
5. _____
6. _____
7. _____
8. _____
9. _____
10. _____
11. _____
12. _____
13. _____
14. _____
15. _____
16. _____
17. _____
18. _____
19. _____
20. _____

Take a Hint
Unique means "one of a kind." That's why calling something "most unique," "very unique," or "quite unique" is redundant. If something is one of a kind, it can't be *very* one of a kind!

127

☰	Make a capital.
/	Make a small letter.
∧	Add something.
ℓ	Take out something.
⊙	Add a period.
¶	New paragraph

PROOFREAD FOR USAGE   Some pronouns can be singular or plural, depending on how they are used.

> Most of the bicycle training was hard, and most of the athletes were young.

Notice that in the first half of the sentence, **most** has a singular meaning, and so the singular verb **was** is used. In the second half of the sentence, **most** has a plural meaning, and so the plural verb **were** is used. Other pronouns that can be singular or plural include *all, any, most, none,* and *some.*

Check for Subject-Verb Agreement   Read each sentence. Correct the four errors in agreement by writing the correct verb.

1. All of the bikers is riding a unicycle.
2. Is any of the events open for amateurs?
3. Some of the participants possesses well-developed biceps.
4. Most of the money raised are going to charity.

1. _____
2. _____
3. _____
4. _____

PROOFREAD A SPORTSCAST   Correct six misspelled words. Also fix two errors in subject-verb agreement.

> Welcome to the bi-weekly Lincoln Park bycycle race. All of the spectators hopes the semi-finals will be exciting. Riders will ride a uncycle in a semecircle. Most of the judging are being done by former riders themselves. Lets cheer them on!

Word List

triple	universal
biweekly	triplets
semicircle	semifinals
unicycle	unique
semisweet	tripod
bifocals	bicentennial
trillion	unify
unison	bicycle
biceps	triangle
semicolon	semiprivate

Personal Words

1. _____
2. _____

WRITE A SPORTSCAST   Write a brief sportscast of an event you have seen or one you make up. Use three list words and a personal word.

biweekly	semicircle
bicycle	semisweet
triangle	semifinals
triple	unison
triplets	universal

Review

WORDS IN CONTEXT   Write the word from the box that completes each sentence.

1. I thought the girls were twins and was surprised to learn they have a sister—they are ___!
2. While some people like bitter chocolate, many like it ___.
3. My little sister has been riding a four-wheeled scooter, but now she wants to ride a ___.
4. A square has four sides, while a ___ has three.
5. The choir sang the first verse in four parts and the second verse in ___.
6. He traced around the coin far enough to make a ___.
7. I can't afford piano lessons every week, so I take them ___.
8. Henry slid safely into third base after hitting a ___.
9. A love for kittens is not ___; some people can't stand them.
10. She qualified during the ___ and is now in the final race.

1. _____
2. _____
3. _____
4. _____
5. _____
6. _____
7. _____
8. _____
9. _____
10. _____

Word *Study*

GREEK AND LATIN ROOTS: BODY WORDS   You know that **bi-** means "two," but what are **ceps** anyway? Words with **ceps** or **cap** in them are related, coming from a Latin word meaning "head." **Biceps** are muscles (in your arm) with two heads or sources. A **capital** is the head of a region. Other "body" word parts are shown in the chart at the right.

Word Parts		
emia, hem	=	blood
ceps, cap	=	head
cor	=	heart
corp	=	body

hemorrhage   cordial   captain   cape   corporation
hemophilia   concord   discord

Write the word from the box above that best fits each clue below. Use your Spelling Dictionary if you need help.

1. a heavy discharge of blood from a blood vessel
2. the leader of a ship
3. a garment usually fastened around the neck
4. group of people with authority to act as a single body
5. disharmony or a pulling apart of hearts
6. harmony or a bringing of hearts together in agreement
7. a blood disorder in which clotting isn't normal
8. heartfelt, warm, and friendly

1. _____
2. _____
3. _____
4. _____
5. _____
6. _____
7. _____
8. _____

129

Latin Roots 2

SPELLING FOCUS

Many words have the Latin roots **vis**, meaning "see"; **dict**, meaning "say" or "speak"; **spect**, meaning "look"; and **aud**, meaning "hear": **vision**, **prediction**, **suspect**, **auditorium**.

■ **STUDY** Say each word. Then read the meaning phrase.

1.	**vision**	having good **vision** with my glasses
2.	**supervision**	**supervision** of study hall
3.	**revise**	must **revise** your report for history class
4.	**prediction**	**prediction** about tomorrow's weather
5.	**contradict**	facts that **contradict** your opinion
6.	**suspect**	a **suspect** in the burglary case
7.	**spectator**	a cheer started by a **spectator**
8.	**auditorium**	spoke to a crowded **auditorium**
9.	**audio-visual**	an **audio-visual** rain forest display
10.	**audit**	will **audit** our financial records

11.	**visible**	**visible** only through a telescope
12.	**provision**	a **provision** in the renter's lease
13.	**dictation**	typed a letter from a **dictation** tape
14.	**verdict**	a **verdict** returned by the jury
15.	**dictator**	obeyed the **dictator** and his cruel law
16.	**spectacle**	**spectacle** of a battle reenactment
17.	**inspector**	spoiled meat found by the **inspector**
18.	**spectacular**	a **spectacular** fireworks display
19.	**audible**	a barely **audible** whisper
20.	**audition**	nervous about the movie **audition**

■ **PRACTICE** Sort the words by writing
- one word containing both **aud** and **vis**
- four other words containing **aud**
- five other words containing **vis**
- five words with **dict**
- five words with **spect**

■ **WRITE** Choose ten phrases to rewrite as sentences.

CHALLENGE!

visibility
valedictorian
introspection
prospective
inaudible

1. _____
2. _____
3. _____
4. _____
5. _____
6. _____
7. _____
8. _____
9. _____
10. _____
11. _____
12. _____
13. _____
14. _____
15. _____
16. _____
17. _____
18. _____
19. _____
20. _____

PROOFREAD A FRIENDLY LETTER

December 15, 19—

Dear Cathy,

When you come to visit for the holidays, you will get to meet the exchange student staying with us. He's studying ecomnics at the university, and sometimes he helps Paul with his algerbra. He is really a uniqe individual. I'm sure you will appriceate his stories of being in a tifoon in India. We have introduced him to our favorite bread, the begal, and he is an enthusiastic spectater at the college football games. See you soon!

Love,
Carolyn

1. _____
2. _____
3. _____
4. _____
5. _____
6. _____
7. _____

PROOFREAD A "HOW-TO" PARAGRAPH

Researching Your Family Tree

When researching your family tree, first consintrate on what you can find out from your family. After that you might get some offical records from your county courthouse. As an alternitive, you might ask your local librarian how to get information, expecially if your library has local histories. If you saspect that an ancestor may have fought in the Civil War, you may get his military record from the National Archives in Washinton. You can also write for a free booklet on how to inishiate a search.

1. _____
2. _____
3. _____
4. _____
5. _____
6. _____
7. _____

PROOFREAD A NOTICE

1. _____
2. _____
3. _____
4. _____
5. _____
6. _____
7. _____

The restoreation of our school auditarium is complete, and the results are spectacleuar! All new audio-visal equipment has been installed, there is provison for many kinds of dramatic presentations, and the stage is now visibel from every seat. Come to our free opening concert Saturday, November 5, at 8 o'clock and make your own evaluatian of this magnificent place!

PROOFREAD A BROCHURE

1. _____
2. _____
3. _____
4. _____
5. _____
6. _____
7. _____

You can give the Lakeside Zoo a boost by adopting one of its residents. We have a lively chimpanzy who wants a friend, a stately camel who could use a helping hand, a cariboo who needs you, and a jagaur, some lions, and a lonely opposum just waiting to be adopted. P.S. Our flamingos over by the laggoon are truely lonesome and would consider it a privilege to be your "adoptees." Why not drop by and help *our* ecomony for a change?

PROOFREAD A THANK-YOU NOTE

1. _____
2. _____
3. _____
4. _____
5. _____
6. _____
7. _____

May 7, 19—

Dear Friends,

We want to thank you for the help you gave us after the tornnado, which almost destroyed our home. You have helped us return to normel by contributing time and money to help restor our house. Although we did not completely ecsape tradgedy, we are well and safe. A trillon thank-yous from

Dave, Marie, and the triplits

(Sam, Sue, and Sara)

PROOFREAD A JOURNAL ENTRY

1. _____
2. _____
3. _____
4. _____
5. _____
6. _____
7. _____
8. _____

Today our class took a trip to the historical society. They have exhibits of a lot of things that once belonged to people in our town. There was a bycicle with a huge front wheel and a little back wheel, a pair of old bifocils that once belonged to the woman who founded our town, an old landtern, a unicicle, a souveneer coffe cup from our town's bicentenial celebration, and some old bones! I'm not sure whose they were! We heard a talk about how the curators evalaute items they receive for display.

STRATEGY WORKSHOP

Choosing the Best Strategy

DISCOVER THE STRATEGY   Use this strategy when you study new words:

Steps for Spelling
1. Look at the word and say it. 2. Spell it aloud. 3. Think about it. 4. Picture it. 5. Look and write. 6. Cover, write, and check it.

Use these strategies on words that give you problems. For each problem word, choose the strategy that works best for you.

Strategies	How to Use Them
Developing Spelling Consciousness	Don't overlook familiar words when you proofread you're writing. (Did you catch the mistake in that last sentence?)
Pronouncing for Spelling	Pronounce the word correctly ("may-on-naise") or make up a secret pronunciation ("cit-ī-zen").
Divide and Conquer	Divide your word into smaller parts: **under/weight tour/na/ment**
Creating Memory Tricks	Link your word with a memory helper that has the same problem letters: (**I am a diamond!**).
Using Meaning Helpers	Pair your word with a shorter, related word. **specialize—special** **invitation—invite**

TRY IT OUT   Tell each speller which strategy you think would work best to help solve each problem.

1. I know how to spell *sherbet,* but I keep writing **sherbert** instead.
2. I keep misspelling the end of *multiple*—the *ple.*
3. I always spell *nuclear* this way: **nucular.**
4. How can I help remember that *appreciate* has two **p's?**
5. *Privilege* has too many letters for me to remember.
6. I keep spelling *eruption* with an **sh** instead of a **t.**
7. Is there another word I could use to help me remember how to spell *reservoir?*
8. New words are hard for me to learn to spell. I just stare at the word list and wonder what to do next.
9. The word *accidentally* is too long for me to remember.
10. I wish I could stop missing easy words like *because* and *always*—words I really do know how to spell.

1. _____
2. _____
3. _____
4. _____
5. _____
6. _____
7. _____
8. _____
9. _____
10. _____

LOOK AHEAD   Look ahead at the next five lessons for list words that might give you problems. Write four of them. Then decide which strategy you will use to help remember each word, and write it next to the word.

Problem Word	Strategy
1. _____	_____
2. _____	_____
3. _____	_____
4. _____	_____

Multisyllabic Words

SPELLING FOCUS

Long words are often easier to spell if you study them syllable by syllable: **con•sid•er•a•tion.**

■ **STUDY** Read each word, carefully pronouncing each syllable. Then read the meaning phrase.

1.	**consideration**	**consideration** for a sick friend
2.	**communication**	**communication** over the telephone
3.	**punctuation**	correct **punctuation** for a quotation
4.	**unbelievable**	an **unbelievable** excuse for being late
5.	**misunderstanding**	a **misunderstanding** of the rules
6.	**competitive**	our team's **competitive** spirit
7.	**encyclopedia**	checked the facts in an **encyclopedia**
8.	**emergency**	stays calm in an **emergency**
9.	**reusable**	keeps **reusable** plastic containers
10.	**calculator**	used a **calculator** to figure percentages

11.	**untrustworthy**	was **untrustworthy** with money
12.	**unpleasantness**	the **unpleasantness** of an argument
13.	**condominium**	move from a house to a **condominium**
14.	**untidiness**	the **untidiness** of her messy room
15.	**ravioli**	ordered **ravioli** at an Italian restaurant
16.	**disagreeable**	avoids crabby, **disagreeable** people
17.	**exaggeration**	an **exaggeration** of the truth
18.	**uncontrollable**	an **uncontrollable** urge to laugh
19.	**decaffeinated**	drank only **decaffeinated** coffee
20.	**instantaneously**	obeyed the order **instantaneously**

■ **PRACTICE** First write the words you think are easy to spell. Then write the ones you think are difficult.

■ **WRITE** Choose two phrases to write in an advertisement, slogan, or saying.

1. _____
2. _____
3. _____
4. _____
5. _____
6. _____
7. _____
8. _____
9. _____
10. _____
11. _____
12. _____
13. _____
14. _____
15. _____
16. _____
17. _____
18. _____
19. _____
20. _____

CHALLENGE!

inappropriately
nonnegotiable
nondiscriminatory
unintimidated
mispronunciation

MAKING CONNECTIONS   Write the list word that is missing from each person's statement.

1. Shopper: "I buy things in ___ containers to reduce waste."
2. Teacher: "You seem confused about the correct ___ to use at the end of a sentence."
3. Real estate agent: "I just sold a ___ in that new building."
4. Librarian: "Try looking in the ___ for that information."
5. Bank supervisor: "Because our employees handle so much money, we can't risk hiring ___ people."
6. Restaurant customer: "I'll have a cup of ___ coffee."
7. Nurse: "Please show ___ for our patients by talking softly."
8. Coach: "We need a more ___ attitude in order to win."
9. Citizen: "I got batteries for my ___ so I can do my taxes."
10. Parent: "Please clean your room; I don't like such ___."
11. First-aid instructor: "In this kind of ___, don't try to move the victim by yourself."
12. Waiter: "Our special tonight is ___ with tomato sauce."

PRONUNCIATIONS   Write the list word for each pronunciation given.

13. kə myü′nə kā′shən
14. in′stən tā′nē əs lē
15. un′kən trō lə bəl
16. dis′ə grē′ə bəl
17. un′bi lē′və bəl
18. un′plez′nt nis
19. eg zaj′ə rā′shən
20. mis′un′dər stan′ding

STRATEGIC SPELLING

Choosing the Best Strategy

Write two list words that you find hard to spell. Which strategy could help you spell each word? Name the strategy and tell why you chose it. Then compare choices with a partner. For a list of strategies, see pages 142–143.

21. _____
22. _____

1. _____
2. _____
3. _____
4. _____
5. _____
6. _____
7. _____
8. _____
9. _____
10. _____
11. _____
12. _____
13. _____
14. _____
15. _____
16. _____
17. _____
18. _____
19. _____
20. _____

Did You Know?
Before the devices we know as calculators were invented, *calculator* referred only to a person who was good at arithmetic.

PROOFREAD FOR PUNCTUATION   Use commas to separate three or more words or phrases in a series. For example:

> Your pet will need a comb, brush, collar, and leash.

Check Commas   Read this advertisement. Write the five words that should be followed by a comma; write the commas after them.

> Dog-walker: I am available for dog-walking every day from 3:00 to 5:00 P.M. I can pick up your pet right at your townhouse apartment condominium, or house. I have experience with dogs of all sizes: poodles spaniels retrievers dachshunds, and Great Danes. My rates are low.

1. _____
2. _____
3. _____
4. _____
5. _____

PROOFREAD AN ADVERTISEMENT   Correct five misspelled words in this advertisement. Some may be words you learned before. Also add three missing commas.

> Avoid the unpleasentness of an uncontrolable, disagreable pet. Don't wait untill it's too late. Bring your dog to Pooch Pet School. Your dog will learn to heel sit lie down, and stay. Teach your pet to obey your commands instantaneously. It's no exageration to say that your dog will learn to be a well-behaved reliable, and trustworthy companion.

Word List

consideration	ravioli
communication	disagreeable
punctuation	encyclopedia
unbelievable	calculator
misunderstanding	emergency
untrustworthy	reusable
competitive	uncontrollable
unpleasantness	decaffeinated
condominium	exaggeration
untidiness	instantaneously

Personal Words

1. _____
2. _____

WRITE AN ADVERTISEMENT   Write an ad for a business you may run someday. Use three list words and a personal word.

Review

DEFINITIONS Write the boxed word that matches each clue.

1. thought given to a decision; thoughtfulness for others
2. a sudden need for immediate action
3. an incorrect meaning; the failure to figure out a correct meaning
4. a book or set of books giving information on all areas of knowledge
5. the marks that make written meaning clear; the use of such marks
6. a machine that solves number problems using various mathematical processes
7. that which can be used again
8. the giving or exchanging of information or news
9. having a desire to get what others are also trying to get
10. that which cannot be accepted as true

> consideration
> communication
> punctuation
> unbelievable
> misunderstanding
> competitive
> encyclopedia
> emergency
> reusable
> calculator

1. _____
2. _____
3. _____
4. _____
5. _____
6. _____
7. _____
8. _____
9. _____
10. _____

Multicultural Connection

ENVIRONMENT All over the world, people choose dwellings that will protect them and make good use of the environment. For example, the Millers bought a condominium in the city. Being close to the bus, train, school, and work is important to them. The condominium owners all try to keep the building in good condition.

Think about the three types of homes below. Then write two reasons that a person would choose to live in each. Tell what would be important to the person and what protection they might need. Use some of the words in the box and add your own.

quiet	water
rivers	climate
religion	wind
school	safety
space	forests
buses	flooding

1. an apartment in a high-rise building _____

_____

_____

2. a home for one family on a large piece of land _____

_____

_____

3. an underground house _____

_____

_____

Related Words 3

SPELLING FOCUS

Sometimes a letter is dropped or changed in words that are related in meaning: **permit**, **permission**; **explain**, **explanation**.

■ **STUDY** Say each pair of related words and notice how the spelling changes. Then read each meaning phrase.

1.	**permit**	doesn't **permit** running in the hall
2.	**permission**	need **permission** to go on the trip
3.	**extend**	will **extend** the school year by a week
4.	**extension**	a long **extension** cord for the lamp
5.	**explain**	will **explain** how to make a pizza
6.	**explanation**	a clear **explanation** of the rules
7.	**pronounce**	can **pronounce** each word clearly
8.	**pronunciation**	the correct **pronunciation** of a word
9.	**curious**	a **curious** person who asks questions
10.	**curiosity**	her **curiosity** about that big box

11.	**collide**	could **collide** with the other train
12.	**collision**	awful wreckage from the **collision**
13.	**expand**	need more space to **expand**
14.	**expansion**	must approve the library's **expansion**
15.	**repeat**	must **repeat** the message for him
16.	**repetition**	boring **repetition** of the same song
17.	**maintain**	will **maintain** good grades all year
18.	**maintenance**	road **maintenance** to fix potholes
19.	**generous**	a **generous** donation to charity
20.	**generosity**	thanked them for their **generosity**

■ **PRACTICE** Sort the words by writing
• four word pairs in which a consonant is changed
• six word pairs in which a vowel letter is changed or dropped
Underline the letters that are changed or dropped.

■ **WRITE** Choose four phrases to rewrite as questions and answers.

1. _____
2. _____
3. _____
4. _____
5. _____
6. _____
7. _____
8. _____
9. _____
10. _____
11. _____
12. _____
13. _____
14. _____
15. _____
16. _____
17. _____
18. _____
19. _____
20. _____

CHALLENGE!

erode	erosion
acclaim	acclamation
emphasis	emphatic

RHYMES Write the list word that rhymes with the underlined word and makes sense in the sentence.

1. Try to <u>retain</u> what I'm about to ___.
2. With its new ___, the house is a <u>mansion</u>.
3. The rules don't ___ that type of <u>wit</u>.
4. If he asks, don't be <u>furious</u>; he can't help being ___.
5. She won't fail to ___ a hand to a <u>friend</u>.
6. Let me ___: please move your <u>feet</u>.
7. The French would <u>denounce</u> the way I ___.
8. Each year, it's a ___; their team wins the <u>competition</u>.
9. Due to popular <u>demand</u>, the store's hours will ___.
10. He blamed the cars' ___ on problems with his <u>vision</u>.
11. Monique struggled to ___ control of the <u>airplane</u>.
12. The principal added an ___ to the student's <u>detention</u>.

DEFINITIONS Write the list word that means the same as the underlined words.

13. My brother's responsible for the <u>upkeep</u> of his car.
14. They could give no <u>reason</u> for the cake's disappearance.
15. I've got Mom's <u>consent</u> to stay past ten o'clock.
16. All the volunteers were <u>unselfish</u> with their time.
17. Eva learns a lot because of her <u>eager desire to know</u>.
18. We were impressed with his <u>willingness to share with others</u>.
19. When players <u>run into each other</u>, they're often injured.
20. Lashon rehearsed his speech using clear <u>sounds for each word</u>.

STRATEGIC SPELLING

Seeing Meaning Connections

repetitive
repeater

21–22. Write the two list words that are related in spelling and meaning to the words in the box.

Then write the word in the box that fits each definition.

23. characterized by repetition
24. any person or thing that repeats

21. _____   23. _____

22. _____   24. _____

1. _____
2. _____
3. _____
4. _____
5. _____
6. _____
7. _____
8. _____
9. _____
10. _____
11. _____
12. _____
13. _____
14. _____
15. _____
16. _____
17. _____
18. _____
19. _____
20. _____

Did You Know?
Collide comes from a Latin prefix that means "together" and a root that means "strike."

149

═	Make a capital.
/	Make a small letter.
∧	Add something.
ℓ	Take out something.
⊙	Add a period.
¶	New paragraph

PROOFREAD FOR CARELESS ERRORS

Do you see the mistake in this sentence?

To have a a friend, you must be one.

The word *a* has been repeated. Correct careless mistakes like this when you proofread.

Check for Repeated Words In each sentence, write the word if it was repeated by mistake. If a sentence is correct, write "Correct."

1. We have a terrific math teacher at at Ridge Junior High.
2. I'm in her pre-algebra class this year.
3. She always gives us us a good explanation of the lesson.
4. She's generous in providing extra help to any any student.
5. In her class, we don't waste time with boring repetition.

1. _____

2. _____

3. _____

4. _____

5. _____

PROOFREAD A DESCRIPTION   Find six misspelled words in this description and write them correctly. Some may be words you learned before. Also correct three careless errors.

> Shaundra and I have been been best freinds ever since kindergarten. She is is thoughtful, generus, and curios. Her curiosity has gotten us both into trouble. Once we took my mom's calculator apart to see how it worked. I can't repete what what Mom said about that! It's fun being aroud Shaundra. I hope we maintane our friendship forever.

Word List

permit	pronounce
permission	pronunciation
generous	extend
generosity	extension
repeat	curious
repetition	curiosity
collide	expand
collision	expansion
maintain	explain
maintenance	explanation

Personal Words

1. _____

2. _____

WRITE A DESCRIPTION   Write a description of someone you've known for a long time. Use two or three list words and a personal word.

Review

THEY SAID IT Write which boxed word each person said.

permit	explanation
permission	pronounce
extend	pronunciation
extension	curious
explain	curiosity

1. Child psychologist: Babies are naturally ___ about their world.
2. Math teacher: Be prepared to ___ how to solve the problem.
3. Judge: Your ___ leaves too many questions to be believed.
4. Science teacher: A good scientist has a strong sense of ___.
5. English teacher: I will ___ your paper's deadline for one week.
6. Language teacher: Here is the way to ___ that word.
7. Driving examiner: This card will ___ you to practice driving.
8. Electrician: It is better to rewire a room than to use a lot of ___ cords.
9. Principal: You have my ___ to put up the display.
10. Detective: Your choice of words and ___ prove you aren't from this part of the country.

1. _____
2. _____
3. _____
4. _____
5. _____
6. _____
7. _____
8. _____
9. _____
10. _____

Word *Study*

LATIN ROOT: *ten* The list words *extend* and *extension* and the words in the box have the root **ten** (also spelled **tend, tens,** and **tent**), which comes from the Latin word *tendere,* "to stretch."

Complete the word web with the words in the box. Use the Spelling Dictionary if you need help.

tendon
pretentious
intensify
contend

"strengthen; increase"
1. _____

"making claims to excellence or importance"
2. _____

tendere— "to stretch"

"work hard against difficulties; struggle"
3. _____

"a tough cord of tissue that joins a muscle to a bone"
4. _____

Complete each sentence with a word from the box.

5. Pollution in the area may ___ if another factory is built there.
6. Farmers had to ___ with rising water in their fields during last summer's flood.
7. I was embarrassed by my friend's ___ behavior.
8. A ___ in Ray's hand was almost severed in the accident.

5. _____
6. _____
7. _____
8. _____

Latin Roots 3

Many words are made up of the Latin roots **mov**, **mot**, and **mob**, meaning "move"; **mit** and **miss**, meaning "send"; and **ced** and **cess**, meaning "go," "move," or "yield": im**mov**able, sub**mit**, pro**ced**ure.

■ **STUDY** Say each word. Then read the meaning phrase.

1.	**immovable**	as **immovable** as a mountain
2.	**emotion**	the powerful **emotion** of grief
3.	**locomotion**	awkward **locomotion** on crutches
4.	**mobile**	two **mobile** classrooms near the school
5.	**submit**	will **submit** her sculpture to the judges
6.	**missile**	prepared for the **missile** launch
7.	**dismissal**	early **dismissal** from school
8.	**procedure**	the **procedure** to register for classes
9.	**intercede**	will **intercede** to stop the argument
10.	**concession**	his **concession** that he was wrong

11.	**motivate**	can **motivate** them to do their best
12.	**motive**	a hidden **motive** for acting friendly
13.	**commotion**	startled by **commotion** in the hall
14.	**immobilize**	must **immobilize** your broken finger
15.	**transmitted**	a disease **transmitted** by bacteria
16.	**remit**	shall **remit** payment with my order
17.	**intermittent**	an **intermittent**, not constant, sound
18.	**receding**	left behind by the **receding** water
19.	**procession**	a **procession** of marching soldiers
20.	**predecessor**	the new principal's **predecessor**

■ **PRACTICE** Sort the words by writing
- eight words with **mov, mot,** or **mob**
- six words with **mit** or **miss**
- six words with **ced** or **cess**

■ **WRITE** Choose three phrases to include in a paragraph.

1. _____
2. _____
3. _____
4. _____
5. _____
6. _____
7. _____
8. _____
9. _____
10. _____
11. _____
12. _____
13. _____
14. _____
15. _____
16. _____
17. _____
18. _____
19. _____
20. _____

CHALLENGE!

promotional
missionary
commissary
antecedent
accessible

WORD ASSOCIATION   Write the list word suggested by each group of words. Use your Spelling Dictionary if you need help.

1. method, steps
2. line of people, orderly march
3. feeling, happiness, anger
4. act of movement, walking, flying
5. admission, acknowledgment
6. send money, make payment
7. moving easily, changing easily
8. off-and-on, not continuous
9. bustle, confusion
10. fix firmly, make motionless
11. going backward, withdrawing
12. give in, yield, surrender

SYLLABLES   Write the list words whose last syllables are given below.

13. __ ▪ sile
14. __ ▪ __ ▪ cede
15. __ ▪ __ ▪ vate
16. __ ▪ __ ▪ __ ▪ ble

17. __ ▪ __ ▪ __ ▪ sor
18. __ ▪ tive
19. __ ▪ __ ▪ ted
20. __ ▪ __ ▪ al

STRATEGIC SPELLING

Seeing Meaning Connections

| motivational |
| motivate |
| unmotivated |

Write the list word that is related in spelling and meaning to the words in the box.

21. _____

Then use the words in the box to complete the paragraph.

After last year's losing record, the Western Wildcats were an (22) group of soccer players. For weeks, the new coach tried to find a way to (23) them. In desperation, the coach finally decided to hire a professional speaker to give the team a (24) talk.

22. _____   24. _____

23. _____

1. _____
2. _____
3. _____
4. _____
5. _____
6. _____
7. _____
8. _____
9. _____
10. _____
11. _____
12. _____
13. _____
14. _____
15. _____
16. _____
17. _____
18. _____
19. _____
20. _____

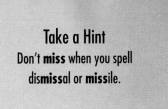

Take a Hint
Don't **miss** when you spell
dismissal or **miss**ile.

153

≡	Make a capital.
/	Make a small letter.
∧	Add something.
ℯ	Take out something.
⊙	Add a period.
¶	New paragraph

PROOFREAD FOR PUNCTUATION

Use commas correctly in the heading, greeting, and closing of a letter. For example:

611 Birch Lane
Hopkins, MN 55345
June 4, 19__

Dear Jeff,

Check for Commas Read these parts of a heading, greeting, and closing. Write each part correctly.

1. Amarillo TX 79107
2. May 31 19__

3. Dear Uncle John
4. Your nephew

1. _____

2. _____

3. _____

4. _____

PROOFREAD A LETTER

Correct four misspelled words in this body of a letter. Also add two missing commas.

153 Grace Street
Ithaca, NY 14851
June 5, 19__

Dear Band Member

Once again band members will run the consesion stand at are football games. The proceedure will be explained prior to this week's game. Please submitt your name to me if you can help.

Sincerely

Mr. James Bestman

Word List

procedure	concession
procession	missile
remit	commotion
dismissal	motive
immovable	intercede
motivate	transmitted
mobile	immobilize
receding	intermittent
emotion	predecessor
submit	locomotion

Personal Words

1. _____

2. _____

WRITE A LETTER

Write a friendly letter to your classmates. Try to use two list words and a personal word.

Review

CROSSWORD PUZZLE
Use the clues to help you fill in the puzzle with words from the box.

immovable	missile
emotion	dismissal
locomotion	procedure
mobile	intercede
submit	concession

Across
2. cannot have location changed
6. the act or power of going from place to place
8. an object or weapon that is thrown or shot (for example, a self-propelled rocket)
9. to yield to the power or authority of someone else
10. a way of doing things

Down
1. anything granted or yielded
3. a strong feeling of any kind
4. the condition or act of being sent away or removed
5. to plead or ask a favor for someone else
7. easy to move

Using a Dictionary

SYNONYM STUDIES
To be sure you are using synonyms correctly, look for **synonym studies** in dictionary entries. If you look up the word *motive*, for example, it will refer you to a synonym study under the entry for *reason*.

Write the synonyms that best complete the questions. Use the synonym study to help you decide.

1. What is the ___ that all this furniture is smashed?
2. What was the criminal's ___ for stealing the jewelry?
3. Is there a particular ___ you left your house unlocked?
4. Is lack of security a ___ of the thief's break-in?
5. Do you think keeping would-be thieves away is a good ___ for having a dog?

> **Syn.** *n.* **1 Reason, cause, motive** mean that which makes something happen. **Reason** applies to a ground or occasion that explains why something has happened: *The reason they went to Arizona was the climate.* **Cause** applies to a person, thing, incident, or condition that directly brings about an action or happening: *The cause of his new diet was his doctor's warning about the dangers of being overweight.* **Motive** applies to the feeling or desire that makes a person do what he or she does: *His motive was to regain his health.*

1. _____
2. _____
3. _____
4. _____
5. _____

155

Prefixes de-, dis-, non-, un-

The prefixes **de-**, **dis-**, **non-**, and **un-** mean "not" or "the opposite of." They give the base word a negative meaning: **un + breakable = not breakable.**

■ **STUDY** Read each word and notice its prefix. Then read the meaning phrase.

1.	**deodorant**	will buy **deodorant** at a drugstore
2.	**decrease**	advised a **decrease** in TV viewing
3.	**discontinue**	may **discontinue** the long tradition
4.	**disrespect**	showed **disrespect** by laughing
5.	**nonviolent**	peaceful, **nonviolent** protest
6.	**nonstop**	talked **nonstop** for an entire hour
7.	**nonfiction**	a **nonfiction** book about Japan
8.	**unbreakable**	a strong, sturdy, **unbreakable** toy
9.	**undefeated**	**undefeated** for twenty-seven games
10.	**unfortunately**	**unfortunately,** didn't know in time

11.	**dehydrate**	could **dehydrate** from lack of water
12.	**decline**	politely **decline** to help
13.	**disability**	had a physical **disability**
14.	**disgraceful**	**disgraceful** lack of fair play
15.	**discourage**	won't let the rain **discourage** us
16.	**nonexistent**	**nonexistent** ghosts
17.	**nonprofit**	a **nonprofit** group that builds homes
18.	**nonpoisonous**	a **nonpoisonous** garter snake
19.	**unemployment**	the problems of **unemployment**
20.	**unconscious**	fell and lay **unconscious**

■ **PRACTICE** Sort the words by writing
- five words with **un-**
- five words with **dis-**
- six words with **non-**
- four words with **de-**

■ **WRITE** Choose ten phrases to rewrite as sentences.

1.
2.
3.
4.
5.
6.
7.
8.
9.
10.
11.
12.
13.
14.
15.
16.
17.
18.
19.
20.

CHALLENGE!

dehumidifier
disenchanted
nonessential
unpredictable
unbusinesslike

HIDDEN WORDS   Each word below is the base of a list word. Write the list word.

1. fortunate
2. poison
3. break
4. grace
5. employ
6. odor
7. defeat
8. exist

CONTEXT CLUES   Write the list word that completes each sentence. Use your Spelling Dictionary if you need help.

9. Most charities are ___ organizations.
10. Each apartment is designed so that a person with a physical ___ can live there independently.
11. Gerard had to politely ___ the invitation because he was ill.
12. You can buy packets of dried food or ___ your own food.
13. Rescuers pulled the ___ driver from his badly damaged car.
14. To cut costs, the company will ___ the practice of giving each employee a turkey at Thanksgiving.
15. The ___ in the number of daylight hours each fall means fewer outdoor activities.
16. She wrote a ___ book about her life as a reporter.
17. Don't let one failure ___ you from trying to reach your goal.
18. Read a thick book if you're flying ___ from coast to coast.
19. The students organized a ___ demonstration for peace.
20. She showed ___ by disobeying the family rules.

STRATEGIC SPELLING

Building New Words

Make new words by adding the prefixes to these base words: *arm, breakable, color, toxic, advantage, fattening, comfort, smoker.*

Add dis-

21. _____
22. _____
23. _____
24. _____

Add non-

25. _____
26. _____
27. _____
28. _____

1. _____
2. _____
3. _____
4. _____
5. _____
6. _____
7. _____
8. _____
9. _____
10. _____
11. _____
12. _____
13. _____
14. _____
15. _____
16. _____
17. _____
18. _____
19. _____
20. _____

Take a Hint
Nonfiction is a single word, just as *fiction* is. Never hyphenate it or make it two words.

| Make a capital. |
| Make a small letter. |
| Add something. |
| Take out something. |
| Add a period. |
| New paragraph |

PROOFREAD FOR USAGE   Avoid sentence **fragments.** Make sure each sentence has a subject and verb and makes sense.

I was talking to the sales clerk about video games. Because my sister wants a new one for her birthday.

Check for Sentence Fragments Read each item below. If it is a fragment, write "F." If it is a complete sentence, write "Correct."

1. Because most video games are quite expensive.
2. Players can try out the latest game before they buy it.
3. Parents prefer to buy nonviolent video games.
4. With less money to spend in times of high unemployment.
5. Whenever games don't sell well.

1. _____

2. _____

3. _____

4. _____

5. _____

PROOFREAD A NEWS ARTICLE   Correct five misspelled words in the news article. Also fix three sentence fragments.

Word List

unbreakable	nonviolent
unemployment	nonstop
undefeated	nonexistent
unfortunately	nonprofit
unconscious	nonfiction
discontinue	nonpoisonous
disrespect	dehydrate
disability	deodorant
disgraceful	decrease
discourage	decline

Personal Words

1. _____

2. _____

Top Secret Toy Invented

Behind a veil of secrecy. Researchers in the toy industry announced the invention of the perfect toy. It promises to be everthing a child could hope for. It's guaranteed to be unbreakeable, it runs none stop without batteries. Unfortunatly, the new product will cost alot more than ordinary toys. As production increases. Its cost is expected to decline.

WRITE A NEWS ARTICLE   What do you think the perfect toy could be? Write a news article that identifies it. Use three list words and a personal word.

Review

ANALOGIES Write the word from the box that completes each analogy.

deodorant	nonstop
decrease	nonfiction
discontinue	unbreakable
disrespect	undefeated
nonviolent	unfortunatel

1. Fairy tale book is to fantasy as science book is to ___ .
2. Pane of glass is to fragile as sheet of steel is to ___ .
3. Mouthwash is to bad breath as ___ is to sweat.
4. City street is to stop and go as interstate highway is to ___ .
5. Cancel is to credit card as ___ is to magazine subscription.
6. "I won the prize" is to luckily as "I missed the bus" is to ___ .
7. War is to destructive as compromise is to ___ .
8. Applauding the speaker is to honor as interrupting the speaker is to ___ .
9. Hose is to fill up as drain is to ___ .
10. A record of 0 and 10 is to winless as a record of 10 and 0 is to ___ .

1. _____
2. _____
3. _____
4. _____
5. _____
6. _____
7. _____
8. _____
9. _____
10. _____

Word *Study*

FIGURATIVE LANGUAGE: HYPERBOLE

One way to add emphasis or humor to speech and writing is by using **hyperbole** (hī pėr′bə lē), or exaggeration. Read the first sentence; then notice how the underlined hyperboles improve the second version.

Lydia was so happy that she almost felt unconscious. She even kissed her dog!

Lydia was so happy that <u>her head floated past Mars</u>. She gave her dog <u>a million kisses</u>!

Replace the underlined words below with your own hyperboles.

A man came into the yard. He was so tall that (1) <u>he must have been over six and a half feet</u>. "I saw your sign," he said. "I want to buy that one." He pointed down at Muggy, the last of Big Dog's new puppies. It was so ugly (2) <u>no one else wanted it</u>. Dad began to talk (3) <u>fast</u>. "This dog isn't much to look at but his nature is (4) <u>as sweet as can be</u>," he said. At this, Muggy looked (5) <u>very scared</u> and moved closer to Big Dog. "Will he be a good watchdog?" asked the man. Dad said, "This little fellow is so fierce that (6) <u>your home will be very safe</u>." With that, the man paid Dad, took Muggy, and turned to leave. Big Dog said good-by with a howl that (7) <u>was very loud</u>.

1. _____
_____
2. _____
_____
3. _____
_____
4. _____
_____
5. _____
_____
6. _____
_____
7. _____
_____

Unusual Spellings

Some words have letter combinations that are unusual in
English: **rhyme, crescent, foreign, raspberry, asthma.**

■ **STUDY**   Say each word and notice its spelling. Then read
the meaning phrase.

1.	**rhyme**	wants the poem to **rhyme**
2.	**rhythm**	will beat the **rhythm** on a drum
3.	**crescent**	curving, **crescent** shape of the moon
4.	**adolescent**	the **adolescent** years from 12 to 20
5.	**conscious**	became **conscious** again after fainting
6.	**foreign**	**foreign** money from several countries
7.	**cologne**	the scent of **cologne** from his face
8.	**raspberry**	kept **raspberry** sherbet in the freezer
9.	**asthma**	breathing problems due to **asthma**
10.	**vehicle**	four-wheel-drive **vehicle** for the snow

11.	**rhinoceros**	saw a horned **rhinoceros** in Africa
12.	**rhinestone**	only a **rhinestone,** not a real diamond
13.	**fluorescent**	**fluorescent** lights in the ceiling
14.	**reign**	the long **reign** of Queen Victoria
15.	**afghan**	a warm **afghan** covering his legs
16.	**psychology**	study of the mind, called **psychology**
17.	**psychiatrist**	a **psychiatrist** who treats depression
18.	**pneumonia**	had **pneumonia** in both lungs
19.	**heirloom**	the antique, **heirloom** ring
20.	**shepherd**	a **shepherd** surrounded by sheep

■ **PRACTICE**   Sort the words by first writing those that you
know how to spell. Then write the words you need to study.

■ **WRITE**   Choose three phrases to write in a rhyme, riddle, or
dialogue.

1. _____
2. _____
3. _____
4. _____
5. _____
6. _____
7. _____
8. _____
9. _____
10. _____
11. _____
12. _____
13. _____
14. _____
15. _____
16. _____
17. _____
18. _____
19. _____
20. _____

CHALLENGE!

rhapsody
acquiesce
arraignment
pseudonym
graham cracker

CLASSIFYING   Write the list word that belongs in each group.

1. adult, infant, ___
2. elephant, hippopotamus, ___
3. apple, cherry, ___
4. blanket, shawl, ___
5. ultraviolet, infrared, ___
6. geology, biology, ___
7. pediatrician, biologist, ___

MAKING INFERENCES   Write the list word that fits each clue.

8. The moon's phases include full, new, quarter, and this shape.
9. This describes a country other than your own.
10. This person spends the day surrounded by animals.
11. You ride in or on this to go faster than you can walk.
12. A person with this disease may need to carry medicine for an unexpected attack.
13. In a poem, some lines may do this.
14. This describes a monarch's rule.
15. A person might buy this on a piece of jewelry.
16. A grandparent or parent may pass this down to you.
17. If perfume is too strong for you, you might prefer this.
18. The Greek word *pneumōn,* meaning "lung," is the root word for the name of this disease.
19. This is what you are when you are awake.
20. A drummer needs to have a good sense of this.

1. _____
2. _____
3. _____
4. _____
5. _____
6. _____
7. _____
8. _____
9. _____
10. _____
11. _____
12. _____
13. _____
14. _____
15. _____
16. _____
17. _____
18. _____
19. _____
20. _____

STRATEGIC SPELLING

Choosing the Best Strategy

Write two list words that you find hard to spell. Which strategy could help you spell each word? Name the strategy and tell why you chose it. Then compare choices with a partner. For a list of strategies, see pages 142–143.

21. _____

_____

22. _____

_____

Did You Know?
The word *rhinestone* originally referred to gemstones made of quartz from the Rhine River in Europe. Most rhinestones today are made of glass.

■ PROOFREADING AND WRITING

≡	Make a capital.
/	Make a small letter.
∧	Add something.
ℓ	Take out something.
⊙	Add a period.
¶	New paragraph

PROOFREAD FOR CARELESS ERRORS

Do you see the careless spelling mistake in this sentence?

The reign of King Rykor brought paece to Galaxy 679.

In the word *peace*, the letters **e** and **a** were reversed. When you proofread, watch out for reversed letters.

Check for Reversed Letters Correct the five careless misspellings.

Our voyage to Galaxy 679 had bene uneventful. Now we eagerly awatied our arrival. Our destination sparkled like a rhinestone befoer us. Three crescent moons hung in the nihgt sky. Then, a violent explosion rocked uor spaceship.

PROOFREAD A STORY   Correct eight misspelled words in this part of a story. Three are careless errors with reversed letters.

1. _____

2. _____

3. _____

4. _____

5. _____

> We where forced to flee Galaxy 679 in our badly damaged space vehicle. Pursued by rebel forces, we sought a place to hide. The flouresent ligths in the cabin dimmed as we entered the atmosphere. In moments we wuold land upon its rock-strewn, foreighn landscape. I suddelny became concious of the dryness in my throat and the strong rythum of my heartbeat.

Word List

rhinoceros	shepherd
psychology	rhythm
crescent	reign
vehicle	raspberry
foreign	afghan
pneumonia	cologne
adolescent	rhinestone
rhyme	asthma
heirloom	psychiatrist
fluorescent	conscious

Personal Words

1. _____

2. _____

WRITE A STORY   Write the beginning of a science-fiction story. Try to use two or three list words and a personal word.

rhyme	foreign
rhythm	cologne
crescent	raspberry
adolescent	asthma
conscious	vehicle

Review

CONTEXT CLUES   Use the context to help you write the best word from the box.

1. Put on this ___ to give you an appealing scent.
2. Some countries have a star and a ___ moon on their flags.
3. A sudden ___ of thumps may mean a problem with a car tire.
4. As some people wake up, they become ___ quite slowly!
5. The lunar rover, which allowed astronauts on the moon to travel several miles, was an odd-looking ___.
6. My sister gets ___ after running around in cool night air.
7. They always enjoy traveling to ___ countries.
8. Grape jam is all right, but I *really* enjoy ___ jam.
9. While childhood may be pleasant, the ___ years can be very stressful.
10. Poets have trouble finding words that ___ with "orange."

1. _____
2. _____
3. _____
4. _____
5. _____
6. _____
7. _____
8. _____
9. _____
10. _____

Word *Study*

IDIOMS   "Put your best foot forward." When you hear this advice, you know someone is telling you to do your best, not where to put your feet. An expression whose meaning can't be understood from the ordinary meanings of the words in it is an **idiom.** You'll find idioms in the dictionary listed under the most important word. *Put your best foot forward* is under *foot.*

black out
see red
out of the blue
in the pink
hit the nail on the head
go to one's head
lose one's head
put our heads together

Many idioms use colors. Write the "color" idiom that completes each sentence. Use the Spelling Dictionary.

1. I had pneumonia last week, but now I'm ___.
2. If you practice football in extreme heat, you might ___.
3. The news that we were moving to Alaska came ___.
4. Mr. Wills will be so angry he'll ___ when I tell him about the window I broke.

Many idioms also use words that refer to parts of the body. Write the idiom with *head* that goes with each meaning below.

5. get overly excited
6. plan or plot with others
7. do something just right
8. make one conceited

1. _____
2. _____
3. _____
4. _____
5. _____
6. _____
7. _____
8. _____

Review

Lesson 31: Multisyllabic Words
Lesson 32: Related Words 3
Lesson 33: Latin Roots 3

Lesson 34: Prefixes de-, dis-, non-, un-
Lesson 35: Unusual Spellings

REVIEW WORD LIST

1. communication
2. competitive
3. condominium
4. disagreeable
5. exaggeration
6. ravioli
7. reusable
8. unbelievable
9. uncontrollable
10. unpleasantness
11. untrustworthy
12. collide
13. collision
14. curiosity
15. curious
16. explanation
17. extend
18. generous
19. maintain
20. permission
21. pronunciation
22. repetition
23. immovable
24. intermittent
25. missile
26. motivate
27. motive
28. procedure
29. procession
30. receding
31. disability
32. discourage
33. disrespect
34. nonfiction
35. nonprofit
36. nonstop
37. unbreakable
38. undefeated
39. unfortunately
40. afghan
41. cologne
42. conscious
43. crescent
44. foreign
45. heirloom
46. raspberry
47. rhinestone
48. rhythm
49. shepherd
50. vehicle

■ PROOFREADING

Find the spelling errors in each passage and write the words
correctly. All passages have seven errors except the last one,
which has eight.

1. _____
2. _____
3. _____
4. _____
5. _____
6. _____
7. _____

PROOFREAD AN EXPOSITORY PARAGRAPH

Many science-fiction writers have written stories about
robots, comunication satellites, invasions from outer space
(often by disagreeible aliens), the colision of planets, and
time travel. Today some early science fiction seems like non
fiction. In Twenty Thousand Leagues Under the Sea,
published in 1870, Jules Verne described an underwater
vehickle many years before the development of nuclear-
powered submarines, and many of the almost unbeleivable
descriptions of space travel, reuseable satellites, and robots
by later writers have become fact.

PROOFREAD A JOURNAL ENTRY

Tonight we boarded a non stop flight to the first foriegn country I have ever visited. As I watched the ground receeding, I was concsious of feeling homesick already. From my window seat, I could see a crecsent moon, and I felt as if I were on a missal hurtling through space. The rythm of the engines soon lulled me to sleep, however.

1. _____
2. _____
3. _____
4. _____
5. _____
6. _____
7. _____

PROOFREAD A BOOK REVIEW

Review by Dan O'Brien

In <u>The Secret of the Old Mine</u>, two boys stumble on an abandoned gold mine in Arizona. They almost colide with an old prospector who gives them permissian to explore, but their curiosite leads to trouble. Once inside, they soon find the entrance blocked by imovable timbers. The genirous old prospector has apparently turned out to be

untrusworthy. Suddenly, they begin to hear intermmitent tapping from deep within the mine, and the noise comes closer and closer until.... You will have to read the book to find out what happens.

1. _____
2. _____
3. _____
4. _____
5. _____
6. _____
7. _____

PROOFREAD A MEMO

1. _____
2. _____
3. _____
4. _____
5. _____
6. _____
7. _____

To: Production Staff

From: Miss Kelly

   Below is a list of props and costumes needed for our production of "The Royal Wish." Please see me if you are unable to find the following articles. Do not bring valuable items! All items will be returned to their owners.

unbreakible cup

man's house slippers

empty colone bottle

old afgan

velvet fabric in orange or rassberry color

sandals that a sheperd would wear (size 9)

old picture frame (supposed to look like an hairloom)

costume jewelry, especially rinestone jewelry

PROOFREAD A FRIENDLY LETTER

1. _____
2. _____
3. _____
4. _____
5. _____
6. _____
7. _____

March 30, 19—

Dear Sylvia,

   Have you ever eaten small pasta squares filled with cheese or meat? Then you know how good ravoili is. That is what Aunt Sophie fixed last night for dinner. I'm enclosing her recipe. The proceedure is rather complicated, but I don't want to descourage you. Maybe you will have an uncontrolable urge to cook! I was cureous to know why Aunt Sophie sold her restaurant, and her explanetion was that she seemed to be running a non profit business. Poor Aunt Sophie!

Your cousin,

Myra

PROOFREAD A NOTICE

1. _____
2. _____
3. _____
4. _____
5. _____
6. _____
7. _____

To Whom It May Concern

I regret the unplaesentness which occurred outside the condonimium last evening. Although it is true that my four-year-old nephew was able to set off the fire alarm, it is an exagerration to claim, as some have, that he then said, "I woke up the mummies." His motef was in no way connected with the precession through the building lobby of people in

their night clothes. Allowing for a child's pronounciation, I believe that he said, "I woke up Mommy." I am sure he meant no disrispect.

Apt. 21C

PROOFREAD A SPORTS STORY

1. _____
2. _____
3. _____
4. _____
5. _____
6. _____
7. _____
8. _____

Bees Sting Hornets

The Bees have gained a competetive edge this year despite the repitition of some of last year's faults, and they soundly beat the undifeated Hornets in Friday's game, 57-42. Apparently Coach Walker has been able to motevate the team, although unfortunatley, Chrissie Taylor was sidelined with a minor disibility. Steffi Baker scored twelve points for the Bees, and if she can manetain this strength, the Bees should exstend their winning streak when they play the Seals next week.

Cross-Curricular Lessons

🖐 SOCIAL STUDIES

🍎 HEALTH

💡 SCIENCE

📖 READING

➗ MATHEMATICS

topographic map
thematic map
political map
physical map
contour map
boundaries
cartographers
projection
distortion
elevations

_____

_____

1. _____

2. _____

3. _____

4. _____

5. _____

6. _____

7. _____

8. _____

9. _____

10. _____

Map Skills

How many types of maps do you think there are—five or ten, maybe? Actually, there are hundreds, each type useful in its own way. The list words relate to maps and map making. Add other words about maps to the list. Then do the activity. Use your Spelling Dictionary if you need it.

■ GETTING AT MEANING

Map Captions Mr. Grant's class is putting together a bulletin-board display on maps and map making. Look over the maps. Then use list words to complete the captions for the display.

A map that shows in some way the physical features of the earth's surface is called a **(4).** One kind of map for this purpose is a **(5).** It comes from the Greek words *topos,* meaning "place," and *graphein.* This map uses colors to show the **(6)** of land above sea level.

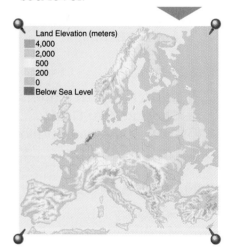

Carta is a Latin word for "chart" or "map." *Graphein* is a Greek word meaning "to write." That explains why map makers are also called **(1).** Map makers create different maps for different purposes. For example, a **(2)** like this one shows the locations of states or countries. It may also show capitals, and other large cities. It also shows the borders, or **(3),** between states or countries.

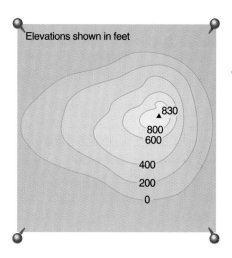

Elevations shown in feet

830
800
600
400
200
0

This **(7)** shows land height by means of lines that connect places with the same elevation. The distances between the contour lines indicate how steeply the land rises or falls.

Some maps show special topics, subjects, or themes, such as population density, yearly rainfall, and natural resources. The general name for this kind of map is **(8)**.

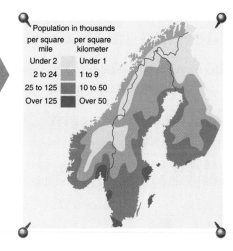

Population in thousands	
per square mile	per square kilometer
Under 2	Under 1
2 to 24	1 to 9
25 to 125	10 to 50
Over 125	Over 50

N
W   E
S

Europe   Asia

Africa

Australia

One way to make a map is to use a transparent globe with a light inside it. The light projects the globe's lines of latitude and longitude onto a sheet of paper, where they can be traced. For this reason, any flat map that shows latitude and longitude lines is called a **(9)**. Because cartographers must "cut" or "stretch" the images from a globe to make a flat map, every map has some error, or **(10)**.

PLAN A TRIP

Obtain a road map of your state. Use the map to plan a car trip to the state capital or to another city that's some distance away. Write up your travel plan, or itinerary, including what roads you'll take, what direction you'll go, how many miles you'll travel, what cities and towns you'll drive through, and what natural features (such as rivers) you'll drive past or over.

ivory
conquistadors
cinnamon
merchants
pepper
spices
Spaniards
circumnavigate
Portuguese
navigators

_____

_____

European Explorations

As early as the 1200s, Europeans were exploring the world for new trade routes, new lands, and new riches. The list words tell of the great age of European exploration, which began in the 1400s. Add other related words to the list, and then do the activities. Use your Spelling Dictionary for help if you need it.

■ GETTING AT MEANING

Who Are They? Read each description carefully. Use the clues to help you write the list word that best fits each one.

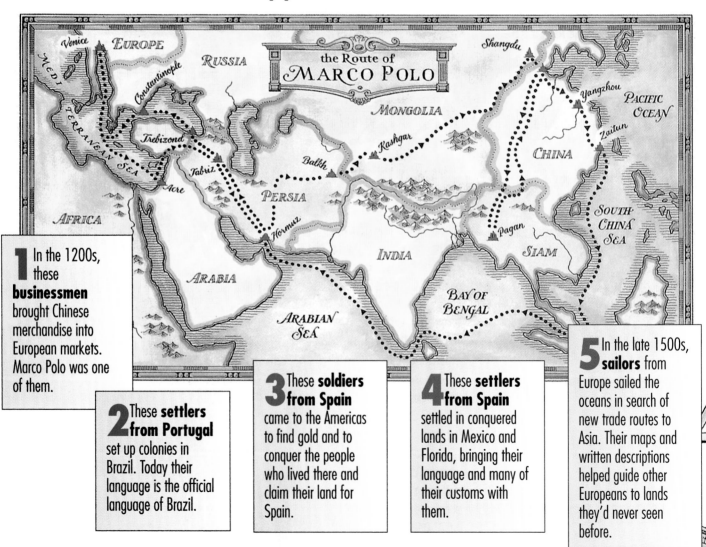

1 In the 1200s, these **businessmen** brought Chinese merchandise into European markets. Marco Polo was one of them.

2 These **settlers from Portugal** set up colonies in Brazil. Today their language is the official language of Brazil.

3 These **soldiers from Spain** came to the Americas to find gold and to conquer the people who lived there and claim their land for Spain.

4 These **settlers from Spain** settled in conquered lands in Mexico and Florida, bringing their language and many of their customs with them.

5 In the late 1500s, **sailors** from Europe sailed the oceans in search of new trade routes to Asia. Their maps and written descriptions helped guide other Europeans to lands they'd never seen before.

What Is It? Read each description carefully. Use the clues to help you write the list word that best fits each one.

6. This word means **"to sail around."** In 1522, Ferdinand Magellan's crew became the first to do this by sailing all the way around the earth.

7. In addition to trade routes, explorers sought various **plant substances** that would strongly flavor and scent food to make it taste better.

8. One of these substances was made from the dried bark of East Indian laurel trees. This **reddish-brown substance** is often used to flavor apples and other cooked fruits.

9. Another of these substances has a hot, spicy taste that comes from the **black berries** of a tropical vine.

10. Another thing some explorers sought was the **hard white substance** that elephants' and walruses' tusks are made of.

1. _____
2. _____
3. _____
4. _____
5. _____

S P I C E   I T   U P !

European food was pretty bland until Asian spices such as cinnamon, nutmeg, clove, ginger, and pepper were introduced. Draw a map containing symbols that show where each spice came from. Which spices have you tasted?

6. _____
7. _____
8. _____
9. _____
10. _____

oasis
Turkish
caravans
Christianity
monotheistic
Judaism
nomadic
Islam
arid
Arabic

_____

_____

1. _____

2. _____

3. _____

4. _____

5. _____

6. _____

7. _____

8. _____

9. _____

10. _____

The Middle East

The list words tell about the Middle East, a large region that covers parts of northeastern Africa, southwestern Asia, and southeastern Europe. If you can, add related words to the list. Then do the activities. Use your Spelling Dictionary if you need help.

■ GETTING AT MEANING

A Travel Journal Use list words to complete the travel journal.

Much of the vast region we call the Middle East is part of the Arab world, where **(1)** is the official language. However, most people in Iran speak Farsi, or Persian. Hebrew is the language of Israel. In Turkey and parts of Cyprus, **(2)** is mostly spoken.

Hot, dry deserts cover much of the Middle East. In desert areas, the land is too **(3)** for raising crops.

A fertile, green **(4)** does occasionally appear, however. Here, date palms and other plants grow in soil moistened by springs.

174

At such a place, **(5)** people traveling in **(6)** with their camels pause for rest and refreshment before moving on.

The Middle East is the birthplace of three of the world's great religions: Christianity, Judaism, and Islam. All three religions are **(7)**, meaning their followers believe in only one God.

THE WORLD'S FIRST CIVILIZATION

In addition to being the birthplace of three great religions, the Middle East is the birthplace of the world's first civilization. The Sumerian civilization developed about 3500 B.C. Research Sumer and find out why historians and archaeologists classify it as a civilization. Present your findings in a series of illustrated panels.

Christians follow **(8),** the religion based on the teachings of Jesus Christ.

Jews follow the religion of **(9),** which is based on the teachings of Moses and the Biblical prophets.

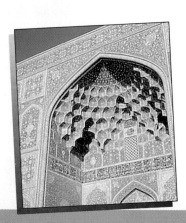

The religion of **(10)** is based on the teachings of Muhammad.

efficient
bronze
extends
ancestors
flourishes
amasses
lucrative
terra cotta
prosperity
usurps

_____

_____

Famous African Kingdoms

Powerful trading kingdoms have been a large part of African history. The list words relate to those kingdoms. If you can, add other words to the list. Then do the activities. Use your Spelling Dictionary if you need help.

■ GETTING AT MEANING

Context Clues Use context clues in the paragraph to complete the caption and the labels with list words.

1. _____

2. _____

3. _____

Artists of the West African kingdom of Benin fashioned splendid sculptures of their rulers. Some sculptors worked in **bronze,** a metal made from copper and tin. Others used **terra cotta,** a hard, waterproof clay. The artists probably were influenced by the neighboring Yoruba people. Today many African Americans count Yoruba artists among their **ancestors.**

These sculptures display the talent and influence of skilled artists, many of whom were **(1)** of today's African Americans.

Head made of the clay known as **(2)**

Head made of the metal known as **(3)**

Synonyms

Write the list word that has the same meaning as each underlined word or phrase.

A.D. 700–1200:
The Ghana Empire **(4)** <u>accumulates</u> wealth due to an **(5)** <u>effective</u> government and a well-trained army that keeps the trade route safe.

A.D. 1200–1500:
The Mali Empire conquers the Ghana Empire and **(6)** <u>expands</u> its borders westward. Tombouctou, Mali's capital, **(7)** <u>develops vigorously</u> and becomes a famous trading and cultural center.

A.D. 1350–1600:
The Songhai Empire gradually **(8)** <u>seizes</u> Mali's territory. By 1400, Songhai is the wealthiest West African kingdom. It controls the most **(9)** <u>profitable</u> Saharan trade routes across the Sahara.

A.D. 700–1800:
To the east, the Kanem Empire develops. Its **(10)** <u>wealth</u> depends on trade in copper, horses, salt, and ivory. The Kanem Empire becomes one of the longest-lasting empires in history.

4. _____

5. _____

6. _____

7. _____

8. _____

9. _____

10. _____

EXPRESS YOURSELF

Africans, like people of other cultures, have long expressed their feelings and beliefs through art. Imagine a work of art that expresses a belief, hope, dream, fear, or any other feeling that is important to you. Write a brief description of this work of art. If you can, go ahead and create it and share it with the class.

Buddhism
Calcutta
caste
Ganges River
Himalayas
Hinduism
New Delhi
reincarnation
sacred
soul

_____

_____

India

The list words tell about the geography and religions of India, a huge and diverse country in South Asia. Add other words about India to the list, and then do the activities. Use your Spelling Dictionary if you need help.

■ GETTING AT MEANING

Map Labels Read the description of India. Then use list words to label the map.

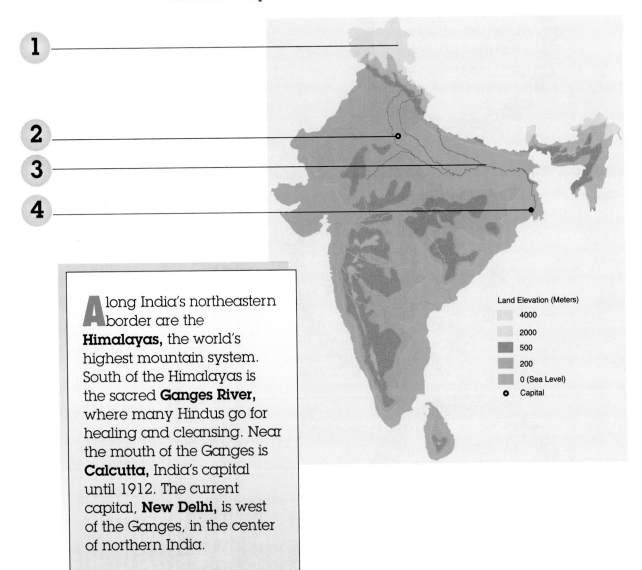

1 _____

2 _____

3 _____

4 _____

Land Elevation (Meters)

4000
2000
500
200
0 (Sea Level)
○ Capital

Along India's northeastern border are the **Himalayas,** the world's highest mountain system. South of the Himalayas is the sacred **Ganges River,** where many Hindus go for healing and cleansing. Near the mouth of the Ganges is **Calcutta,** India's capital until 1912. The current capital, **New Delhi,** is west of the Ganges, in the center of northern India.

Related Words Read about India's religions. Then write the list word that fits with each group of words.

> **Hinduism,** India's major religion, teaches that each person is born into a certain class, or **caste,** which has its own rules for behavior.
>
> Hindus also believe in **reincarnation,** in which the **soul** is reborn in another life form after the body dies. This process is repeated until the soul reaches spiritual perfection.
>
> The religion of **Buddhism** stresses nonviolence and compassion. These **sacred** ideals were handed down by Buddha, the "Enlightened One," about 2,500 years ago.
>
> 5. spirit, essence, everlasting _____
>
> 6. class, system, status _____
>
> 7. rebirth, immortal, renewal _____
>
> 8. nonviolence, compassion _____
>
> 9. reincarnation, caste system _____
>
> 10. holy, honored, revered _____

TANDOORI MURG, ANYONE?

India is known for its wide variety of tasty and often colorful foods. *Tandoori Murg,* for instance, is chicken marinated in a spicy yogurt sauce and roasted over coals. The spice mixture turns the meat a fiery red. Learn about other Indian foods, such as *naan, papadams, rayta, cachumbar,* and *uppuma.* Has anyone in your class done any Indian cooking? Perhaps he or she could bring in a sample for everyone to taste.

umbrellas
wheelbarrow
paper
suspension bridges
mechanical clock
magnetic compass
decimal system
gunpowder
fireworks
porcelain

_____

_____

Ancient Chinese Inventions

The list words name ancient Chinese inventions that have influenced life around the world for thousands of years. Add other words about ancient China to the list. Then do the activities. Use your Spelling Dictionary if you need it.

■ GETTING AT MEANING

What Is It? Write the list word that each fact describes.

1 In the 1500s, European explorers used this to find their way to distant lands. It was invented in China four hundred years earlier.

2 The first ones were made from silk or oiled paper to protect people from sun and rain.

3 Today, as in ancient times, fine bowls and vases are made from this.

4 This invention was—and is—used for hauling supplies. In ancient China it was known as "wooden ox and gliding horse."

5 This was developed primarily from saltpeter, sulfur, and carbon. It led to the development of the cannon.

6 The Chinese developed this computation system 2,300 years before it finally was adopted in the West.

7 The first one consisted of a giant wheel turned by water that flowed into scoops. The wheel automatically rotated once every twenty-four hours.

8 The Chinese first made this from tree bark. Later, they found it was easier to write on when it was made from a pulp mixture of pounded rags, rope, and old fish nets.

9 These roadways, held up by cables, span valleys and rivers in countries all over the world.

10 The ancient Chinese first made these by throwing pieces of bamboo into fire and watching them explode.

1. _____

2. _____

3. _____

4. _____

5. _____

6. _____

7. _____

8. _____

9. _____

10. _____

DID YOU KNOW?

The ancient Chinese recorded some of the earliest accurate astronomical observations in the world. One such recording was of the first exploding star, or supernova, in A.D. June 1054. The Chinese reported that the reddish-white flares of the star could be seen for twenty-three days and nights. The remains of that explosion can still be seen today and are called the Crab Nebula.

Word Association Write the list word that each group of words suggests to you.

11. cherry bombs, Roman candles, sparklers
12. ones, tens, hundreds, thousands
13. north, south, east, west
14. cups, saucers, plates, figurines
15. hourglass, sundial, chronometer

11. _____

12. _____

13. _____

14. _____

15. _____

Hokkaido
isolated
samurai
Honshu
calligraphy
scrolls
Sapporo
tea ceremony
kimonos
Tokyo

_____

_____

Japan

Japan is a nation of contrasts: a modern industrial giant that maintains a strong respect for tradition. The list words tell about Japan. If you can, add other words to the list. Then do the activities. Use your Spelling Dictionary if you need it.

■ GETTING AT MEANING

A Letter from Japan Complete the letter with list words. Use the map for help.

1. _____

2. _____

3. _____

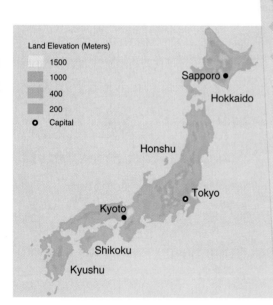

Land Elevation (Meters)
1500
1000
400
200
○ Capital

Sapporo ●
Hokkaido
Honshu
Tokyo
Kyoto ●
Shikoku
Kyushu

July 12, 19__

Dear Grandma and Grandpa,

Greetings from Japan! Mom has been pretty busy with meetings, but Dad and I are seeing the sights and learning about the country.

Our plane flew into **(1)**, the capital, which is the fourth largest city in the world. Did you know that almost 8,500,000 people live there? I didn't. I also didn't know that Japan is made up of four large islands and thousands of smaller islands! The largest of the four main islands is **(2)**, which is where Tokyo is. The second largest island is **(3)**. We're planning a short trip there to see the city of **(4)**, which is famous for its botanical gardens.

I'm learning something about Japan's history too. In the past, being surrounded by water helped keep the Japanese separated from other people and places. To add to that, the government cut off all contact with other countries in the 1630s. Japan was completely **(5)** from the rest of the world for almost 225 years!

Dad says I have to stop now. We're going to the mountains today. I'll write again soon.

Love,

Jason

4. _____

5. _____

Items of Japanese Culture Read the following passages about Japanese traditions. Then label each picture with the correct list word.

(6) _____ were Japanese warriors who were also

accomplished in Japanese arts. A samurai might produce

elegant **(7)**  , or decorative handwriting.

He might also paint historical tales or legends on

long paper **(8)** . Many samurai also knew how

to conduct a perfect **(9)** 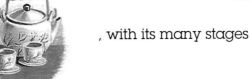 , with its many stages

and utensils.

Today, the arts practiced by the samurai honor Japanese

traditions. They are as much symbols of Japan as are the

beautiful **(10)**  worn by both men and women

for holidays and special ceremonies.

6. _____

7. _____

8. _____

9. _____

10. _____

183

kangaroos
Tasmania
koalas
Great Barrier Reef
marsupials
dingo
boomerangs
eucalyptus
Canberra
kookaburra

_____

_____

1. _____

2. _____

3. _____

4. _____

5. _____

6. _____

7. _____

8. _____

9. _____

10. _____

Australia

The list words tell about Australia, the only populated continent that lies completely "down under," or south of the Equator. Add other words that you know about Australia, and then do the activity. Use your Spelling Dictionary for help if you need it.

▋ GETTING AT MEANING

Picture Clues Use the map, pictures, and captions to help you fill in the blanks with list words.

1. The largest inland city in Australia, _____, is also the country's capital.
2. Off the southeastern coast of Australia lies the island of _____, home of the animal called the Tasmanian devil.
3. Spanning over 1,250 miles, the _____ is the largest coral reef in the world and one of Australia's most popular tourist attractions.

Kangaroos, like koalas and other marsupials, give birth to tiny babies who then develop inside the mother's pouch. Adult kangaroos use their powerful hind legs to hop high and fast.

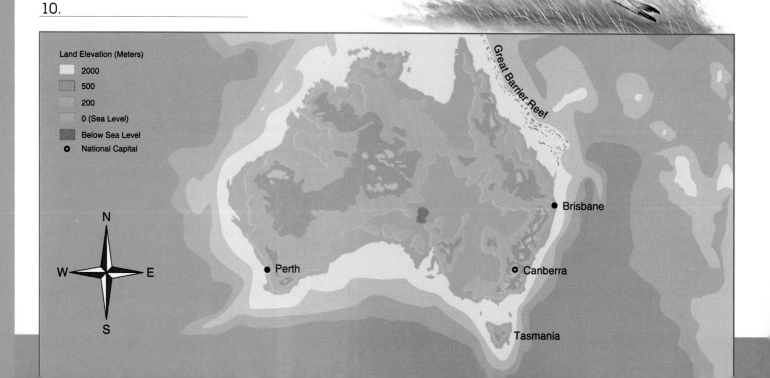

Land Elevation (Meters)

2000
500
200
0 (Sea Level)
Below Sea Level
⊙ National Capital

Great Barrier Reef

N
W — E
S

• Perth

• Brisbane

⊙ Canberra

Tasmania

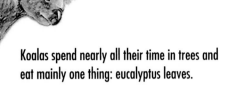

Koalas spend nearly all their time in trees and eat mainly one thing: eucalyptus leaves.

4. The Australians have a popular song about the _____, a bird with a harsh, cackling voice.

5. Australian _____ sleep in trees during the day and come down only to move to other trees.

6. Koalas get most of their nourishment—both liquids and solids—from the leaves and young shoots of _____ trees.

7. Large _____ can hop up to forty miles per hour and can leap over obstacles six feet high.

8. Kangaroos, koalas, and most of the world's other pouch-bearing _____ live in Australia or on nearby islands.

9. If a wild _____ is caught as a puppy, it can be trained to be a good pet.

10. Although they were originally used as weapons in Australia, _____ are now thrown mostly for sport.

The large bird known as the kookaburra and the dog known as the dingo are just two of the animals that are found in the Australian wild.

DISCOVER AUSTRALIA'S UNIQUE ANIMALS

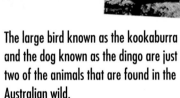

Kangaroos, koalas, kookaburras, and dingoes are only four of Australia's unique animals. Others include bandicoots, emus, platypuses, wombats, and Tasmanian devils.

Choose one animal to learn more about. Share your discoveries through an illustration or photograph and a list of the animal's characteristics.

The Aborigines—the first people to live in Australia—traditionally have used boomerangs for hunting and other tasks.

diversity
monsoons
volcanic
agrarian
festivals
animism
urbanized
batik
metropolis
silt deposits

_____

_____

Southeast Asia

The list words tell about the geography and ways of life of the mainland and island countries that form Southeast Asia. If you can, add related words to the list. Then do the activities. Use your Spelling Dictionary if you need help.

■ GETTING AT MEANING

Passage Completion Complete the following passages with words from the list.

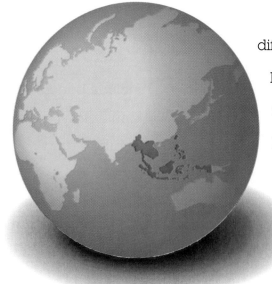

The ten countries of Southeast Asia are known for the differences in their geography, languages, and customs. Despite this **(1),** however, most of the region's people live in rural areas and share an agricultural, or **(2)** lifestyle, raising rice on small plots of land.

Each of the countries has at least one major metropolitan area, or **(3).** However, Singapore is so highly **(4)** that everyone lives in cities!

Depending upon where they live, Southeast Asians hold

different celebrations, or **(5).** Country dwellers celebrate holidays corresponding to the farming seasons, while city folk celebrate a variety of religious and ethnic holidays.

1. _____

2. _____

3. _____

4. _____

5. _____

Cause and Effect Use the following facts to complete the chart with list words.

FACT: Many of Southeast Asia's rural people offer small sacrifices and carry out other practices based on **animism,** the belief that all natural objects have a spirit, or soul.

FACT: **Monsoons,** seasonal winds that bring much rain, often cause flooding and damage. However, they also help farmers grow rice, which needs a great deal of water.

FACT: In the island countries of Southeast Asia, **volcanic** ash from erupting volcanoes makes the soil very fertile.

IT'S NICE— IT'S RICE

More than half the world's people rely on rice as their major food. Look through cookbooks for rice-dish recipes. Try to find at least one recipe that comes from Asia. With a group of classmates, hold a "rice cook-off," in which each of you brings a different rice dish for tasting, and the group votes for its favorite.

CAUSE	EFFECT
river systems carrying **(6)**	fertile soil on mainland
(7) ash from active volcanoes	fertile soil on islands
(8) believed in by rural people	offering of sacrifices to keep away natural disaster
(9) with high winds and rain	flooding, damage, moisture for rice crop
(10) method used on cloth	colored designs

FACT: Three great rivers— the Mekong, the Irrawaddy, and the Red— drain the mainland countries of Southeast Asia. They also carry **silt deposits** that enrich the soil.

FACT: The Southeast Asian country of Indonesia is world famous for

batik, a method of forming colored designs on cloth using dye and wax.

6. _____

7. _____

8. _____

9. _____

10. _____

calories
anorexia nervosa
bulimia
pellagra
niacin
amino acids
acne
fatigue
proteins
leukemia

_____

_____

Nutritional Needs

How vital is nutrition to good health? The activity below will help you answer this question. Think of two other words about nutrition or health and add them to the list. Then do the activity. Use your Spelling Dictionary if you need help.

■ GETTING AT MEANING

Word Histories Use the italicized words to help you complete the paragraphs with list words.

The Latin word *calor* means "heat." We all need to obtain

(1) from our food in order to provide our bodies with heat, or

energy.

The Latin word *pellis* means "skin." A disease in which the skin

becomes inflamed due to a lack of B complex vitamins is called

(2). It can be cured by taking **(3),** whose name comes from the

term *nicotinic acid.*

The need to eat constantly is called **(4),** from the Greek *bous*

and *limos,* meaning "ox hunger." The need to keep losing weight

no matter how thin you get

is called **(5),** from the

Latin *an* and *orexis,*

meaning "without a

desire for something."

1. _____
2. _____
3. _____
4. _____
5. _____
6. _____
7. _____
8. _____
9. _____
10. _____

The Greek word *protos* means "first." The all-important compounds our bodies need to function well are called **(6).** They are made from chemicals called **(7).** This term comes from the Latin *amine.*

The Greek *aknē* means the same as the English **(8):** "eruption" or "point."

From the Latin *fatigare,* "to tire," comes the English **(9).** Occasionally people are tired because their bodies produce too many white blood cells. They have a disease called **(10),** from the Greek *leukos* and *haima,* meaning "white blood."

DID YOU KNOW?

British sailors are often called "limeys" because they used to drink lime juice to prevent scurvy, a disease caused by a lack of vitamin C.

consumer
dermatologist
sunscreen
evaluate
protection
deodorant
floss
conditioner
fluoride
persuade

_____

_____

Personal Health Concerns

Everywhere we turn, we see products meant to improve our health and appearance. Not all those products live up to their claims, however. Add two more health-related words to the list. Then do the activities. Use the Spelling Dictionary if you need help.

■ GETTING AT MEANING

An Editorial Use list words to complete the editorial.

THE HEALTH TIMES

BE A WISE HEALTH CONSUMER

When it comes to health, it's important to shop wisely. You, the consumer, must **(1)** health-care ads carefully, judging their claims. Separate useful information from words that are only meant to **(2)** you to buy. For example, it's helpful to know if a product offers real **(3)** from the sun's rays; but be wary of ads that promise beauty or popularity.

1. _____
2. _____
3. _____
4. _____
5. _____
6. _____
7. _____
8. _____
9. _____
10. _____

Would You Buy It? Complete each ad with a list word. As you do, evaluate it. Think about what useful information it gives you versus words meant only to flatter and persuade. Write a plus (+) next to your answers for ads that you think give useful information and a minus (–) next to the ones that don't.

As a smart **(4)**, you want to buy only the best products. For effective protection from odor, use **NO SWEAT**, the best **(5)** money can buy.

Dr. Scott, the **(6)**, wants you to take care of your skin. She recommends **BLOCKOUT**, the **(7)** that protects your skin from the sun's harmful rays.

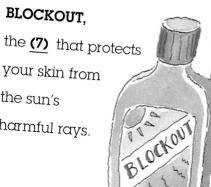

Of course you want to have the softest, silkiest hair possible! Use **SILKY (8)** and people will notice.

Your teeth are already clean and strong because you use **CAVITY-AWAY (9)** toothpaste. Now clean between your teeth with **EASY-PULL (10)**.

AND NOW, A WORD FROM OUR SPONSOR

Make up a health-care or grooming product that you would like to have—something that would do everything it was supposed to do. Then design an ad for your product.

splint
heatstroke
lifeguard
lightning
shock
life jacket
sprain
frostbite
hypothermia
fracture

_____

_____

Preventing Emergencies

The best way to prevent emergencies is to be prepared. What are some things you can do? Add two more words to the list, and then do the activities. Use your Spelling Dictionary if you need help.

■ GETTING AT MEANING

Safety First Complete these public safety announcements with list words.

Water Safety Tips Sun . . . sand . . . water! There's nothing like a day at the beach! The following tips should make your day *safe* as well as fun.

1. For your protection, always choose a beach with a _____ on duty.

2. If it starts to thunder and _____, get out of the water immediately.

3. If you decide to go for a boat ride, always wear a _____ for extra protection.

4. Know when it's time to go home! Too much heat, sun, or humidity can cause _____.

1. _____
2. _____
3. _____
4. _____
5. _____
6. _____
7. _____
8. _____
9. _____
10. _____

Safe Skiing Here are some snow-ski safety tips. First, dress warmly to ward off the icy bite of cold and wind, which can give your skin damaging **(5)**. If you get too cold, seek shelter. Exposure to cold and damp can cause **(6)**, a lowering ("hypo-") of the heat ("therm") of your body.

If someone stretches or tears tissues in an ankle but does not break it, wrap the **(7)** firmly with an elastic bandage. If someone cracks or breaks a bone, have a paramedic set the **(8)** in a sturdy **(9)**. If the injury is serious, try to keep the victim from going into **(10)** by keeping him or her warm and dry until help arrives.

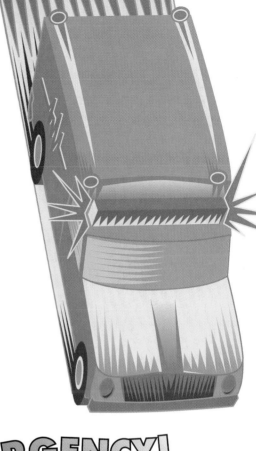

EMERGENCY! EMERGENCY!

Interview a paramedic, emergency-room worker, or school nurse about what to do during different kinds of emergencies. Arrange your notes into a booklet that you can display in your class or school library.

particulates
pollution
acid rain
scrubber
ground water
decibel
carbon monoxide
smog
fuel
hazardous waste

_____

_____

Your Environment

Many factors cause environmental pollution, and many solutions are needed to reduce it. Add two words of your own to the list. Then do the activity. Use your Spelling Dictionary if you need help.

■ GETTING AT MEANING

It's a Puzzlement! Read the clues on page 195. Use them to complete the puzzle with list words.

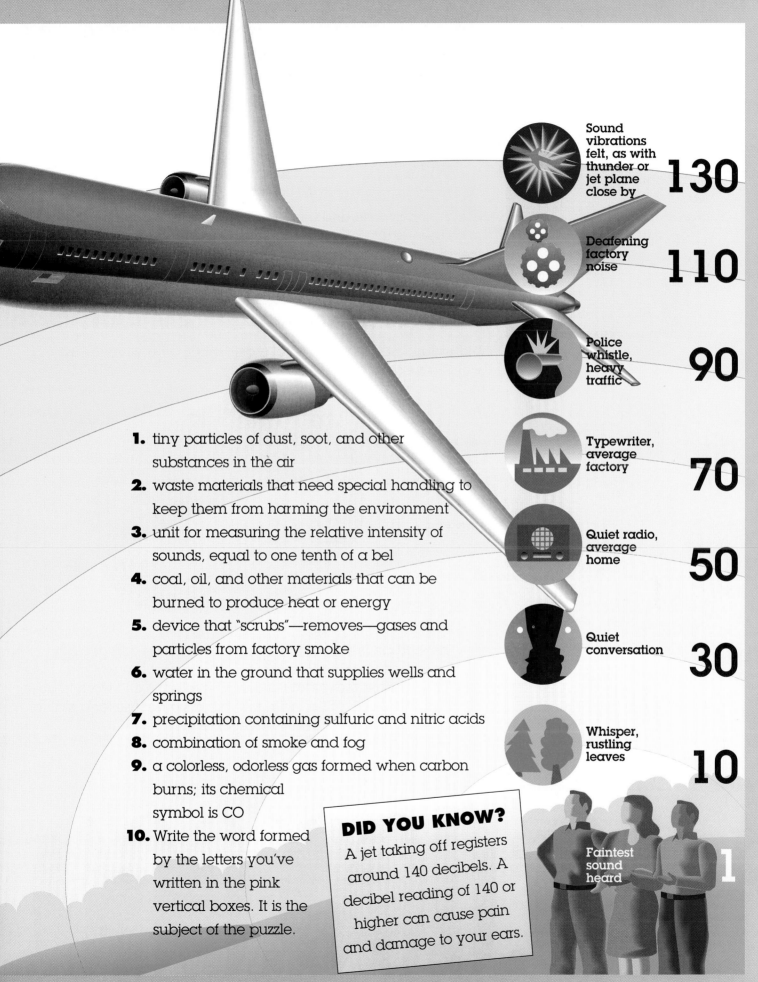

1. tiny particles of dust, soot, and other substances in the air
2. waste materials that need special handling to keep them from harming the environment
3. unit for measuring the relative intensity of sounds, equal to one tenth of a bel
4. coal, oil, and other materials that can be burned to produce heat or energy
5. device that "scrubs"—removes—gases and particles from factory smoke
6. water in the ground that supplies wells and springs
7. precipitation containing sulfuric and nitric acids
8. combination of smoke and fog
9. a colorless, odorless gas formed when carbon burns; its chemical symbol is CO
10. Write the word formed by the letters you've written in the pink vertical boxes. It is the subject of the puzzle.

130 — Sound vibrations felt, as with thunder or jet plane close by

110 — Deafening factory noise

90 — Police whistle, heavy traffic

70 — Typewriter, average factory

50 — Quiet radio, average home

30 — Quiet conversation

10 — Whisper, rustling leaves

1 — Faintest sound heard

DID YOU KNOW?

A jet taking off registers around 140 decibels. A decibel reading of 140 or higher can cause pain and damage to your ears.

biology
tissue
skin
cell
nucleus
cell membrane
permeable
receptor
organ
cytoplasm

_____

_____

The Cell

Everything you do and think is done by cells—structures too small to be seen without a microscope. Add more words about cells to the list. Then do the activities. Use the Spelling Dictionary if you need help.

■ GETTING AT MEANING

Diagrams Use this diagram of a cell to help you write the list word that each sentence describes.

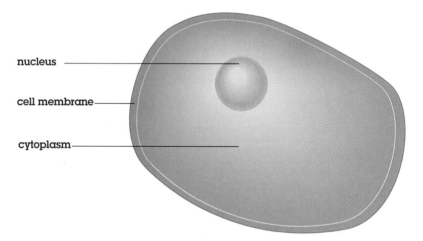

nucleus

cell membrane

cytoplasm

1. _____

2. _____

3. _____

1. This surrounds the outside of the cell. Nothing can get in or out without passing through it.
2. This is right in the middle of things. It tells the cell what to do.
3. Most of the cell is filled with this. It is a storehouse for building materials. Shake it, and it shivers like jelly.

10,000,000,

Name That Word Write the list word that each item describes. Use the boldfaced words to help you.

4. This covers a grape. It also covers your body.
5. This is an adjective that describes a membrane full of small holes that can be easily **penetrated.**
6. This is a small room where prisoners are kept. It is also the basic structure of living things.
7. This is a type of cell that's especially **receptive** to stimuli.
8. You can use this to wrap presents. It is also a mass of cells that performs a specific function.
9. This is a group of living tissues **organized** to perform some specific function.
10. **Psychology** is the study of the mind, but this is the study of life and living things.

4. _____

5. _____

6. _____

7. _____

8. _____

9. _____

10. _____

ACROSTIC

An acrostic is an arrangement of words in which one letter of each line helps to spell a word. Write an acrostic for one of the list words. See the example for *skin* below.

Smooth and rough

Blac**K**, pink, yellow, brown

Wr**I**nkles and lines

Contai**N**s your blood and bones

Did You Know?

The adult human body is made up of some 10 *trillion* cells!

genetic
heredity
environment
dominant
recessive
genes
mitosis
meiosis
DNA
traits

_____

_____

Genetics

Genetics explains why family members often have similar characteristics. The list words all relate to genetics. Can you add two more words to the list? Use your Spelling Dictionary as you do the activities.

■ GETTING AT MEANING

Drawing Conclusions Read the paragraphs below. Then use list words to answer the questions.

Your opinions and interests are influenced by the world you live in—your **environment.** But features such as the color of your hair and eyes are a result of **heredity**—the passing of characteristics from your parents to you.

The key to heredity is **DNA,** a kind of blueprint for what's been transmitted to you through heredity. When most cells divide—**mitosis**—each of the two new cells has the same DNA as the original cell. But when cells divide to produce sperm or eggs—**meiosis**—each new cell contains only half of the DNA of the original cell. Later, when sperm and egg join, the offspring gets a full set of DNA, half from each parent.

1. What chemical in your cells carries the master plan for your body?
2. Are the physical differences and similarities between a parent and a child the result of mitosis or meiosis?
3. As you grow, your body cells multiply. Almost all those cells contain the same set of DNA. Is this a result of mitosis or meiosis?
4. What has the most influence on the kind of music you like—environment or heredity?
5. Is the shape of your nose most influenced by your environment or heredity?

1. _____

2. _____

3. _____

4. _____

5. _____

Using Diagrams Use the paragraph and the diagrams to answer the questions with list words.

DNA contains **genes** that determine physical and mental **traits.** For any one **genetic** trait—for example, hair color—you receive at least one gene from your mother and one from your father. If the genes are different, the **dominant** genes determine your hair color, but the **recessive** genes are still present in your DNA, and you can pass them on to your own child. This simplified diagram shows the possible gene combinations for hair color that two dark-haired parents can pass on to their children.

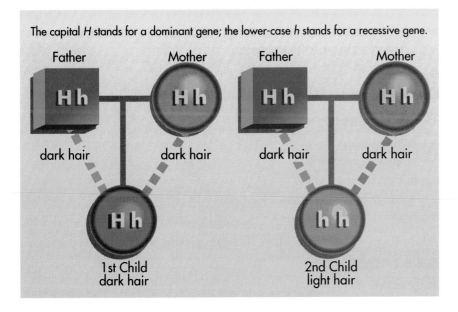

The capital *H* stands for a dominant gene; the lower-case *h* stands for a recessive gene.

Father	Mother	Father	Mother
H h	**H h**	**H h**	**H h**
dark hair	dark hair	dark hair	dark hair

H h
1st Child
dark hair

h h
2nd Child
light hair

6. Height, skin color, and the shape of your eyes are all examples of physical _____.
7. You can tell from the diagrams that the two _____ the second child inherited were both for blonde hair.
8. From the diagrams, you can infer that the gene for brown hair is _____.
9. From the diagrams, you can infer that the gene for blonde hair is _____.
10. A disease caused by a gene inherited from one or both parents is called a _____ disease.

JUST LOOK AT YOU NOW

Bring in a picture of yourself when you were little. Put it on a bulletin board display with pictures of the rest of the class. Write down who you think is in each picture. Which physical traits does each person have now that were or were not evident then?

6. _____

7. _____

8. _____

9. _____

10. _____

classification
kingdom
phylum
class
order
family
genus
species
scientific name
common name

_____

_____

Taxonomy

Scientists classify living things into groups and subgroups, beginning with kingdoms and ending with species. This system of classification is called **taxonomy.** If you can, add two words to the list. Then do the activities. Use the Spelling Dictionary if you need help.

■ GETTING AT MEANING

Crossword Puzzle Use the taxonomy table for leopards to help you fill in the puzzle with list words.

TAXONOMY TABLE: Classification of Leopards

COMMON NAME: leopard **SCIENTIFIC NAME:** *Panthera pardus*

GROUPS AND SUBGROUPS

KINGDOM (ANIMAL)

FACT: Scientists classify living organisms into five groups or kingdoms. The leopard belongs to the animal kingdom.

PHYLUM (CHORDATE)

FACT: The animal kingdom is divided into several phyla (plural). The leopard's phylum (singular) is called chordate.

CLASS (MAMMAL)

FACT: Chordates are divided into classes. The leopard belongs to the mammal class.

ORDER (CARNIVORE)

FACT: Some mammals are carnivores—meat-eaters. The leopard belongs to this order.

FAMILY (FELIDAE)

FACT: Each order is divided into families. The leopard's family, *Felidae,* contains catlike animals.

GENUS (PANTHERA)

FACT: Each family is further divided into genera (plural). The leopard's genus (singular) is *Panthera.* Lions and tigers belong to this same genus.

SPECIES (PANTHERA PARDUS)

FACT: Each genus is divided into several species. The leopard is the species *Panthera pardus.* Lions and tigers are different species.

DISCOVERING YOURSELF

Suppose you were a just-discovered organism. Write or draw a description of yourself. Give yourself a Latin genus and species name. (Consult an encyclopedia or your life-science book for help.)

Across

1 the process of putting living organisms into groups and subgroups
4 the subgroup into which classes are divided
5 leopards and lions are not the same one
8 *Panthera* is an example of this subgroup
9 the kind of name that people commonly give to plants and animals

Down

1 mammal is an example of this subgroup
2 the kind of name that life scientists give to living things
3 *Felidae* is an example of this subgroup
6 one of the five largest groups into which organisms are classified
7 the leopard's is known as chordate

virus
bacteria
host
pathogens
toxin
vaccine
antibiotic
immune system
antibodies
decomposition

_____

_____

Viruses and Bacteria

1. Invasion by a Flu Virus

Flu **virus** enters nose and mouth.

You don't get the flu.

Virus invades **host** cell and begins to reproduce.

Your **immune system** produces **antibodies** that arm your body against the virus.

Tiny organisms can cause big health problems. If you've ever had a cold or the mumps, you've been invaded by a virus. If you've ever had an infection, you've been invaded by viruses or bacteria. Add two more words to the list. Then use the art and your Spelling Dictionary to do the activities.

2. Vaccination Against the Flu

You receive a **vaccine** made of weak or dead viruses.

You get the flu.

■ GETTING AT MEANING

Context Clues Use the art and the list words in it to help you complete the sentences.

1. _____

2. _____

3. _____

1. Wendy had been skipping meals and not sleeping much. She felt tired and run-down. Her _____, or natural defense against disease, was weak.
2. Wendy went to a doctor to be inoculated with a _____ against a kind of flu common that winter.
3. Unfortunately, later that winter she was exposed to a different kind of flu _____.

4. Since her immune system had not developed ___ to this virus, it was able to multiply.

5. The cells lining her throat were a perfect ___ for the invading virus, and she was sick for a week.

4. _____

5. _____

Defining Words Use the chart to help you write a list word for each definition.

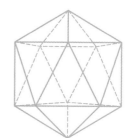

ACTIONS OF BACTERIA	
HELPFUL	**HARMFUL**
Bacteria cause **decomposition** of dead plants and animals.	Bacteria grow on food and produce a **toxin** that causes food poisoning.
Bacteria cause the sharp taste of yogurt and cheeses.	Some bacteria are **pathogens,** which cause diseases. An **antibiotic** such as penicillin can kill such bacteria and cure the diseases.

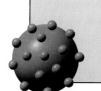

6. microscopic one-celled organisms that can be helpful or harmful
7. chemical that cures illnesses by preventing the growth of bacteria
8. a poison
9. process of breaking down organic materials
10. agents that produce diseases

6. _____   9. _____

7. _____   10. _____

8. _____

A VIRUS MODEL

What does a virus look like? You can make a simple model of one type of virus. Trace one of the triangles on this page. Then cut twenty of them from lightweight cardboard. Tape the triangles together in the pattern shown. Fold and tape the pattern along each edge to form a solid figure with twenty sides. Poke a toothpick into each of the twelve vertices (where five triangles meet). Glue cotton to the tip of each toothpick. Then imagine it hundreds of thousands of times smaller!

skeleton
bone
joints
fixed joint
gliding joint
hinge joint
pivot joint
ball-and-socket joint
cartilage
ligaments

_____

_____

The Skeletal System

Did you know that there are 206 bones in your body? Do you know any of their names? Add them to the list. Then do the activities. Use your Spelling Dictionary if you need help.

■ GETTING AT MEANING

Picture Clues Look at the pictures and use the clues to write the correct list words.

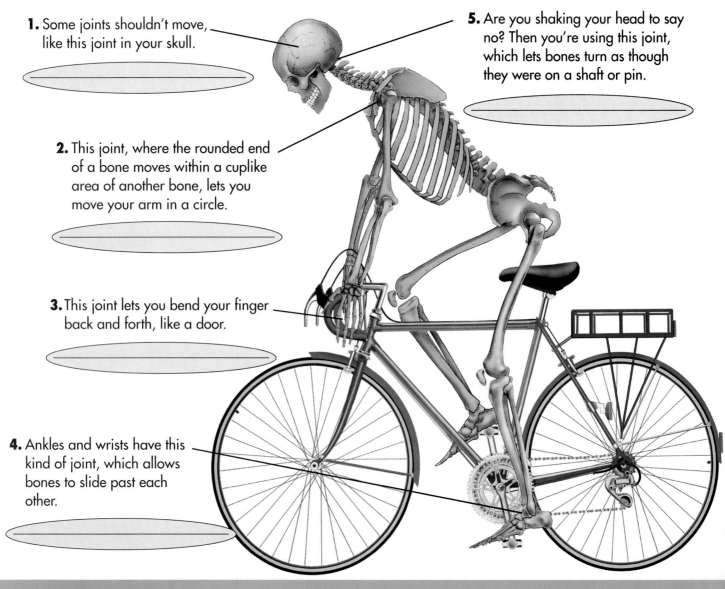

1. Some joints shouldn't move, like this joint in your skull.

2. This joint, where the rounded end of a bone moves within a cuplike area of another bone, lets you move your arm in a circle.

3. This joint lets you bend your finger back and forth, like a door.

4. Ankles and wrists have this kind of joint, which allows bones to slide past each other.

5. Are you shaking your head to say no? Then you're using this joint, which lets bones turn as though they were on a shaft or pin.

Paragraph Completion Complete the doctor's lecture with words from the list. Use the pictures and labels to help you.

Today's lecture will begin our study of the human **(6),** without which we would all be floppy piles of flesh. Think about it— without the femur, a **(7)** in your leg, you wouldn't be able to stand up! And because you have **(8)** where two bones meet, or join, you can throw a ball, bend to pick up a book, and grab a fork so you can eat! And what holds those bones together? Tough bands of tissue called **(9)** do. Also, your body has **(10)** at the ends of bones to keep them from rubbing together and grinding away.

6. _____

7. _____

8. _____

9. _____

10. _____

LABEL ART

Many of the movements performed by the joints in your body are duplicated in things all around you. Write which joint in the human body is duplicated by the common items pictured below.

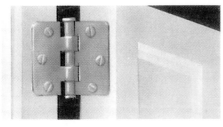

a. _____

b. _____

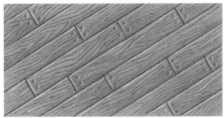

c. _____

digestion
salivary glands
esophagus
stomach
gastric glands
liver
bile
gall bladder
pancreas
intestines

_____

_____

Digestion

Have you ever wished your stomach wouldn't rumble? Do you ever hiccup at the wrong time? That's not surprising. You do not have voluntary control over your digestive system. Without it, though, the food you eat would be of no value to your body. Add other words to the list that describe digestion. Then do the activity. Use your Spelling Dictionary if you need help.

■ GETTING AT MEANING

The Digestion Game Study the diagram of the human digestive system. Then use it to help you match the definitions with words from the list.

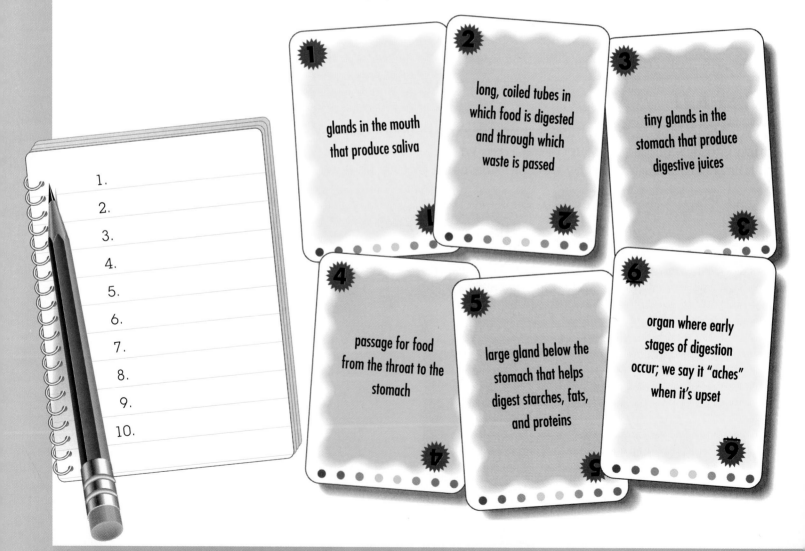

1.
2.
3.
4.
5.
6.
7.
8.
9.
10.

1 glands in the mouth that produce saliva

2 long, coiled tubes in which food is digested and through which waste is passed

3 tiny glands in the stomach that produce digestive juices

4 passage for food from the throat to the stomach

5 large gland below the stomach that helps digest starches, fats, and proteins

6 organ where early stages of digestion occur; we say it "aches" when it's upset

The Human Digestive System

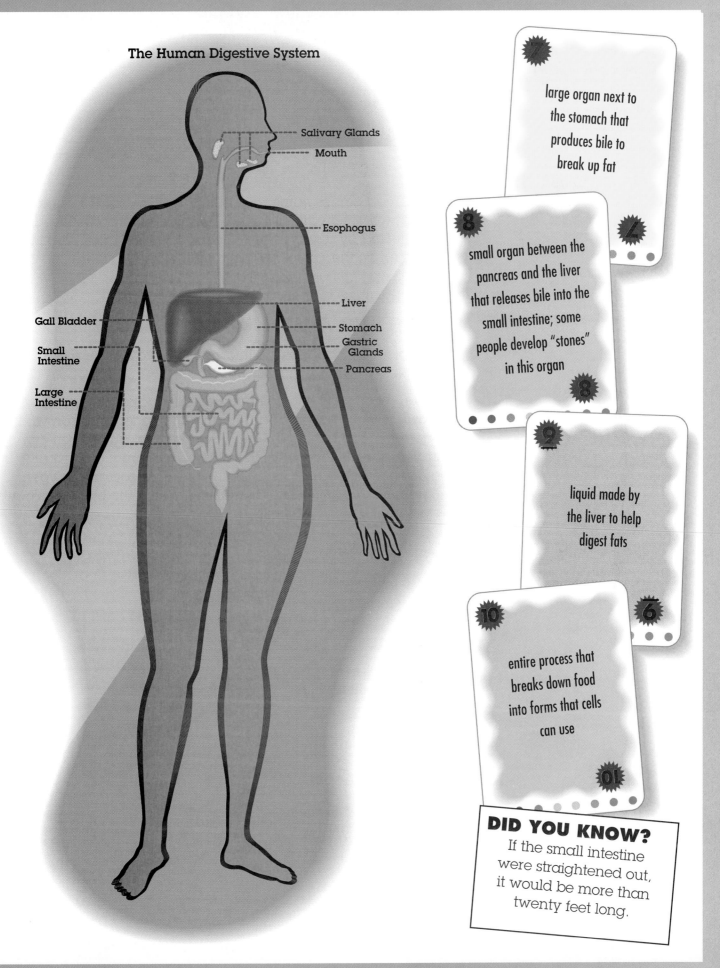

Salivary Glands
Mouth
Esophogus
Liver
Gall Bladder
Stomach
Gastric Glands
Small Intestine
Pancreas
Large Intestine

7 large organ next to the stomach that produces bile to break up fat

8 small organ between the pancreas and the liver that releases bile into the small intestine; some people develop "stones" in this organ

9 liquid made by the liver to help digest fats

10 entire process that breaks down food into forms that cells can use

DID YOU KNOW?
If the small intestine were straightened out, it would be more than twenty feet long.

plasma
hemoglobin
platelets
fibrin
hemophilia
leukemia
anemia
sickle cell anemia
red blood cells
white blood cells

_____

_____

1. _____

2. _____

3. _____

4. _____

5. _____

6. _____

7. _____

8. _____

9. _____

10. _____

Blood

Your blood carries nutrients and oxygen to your cells, and it carries wastes away. Like other tissues in your body, blood can be affected by disease. Add two more words about blood to the list. Then do the activities. Use your Spelling Dictionary if you need help.

■ GETTING AT MEANING

Complete a Chart Use the information below to help you complete the chart with list words.

When a person has **leukemia,** the body makes abnormal **white blood cells** that cannot fight harmful bacteria. A person with **anemia** may not have enough **hemoglobin,** an oxygen-carrying protein in **red blood cells.** In **sickle cell anemia,** abnormally shaped red blood cells reduce the flow of blood and oxygen. **Hemophilia** is an inherited disease in which the blood has trouble clotting.

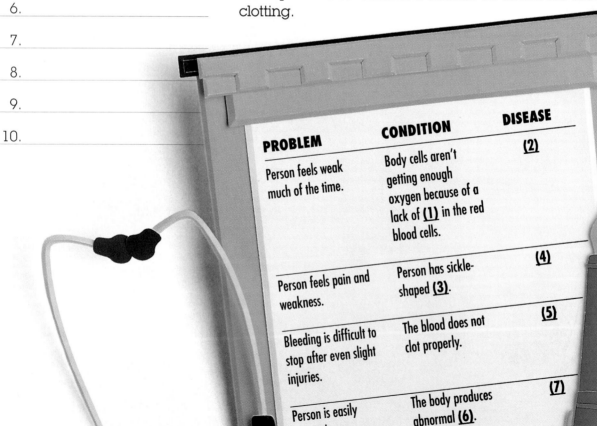

PROBLEM	CONDITION	DISEASE
Person feels weak much of the time.	Body cells aren't getting enough oxygen because of a lack of **(1)** in the red blood cells.	**(2)**
Person feels pain and weakness.	Person has sickle-shaped **(3)**.	**(4)**
Bleeding is difficult to stop after even slight injuries.	The blood does not clot properly.	**(5)**
Person is easily infected.	The body produces abnormal **(6)**.	**(7)**

The Process of Blood Clotting Use the diagram to help you complete the description with list words.

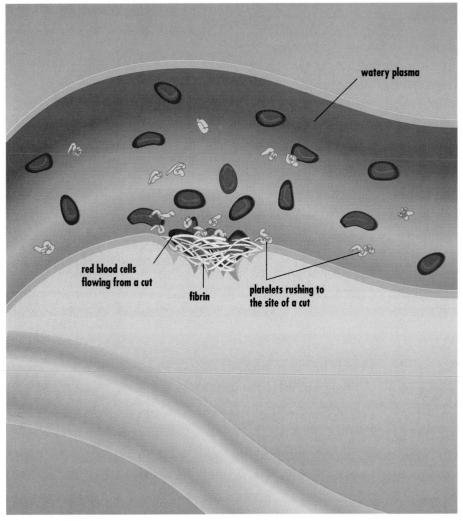

watery plasma

red blood cells flowing from a cut

fibrin

platelets rushing to the site of a cut

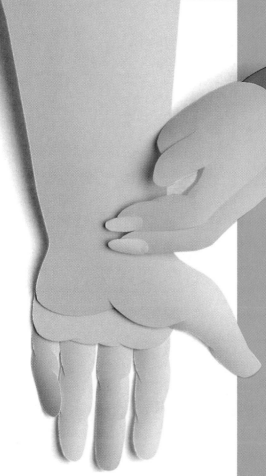

8. Blood components are carried freely through the body in the liquid part of the blood, called _____.
9. When a blood vessel is damaged, small grainy cells called _____ pile up at the site of the injury and break apart, releasing chemical messages.
10. Those chemical messages start the growth of a threadlike network of protein called _____ that seals the wound by trapping the red blood cells until a clot forms.

TAKING YOUR PULSE

The pulse you feel at your wrist, neck, or temple is your blood being pumped through your arteries. Place your fingers lightly on your wrist or neck. Count each beat for fifteen seconds. Then multiply the number of beats by four. This is your pulse rate per minute. Take your pulse after different activities. Which activities cause your pulse rate to speed up or slow down?

ecosystem
ecologist
populations
biosphere
community
niche
producers
consumers
food chain
habitat

_____

_____

Ecology

Ecology is the study of living things "in their homes." Add two more words about ecology to the list. Then do the activity. Use your Spelling Dictionary if you need help.

■ GETTING AT MEANING

Applying Concepts Use the paragraph and the illustration to help you complete each sentence with a list word.

The **ecosystem** of a pond is made up of everything in and around it, including water, mud, wind, heat, and sunlight. **Populations** of fish, ducks, cattails, and other species live in this pond **community.** Each species lives in its own **habitat.** Some species live on the bottom. Some swim through the water. Others live on the pond's surface. Each species has its own **niche,** or role to play, in this pond community.

1. Aquatic plants fill an important _____ in the community, providing food, shelter, and oxygen for the fish and animals.
2. The ducks feed on plants in part of their _____, the surface of the pond.
3. If the pond is polluted and most of the plants die, the _____ of ducks and fish will decline too.
4. Plants produce their own food. They do not have to eat other living things. This makes them _____.

1. _____
2. _____
3. _____
4. _____
5. _____
6. _____
7. _____
8. _____
9. _____
10. _____

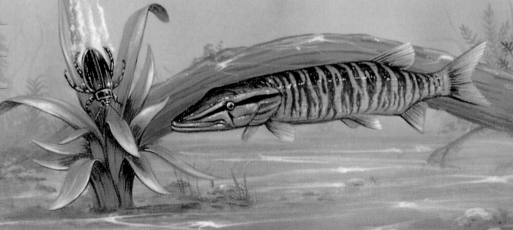

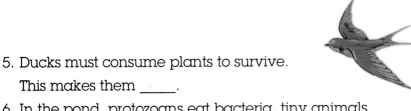

5. Ducks must consume plants to survive.
   This makes them _____.
6. In the pond, protozoans eat bacteria, tiny animals
   eat the protozoans, and fish eat these tiny animals.
   This feeding pattern is called a _____.
7. If many of the ducks in a pond started to die suddenly, you
   might call in an _____ to study the problem.
8. Woodpeckers, black snakes, and pine trees all living together
   in a forest is another example of a _____.
9. If you studied the birds, animals, trees, soil, and weather
   conditions in a forest, you would be studying its _____.
10. The total of all the communities on the earth and the
    environments in which they live is called the _____, a word
    that literally means the "sphere" of all "life."

DID YOU KNOW?

For centuries, Hawaii had no snakes. But in recent years, as more and more people have traveled to Hawaii, snakes have come with them. Now Hawaii is home to snakes and other organisms that are not native to the islands. The snakes feed on many of Hawaii's endangered birds. Because the snakes have no natural predators, ecologists are trying to control them before Hawaii's unique ecosystem suffers irreversible damage.

Animal Behavior

innate behavior
instinct
learned behavior
reflex action
memory
positive reinforcement
trial-and-error learning
reasoning
short-term memory
long-term memory

_____

_____

Animal behavior is the study of how animals act in their environment. Add two more words about animal behavior to the list. Then do the activity.

■ GETTING AT MEANING

Identifying Situations Use the pictures and the definitions to help you write the correct list word from each pair of parentheses. You will use some words more than once.

innate behavior behavior that does not have to be learned

learned behavior behavior that changes as a result of experiences

instinct complex behavior, often involving a series of steps, that does not have to be learned

reflex action behavior that happens automatically in response to a change or condition

1. (learned behavior, innate behavior)

2. (learned behavior, innate behavior)

3. (learned behavior, innate behavior)

4. (learned behavior, innate behavior)

5. A horse blinks when dust blows into its eyes. (reflex action, instinct)

6. A bird builds a nest. (reflex action, instinct)

7. Butterflies migrate south. (reflex action, instinct)

memory ability to store and retrieve knowledge

reasoning using past learning in new situations or to solve a problem

8. You know the multiplication tables. (memory, reasoning)
9. You figure out how much it will cost to buy ten thirty-cent stamps. (memory, reasoning)
10. After learning how rust forms, you decide to stop leaving your bike out in the rain. (memory, reasoning)

positive reinforcement reward for certain behaviors

trial-and-error learning method of learning by correcting mistakes through practice

short-term memory ability to store and recall knowledge for only a short time

long-term memory ability to store and recall knowledge over a long period of time

11. You call your best friend every day. You never look up the number. You know it by heart. (long-term memory, short-term memory)
12. You look up a phone number in the directory. You remember the number only long enough to dial it. (long-term memory, short-term memory)
13. A child doing a jigsaw puzzle will try every piece until he finds the piece that fits the space. (trial-and-error learning, positive reinforcement)

1. _____
2. _____
3. _____
4. _____
5. _____
6. _____
7. _____
8. _____
9. _____
10. _____
11. _____
12. _____
13. _____
14. _____
15. _____

14. (trial-and-error learning, positive reinforcement)

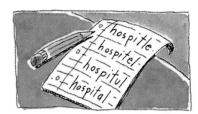

15. (trial-and-error learning, positive reinforcement)

GETTING IN SHAPE

Trace the shape of the figure at the right. Cut out four exact copies of it. Put together the four pieces to form a perfect square with no spaces. Allow yourself ten minutes. After ten minutes, take apart the puzzle and put it away somewhere. Wait five minutes. Then try to solve the puzzle again. Can you do it? What kind of behavior is this?

DID YOU KNOW?

Most pets and circus animals are trained by positive reinforcement. The animals learn to associate words, whistles, or motions with certain behaviors. The animals often receive food after they have correctly completed a task.

dialogue
camaraderie
resources
limelight
apprehensive
contemporary
infatuation
pursuit
despises
encourages

_____

_____

Learning What Matters

Many stories of young people growing up deal with decisions about what really matters. The list words all relate to matters of importance. Add some words of your own to the list. Then do the activity. Use your Spelling Dictionary if you need help.

■ GETTING AT MEANING

Plot Summaries Use a list word to complete the description of each book. Then think about which book you would most enjoy reading.

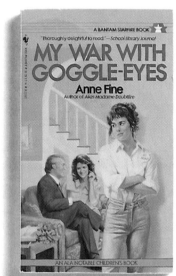

My War with Goggle-Eyes by Anne Fine (Little, Brown, 1989).

Kitty loathes and **(1)** the boring, middle-aged man her mother is dating. What's worse, the man is always around their house. "He's horrible," Kitty explains. "He's slimy and creepy and revolting. He makes me absolutely sick." Part of the fun of this novel is its realistic **(2).**

Baseball in April and Other Stories by Gary Soto (Harcourt, 1990).

Manuel dreams of being in the **(3)** at the school talent show—and not goofing up as he usually does! Yollie is skeptical of her mother's plan for making an old dress look new. These short stories about present-day life are **(4),** funny, and hard to resist.

1. _____

2. _____

3. _____

4. _____

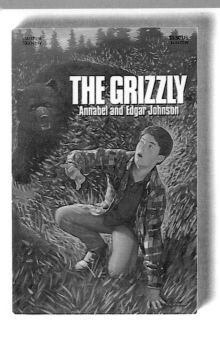

The Grizzly by Annabel and Edgar Johnson (Harper, 1973).

David has always been afraid of his father, whom he hasn't seen in years. When his father proposes taking him camping, David is nervous and **(5).** But the trip takes an unexpected turn when a grizzly attacks their camp. As David draws on inner strength and **(6)** he never knew he had, he comes to a more realistic view of his father.

The Mouse Rap by Walter Dean Myers (Harper, 1990).

"You can call me Mouse, 'cause that's my tag
I'm into it all, everything's my bag
You know I can run, you know I can hoop
I can do it alone, or in a group."

A Harlem summer is exciting when Mouse is around. There is affection and **(7)** between Mouse and his friends, and the action heats up as they all go in **(8)** of hidden treasure.

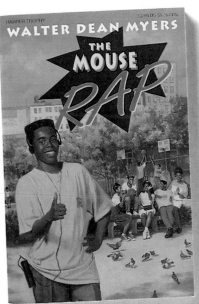

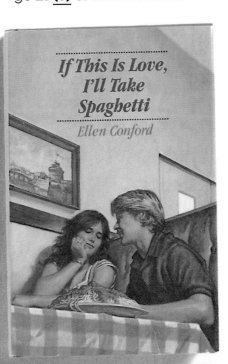

If This Is Love, I'll Take Spaghetti by Ellen Conford (Macmillan, 1983).

Whether it's love or just **(9),** Ellen Conford finds humor in the problems of being a teenaged girl. Meeting your favorite rock star, feeling too shy to talk to the boy you like, and falling off your diet are some of the events described. With her upbeat, positive tone, the author **(10)** us to feel that even the worst days of an adolescent can have a happy ending.

5. _____

6. _____

7. _____

8. _____

9. _____

10. _____

FRIENDSHIP DAY

We observe Mother's Day, Father's Day, Sweetest Day, and Valentine's Day. How about a day to celebrate friendship? Design a poster for "Friendship Day," with a symbol, picture, or slogan that expresses the importance of friendship.

artist
career
farmer
judge
photographer
reporter
scientist
surgeon
teacher
writer

_____

_____

Chasing Your Goals

If you set your mind to it, you can be anything you want to be. What career or careers would you like to pursue? Add those job names to the list. Then do the activities. Use your Spelling Dictionary if you need help.

Want Ads Complete the circled want ads with list words.

CLASSIFIEDS

The Youngstown Times

Sunday, April 11, 1993

Our company is one of the fastest-growing in the industry and we need the right individual to join our winning team. If that is you, Call Mr. Rosa. 555–4949

Brown & Sharp Screw Machine Set-Up Person wanted. Must have min. 5 yrs exp, have own tools, and read from blueprints. Bensenville. 555–8450

1. _____

2. _____

3. _____

4. _____

Meat Wrapper and Stockperson needed. Exp'd. only Call 345–555–5958.

Wanted: Someone who knows how to use lenses and film to take the very best pictures of people and pets. If you're a skilled **(1)**, call today! 312–555–4567.

Food broker looking for sales person to call on food retail accounts in city of Chicago. Must have degree, preferably in marketing. Send resume to: PMI, 500 Waters Edge, New York, NY 60605. Attn: Mark Wesley

Driver/semi. Apply in person, 3201 South Pulan, Youngstown, Ohio

If you'd like to help students find jobs that best suit their abilities and training, give us a call. You just may become our next **(2)** counselor. 555–8170.

Hairstylist/nail tech-Must be licensed. Full or part time. Call 393–555–3838

Do you ever read magazine articles and think "I could write like that!"? Well, our new publication is looking for a **(3)**. Fax us a writing sample of your best work. 555–8312.

Firefighter positions available, Class 2020, when available. Call Ms. Ferris: 912–555–4844.

Telemarketing Sales Qualifications include

The Burb Times, the greatest newspaper in Jefferson County, is looking for a **(4)** to cover farm news in the Tri-State area. 555–7071

Aggressive, self-motivated individual being sought in the Berwyn/Brookfield area for an outstanding sales management position selling the Midwest's largest newspaper. Must have ability to work independently and own reliable transportation. Call 312–555–1234.

Well-known home improvement company seeking aggressive type personalities for immediate telemarketing positions. Will pay you top hourly pay plus commission. Next to Washington Bridge and train. 800-969-9694

Tools of the Trade We associate certain tools with certain jobs. For example, when we think of a writer, we might picture a typewriter or word processor. Write the list word suggested by each "tool of the trade."

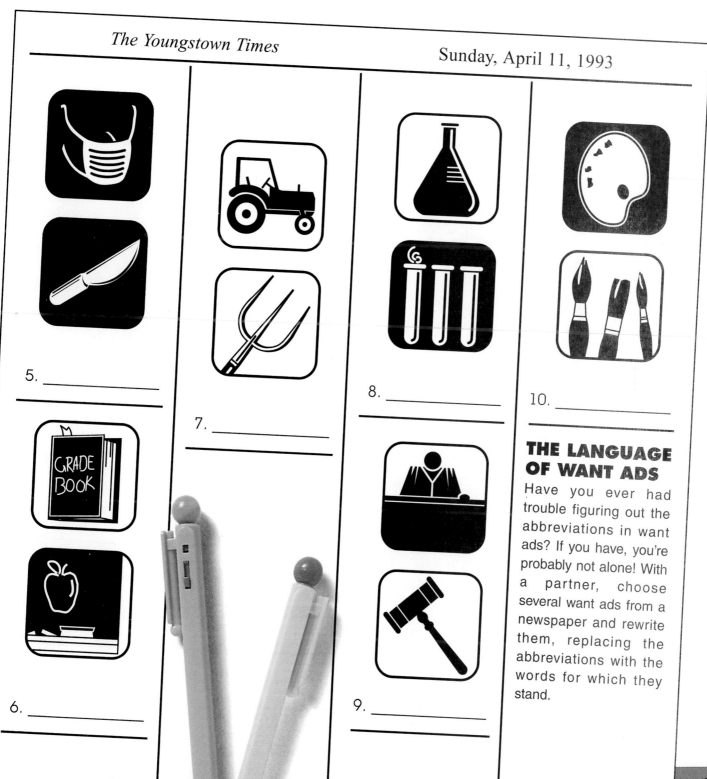

The Youngstown Times

Sunday, April 11, 1993

5. _____

6. _____

7. _____

8. _____

9. _____

10. _____

THE LANGUAGE OF WANT ADS

Have you ever had trouble figuring out the abbreviations in want ads? If you have, you're probably not alone! With a partner, choose several want ads from a newspaper and rewrite them, replacing the abbreviations with the words for which they stand.

bizarre
nightmare
gods
goddesses
monsters
dazzling
exaggeration
challenges
gigantic
invisible

_____

_____

Tales of the Imagination

The words in the list can be used to create imaginative characters and stories. Add two more words to the list and then do the activities.

■ GETTING AT MEANING

Creating Characters Help the writer create characters for a story. Fill in each blank with a list word.

Creating characters isn't easy. It's one of a writer's toughest **1.** _____.
Let's see, I could model some characters after those powerful beings from myths who ruled over heaven and earth, the **2.** _____ and
3. _____.

I'll also need to create some strange and horrible-looking **4.** _____.
They must be so scary that my readers will think these characters stepped out of a
5. _____. I'll call one Monstrophagus.
He'll be an ape that's so **6.** _____ that his shadow covers an entire city.

Yes, and I'll create a woman who can be heard but can't be seen. This **7.** _____ woman will invent all sorts of unusual ways to scare her unsuspecting victims.

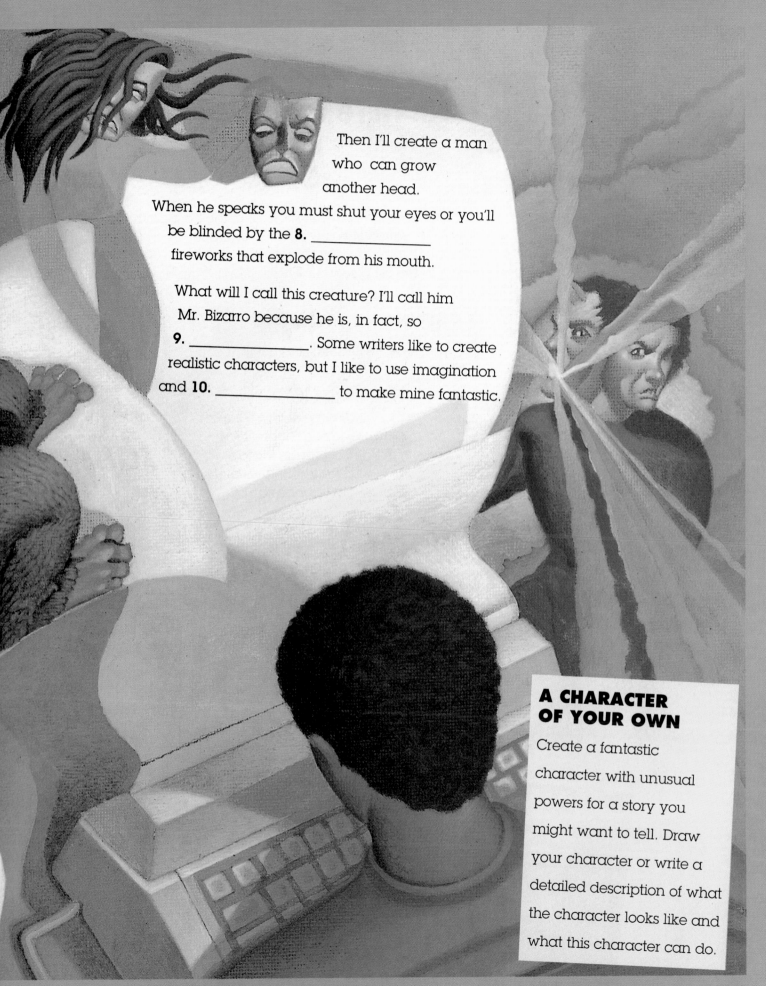

Then I'll create a man who can grow another head. When he speaks you must shut your eyes or you'll be blinded by the **8.** _____ fireworks that explode from his mouth.

What will I call this creature? I'll call him Mr. Bizarro because he is, in fact, so **9.** _____. Some writers like to create realistic characters, but I like to use imagination and **10.** _____ to make mine fantastic.

A CHARACTER OF YOUR OWN

Create a fantastic character with unusual powers for a story you might want to tell. Draw your character or write a detailed description of what the character looks like and what this character can do.

plague
pilgrimage
illuminated manuscripts
nomads
dowry
immunized
space shuttle
word processor
commute
pension plan

_____

_____

From Here to There

How was life different back there, in the past, from life here and now? The word list is a mix of words about life in the past and the present. Before you do the activities, see if you can add two more words to the list. Use your Spelling Dictionary if you need help.

■ GETTING AT MEANING

Comparisons Write the list word that completes each incomplete sentence.

In Medieval Europe, Christian monks copied books by hand. These beautifully illustrated (or "illuminated") books were called illuminated manuscripts.

When a deadly disease swept through Mexico City in 1736, the plague killed nearly one-third of the city's inhabitants.

Today, children are **(2)** against many diseases, and plagues are less common.

Today, we write letters, school reports, and books on computers, using a **(1)**.

Early humans lived as nomads, moving from place to place in search of fresh grazing land for their herds.

Today, people usually live in one place, but they **(3)** from home to work every day, often spending hours on the road.

When a Muslim in the tenth century went on a pilgrimage to Mecca, the center of the Islamic religion, the pious journey might have taken several years.

1. _____

2. _____

3. _____

4. _____

5. _____

Today, a **(4)** can take off, orbit the earth, launch a satellite, and return to earth in two days' time.

In Medieval Europe, a father saved for his daughter's dowry—money, land, or goods that she took to her marriage.

Today, many workers save for retirement through a company **(5)**.

Word Associations Write the list word that is associated with each group of words. Use the information in items 1 to 5 to help you.

6. money, land, bride _____

7. handwritten, monks, Medieval _____

8. travel, religious, long distance _____

9. illness, death, many people _____

10. wandering, pastures, unsettled _____

WHAT WAS LIFE LIKE THEN?

Interview an older family member or neighbor about his or her childhood. Ask about fashions, entertainment, travel, and anything else you are interested in. Report back to your class on how life was different then from now.

supplementary
translation
transformation
congruent
line of symmetry
rotation
reflection
tessellation
complementary
symmetric

_____

_____

Geometry

Geometric figures are all around us. The list words are geometric terms. Add two more of your own. Then do the activities. Use your Spelling Dictionary if you need help.

■ GETTING AT MEANING

Diagrams Artistic designs often are made by transforming one simple figure over and over—by flipping, sliding, or turning it without changing its shape or size. The four illustrations on this page show some of these transformations. Write the list word from the illustrations that each item refers to.

TRANSFORMATIONS

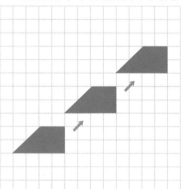

Translation (slide)

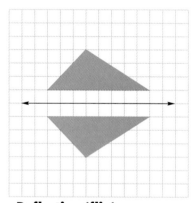

Reflection (flip)

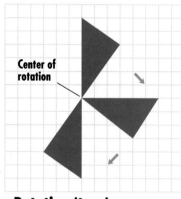

Center of rotation

Rotation (turn)

1. _____

2. _____

3. _____

4. _____

5. _____

1. You fold a piece of paper in half. Along the fold, you cut out the shape of half a heart. When you unfold it, you're holding a whole heart, with one half a mirror image of the other.

2. A table faces north with one leg at the room's exact center. You turn it until it faces northeast with the same leg still at the room's exact center.

3. You see the image of a cat standing at the left edge of your TV screen. The image slides to the middle of the screen and stays there.

4. You notice that the design of your bathroom tile is a series of polygons with no gaps between them.

5. You make this whenever you change a geometric figure by translation, reflection, or rotation of that figure.

TESSELLATION

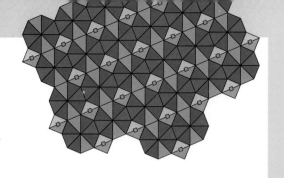

Applying Concepts The next set of diagrams shows another way to talk about transformations. Write the list word from the diagrams that completes each item.

Line of
Symmetry

Symmetric Figure

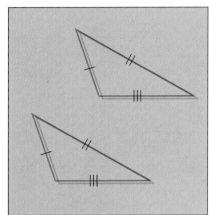

Congruent Figures

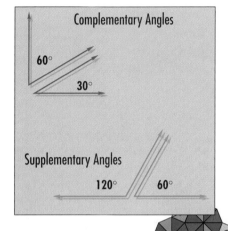

Complementary Angles

60°

30°

Supplementary Angles

120°   60°

6. If you fold a shape down the middle and the two halves match, then you know the figure is ____.

7. The figures shown in the translation are the same size and shape; therefore, the figures are ____.

8. Imagine a pie cut into four equal pieces. The angles formed by two adjacent pieces are ____ angles.

9. Imagine a pie cut into eight equal pieces. The angles formed by two adjacent pieces are ____ angles.

10. If you could fold a football field in half, the fifty-yard line would be the ____.

6. _____

7. _____

8. _____

9. _____

10. _____

CAPITAL SYMMETRY

Some capital letters are symmetric. For example, M has a vertical line of symmetry, and D has a horizontal line of symmetry. Find other symmetric capital letters and tell whether each line of symmetry is vertical or horizontal. Do any letters have both horizontal and vertical lines of symmetry? Do any letters have diagonal lines of symmetry?

milliliter
milligram
centiliter
centigram
deciliter
decigram
dekaliter
dekagram
kiloliter
kilogram

_____

_____

Measurement

In the metric system, the liter is the basic unit of capacity and the gram is the basic unit of mass, or weight. Add other metric system measurement words to the list. Then do the activities. Use the Spelling Dictionary if you need help.

■ GETTING AT MEANING

Picture and Chart Clues Study the picture and the chart of metric units. Then choose the correct word from the parentheses to fill in each blank.

one thousand	ten	one	one tenth	one hundredth	one thousandth
kiloliter	dekaliter	liter	deciliter	centiliter	milliliter
kilogram	dekagram	gram	decigram	centigram	milligram

DAVE'S GENERAL *Store*

DAIRY CASE

This carton holds about 1 liter of milk. The milk weighs about 1 kilogram.

This carton holds a little more than 2 deciliters of milk.

AISLE 1

AISLE 2

PAPER CLIPS 10 for 10¢

An eyedropper holds about one **(1)**. (milliliter, dekaliter)

A soup spoon has a capacity of about one **(2)**. (kiloliter, centiliter)

A small juice glass holds about one **(3)**. (deciliter, milliliter)

Ten paper clips weigh about one **(4)**. (dekagram, decigram)

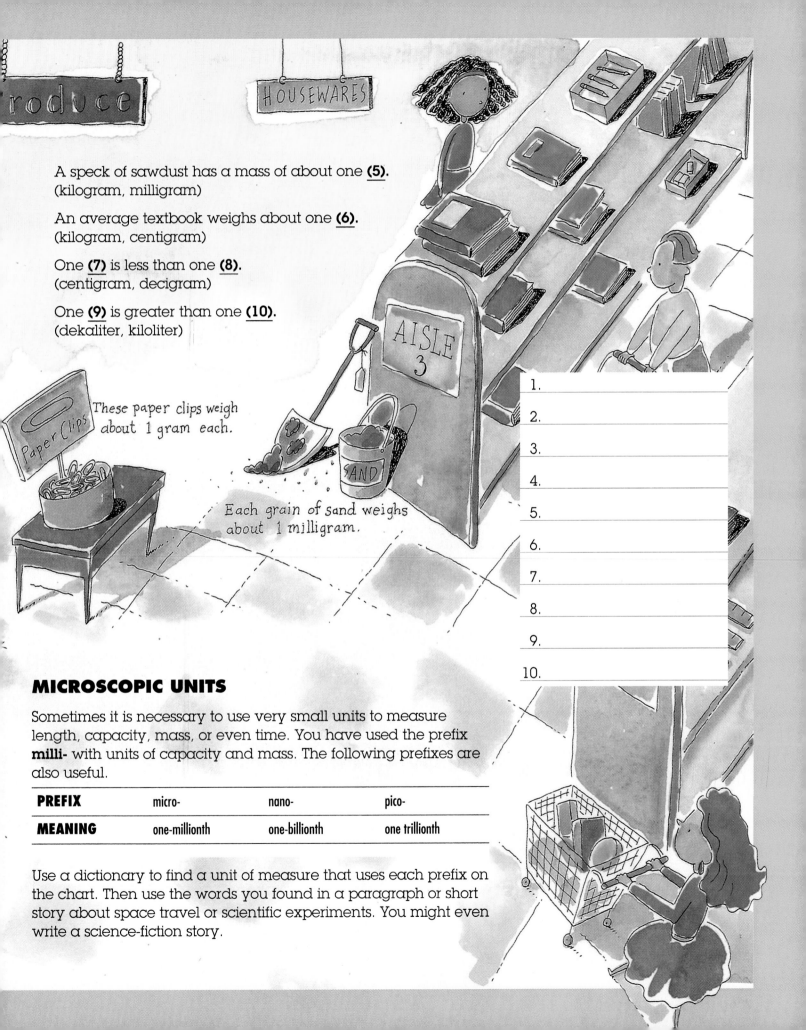

A speck of sawdust has a mass of about one **(5)**. (kilogram, milligram)

An average textbook weighs about one **(6)**. (kilogram, centigram)

One **(7)** is less than one **(8)**. (centigram, decigram)

One **(9)** is greater than one **(10)**. (dekaliter, kiloliter)

These paper clips weigh about 1 gram each.

Paper Clips

AISLE 3

SAND

Each grain of sand weighs about 1 milligram.

1.
2.
3.
4.
5.
6.
7.
8.
9.
10.

MICROSCOPIC UNITS

Sometimes it is necessary to use very small units to measure length, capacity, mass, or even time. You have used the prefix **milli-** with units of capacity and mass. The following prefixes are also useful.

PREFIX	micro-	nano-	pico-
MEANING	one-millionth	one-billionth	one trillionth

Use a dictionary to find a unit of measure that uses each prefix on the chart. Then use the words you found in a paragraph or short story about space travel or scientific experiments. You might even write a science-fiction story.

Statistics

random sample
represent
compare
range
mean
median
mode
double bar graph
horizontal scale
vertical scale

_____

_____

The words on the list are used in collecting, organizing, and presenting statistical data. If you can, add more words. Then do the activities. Use your Spelling Dictionary if you need help.

■ GETTING AT MEANING

Charts First study the chart below. Then complete items 1–4, using the four list words and the data:

mode   mean
median   range

DATA:
3, 10, 3, 5, 9

DATA	MEAN	MEDIAN	MODE	RANGE
0, 1, 9, 15, 5	$(0+1+9+15+5) \div 5 = 6$	0, 1, **5**, 9, 15	none	$15 - 0 = 15$
3, 7, 10, 6, 4, 7, 5	$(3+7+10+6+4+7+5) \div 7 = 6$	3, 4, 5, **6**, 7, 7, 10	7	$10 - 3 = 7$

1. _____

2. _____

3. _____

4. _____

1. To find the _____, divide 30 (3 + 10 + 3 + 5 + 9) by 5.
2. The _____ for this set of data is 3.
3. The _____ is 10 – 3, or 7.
4. The _____ is 5.

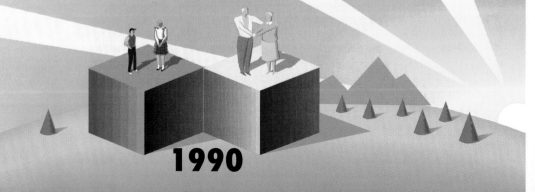

1990

226

Stories Read Story A and complete Story B with list words.

STORY A

Randy's and Rita's math groups had statistics projects to complete. Randy's group gathered a **random sample** of thirty students to **represent** all the seventh graders in school. These thirty students voted for their favorite sport to watch and their favorite sport to play. Randy's group made a **double bar graph** to **compare** their results. The graph's **horizontal scale** shows the five sports voted on, while the **vertical scale** shows how many students voted for each sport.

Favorite Sports

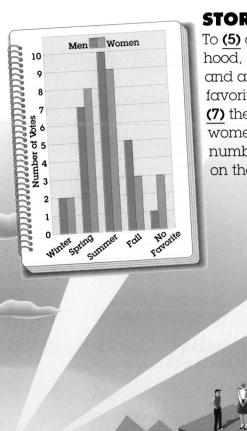

STORY B

To **(5)** all the adults in their neighborhood, Rita's group chose a **(6)** of fifty and asked them to vote on their favorite season. The group decided to **(7)** the responses of men with those of women, using a **(8).** The **(9)** shows the number of votes for each choice listed on the **(10)**.

5. _____

6. _____

7. _____

8. _____

9. _____

10. _____

DID YOU KNOW?

In 1990 the United States population figures showed about the same number of people in the age range of 5–13 as in the 65 and over age range. The U.S. Bureau of the Census has predicted that in the year 2080 there will be about three times as many people in the 65 and over range as in the 5–13 range.

2080

Integers and Coordinates

integers
positive
negative
opposite
absolute value
number line
quadrant
coordinates
origin
axes

_____

_____

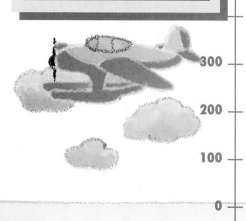

The list words are all used for locating points on a coordinate plane or number line. Add two more words to the list. Then do the activities. Use your Spelling Dictionary if you need help.

■ GETTING AT MEANING

Integers on a Number Line Integers are positive and negative whole numbers and zero. Each integer has an opposite (-1 and 1, 3 and -3, and so on), except for zero. An integer's absolute value is its distance from zero on a number line. Use the illustration below to help you fill in the blanks with list words.

300
200
100
0
−100
−200
−300
−400

1. To record the altitude of the seaplane, you would write a _____ number.

2. To record the depth of the diver, you would write a _____ number.

3. To record the depths of the fish and diver and the altitudes of the bird and seaplane, you would write four different _____.

4. You can determine these depths and altitudes by looking at the _____ on the left side of the picture.

1. _____

2. _____

3. _____

4. _____

5. _____

6. _____

7. _____

8. _____

9. _____

10. _____

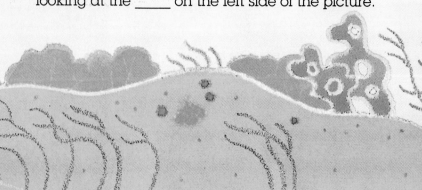

Coordinate Plane Use the graph to help you fill in the blanks with list words.

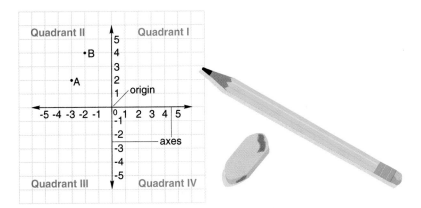

The coordinates for point A are (-3, 2).

7. Point B is located in the second _____ of the plane.
8. To reach point B, start where the axes intersect, at the _____, and move 2 units to the left and 4 units up.
9. The _____ for point B are (-2, 4).
10. These numbers are listed on the horizontal and vertical _____ of the plane.

COORDINATE NEIGHBORHOODS

Make a coordinate plane that represents the neighborhood where you live or go to school. Use your home or your school as the origin and locate parks, libraries, stores, or government buildings on the grid. Let each unit on the grid represent one block, or some other reasonable unit.

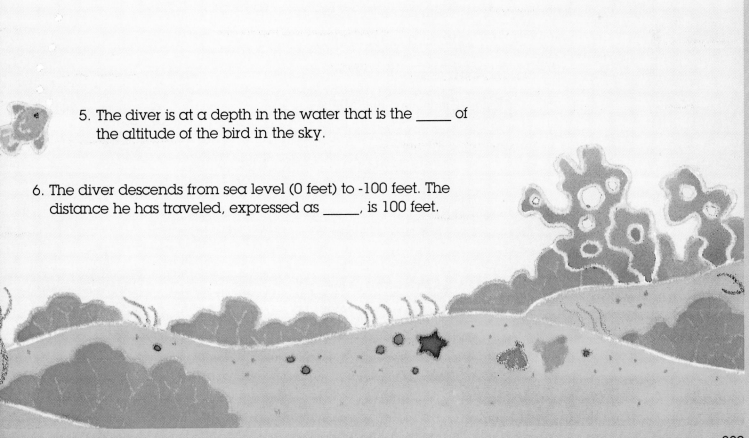

5. The diver is at a depth in the water that is the _____ of the altitude of the bird in the sky.

6. The diver descends from sea level (0 feet) to -100 feet. The distance he has traveled, expressed as _____, is 100 feet.

Writer's Handbook

INTRODUCTION

Above all, writers want their work to be clear to their readers.
Spelling and punctuating correctly are two ways to help your
readers understand what you want to say. What else can you do
to make your writing clear? This handbook will tell you more
about how to become a better writer.

CONTENTS

The Writing Process

This section answers some of the questions you might have about the five steps of the writing process: **prewriting, drafting, revising, proofreading,** and **presenting.**

1. PREWRITING

What should I do before I begin writing?

Just as mapping out where you want to go can help make a road trip go more smoothly, "mapping out" what you want to say can help make your writing go more smoothly. Before you begin writing, take some time to plan ahead.

- **Decide what to write about.** If you are having trouble deciding what to write about, you might come up with some ideas by going through your writing journal and rereading your thoughts, feelings, and observations. You also might try looking through books, magazines, or newspapers for ideas.
- **Determine your purpose and audience.** What will be your purpose for writing? Do you want to express certain feelings or opinions? describe or explain something? inform, persuade, or entertain? Who will be your audience? Will you address a specific person or group, or are you writing only for yourself?
- **Narrow your topic.** To make sure all your ideas really do focus on a specific topic, you might develop a written outline, create a web, or write down questions.
- **Gather information about your topic.** Depending on what you're writing about, you might take notes from different sources; conduct interviews; list points you want to make; arrange events on a time line; or note how things look, sound, smell, taste, and feel.
- **Organize your information.** Depending on your type of writing and your purpose for writing, you will need to organize by time order, spatial order, or order of importance.

2. DRAFTING

How do I actually begin writing?

Gather up your materials—including your writing journal, your prewriting notes, and any other resources you'll need—and find a quiet, comfortable, well-lit place. Plan on writing for at least twenty minutes. If you have trouble getting started, these strategies might help:

- **Set a goal.** Tell yourself you'll write a certain amount, or for a certain amount of time, and then try to stick to it.
- **Tune out distractions,** such as radio, TV, or conversations. Concentrate on the task at hand.
- **Review your resources.** Examine your notes or your writing journal to come up with an idea for a good opening line or paragraph.
- **Get started!** Don't worry about perfect spelling, punctuation, or capitalization now. You will work on them later. For now, just begin with a sentence that is direct and interesting, and that states your main idea. Then let your ideas flow freely.

3. REVISING

How do I revise my writing?

When you revise, you reread what you have written, looking for ways to improve it. To begin revising, you might do the following:

- **Read your draft to yourself** to catch errors such as unclear or unnecessary ideas, or ideas that are out of order.
- **Have a conference** with other students or with your teacher. Read your draft aloud and ask for reactions. Did your listeners understand what you were trying to say? Can they suggest ways to improve your draft?

What kinds of questions should I ask?

The questions you ask will depend on your purpose, audience, and type of writing. Here are some points to consider:

Ask these questions!

- Does each paragraph have a topic sentence that sets up or states the main idea of the rest of the paragraph?
- Do all my details support the main idea?
- Are they all in the correct order?
- Can I delete any extra words or replace any inexact ones?
- Do I need to delete any unnecessary information?
- Do I need to add or rearrange any information?
- Are all my facts and figures correct?
- Have I used language appropriate for my audience and type of writing?
- Does my writing have a clear beginning, middle, and end?

What kinds of changes should I make?

Try making these changes to clarify your writing:

- **Add or subtract** words or ideas.
- **Move** words, sentences, or paragraphs.
- **Replace** words or ideas that are unclear or inexact.

4. PROOFREADING

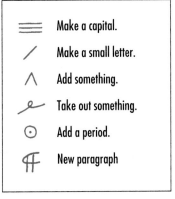

Why should I proofread, and when and how should I do it?

You should proofread to correct errors in usage, punctuation, capitalization and spelling. Proofread once after revising your first draft. Then, after finishing your final draft, proofread it one last time to make sure everything is as perfect as you can make it.

Use proofreading symbols such as the ones on this page to clearly indicate any corrections needed.

What kinds of things should I look for when I proofread?

Here are some things to look for when you proofread:

- Did I capitalize the first word of each sentence?
- Did I capitalize all proper nouns and proper adjectives?
- Is each sentence correctly punctuated?
- Have I avoided fragments and run-on sentences?
- Did I keep the correct verb tense throughout?
- Do all my subjects and verbs agree?
- Did I check carefully for spelling?
- Did I indent every paragraph?
- If there is a special format for this kind of writing, have I followed it?
- Is my handwriting clear and legible?

Check for these possible errors!

5. PRESENTING

How should I present my final work?

For regular assignments, these steps are often used:

- Copy your final draft neatly on one side of white, lined paper.
- If you are using a computer, make final corrections to your rough draft and print out a new version.
- Put your name, subject, and date in the top right-hand corner.
- Skip a line (or add an extra return) and write or type the title of your piece. Center it on the line.
- Leave an inch margin on the sides and bottom of the paper.

Special ways to present your writing include displaying it on a bulletin board, binding it in an illustrated book or magazine, reading it aloud, and submitting it for publication.

Taking Writing Tests

The following tips should help make taking writing tests easier.

GENERAL GUIDELINES FOR WRITING TESTS

- **Listen carefully to instructions.** Pay close attention to find out how much time you have, what kind of writing utensil you should use, when you should begin and end, and any other special instructions.
- **Read the assignment and identify the key words.** Before you begin writing, make sure you understand what the directions are asking you to do. Here are some key words that often appear in test directions:

Look for these
key words!

Categorize or *Classify:* Sort ideas or facts into groups.
Compare and Contrast: Point out similarities (compare) and differences (contrast).
Defend: Give evidence to show why a view is right.
Define: Tell what something is or means.
Describe: Create a word picture with details and examples.
Discuss: State varying ideas about a given topic.
Evaluate: Give your opinion, with supporting details or reasons, on whether an idea is good or bad, right or wrong.
Explain: Make something clear by explaining cause and effect or by giving examples or steps.
Summarize: State main points, or retell important parts of a story.

- **Plan how you'll use your time.** Take time at the start to map out what you will write and at the end to reread and catch any errors.
- **Write a strong opening** to catch your readers' attention. Be sure it specifically addresses the topic of the assignment.
- **Use specific facts and details** to help develop your ideas. Be sure to put them into the proper order or form.
- **Take time to wrap things up.** Don't stop writing just because your time is up. Write a strong conclusion that pulls everything together.

WRITING A CHARACTER SKETCH

A character sketch is a description of a fictional character or a person from real life. In it, the writer describes the character's appearance, actions, and special qualities.

KEY WORDS IN ASSIGNMENTS
- "**Describe** a character from . . ."
- "**Tell about** your best friend . . ."

SAMPLE ASSIGNMENTS
- Write a character sketch about someone you like and admire. Describe what this person looks like. Then tell what it is about this person that you like and admire, and why.
- Who is your favorite character from books or movies? Write a character sketch describing what this character looks like and what this character said and did that showed his or her unique qualities.

A PLAN OF ATTACK
- Before you write, think about the subject of your character sketch. Jot down details and incidents that help illustrate his or her appearance and uniqueness.
- Begin your writing with a topic sentence that tells who you will be describing.
- When you describe something the character has done, use **time order** to organize your description. When you describe appearance, use **spatial order,** proceeding from head to toe, or vice versa.
- To signal time order, use clue words such as *first, then,* and *later.* To signal spatial order, use clue words such as *above, near,* and *below.*
- Use figurative language and exact, vivid words to "sketch" the clearest possible picture for your readers.

FOLLOW-UP CHECKLIST
- Does your topic sentence clearly identify the person you described?
- Have you chosen the proper organization for your character sketch?
- Have you used clue words to help signal that order?
- Are your punctuation, capitalization, spelling, and usage correct?

WRITING ABOUT CAUSE/EFFECT

A cause is what makes something happen. An effect is what happens because of the cause. When you write about cause/effect relationships, you tell why things happened or why they are the way they are.

KEY WORDS IN ASSIGNMENTS

- "What **caused** . . ."
- "**What happened** when . . ."
- "Explain the **effects** of . . ."

SAMPLE ASSIGNMENTS

- Uh oh—you were having such a good time outdoors that you stayed out in the sun too long. Explain the effects that overexposure to the sun can have on your body.
- Every day you see and hear ads for different products. What effects do those ads have on consumers? Describe a popular ad and explain the effects its makers want it to have on consumers like you.

A PLAN OF ATTACK

- Before you write, make a word web. In the center, write the cause or causes in a large circle (for example, *sun*). Draw lines branching out from the center, and at the end of each line write an effect (for example, *skin cancer, dehydration,* or *blisters*).
- Look over your effects. Are they accurate? Is it reasonable to conclude that these effects follow from the cause?
- Begin your writing with a topic sentence that states the cause/effect relationship or relationships that you will be describing.
- Use transition words and phrases such as *because, since, as a result,* and *consequently* to signal cause/effect relationships.

FOLLOW-UP CHECKLIST

- Are your facts accurate? Are your conclusions reasonable?
- Does your topic sentence clearly state the cause/effect relationship or relationships you described?
- Have you used transition words and phrases to clearly signal these relationships?
- Are your punctuation, capitalization, spelling, and usage correct?

WRITING INSTRUCTIONS

Instructions are step-by-step directions that tell readers how to do something. The steps are arranged in a specific order so that readers can follow them easily and correctly.

KEY WORDS IN ASSIGNMENTS

- "Explain **how to** . . . "
- "**List the steps** to follow to . . . "
- "Tell what you **need** to . . . "

SAMPLE ASSIGNMENTS

- You have to give a demonstration speech to your English class about how to make your favorite food—a main dish, a party snack, or a dessert. Write the instructions you will give during your speech. Be sure to list all the ingredients.
- What was your favorite game when you were little—hide-and-go-seek, kickball, capture the flag? Pick a favorite game. Now imagine that you must explain to a five-year-old how it's played. Write your instructions step by step. Be sure to make them clear and simple.

A PLAN OF ATTACK

- Before you write, think through each step of the instructions. Then list the steps in order, making sure to include any materials required.
- When you begin writing, start with a topic sentence that states what your instructions are for. Then tell what materials you'll need.
- Organize the steps in **sequential order**. Tell what you will do first, next, and so on.
- Use clue words and phrases such as *first, next, then, after that,* and *finally* to make the sequential order clear.

FOLLOW-UP CHECKLIST

- Does your topic sentence tell what the instructions are for?
- Are your steps arranged in the proper sequence or order?
- Have you used clue words and phrases to help signal that order?
- Have you included all the materials or ingredients?
- Are your punctuation, capitalization, spelling, and usage correct?

WRITING A DETAILED EXPLANATION

A detailed explanation uses related details to explain a main idea. Often, these related details are made up of examples or reasons.

KEY WORDS IN ASSIGNMENTS

- "Give **examples** to explain how . . ."
- "Tell **how** the . . ."
- "Explain the **reasons why** . . ."

SAMPLE ASSIGNMENTS

- Sometimes small children can be annoying. Think of examples from your experience that illustrate this statement. Use these examples to help you write an explanation of how small children can be annoying.
- Millions of people have pets. What do pets give back to the people who own and take care of them? Write an explanation of why people have pets. Use reasons and examples to make your explanation clear.

A PLAN OF ATTACK

- Before you write, list reasons or examples you can use to explain your main idea.
- Organize them by **order of importance,** from least important (weakest) to most important (strongest) or from most important to least important.
- Begin with a topic sentence that clearly states what you will explain. Then deal with your examples or reasons one at a time, in the order you have them listed.
- Use clue words and phrases that signal each new reason or example, such as *for example, for this reason, because,* and *this shows.*

FOLLOW-UP CHECKLIST

- Have you stated your main idea in a topic sentence?
- Do all your reasons and examples relate to the main idea?
- Have you kept to the pattern of organization you've chosen?
- Have you used clue words and phrases that signal each new reason or example?
- Are your punctuation, capitalization, spelling, and usage correct?

WRITING A PERSONAL NARRATIVE

A personal narrative tells about something you have done, felt, or experienced.

KEY WORDS IN ASSIGNMENTS

- "What did you **do** when . . . ?"
- "Write how you **felt** when . . ."
- "Tell **what happened** when . . ."

SAMPLE ASSIGNMENTS

- Describe a time when you learned how to do something new, such as ride a bike, cook a meal, or build something. Write about what you did, thought, and felt during your learning experience.
- We all have times when, for one reason or another, we're embarrassed. Think about an embarrassing moment you've had. Write about what happened and how you felt as it was happening.

A PLAN OF ATTACK

- Before you write, narrow your topic to one particular learning experience or embarrassing moment.
- Next, relive the experience in your mind and jot down some words and phrases that explain exactly what you were doing, thinking, and feeling at the time.
- Then use the words and phrases to write a rough outline for your narrative. Be sure to include a beginning, a middle, and an end.
- As you write your narrative, keep your readers in mind. Imagine you are introducing yourself to them as you relate your story.

FOLLOW-UP CHECKLIST

- Does your narrative have a beginning, a middle, and an end?
- Does the beginning grab your readers' attention and tell them what you will be writing about?
- Did you "capture the moment" by using exact words and phrases to describe your thoughts and feelings?
- Do your subjects and verbs agree throughout?
- Are your punctuation, capitalization, spelling, and usage correct?

WRITING AN EDITORIAL

An editorial is a magazine or newspaper article that gives the editor's or publisher's opinion about a particular topic or issue.

KEY WORDS IN ASSIGNMENTS

- "**State your opinion** of . . . "
- "**What do you think** (or **How do you feel**) about . . . "

SAMPLE ASSIGNMENTS

- You are the editor of the school newspaper. Your school has a budget crisis, and some members of the community have proposed eliminating all field trips as a way to save money. Write an editorial that states your opinion of this suggestion. Give reasons to support your opinion.
- Some of the teachers in your school have proposed changing the grading system from letter grades to written evaluations. They believe this will allow them to be more specific about student strengths and weaknesses. What do you think of their proposal? State your opinions in an editorial.

A PLAN OF ATTACK

- Before you begin writing, evaluate the proposal you have chosen to discuss. Do you agree or disagree? Why? What alternatives are there? Jot down several reasons that support your opinion.
- Look over your reasons and make sure they really do support your point of view. Cross out any that don't.
- Begin your editorial with a topic sentence that states your opinion.
- Organize your supporting reasons by **order of importance.** Make them build from least important (weakest) to most important (strongest) or from most important to least important.
- Avoid personal attacks—focus on the issues, not whether you like or dislike the person who is making the proposal.

FOLLOW-UP CHECKLIST

- Does your topic sentence clearly state your opinion or point of view?
- Do your reasons strongly support your opinion?
- Do you stick to the pattern of organization you've chosen?
- Have you included only information that is relevant to your argument?
- Are your punctuation, capitalization, spelling, and usage correct?

Rules, Guidelines, and Models

CAPITALIZATION

Capitalize the following in your writing:

Names, initials, and titles used with names:

> Rev. Frank Harrison, Sr.   Ms. Edith A. Fleming

Proper adjectives:

> Mexican food   European diplomat   African literature

The pronoun *I*:

> Ginny and I are second cousins.

Names of cities, states, countries, continents:

> St. Cloud   New Hampshire   Algeria   North America

Names of lakes, rivers, mountains, structures, organizations:

> Lake Okeechobee   Great Wall of China
>
> Great Smoky Mountains   Red Cross

Names of streets and street abbreviations:

> Maple St.   S. Mason   Sycamore Ave.   Old Orchard Rd.

Days, months, holidays, special events:

> Thursday   Fri.   February   Aug.
>
> Veterans Day   Octoberfest   New Year's Day

First, last, and all important words in movie, book, story, play, and TV show titles:

> The Pink Panther   A Tale of Two Cities
> "The Pit and the Pendulum"

First word in the greeting and closing of a letter:

> My dear sister,   Very truly yours,

First word in a sentence:

> What a great day it is!

First word inside quotation marks:

> Selena asked, "Are we going to go to the library now?"

First word of each main topic and subtopic in an outline:

> I. Special ways that animals communicate
>   A. Sounds they make
>   B. Movements

Both letters of the United States Postal Service state abbreviations:

AL (Alabama)	**LA** (Louisiana)	**OH** (Ohio)
AK (Alaska)	**ME** (Maine)	**OK** (Oklahoma)
AZ (Arizona)	**MD** (Maryland)	**OR** (Oregon)
AR (Arkansas)	**MA** (Massachusetts)	**PA** (Pennsylvania)
CA (California)	**MI** (Michigan)	**RI** (Rhode Island)
CO (Colorado)	**MN** (Minnesota)	**SC** (South Carolina)
CT (Connecticut)	**MS** (Mississippi)	**SD** (South Dakota)
DE (Delaware)	**MO** (Missouri)	**TN** (Tennessee
FL (Florida)	**MT** (Montana)	**TX** (Texas)
GA (Georgia)	**NE** (Nebraska)	**UT** (Utah)
HI (Hawaii)	**NV** (Nevada)	**VT** (Vermont)
ID (Idaho)	**NH** (New Hampshire)	**VA** (Virginia)
IL (Illinois)	**NJ** (New Jersey)	**WA** (Washington)
IN (Indiana)	**NM** (New Mexico)	**WV** (West Virginia)
IA (Iowa)	**NY** (New York)	**WI** (Wisconsin)
KS (Kansas)	**NC** (North Carolina)	**WY** (Wyoming)
KY (Kentucky)	**ND** (North Dakota)	

PUNCTUATION

Use **periods**

- to end sentences that make statements or sentences that make commands or requests:

    I've got a ladybug in my hand.
    Let me see it.

- after most abbreviations:

    Mon. Blvd. Gen. Aug. Dr. A.M.

Use **exclamation marks**

- after sentences that show strong feeling:

    This movie is incredibly funny!

Use **question marks**

- after sentences that ask questions:

   How are you feeling today?

Use **commas**

- between the day and the year in a date:

   April 27, 1881

- between the day and the month in a date:

   Sunday, June 19

- to set off a date from the rest of a sentence:

   On March 1, 1987, my little sister was born.
   Can you come to the party on Saturday, September 22?

- between the name of a city and state:

   Columbus, Ohio

- to set off an address from the rest of a sentence:

   Juan is moving to 16 Scott Street, Taos, New Mexico,
      next week.

- after the greeting and closing of a friendly letter:

   Dear Wendell,   Your friend,

- between a series of words in a sentence:

   I packed my pajamas, robe, and slippers for the trip.

- before the conjunction that joins a compound sentence:

   I am on a swim team, and my brother is on a soccer team.
   We knocked on the door, but no one answered.

- after introductory words or phrases:

   No, I don't want onions on my hamburger.
   As you know, they are one of my least favorite foods.

- to set off interrupting words or phrases:

   Pickles, incidentally, are another of my least favorite foods.

- to separate a noun of address from the rest of a sentence:

   Would you like me to help you with that, Mr. Lee?
   Sam, how kind of you to ask!
   Are you coming with us, Delores, or are you staying here?

- before quotation marks or inside the end quotation marks:

   Samantha asked, "When is our homework assignment
      due?"
   "It's due next Thursday," answered Armando.

- to set off appositives (words or phrases that identify or explain nouns):

    I saw Mrs. Hallmann, my math teacher, at the hospital today.

    She was visiting her brother, Mr. Geils.

- after mild interjections (words that express feeling):

    Hey, did you see that?

Use **quotation marks**

- around the exact words someone used when speaking:

    "I've finished all my homework," said Tony.

- around titles of stories, poems, songs, and articles:

    "Frozen Fire"   "Birdsong"   "Gift of the Incas"

Underline or **italicize** titles of books and movies:

The Invisible Man   *The Bad News Bears*

Use **apostrophes**

- to form the possessive of a noun:

    people's   girls'   bus's

- in contractions in place of dropped letters.

    he's (he is)   it'll (it will)   we've (we have)

Use **colons**

- between hours and minutes to indicate time:

    2:45   12:50

- after the greeting in a business letter:

    Dear Century Homes: Dear Mr. Trask:

BUSINESS LETTER FORM

You might write a business letter to ask for information about particular products or services. You might also want to register a complaint or give opinions or suggestions.

Since you usually write business letters to people you don't know, your tone should be formal, and you should be as brief and to-the-point as possible.

Study the business letter below. Notice its five parts, and how each of those parts is capitalized and punctuated.

469 Hastings Street
Chicago, IL 60641
November 18, 19—

Heading

Manager
Al's Grocery
711 East Kensington Avenue
Chicago, IL 60641

Inside Address

Dear Manager:

Greeting

My family has shopped at Al's Grocery for many years. Recently, I was shocked to find that my favorite cereal, "Flakey Flakes," has disappeared from your shelves. The clerk I talked to said you no longer carry that item. I am writing to ask you to reconsider that decision.

Body

"Flakey Flakes" is a healthful cereal, full of whole grains and fruits. It is low in sugar and salt, and it tastes good too. My parents usually buy two boxes a week for my sister and me, and several of my friends also buy it. We all hope you will continue to stock "Flakey Flakes" so that we don't have to go to another store to buy it.

Thanks for paying attention to my suggestion. I hope you will consider it.

Sincerely,

John Ragsdale

John Ragsdale

Closing

Dictionary Handbook

Understanding and Using the Dictionary

Have you ever stopped while you were writing to wonder how to spell a word, or while you were reading to wonder what a certain word meant or how to pronounce it? You can find the answers to questions like these when you know how to use a dictionary. This handbook will help you do this.

1. How do I look up a word quickly?

The **entry words** in a dictionary are arranged in alphabetical order. To find a word quickly, use the pairs of words at the top outside corner of each page—the **guide words.** They tell you the first and last entry words on that page. If your word falls between the guide words, then you know it's somewhere on that page.

For example, if the guide words are **fly l fog,** you'll find *focus* on that page, but to find *fish* you'll have to turn back a few pages.

Exercise 1   Write two entry words that would appear on the same dictionary page as each set of guide words.

1. beam l bristle
2. sea l storm
3. acid l attitude
4. canary l cartilage
5. random l rubber
6. limp l live
7. fiddle l fumble
8. staff l stockade

2. How do I look up a word I don't know how to spell?

The key is finding out how the word begins. For example, suppose you need to correct this misspelling: "He wanted to become a *sitizen.*" How else might the word begin? Think about what letters could make the sound /s/ at the beginning of this word. You know that the letters **s** and **c** are common spellings of this sound, so you try them out.

1. _____

2. _____

3. _____

4. _____

5. _____

6. _____

7. _____

8. _____

First, you try *sitizen.* You look through the **guide words** until you find the page headed **sir | size,** but *sitizen* isn't there. So you try *citizen,* and there it is on the page headed **cistern | civilize.**

Exercise 2   Use your Spelling Dictionary to find out which one of each pair is spelled correctly. Write the correct spelling and the guide words from the dictionary page where each is found.

1. neumonia—pneumonia
2. cardigan—kardigan
3. rinestone—rhinestone
4. exception—ekception
5. shandelier—chandelier
6. etymology—etimology

3. What do I do if I still can't find the word?

Most dictionaries have a **spelling chart** that shows all the possible spellings for each English sound. The part of the chart for the sound /k/ is shown.

k   **c**oat, **k**ind, ba**ck**, e**ch**o, a**ch**e, **q**uit, a**cc**ount, anti**que**, e**x**cite, a**cq**uire

Notice that there are ten possible spellings for this sound in English. Use the spelling chart if you still can't find a word after you've looked up every spelling you can think of.

Exercise 3   Use the spelling chart called "Spellings of English Sounds" at the beginning of your Spelling Dictionary to answer these questions.

1. How many ways can the sound /t/ be spelled?
2. Which word in the chart has the sound /ėr/ spelled the same as in *germ?*
3. Which word in the chart has the sound /m/ spelled the same as in *dumb?*
4. How many ways can the sound /ou/ be spelled?
5. What are the four ways that the sound /ch/ can be spelled?
6. What are the five ways that the sound /z/ can be spelled?

1. _____

2. _____

3. _____

4. _____

5. _____

6. _____

1. _____

2. _____

3. _____

4. _____

5. _____

6. _____

4. How do I know which definition fits my word?

Many words have more than one meaning. In fact, a word like *take* has dozens of meanings. You can use the **context** of the word, the **parts of speech** labels, and the **illustrative phrases** and **sentences** provided to help you choose the proper **definition** of your word. What is the definition of the word *limelight* in this sentence: "The famous actress is in the limelight again for donating one million dollars to her favorite charity."

> **lime■light** (līm′līt′), *n.* **1** an intense white light produced by heating a piece of lime in a flame, formerly used in a theater to light up certain persons or objects on the stage and draw attention to them. **2** fixture that produced this light. **3** center of public attention and interest. —**lime′light′er**, *n.*

From the context of the sentence, you know that the definition you are looking for means "center of public attention." Reading the definitions, you can see that the one you want is definition 3: center of public attention or interest.

1. _____
2. _____
3. _____
4. _____
5. _____

Exercise 4   Write the part of speech and the number of the definition that fits the italicized word in each sentence. Use your Spelling Dictionary.

1. Sue's *account* of the accident was very accurate.
2. Randy said his stay in the hospital was a real *nightmare*.
3. Gina memorized the *combination* to her gym locker.
4. The heart is a very important *organ* of the body.
5. Martin's eyes were *coffee* brown.

5. How can I find out how to pronounce a word?

You can use a dictionary to help you pronounce words that may be unfamiliar to you. The entry word is broken into **syllables.** Right after it comes the pronunciation, enclosed in parentheses: **fa■tigue** (fə tēg′). The **accent mark** tells you which syllable to emphasize.

The **pronunciation key,** which appears on every page in most dictionaries, shows how to sound out the pronunciations.

Some words can be said in more than one way. For example, two pronunciations are given in your Spelling Dictionary for *congruent* (kən grü′ənt *or* kong′grü ənt). The pronunciation (kən grü′ənt) is given first, not because it is more correct than (kong′grü ənt), but because it is used by more people. If you say (kong′grü ənt) however, you are just as correct as those people who say (kən grü′ənt).

Exercise 5 Write the word that each pronunciation represents. Use the pronunciation key below to help you.

1. (jī gan′tik)
2. (prə tekt′)
3. (hed′āk′)
4. (rek′tang′gəl)
5. (bāzh)
6. (jag′wär *or* jag′yü är)
7. (ab′sə lüt)
8. (jėr′nl)
9. (kon′shəs)
10. (ri krüt′)

a	hat	ī	ice	u̇	put	ə stands for	
ā	age	o	not	ü	rule	a	in about
ä	far, calm	ō	open	ch	child	e	in taken
âr	care	ȯ	saw	ng	long	i	in pencil
e	let	ô	order	sh	she	o	in lemon
ē	equal	oi	oil	th	thin	u	in circus
ėr	term	ou	out	ᴛʜ	then		
i	it	u	cup	zh	measure		

1. ___
2. ___
3. ___
4. ___
5. ___
6. ___
7. ___
8. ___
9. ___
10. ___

6. How do I find the correct spelling for a word that is not an entry word?

Sometimes when you add endings such as **-ed**, **-ing**, **-s**, and **-es** to words the spelling changes. These are not listed as entry words. To find the correct spellings of these forms, look up the base word and find the **related forms** in the entry.

Exercise 6 In your Spelling Dictionary, look up the base word of each misspelled related form. Write the related form correctly.

1. characterizeing
2. portfolioes
3. uglyness
4. paralysises
5. positivly
6. communitys

1. ___
2. ___
3. ___
4. ___
5. ___
6. ___

7. What if my dictionary lists two ways to spell a word?

Some words may be spelled in more than one way. Sometimes this is shown in a single entry, with the more common spelling first: *savanna* **or** *savannah.* Other times, different spellings are listed as separate entries, and the definition is given under the more common spelling:

judg▪ment (juj′mənt), *n.* **1** result of judging; opinion or estimate: *It was a bad plan in our judgment.* **2** ability to form sound opinions; power to judge well; good sense. **3** act of judging. **4** decision, decree, or sentence given by a judge or court. **6** decision made by anyone who judges. **7** criticism; condemnation: *pass judgment on one's neighbors.* **8** misfortune thought of as a punishment from God. Also, **judgement.**

judge▪ment (juj′mənt), *n.* judgment.

1. _____

2. _____

3. _____

4. _____

Exercise 7   Look up these words in your Spelling Dictionary. Write the more common spelling for each word.

1. détente, detente
2. fulfil, fulfill
3. Halloween, Hallowe'en
4. medallist, medalist

8. How do I find out where a word in our language came from originally?

An explanation of a word's origin is called an **etymology.** A word's etymology is usually found at the end of the entry, enclosed in brackets. Read this entry for *erode.*

> **e▪rode** (i rōd'), *v.,* **e rod ed, e rod ing.** —*v.t.* **1** eat or wear away gradually; eat into: *Running water erodes soil and rocks.* **2** form by a gradual eating or wearing away: *The stream eroded a channel in the solid rock.* —*v.i.* be worn away or eaten out. [< Latin *erodere* < *ex-* away + *rodere* gnaw]

1. _____

2. _____

3. _____

4. _____

5. _____

6. _____

7. _____

8. _____

Exercise 8   Use your Spelling Dictionary to find the etymologies of the following words. Write the language, languages, or other source each word came from.

1. yogurt
2. bagel
3. typhoon
4. coffee
5. reservoir
6. chimpanzee
7. tornado
8. pretzel

9. What else can I find in a dictionary entry?

Sometimes an entry is followed by a **synonym study.** These explain subtle differences between words that are closely related in meaning. Look at this entry for the word *motive:*

> **mo▪tive** (mō'tiv), —*n.* **1** thought or feeling that makes one act; moving consideration or reason; incentive: *My motive in taking the trip was a wish to travel.*
> **Syn.** *n.* **Motive, reason,** and **cause** mean that which makes something happen. **Motive** applies to the feeling or desire that makes a person do what he or she does: *His motive was to regain his health.* **Reason** applies to a ground or occasion that explains why something has happened: *The reason they went to Arizona was the climate.* **Cause** applies to a person, thing, incident, or condition that directly brings about an action or happening: *The cause of his new idea was his doctor's warning about the dangers of being overweight.*

Exercise 9   Use **motive, reason,** and **cause** each in a sentence to illustrate their differences in meaning.

1. _____

2. _____

3. _____

10. Why are there two different entries for some words?

These words are homographs. A **homograph** is a word that is spelled the same as another word but has a different origin and meaning. Look at the two entries for *rill*.

> **rill**[1] (ril), *n.* a tiny stream; a little brook. [< Dutch *ril* groove, furrow]
> **rill**[2] or **rille** (ril), *n.* a long, narrow valley on the surface of the moon. [< German *Rille* furrow]

If you look at the etymologies of the two words, you will see that rill[1] is originally from the Dutch word *ril* and rill[2] (or rille) is originally from the German word *Rille*.

Exercise 10   Use a dictionary to look up these homographs. Explain the differences in their origins and meanings. (Note: The word *cape* will be the only word with a complete homograph entry in your Spelling Dictionary.)

1. cape[1], cape[2]
2. keen[1], keen[2]
3. snare[1], snare[2]
4. loaf[1], loaf[2]
5. box[1], box[2], box[3]
6. gore[1], gore[2], gore[3]

1. _____

_____

2. _____

_____

3. _____

_____

4. _____

_____

5. _____

_____

6. _____

_____

Spelling Dictionary

Parts of a Dictionary Entry

2   **3**
↓   ↓

1 ⟶ **break** (brāk), *v.*, **broke, bro•ken,** ⟵ **4**
break•ing, *n.* —*v.t.* **1** make something ⟵ **5**
come to pieces by a blow or pull: *She
broke the fragile vase.* See synonym ⟵ **6**
study below. **2** damage; injure. **3 break** ⟵ **7**
with, stop being friends with. —*n.* **1** a
broken place; gap; crack. **2** a forceful
and sudden separation of parts. [Old ⟵ **8**
English *brecan*] —**break′a•ble,** *adj.* ⟵ **9**

10 →   **Syn.** *v.t.* **1** Break and **shatter** mean to
make something come or go to pieces.
Break means to divide something into
two or more pieces by pulling, hitting,
dropping, or striking it: *I broke the handle off a cup.* **Shatter** means to break
suddenly into a number of pieces that fly
in all directions: *I shattered the cup
when I dropped it on the floor.*

1 Entry word
2 Pronunciation
3 Part-of-speech label
4 Inflected forms
5 Definitions
6 Illustrative sentence
7 Idiom
8 Etymology
9 Run-on entry
10 Synonym study

Full Pronunciation Key

a	hat, cap	**i**	it, pin	**p**	paper, cup	**v**	very, save
ā	age, face	**ī**	ice, five	**r**	run, try	**w**	will, woman
ä	father, far			**s**	say, yes	**y**	young, yet
â	care, hair	**j**	jam, enjoy	**sh**	she, rush	**x**	zero, breeze
		k	kind, seek	**t**	tell, it	**zh**	measure
b	bad, rob	**l**	land, coal	**th**	thin, both		seizure
ch	child, much	**m**	me, am	**ŦH**	then, smooth		
d	did, red	**n**	no, in			**ə**	represents:
		ng	long, bring	**u**	cup, cutter		a in about
e	let, best			**u̇**	run, try		e in taken
ē	equal, be	**o**	hot, rock	**ü**	rule, move		i in pencil
ėr	term, learn	**ō**	open, go				o in lemon
		ȯ	all, saw				u in circus
f	fat, if	**ô**	order, store				
g	go, bag	**oi**	oil, voice				
h	he, how	**oi**	house, out				

Spellings of English Sounds*

Symbol	Spellings	Symbol	Spellings
a	at, plaid, half, laugh	ng	long, ink, handkerchief, tongue
ā	able, aid, say, age, eight, they, break, vein, gauge, crepe, beret	o	odd, honest
ä	father, ah, calm, heart, bazaar, yacht, sergeant	ō	open, oak, toe, own, home, oh, folk, though, bureau, sew, brooch, soul
âr	dare, aerial, fair, prayer, where, pear, their, they're	ȯ	all, author, awful, broad, bought, walk, taught, cough, Utah, Arkansas
b	bad, rabbit	ô	order, board, floor, tore
ch	child, watch, future, question	oi	oil, boy
d	did, add, filled	ou	out, owl, bough, hour
e	end, said, any, bread, says, heifer, leopard, friend, bury	p	pay, happy
		r	run, carry, wrong, rhythm
ē	equal, eat, eel, happy, cities, vehicle, ceiling, receive, key, these, believe, machine, liter, people	s	say, miss, cent, scent, dance, tense, sword, pizza, listen
		sh	she, machine, sure, ocean, special, tension, mission, nation
ėr	stern, earth, urge, first, word, journey	t	tell, button, two, Thomas, stopped, doubt, receipt, pizza
f	fat, effort, laugh, phrase	th	thin
g	go, egg, guest, ghost, league	TH	then, breathe
gz	example, exhaust	u	up, oven, trouble, does, flood
h	he, who, jai alai, Gila monster	u̇	full, good, wolf, should
hw	wheat	ü	food, junior, rule, blue, who, move, threw, soup, through, shoe, two, fruit, lieutenant
i	it, England, ear, hymn, been, sieve, women, busy, build, weird		
		v	very, have, of, Stephen
īf	I, ice, lie, sky, type, rye, eye, island, high, eider, aisle, height, buy, coyote	w	will, quick
		y	yes, opinion
		yü	use, few, cue, view, vacuum
j	jam, gem, exaggerate, schedule, badger, bridge, soldier, large, allegiance	z	zero, has, buzz, scissors, xylophone
		zh	measure, garage, division
k	coat, kind, back, echo, ache, quit, account, antique, excite, acquire	ə	alone, complete, moment, authority, bargain, April, cautious, circus, pageant, physician, oxygen, dungeon, tortoise
l	land, tell		
m	me, common, climb, solemn, palm		
n	no, manner, knife, gnaw, pneumonia		

*Not all English spellings of these sounds are included in this list.

A

ab·a·lo·ne (ab/ə lō/nē), *n.* an edible saltwater mollusk with a large, rather flat shell lined with mother-of-pearl, found along the Pacific coast of North America. [< Mexican Spanish *abulón* < Costanoan (an Amerind language of California) *aulun*]

a·ban·don (ə ban/dən), *v.t.* **1** give up entirely; renounce or relinquish: *abandon a career.* **2** leave without intending to return to: *Abandon ship!*

ab·bre·vi·a·tion (ə brē/vē ā/shən), *n.* **1** part of a word or phrase standing for the whole; shortened form: *"Dr." is an abbreviation of "Doctor."* **2** a making shorter; abridgment.

ab·duct (ab dukt/), *v.t.* **1** carry off (a person) by force or by trickery; kidnap. **2** pull (a part of the body) away from its normal position, as to raise an arm upward and outward. [< Latin *abductum* led away < *ab-* away + *ducere* to lead] **—ab·duc/tion,** *n.*

ab·nor·mal (ab nôr/məl), *adj.* away from the normal; deviating from the ordinary conditions, the standard, or a type; markedly irregular; exceptional. **—ab·nor/mal·ly,** *adv.*

ab·so·lute val·ue (ab/sə lüt val/yü), value of a real number regardless of any accompanying sign: *The absolute value of +5, or -5, is 5.*

ac·a·dem·ic (ak/ə dem/ik), *adj.* **1** of or having to do with schools, colleges, universities, and their studies; scholastic: *the academic year.* **2** concerned with general education, especially classical and literary studies, rather than commercial, technical, or professional education.

a·cad·e·my (ə kad/ə mē), *n., pl.* **-mies. 1** place for instruction. **2** a private high school. **3** school for instruction in some special subject: *a military academy.*

ac·cept·a·ble (ak sep/tə bəl), *adj.* **1** likely to be well received; agreeable; welcome. **2** good enough but not outstanding; satisfactory; passable: *an acceptable performance.*

ac·ces·si·ble (ak ses/ə bəl), *adj.* easy to reach, enter, or use; convenient or attainable: *A telephone should be put where it will be accessible.*

abandon (def. 2)
The house is
abandoned.

ac·ci·den·tal (ak/sə den/tl), *adj.* **1** happening by accident; not intended or expected: *an accidental meeting, an accidental death by drowning.* **2** nonessential; incidental. **—ac/ci·den/tal·ly,** *adv.*

ac·claim (ə klām/), *v.t.* welcome with shouts or other signs of approval; praise highly; applaud.

ac·cla·ma·tion (ak/lə mā/shən), *n.* shout of welcome or show of approval by a crowd; applause.

ac·com·mo·date (ə kom/ə dāt), *v.t.,* **-dat·ed, -dat·ing.** have room for; hold comfortably.

ac·com·pa·nist (ə kum/pə nist), *n.* person who plays a musical accompaniment.

ac·com·plice (ə kom/plis), *n.* person who knowingly aids another in committing a crime or other wrong act.

ac·com·plish·ment (ə kom/plish mənt), *n.* **1** something accomplished; completed undertaking; achievement. **2** skill in some social art or grace; acquirement. **3** an accomplishing; fulfillment; completion.

ac·count (ə kount/), *n.* **1** statement telling in detail about an event or thing; description or report: *Give me an account of everything that happened.* **2** statement of money received and spent.
on account of, because of.
on any account, under any conditions; for any reason.

ac·count·a·ble (ə koun/tə bəl), *adj.* **1** liable to be called to account; responsible: *accountable for one's work.* **2** explainable.

ac·count·ant (ə koun/tənt), *n.* person whose profession is examining or interpreting business accounts and financial records.

ac·id rain (as/id rān/), rain containing a dilute solution of sulfuric and nitric acid, created by pollutants emitted during the burning of fossil fuels.

ac·ne (ak/nē), *n.* a chronic skin disease in which the oil glands in the skin become clogged and inflamed, often causing pimples, especially on the face. [< Late Greek *aknē*]

ac·qui·esce (ak/wē es/), *v.i.,* **-esced, -esc·ing.** give consent by keeping silent or by not making objections; accept (the conclusions or arrangements of others); accede: *acquiesce in a decision.*

ac·qui·si·tion (ak′wə zish′ən), *n.*
1 act of acquiring: *the acquisition of skill by practicing.* **2** something acquired or gained; addition to an existing group. [< Latin *acquisitionem* < *acquirere*]

ac·quit·tal (ə kwit′l), *n.* an acquitting; discharge; release.

ac·ti·vate (ak′tə vāt), *v.t.*, **-vat·ed, -vat·ing. 1** make active; cause to act. **2** make radioactive. **3** make capable of reacting or of speeding up a chemical reaction.

a·dapt (ə dapt′), *v.t.* **1** make fit or suitable; adjust: *adapt one's way of working to the needs of the job.* **2** modify or alter so as to make fit or suitable for a different use or a particular place or purpose: *The story was adapted for the movies.* —*v.i.* be adjusted. [< Latin *adaptare* < *ad-* to + *aptus* fitted, suitable]

a·dapt·a·ble (ə dap′tə bəl), *adj.* easily changed or changing easily to fit different conditions; flexible.

ad·her·ent (ad hir′ənt), *n.* a faithful supporter or follower: *an adherent of the conservative party.*

ad·o·les·cence (ad′l es′ns), *n.* **1** growth from childhood to adulthood. **2** period or time of this growth; youth.

ad·o·les·cent (ad′l es′nt), *n., pl.* **ad·o·les·cents.** person growing up from childhood to adulthood, especially a person from about 12 to about 20 years of age.

a·dopt (ə dopt′), *v.t.* **1** take or use as one's own choice: *adopt an idea, adopt a new custom.* **2** take (a child of other parents), as approved by law, and bring up as one's own child.

a·dop·tion (ə dop′shən), *n.* **1** act of adopting: *the adoption of a new name.* **2** fact or condition of being adopted: *offer a child for adoption.*

a·dop·tive (ə dop′tiv), *adj.* adopted: *an adoptive son.*

ad·verse (ad′vėrs′, ad vėrs′), *adj.* unfriendly in purpose or effect; antagonistic; hostile.

ad·ver·tise (ad′vər tīz), *v.,* **-tised, -tis·ing.** —*v.t.* **1** give public notice of in a newspaper or magazine, on the radio or television, etc.; announce. **2** make known or recommend publicly (a product, service, etc.) by praising its good quality in order to create a demand or promote sales: *advertise automobiles.* —*v.i.* **1** ask by public notice (*for*): *advertise for a job.* **2** seek to sell products, etc., by advertising; issue advertising: *It pays to advertise.* [< Middle French *advertiss-*, a form of *advertir* make known < Latin *advertere*]

ad·vice (ad vīs′), *n.* opinion, suggestion, or recommendation as to what should be done; counsel.

ad·vis·a·ble (ad vī′zə bəl), *adj.* to be advised or recommended; wise; sensible; suitable.

ad·vise (ad vīz′), *v.,* **-vised, -vis·ing.** —*v.t.* **1** give advice to; counsel. **2** recommend as a remedy, policy, etc.: *My doctor advised complete rest.* **3** give information to; inform; tell. —*v.i.* give advice; recommend: *I do as you advise.*

ad·vi·sor·y (ad vī′zər ē), *adj.* having the power only to advise, not to determine or direct policy.

af·fect (ə fekt′), *v.t.* have an effect on; act on; influence or change.

af·fec·tion (ə fek′shən), *n.* feeling of warm liking and tender attachment; fondness; love.

af·ghan (af′gən, af′gan), *n.* blanket or shawl made of knitted or crocheted wool, nylon, etc.

a·grar·i·an (ə grer′ē ən), *adj.* **1** having to do with farming land, its use, or its ownership: *agrarian laws.* **2** agricultural.

air·craft (âr′kraft′), *n., pl.* **-craft.** machine for air navigation that is supported in air by its own buoyancy (such as a balloon) or by dynamic reaction of air particles to its surface (such as an airplane), or by reaction to a jet stream.

advertise (def. 2)
advertising a
restaurant's food

afghan
An **afghan** can keep
you warm on a cold day.

a	hat	**ī**	ice	**u̇**	put	**ə** stands for
ā	age	**o**	not	**ü**	rule	**a** in about
ä	far, calm	**ō**	open	**ch**	child	**e** in taken
âr	care	**ȯ**	saw	**ng**	long	**i** in pencil
e	let	**ô**	order	**sh**	she	**o** in lemon
ē	equal	**oi**	oil	**th**	thin	**u** in circus
ėr	term	**ou**	out	**ᴛʜ**	then	
i	it	**u**	cup	**zh**	measure	

al·ge·bra (al′jə brə), *n.* branch of mathematics that uses the operations of arithmetic in dealing with the relations and properties of quantities by the use of symbols and letters, negative numbers as well as ordinary numbers, and equations to solve problems involving a finite number of operations. $x + y = x^2$ is a way of stating, by algebra, that the sum of two numbers equals the square of one of them. [< Medieval Latin < Arabic *al-jabr*, literally, the reduction (of algebraic equations to their simplest terms)]

all-a·round (ȯl′ə round′), *adj.* not limited or specialized; useful in many ways.

al·ter·nate (*v.* ȯl′tər nāt, al′tər nāt; *adj.* ȯl′tər nit, al′tər nit), *v.,* **-nat·ed, -nat·ing,** *adj.* —*v.t.* arrange, do, or perform (two things) each after the other continuously: *alternate work and pleasure.* —*adj.* **1** placed or occurring by turns; first one and then the other: *a flag with alternate red and white stripes.* **2** every other: *The milkman comes on alternate days.*

al·ter·na·tive (ȯl tėr′nə tiv, al tėr′nə tiv), *n.* **1** choice from among two or more things: *She had the alternative of staying in college or going to work.* **2** one of the things to be chosen: *She chose the former alternative and stayed in college.*

a·lum·ni (ə lum′nī), *n.* pl. of **alumnus.**

a·lum·nus (ə lum′nəs), *n., pl.* **-ni.** a graduate or former student of a certain school, college, or university. [< Latin, foster son < *alere* nourish]

a·mass (ə mas′), *v.t.* **a·mass·es, a·massed, a·mass·ing.** heap together; pile up, especially for oneself; accumulate: *amass a fortune.* [< Old French *amasser* < *a-* to + *masse* mass]

a·mi·no (ə mē′nō), *adj.* of or containing the —NH₂ group combined with a nonacid radical.

a·mi·no ac·id (ə mē′nō as′id), *n., pl.* **a·mi·no ac·ids.** any of a number of complex organic compounds containing the amino group ($-NH_2$) and the carboxyl group ($-COOH$) combined with various other elements and groups. Amino acids link together in long chains to form proteins.

ante-bellum (def. 2)

the **ante-bellum**

plantation of Robert E.

Lee's mother

am·phib·i·an (am fib′ē ən), *n.* any of a class of cold-blooded vertebrates with moist, scaleless skin that, typically, lay eggs in water where the young hatch and go through a larval or tadpole stage, breathing by means of gills; the larval forms lose their gills and develop lungs for breathing and limbs. Frogs and toads belong to this class.

an·ces·tor (an′ses′tər), *n., pl.* **an·ces·tors. 1** person from whom one is descended, usually one more remote than a grandparent; forefather. **2** a forerunner; precursor. **3** the early form from which a species or group is descended. [< Old French *ancestre* < Latin *antecessor* < *antecedere* go before]

a·ne·mi·a (ə nē′mē ə), *n.* condition resulting from an insufficiency of hemoglobin or red blood cells or by a loss of blood, characterized by weakness, pallor, palpitation of the heart, and a tendency to fatigue. Also, **anaemia.** [< Greek *anaimia* < *an-* not + *haima* blood]

an·i·mism (an′ə miz′əm), *n.* belief that there are living souls in trees, stones, stars, etc.

an·ni·ver·sar·y (an′ə vėr′sər ē), *n., pl.* **-sar·ies,** *adj.* —*n.* **1** the yearly return of a special date. **2** celebration of the yearly return of a special date. —*adj.* having to do with an anniversary.

an·nu·al·ly (an′yü ə lē), *adv.* coming once a year.

an·o·rex·i·a ner·vo·sa (an′ə rek′sē ə nər vō′sə), condition in which a person chronically avoids food, usually caused by emotional problems and producing extreme thinness and even starvation.

an·te·bel·lum (an′ti bel′əm), *adj.* **1** before the war. **2** before the American Civil War. [< Latin *ante bellum* before the war]

an·te·ced·ent (an′tə sēd′nt), *n.* a previous thing or event; something happening before and leading up to another.

an·thro·pol·o·gy (an′thrə pol′ə jē), *n.* science or study of human beings, dealing especially with their fossil remains, physical characteristics, cultures, customs, and beliefs.

an·ti·bi·ot·ic (an′ti bī ot′ik), *n.* substance produced by a living organism, especially a bacterium or a fungus, that destroys or weakens harmful microorganisms. Penicillin is an antibiotic.

an·ti·bod·y (an′ti bod′ē), *n., pl.* **an·ti·bod·ies.** a protein substance produced in the blood or tissues that destroys or weakens bacteria or neutralizes poisons of organic origin. Antibodies are formed in response to specific antigens.

a·pol·o·gy (ə pol′ə jē), *n., pl.* **-gies.** words of regret for an offense or accident; expressing regret and asking pardon.

ap·pen·dix (ə pen′diks), *n., pl.* **-dix·es** or **-di·ces** (-di sēz). addition at the end of a book or document.

ap·pre·ci·ate (ə prē′she āt), *v.t.,* **-at·ed, -at·ing. 1** think highly of; recognize the worth or quality of; value. **2** be thankful for. **3** have an opinion of the value, worth, or quality of; estimate.

ap·pre·hen·sive (ap′ri hen′siv), *adj.* afraid that some misfortune is about to occur; anxious about the future; fearful.

ap·pren·tice (ə pren′tis), *n., v.,* **-ticed, -tic·ing. —n. 1** person learning a trade or art, especially one bound by a legal agreement to work for an employer for a certain length of time in return for instruction and, formerly, maintenance, but little or no pay. **2** beginner; learner. —*v.t.* bind or take as an apprentice. [< Old French *aprentis* < *aprendre* learn < Latin *apprehendere*]

ap·prox·i·mate (ə prok′sə mit), *adj.* nearly correct. [< Latin *approximatum* approached < *ad-* to + *proximus* nearest] —**ap·prox′i·mate·ly,** *adv.*

A·pril Fools' Day, April 1, a day on which tricks and jokes are played on people; All Fools' Day.

aq·ue·duct (ak′wə dukt), *n.* an artificial channel or large pipe for bringing water from a distance.

Ar·a·bic (ar′ə bik), *n.* the Semitic language of the Arabs, related to Hebrew. Arabic is now spoken chiefly in Arabia, Iraq, Syria, Jordan, Lebanon, and North Africa. —*adj.* of or having to do with the Arabs or their language.

ar·chi·tec·ture (är′kə tek′chər), *n.* **1** science or art of planning and designing buildings. **2** style or qualities that distinguish the buildings of one time, region, or group from those of another: *Greek architecture made much use of columns.*

ar·gue (är′gyü), *v.,* **ar·gued, ar·gu·ing. —v.i. 1** put forward reasons selected so as to support or refute a proposal, etc.; discuss (a point of view) with someone who disagrees. **2** bring forward reasons against anything; dispute. —*v.t.* **1** put forward reasons for or against (something): *argue a question.* **2** try to prove by reasoning. [< Old French *arguer* < Latin *argutare* to chatter < *arguere* make clear]

ar·gu·men·ta·tive (är′gyə men′tə tiv), *adj.* fond of arguing; quarrelsome.

ar·id (ar′id), *adj.* having very little rainfall; dry: *an arid climate.* [< Latin *aridus* < *arere* be dry] —**ar′id·ly,** *adv.* —**ar′id·ness,** *n.*

ar·raign (ə rān′), *v.t.* **1** bring before a court of law to answer an indictment. **2** call to account; find fault with; accuse. [< Anglo-French *arainer* < Old French *a-* to + *raisnier* speak] —**ar·raign′ment,** *n.*

ar·ro·gance (ar′ə gəns), *n.* excessive pride with contempt of others.

ar·thri·tis (är thrī′tis), *n.* inflammation of a joint or joints of the body. Gout is one kind of arthritis.

art·ist (är′tist), *n.* **1** person who paints pictures; painter. **2** person skilled in any of the fine arts, such as music.

as·ter·isk (as′tə risk′), *n.* a star-shaped mark (*) used in printing and writing to call attention to a footnote, indicate the omission of words or letters, etc. —*v.t.* mark with an asterisk. [< Greek *asteriskos,* diminutive of *astēr* star]

as·ter·oid (as′tə roid′), *n.* any of numerous minor planets which revolve about the sun, between the orbits of Mars and Jupiter.

aqueduct

modern **aqueducts**

located in Tasmania

arid

the **arid** land near

Tucson, Arizona

a	hat	**ī**	ice	**u̇**	put		**ə** stands for	
ā	age	**o**	not	**ü**	rule	**a**	in about	
ä	far, calm	**ō**	open	**ch**	child	**e**	in taken	
âr	care	**ȯ**	saw	**ng**	long	**i**	in pencil	
e	let	**ô**	order	**sh**	she	**o**	in lemon	
ē	equal	**oi**	oil	**th**	thin	**u**	in circus	
ėr	term	**ou**	out	**ŦH**	then			
i	it	**u**	cup	**zh**	measure			

asth·ma (az′mə), *n.* a chronic disease of respiration, characterized by intermittent paroxysms of breathing with a wheezing sound, a sense of constriction in the chest, and coughing. [< Greek]

as·trol·o·gy (ə strol′ə jē), *n.* study of the stars to foretell what will happen. [< Greek *astrologia* < *astron* star + *-logos* treating of]

as·tro·naut (as′trə nòt), *n.* pilot or member of the crew of a spacecraft. [< Greek *astron* star + *nautēs* sailor]

astronaut

astronauts completing

eight days of research

as·tron·o·mer (ə stron′ə mər), *n.* an expert in astronomy.

as·tro·nom·i·cal (as′trə nom′ə kəl), *adj.* **1** of or having to do with astronomy. **2** so large as to be beyond comprehension; enormous: *The government has astronomical expenses.*

as·tron·o·my (ə stron′ə mē), *n.* science that deals with the constitution, motions, relative positions, sizes, etc., of the sun, moon, planets, stars, and all other heavenly bodies, as well as with the earth in its relation to them. [< Greek *astronomia* < *astron* star + *nomos* distribution]

at·tend·ant (ə ten′dənt), *n.* **1** person who waits on another, such as a servant or follower. **2** employee who waits on customers. —*adj.* waiting on another to help or serve: *an attendant nurse.*

au·di·ble (ò′də bəl), *adj.* that can be heard; loud enough to be heard.

au·di·ence (ò′dē əns), *n.* **1** people gathered in a place to hear or see: *a theater audience.* **2** any persons within hearing: *a radio audience.*

au·di·o·vis·u·al (ò′dē ō vizh′ü əl), *adj.* of or having to do with both hearing and sight. Schools use motion pictures, slides, and recordings as audio-visual aids in teaching.

au·dit (ò′dit), *v.t.* **1** examine and check (business accounts) systematically and officially. **2** attend (a college class) as a listener without getting academic credit for the course. —*n.* a systematic and official examination and check of business accounts.

avocado (def. 1)

an **avocado** cut

into halves

au·di·tion (ò dish′ən), *n.* **1** a hearing to test the ability, quality, or performance of a singer, actor, or other performer. **2** act of hearing. **3** power or sense of hearing. —*v.i.* sing, act, or perform at an audition.

au·di·to·ri·um (ò′də tôr′ē əm, ò′də tōr′ē əm), *n., pl.* **-to·ri·ums, -to·ri·a** (-tôr′ē ə, -tōr′ē ə). **1** a large room for an audience in a church, theater, school, etc. **2** building especially designed for public meetings, lectures, concerts, etc.

au·ral (ôr′əl), *adj.* of, having to do with, or perceived by the ear. [< Latin *auris* ear] —**au′ral·ly**, *adv.*

au·thor·i·ty (ə thôr′ə tē, ə thòr′ə tē), *n., pl.* **-ties. 1** the right to control, command, or make decisions; power to enforce obedience; jurisdiction. **2** person, body, board, or the like having such power, right, or jurisdiction: *the Transit Authority.* **3** person whose advice or opinion is generally accepted in a particular field or subject; expert. **4** power over the action of others.

au·to·crat (ò′tə krat), *n.* **1** ruler who claims or exerts unrestricted power and uncontrolled authority. **2** person who rules with undisputed sway or supremacy in any group or sphere.

au·to·mo·bile (ò′tə mə bēl′, ò′tə mə bēl′), *n.* a four-wheeled passenger vehicle, for use on roads and streets, that is self-propelled by an internal-combustion engine. —*adj.* of or for automobiles: *an automobile mechanic.*

aux·il·iar·y (òg zil′yər ē, òg zil′ər ē), *adj., n., pl.* **-iar·ies.** —*adj.* **1** giving help or support; assisting: *The army was sent auxiliary troops.* **2** additional; subsidiary: *The main library has several auxiliary branches.* —*n.* a subsidiary group: *a men's club with a women's auxiliary.*

a·verse (ə vèrs′), *adj.* having a strong or fixed dislike; opposed or unwilling: *I am averse to fighting.*

av·o·ca·do (av′ə kä′dō, äv′ə kä′dō), *n., pl.* **av·o·ca·dos. 1** a usually pear-shaped tropical fruit with a dark-green to purplish-black skin and a very large seed. **2** tree that it grows on, of the same family as the laurel.

ax·is (ak′sis), *n., pl.* **ax·es** (ax ēz′). **1** a central or principal line around which parts are arranged symmetrically. The axis of a cone is the straight line joining its apex and the center of its base. **2** any line used for reference, such as the x-axis or the y-axis of a graph.

B

bach·e·lor (bach′ə lər), *n.* man who has not married.

bac·ter·i·a (bak tir′ē ə), *n.pl.* of **bacterium.** a large group of one-celled microorganisms that multiply by fission or by forming spores. Bacteria are classed as either monerans or protists. Certain species cause diseases such as pneumonia and typhoid fever. Others are concerned in such processes as fermentation, nitrogen fixation, etc. [< New Latin, plural of *bacterium* < Greek *baktērion,* diminutive of *baktron* rod]

bad·min·ton (bad′min tən), *n.* game somewhat like tennis but played with a shuttlecock instead of a ball, lighter rackets, and a higher net. [< *Badminton,* the Duke of Beaufort's estate in England, where the game was first played]

ba·gel (bā′gəl), *n.* a hard roll made of raised dough shaped into a ring, simmered in water, and then baked. [< Yiddish *beigel*]

ball-and-sock·et joint (bȯl′ən sok′it joint′), a flexible joint formed by a ball or knob fitting in a socket, such as hip joints, permitting motion in a rotary direction.

ban·dan·na or **ban·dan·a** (ban dan′ə), *n.* a large, gaily colored kerchief or handkerchief, often worn on the head or neck. [< Hindustani *bāndhnū* way of tying cloth so as to produce designs when dyed]

ban·gle (bang′gəl), *n.* **1** a small ornament suspended from a bracelet. **2** a bracelet or anklet without a clasp. [< Hindustani *bangrī* glass bracelet]

bank·rupt (bang′krupt), *n.* person who is declared by a court of law to be unable to pay his or her debts, and whose property is distributed among the people who are owed money. —*adj.* unable to pay one's debts; declared legally unable to pay.

bar mitz·vah (bär′ mits′və), **1** ceremony or celebration held when a Jewish boy becomes thirteen years old, to affirm that he has reached the age of religious responsibility. **2** the boy himself. [< Hebrew *bar miswah,* literally, son of the commandment]

bat mitz·vah (bät′ mits′və), **1** ceremony or celebration held, especially in a Reform or Conservative synagogue, when a Jewish girl becomes thirteen years old to affirm that she has reached the age of religious responsibility. **2** the girl herself. Also, **bas mitzvah.**

ba·tik (bə tēk′, bat′ik), *n.* method of executing designs on textiles by covering the material with wax in a pattern, dyeing the parts left exposed, and then removing the wax. [< Javanese *mbatik*]

bay·ou (bī′ü), *n.* a sluggish, marshy inlet or outlet of a lake, river, or gulf in the south central United States. [< Choctaw *bayuk* creek]

beau·te·ous (byü′tē əs), *adj.* beautiful. —**beau′te·ous·ly,** *adv.*

be·guile (bi gīl′), *v.t.,* **be·guiled, be·guil·ing. 1** trick or mislead (a person); deceive; delude: *Your flattery beguiled me into thinking that you were my friend.* **2** take away from deceitfully or cunningly. **3** win the attention of.

beige (bāzh), *adj.* pale-brown; brownish-gray. —*n.* a pale brown.

be·lieve (bi lēv′), *v.,* **-lieved, -liev·ing.** —*v.t.* **1** accept as true or real: *We all believe that the earth is round.* **2** think (somebody) tells the truth: *My friends believe me.* **3** think; suppose. —*v.i.* **1** have faith (in a person or thing); trust: *We believe in our friends.* **2** accept something as true or existing: *believe in ghosts.* **3** think; suppose.

ben·e·fit (ben′ə fit), *v.i.,* **ben·e·fit·ed, ben·e·fit·ing.** receive good; profit. —*n.* anything which is for the good of a person or thing; advantage. [< Anglo-French *benfet* < Latin *benefactum* good deed < *bene* well + *facere* do]

bagel
A **bagel** makes a good breakfast food.

batik
fabric dyed using **batik**

a	hat	**ī**	ice	**u̇**	put	**ə** stands for	
ā	age	**o**	not	**ü**	rule	**a**	in about
ä	far, calm	**ō**	open	**ch**	child	**e**	in taken
âr	care	**ȯ**	saw	**ng**	long	**i**	in pencil
e	let	**ô**	order	**sh**	she	**o**	in lemon
ē	equal	**oi**	oil	**th**	thin	**u**	in circus
ėr	term	**ou**	out	**ᴛʜ**	then		
i	it	**u**	cup	**zh**	measure		

bi·cen·ten·ni·al (bī′sen ten′ē əl), *adj.*
1 having to do with a period of 200
years or a 200th anniversary.
2 recurring every 200 years. —*n.* a
200th anniversary, celebration.

bi·ceps (bī′seps), *n., pl.* **-ceps** or
-ceps·es. any muscle having two
heads or origins: **a** the large muscle
in the front part of the upper arm,
which bends the forearm. **b** the
corresponding large muscle in
the back of the thigh.

bi·cul·tur·al (bī kul′chər əl), *adj.*
having two distinct cultures
existing side by side.

bi·cy·cle (bī′sik′əl, bī′sə kəl), *n., v.,*
-cled, -cling. —*n.* a lightweight
vehicle consisting of a metal frame
with two wheels, one behind the
other, a handlebar for steering, a
seat for the rider, and pedals.
—*v.i.* ride or travel on a bicycle.

bi·fo·cal (bī fō′kəl, bī′fo′kəl), *adj.*
having two focuses. Bifocal lenses
have two sections of different focal
lengths, the upper for distant, the
lower for near vision. —*n.* **bifocals,**
pl. glasses having bifocal lenses.

bile (bīl), *n.* a bitter, greenish-yellow
liquid secreted by the liver and
stored in the gall bladder. It aids
digestion in the duodenum.
[< French < Latin *bilem*]

bi·lin·gual (bī ling′gwəl), *adj.* **1** able
to speak another language as well
or almost as well as one's own.
2 containing or written in two
languages. —*n.* a bilingual person.

bi·noc·u·lars (bə nok′yə lərz, bī
nok′yə lərz), *n.pl.* a double
telescope joined as a unit for use
with both eyes simultaneously,
such as field glasses and opera
glasses.

bi·ol·o·gy (bī ol′ə jē), *n.* the scientific
study of living organisms, including
their origins, structures, activities,
and distribution. Botany and
ecology are branches of biology.

bi·o·sphere (bī′ə sfir), *n.* the region
on and surrounding the earth that
can support life, including the
atmosphere, water, and soil.

bis·cuit (bis′kit), *n., pl.* **-cuits** or **-cuit,**
adj. —*n.* a kind of bread leavened
with baking powder, soda, or yeast
and baked in small, round forms.

bi·week·ly (bī wēk′lē), *adj., adv., n.,*
pl. **-lies.** —*adj.* **1** happening once
every two weeks. **2** happening
twice a week; semiweekly. —*adv.*
1 once every two weeks. **2** twice
a week. —*n.* newspaper or other
periodical published biweekly.

bone

the **bones** of a hand
and arm

bi·zarre (bə zär′), *adj.* strikingly odd
in appearance or style; fantastic;
grotesque. [< French < Spanish
bizarro brave < Italian *bizzarro*
angry < *bizza* anger]
—**bi·zarre′ly,** *adv.*
—**bi·zarre′ness,** *n.*

black (blak), *adj.* **1** reflecting little or
no light; having the color of coal:
This print is black. **2** Also, **Black.**
having dark skin, eyes, and hair;
having to do with or belonging to
Negroes; Negro. **3** without any
light; very dark. **4** dirty; grimy:
hands black with soot. —*n.* **1** the
darkest color; color of coal. **2** a
black paint, dye, or pigment. Also,
Black. person belonging to a dark-
skinned ethnic group; Negro. —*v.t.*
make black; blacken. —*v.i.*
blackout, a become temporarily
blind or unconscious. **b** darken
completely.

blood pres·sure (blud′ presh′ər),
pressure of the blood against the
inner walls of the arteries, varying
with the strength of the heartbeat,
exertion, excitement, health, age.

blue (blü), *n., adj.,* **blu·er, blu·est,** *v.,*
blued, blu·ing or **blue·ing.** —*n.*
1 the color of the clear sky in
daylight, lying in the color
spectrum between green and
violet. **2** a lighter or darker shade
of this color. **3** a blue pigment or
dye. **4 the blue, a** the sky. **b** the
sea. **5 out of the blue,** from an
unforeseen source; from an
unknown place; completely
unexpectedly. —*adj.* **1** having the
color of the clear sky in daylight
or any variation of this color.
2 having a dull-bluish color; livid:
blue from cold. **3** in low spirits;
sad; gloomy. **4** strict in morals or
religion; puritanical. —*v.t.* **1** make
blue. **2** use bluing on. [< Old
French *bleu*] —**blue′ness,** *n.*

bone (bōn), *n., v.,* **boned, bon·ing,** *adj.*
—*n.* **1** one of the distinct pieces
making up the skeleton of a
vertebrate animal. **2** the hard
tissue forming the substance of the
skeleton. **3** any of various similar
animal substances, as the dentin
of teeth, ivory, or baleen. **4** a pale
beige. **5 feel in one's bones** or **know
in one's bones,** be sure without
knowing why. **6 have a bone to
pick,** have cause for argument or
complaint. —*v.t.* take bones out of:
bone fish. —*v.i.* SLANG. study hard.
—*adj.* pale-beige. [Old English
bān] —**bone′like′,** *adj.*

book·shelf (bùk′shelf′), *n., pl.*
book·shelves (-shelvz). shelf for
holding books.

book·worm (bùk′wèrm′), *n.* **1** person
who is very fond of reading and
studying. **2** any insect larva that
feeds on the bindings or leaves of
books.

boo·me·rang (bü′mə rang′), *n., pl.*
boo·me·rangs. 1 a curved, rather
flat piece of hard wood used as a
weapon. One kind, made and
used by Australian aborigines, can
be thrown so as to curve in flight
and return to the thrower. **2** anything that recoils or reacts to harm
the doer or user. —*v.i.* act as a
boomerang. [< native dialect of
New South Wales]

boul·e·vard (bùl′ə värd, bü′lə värd),
n. a broad street or avenue, often
planted with trees.

bound·ar·y (boun′dər ē), *n., pl.*
bound·ar·ies. a limiting line or
thing; limit; border: *the boundary
between Canada and the United
States.*

brav·er·y (brā′vər ē), *n., pl.* **-er·ies.**
1 quality of being brave;
fearlessness; boldness. **2** fine
clothes; finery.

brib·er·y (brī′bər ē), *n., pl.* **-er·ies.**
1 the giving or offering of a bribe.
2 the taking of a tribe.

brief·case (brēf′kās′), *n.* a flat
container of leather or the like
for carrying loose papers, books,
drawings, etc., without folding.

bro·chure (brō shùr′), *n.* pamphlet.
[< French]

bronze (bronz), *n., adj.,* —*n.* **1** a brown
metal, an alloy of copper and tin.
2 a similar alloy of copper with zinc
or other metals. **3** a yellowish
brown or reddish brown. —*adj.*
1 made of bronze. **2** yellowish-
brown or reddish-brown. [< Middle
French < Italian *bronzo* bell metal]

broth·er-in-law (bruŦH′ər in lò′), *n., pl.*
broth·ers-in-law. 1 brother of one's
husband or wife. **2** husband of
one's sister. **3** husband of the sister
of one's wife or husband.

Bud·dhism (bü′diz əm, bùd′iz əm), *n.*
religion based on the teachings of
Buddha, which maintain that right
living will let people attain a state
free from all desire and pain.

bug (bug), *n., v.,* **bugged, bug·ging.**
—*n.* **1** any of an order of insects,
which are wingless or have a front
pair of wings thickened at the
base, and have a pointed beak for
piercing and sucking. **2** any insect
or other invertebrate somewhat like
a true bug. Ants, spiders, beetles,
and flies are often called bugs.
3 INFORMAL. a disease germ or
microbe: *the flu bug.* **4** a problem
in a computer. —*v.t.* **1** hide a small
microphone in (a room, telephone,
etc.). **2** SLANG. annoy; irritate.

bu·lim·i·a (byü lim′ē ə), *n.* an eating
disorder characterized by food
binges followed by forced
vomiting. [< New Latin < Greek
boulimia extreme hunger < *bous*
ox, cow + *limos* hunger]

bul·le·tin (bùl′ə tən), *n.* **1** a short
statement or account of late news
or events, issued for the information
of the public, especially by an
authority: *a weather bulletin.*
2 magazine or newspaper
appearing regularly, especially
one published by a club or society.
[< Middle French < Italian
bullettino, diminutive of *bulla* bull]

brochure
brochures from
historical sites

c

cab·ri·o·let (kab′rē ə lā′), *n.*
1 formerly, an automobile
resembling a coupe, but having
a convertible top. **2** a light,
one-horse, two-wheeled carriage.
[< French < *cabrioler* to caper]

cab·i·net (kab′ə nit), *n.* **1** piece of
furniture with shelves or drawers
to hold articles for use or display:
*a supply cabinet, a filing cabinet,
a china cabinet.* **2** Also, **Cabinet.**
group of advisers chosen by the
head of a government to aid in
administration. [< Middle French]

bronze (*adj.* def. 1)
a **bronze** statue of
Thomas Jefferson

a	hat	**ī**	ice	**ù**	put	**ə** stands for	
ā	age	**o**	not	**ü**	rule	**a**	in about
ä	far, calm	**ō**	open	**ch**	child	**e**	in taken
âr	care	**ȯ**	saw	**ng**	long	**i**	in pencil
e	let	**ô**	order	**sh**	she	**o**	in lemon
ē	equal	**oi**	oil	**th**	thin	**u**	in circus
ėr	term	**ou**	out	**ŦH**	then		
i	it	**u**	cup	**zh**	measure		

caf·e·ter·i·a (kaf′ə tir′ē ə), *n.* restaurant where people wait on themselves. [< Mexican Spanish *cafeteria* coffee shop < *café* coffee]

cal·cu·la·tor (kal′kyə lā′tər), *n.* machine that calculates, especially one that solves difficult problems in calculation.

Cal·cut·ta (kal kut′ə), *n.* seaport in E. India, near the Bay of Bengal. It was formerly the capital of India. 3,149,000. —**Cal·cut′tan,** *adj., n.*

cal·lig·ra·phy (kə lig′rə fē), *n.* 1 handwriting. 2 beautiful handwriting. [< Greek *kalligraphia* < *kallos* beauty + *graphein* write]

cal·or·ie (kal′ər ē), *n., pl.* **cal·or·ies.** 1 the quantity of heat energy necessary to raise the temperature of a gram of water one degree Celsius; small calorie. 2 Also, **Calorie.** unit of energy equal to 1000 calories; kilocalorie.

calf (kaf), *n., pl.* **calves.** 1 a young cow or bull. 2 a young elephant, whale, deer, seal, etc.

ca·ma·ra·der·ie (kä′mə rä′dər ē), *n.* friendliness and loyalty among comrades; comradeship. [< French]

Can·ber·ra (kan′ber ə, kan′bər ə), *n.* capital of Australia, in the SE part. 166,000.

can·di·date (kan′də dāt, kan′də dit), *n.* 1 person who seeks, or is proposed for, some office or honor: *There are three candidates for president of the club.* 2 person who is studying for a degree: *a doctoral candidate.* 3 person applying for a position: *There were twenty candidates for the job.*

cape[1] (kāp), *n.* an outer garment, or part of one, without sleeves, worn falling loosely from the shoulders and often fastened at the neck. [< French < Spanish *capa* < Late Latin *cappa* cap, hood]

cape[2] (kāp), *n.* point of land extending into the water. [< Old French *cap* < Provençal < Latin *caput* head]

cap·i·tal (kap′ə tel), *n.* 1 city where the government of a country, state, or province is located. 2 capital letter. [< Latin *capitalem* chief; punishable by death < *caput* head]

Cap·i·tol (kap′ə tel), *n.* 1 the building at Washington, D.C., in which Congress meets. 2 Also, **capitol.** the building in which a state legislature meets.

cap·tain (kap′tən), *n.* 1 head of a group; leader or chief: *Robin Hood was captain of his band.* 2 commander of a ship. 3 an army, air force, or marine officer ranking next below a major and next above a first lieutenant. 4 a navy officer ranking next below a rear admiral and next above a commander. 5 a police or fire department officer ranking next above a lieutenant. 6 leader of a team in sports. [< Old French *capitaine* < Late Latin *capitaneus* chief < Latin *caput* head]

car·a·van (kar′ə van), *n. pl.* **car·a·vans.** 1 group of merchants, pilgrims, etc., traveling together for safety through difficult or dangerous country. 2 the vehicles or beasts of burden used by such a group. 3 a closed truck or van. [< Old French *caravane* < Persian *kārwān*]

car·bon mo·nox·ide (kär′bən mo nok′sīd), a colorless, odorless, very poisonous gas, formed when carbon burns with an insufficient supply of air. *Formula:* CO

car·di·gan (kär′də gən), *n.* a knitted jacket or sweater that buttons down the front. [< Earl of *Cardigan,* 1797–1868, British general]

ca·reer (kə rir′), *n.* 1 a general course of action or progress through life: *It is interesting to read of the careers of great men and women.* 2 way of living; occupation; profession: *She planned to make law her career.* —*adj.* following a certain occupation or profession through-out life: *a career diplomat.* [< Middle French *carrière* racecourse < Latin *carrus* wagon]

car·go (kär′gō), *n., pl.* **car·goes** or **car·gos.** load of goods carried on a ship or aircraft; freight.

car·i·bou (kar′ə bü), *n., pl.* **-bous** or **-bou.** the reindeer of northern regions of the New World and Siberia. [< Canadian French; of Algonquian origin]

car·ti·lage (kär′tl ij), *n.* 1 a tough, elastic substance forming parts of the skeleton of vertebrates; gristle. Cartilage is more flexible than bone and not as hard. The external ear consists of cartilage and skin. 2 part formed of this substance. [< Latin *cartilago*]

car·tog·ra·pher (kär tog′rə fər), *n. pl.* **car·tog·ra·phers.** maker of maps or charts.

cafeteria

selecting a meal in the

cafeteria

caste (kast), *n.* **1** one of the social classes into which Hindus are divided. By tradition, a Hindu is born into a caste and cannot rise above it. **2** an exclusive social group; distinct class. **3** a social system having distinct classes separated by differences of birth, rank, wealth, or position. **4** the position which caste confers: *renounce caste.* [< Portuguese *casta* race, class, animal species < Latin *castus* pure, chaste]

cat·e·go·ry (kat′ə gȯr′ē, kat′ə gōr′ē), *n., pl.* **-ries.** group or division in a general system of classification; class: *She places all people into two categories: those she likes and those she dislikes.*

cause (kȯz), *n.* **1** whatever produces an effect; person, thing, or event that makes something happen: *The flood was the cause of much damage.* **2** reason or occasion for action; ground; motive: *cause for celebration.* See **reason** for synonym study. **3** good reason; reason enough: *He was angry without cause.*

cau·tion (kȯ′shən), *n.* **1** great care; regard for safety; unwillingness to take chances; prudence: *Use caution in crossing streets.* **2** a warning: *A sign with "Danger" on it is a caution.* —*v.t.* urge to be careful; warn. [< Latin *cautionem* < *cavere* beware]

cel·e·brate (sel′ə brāt), *v.,* **-brat·ed, -brat·ing.** —*v.t.* **1** observe (a special time or day) with the proper ceremonies or festivities: *We celebrated my birthday with a party.* **2** perform publicly with the proper ceremonies and rites: *The priest celebrates Mass in church.* —*v.i.* **1** observe a festival or event with ceremonies or festivities: *On my birthday I was too sick to celebrate.* **2** INFORMAL. have a good time. [< Latin *celebratum* observed by many < *celeber* frequented, crowded] —**cel′e·bra′tor,** *n.,* —**cel′e·bra·tor′y** (sel′ə brə tôr′ē), *adj.*

cell (sel), *n.* **1** a small room in a prison, convent, or monastery. **2** the basic unit of living matter, of which all plants, animals, etc., are made. Cells are generally microscopic, contain a central nucleus with chromosomes surrounded by cytoplasm, and are enclosed by a cell wall or cell membrane. [< Latin *cella* small room]

cell mem·brane (sel′ mem′brān), the thin membrane that forms the outer surface of the protoplasm of a cell.

cem·e·ter·y (sem′ə ter′ē), *n., pl.* **-ter·ies.** place for burying the dead; graveyard. [< Latin *coemeterium* < Greek *koimeterion,* originally, sleeping place < *koiman* lull to sleep]

cen·te·nar·i·an (sen′tə ner′ē ən), *n.* person who is 100 years old or more.

cen·ten·ni·al (sen ten′ē əl), *n.* a 100th anniversary.

cen·ti·gram (sen′tə gram), *n.* unit of mass equal to 1/100 of a gram.

cen·ti·li·ter (sen′tə lē′tər), *n.* unit of volume equal to 1/100 of a liter.

cer·tain·ty (sėrt′n tē), *n., pl.* **-ties. 1** a being certain; freedom from doubt. **2** something certain; a sure fact.

chain re·ac·tion (chān′ rē ak′shən), **1** a self-sustaining nuclear reaction occurring when a fissionable nucleus absorbs a neutron and splits, releasing atomic energy and additional neutrons. These neutrons split other fissionable nuclei releasing more energy and more neutrons. **2** any series of events or happenings, each caused by the preceding one or ones.

chal·lenge (chal′ənj), *n., pl.* **chal·leng·es. 1** a call to a game or contest. **2** anything that claims or commands effort, interest, feeling, etc. [< Old French *chalenger* < Latin *calumniari* to slander < *calumnia* false accusation]

cha·me·le·on (kə mē′lē ən, kə mē′lyən), *n.* **1** a small lizard that can change the color of its skin to blend with the surroundings. **2** a changeable or fickle person.

cemetery
a Japanese **cemetery**

a	hat	ī	ice	u̇	put	ə stands for	
ā	age	o	not	ü	rule	a	in about
ä	far, calm	ō	open	ch	child	e	in taken
âr	care	ȯ	saw	ng	long	i	in pencil
e	let	ô	order	sh	she	o	in lemon
ē	equal	oi	oil	th	thin	u	in circus
ėr	term	ou	out	ᴛʜ	then		
i	it	u	cup	zh	measure		

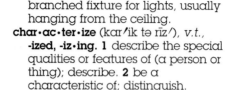

chan·de·lier (shan'də lir'), *n.* a branched fixture for lights, usually hanging from the ceiling.

char·ac·ter·ize (kar'ik tə rīz'), *v.t.,* **-ized, -iz·ing. 1** describe the special qualities or features of (a person or thing); describe. **2** be a characteristic of; distinguish. **3** give character to.

chauf·feur (shō'fər, shō fèr'), *n.* person whose work is driving an automobile, usually as the employee of a private person or company. —*v.t.* act as a chauffeur to; drive around. [< French, literally, stoker < *chauffer* to heat; the term arose in the days of steam automobiles]

chef (shef), *n. pl.* **chefs. 1** a head cook. **2** any cook.

chem·ist (kem'ist), *n.* **1** an expert in chemistry. **2** BRITISH. druggist.

chim·pan·zee (chim'pan zē', chim pan'zē), *n.* an anthropoid ape of equatorial Africa, smaller than a gorilla and the most intelligent. [< Bantu (Angolan dialect) (*kivili*)-*chimpenze* ape]

choc·o·late (chók'lit, chók'ə lit; chok'lit, chok'ə lit), *n.* **1** substance made by roasting and grinding cacao seeds. **2** drink made of chocolate with hot milk or water and sugar. **3** candy made of chocolate. **4** a dark brown. —*adj.* **1** made of or flavored with chocolate. **2** dark-brown. [< Mexican Spanish < Nahuatl *chocolatl*]

chris·ten·ing (kris'n ing), *n.* act or ceremony of baptizing and naming: baptism.

Chris·ti·an·i·ty (kris'chē an'ə tē), *n.* the religion based on the teachings of Christ as they appear in the Bible; Christian religion.

Christ·mas (kris'məs), *n.* **1** the yearly celebration of the birth of Christ; Dec. 25. **2** season of Christmas.

chron·o·graph (kron'ə graf), *n.* instrument for measuring very short intervals of time, such as a stop watch.

chron·o·log·i·cal (kron'ə loj'ə kəl), *adj.* arranged in order of time.

cin·na·mon (sin'ə mən), *n.* **1** spice made from the dried, reddish-brown inner bark of a laurel tree of the East Indies. **2** this bark. **3** tree yielding this bark. **4** a light, reddish brown. —*adj.* **1** flavored with cinnamon. **2** light reddish-brown. [< Latin < Greek *kinnamon*; of Semitic origin]

chef (def. 1)

The **chef** is preparing a large meal.

cir·cum·nav·i·gate (sėr'kəm nav'ə gāt), *v.t.,* **-gat·ed, -gat·ing.** sail around: *Magellan's ship circumnavigated the earth.* —**cir'cum·nav'i·ga'tor,** *n.*

ci·ta·tion (sī tā'shən), *n.* **1** quotation or reference given as an authority for facts or opinions. **2** act of citing. **3** honorable mention for bravery in war. **4** specific mention in an official dispatch. **5** commendation of a civilian for public service by some official or institution. **6** summons to appear in court.

ci·vil·ian (sə vil'yən), *n.* person who is not in the armed forces. —*adj.* of civilians; not of the armed forces.

civ·i·lize (siv'ə līz), *v.t.,* **-lized, -liz·ing. 1** change from a primitive way of life; train in culture, science, and art: *The Romans civilized a great part of their world.* **2** improve in culture and good manners; refine.

class (klas), *n.* **1** group of persons or things alike in some way; kind; sort. **2** group of students taught together: *an art class.* **3** a meeting of such a group. **4** rank or division of society: *the middle class.* **5** system of ranks or divisions in society. **6** high rank in society. **7** grade or quality. **8** (in biology) a primary group of related organisms ranking below a phylum or division and above an order. —*v.t.* put in a class or group; classify. —*v.i.* be in a class or group. [< Latin *classis* class, collection]

clas·si·fi·ca·tion (klas'ə fə kā'shən), *n.* **1** act or process of arranging in classes or groups; grouping according to some system. **2** result of classifying; a systematic arrangement in groups or classes.

co·coa (kō'kō), *n.* **1** powder made by roasting, grinding, and removing some fat from the kernels of cacao seeds. **2** drink made of this powder with milk or water and sugar. **3** the plant itself. **4** a dull-brown color, lighter than chocolate. [variant of Spanish *cacao*]

cof·fee (kó'fē, kof'ē), *n.* **1** a dark-brown drink made from the roasted and ground seeds of a tall, tropical evergreen shrub of the same family as the madder. **2** coffee beans. **3** the plant itself. **4** the color of coffee; a dark brown, darker than chocolate. [< Italian *caffè*]

col·lide (kə līd′), *v.,* **-lid·ed, -lid·ing.**
—*v.i.* **1** come violently into contact; come together with force; crash: *Two large ships collided in the harbor.* **2** clash; conflict. —*v.t.* bring violently into contact; smash together: *The stunt drivers collided their cars.* [< Latin *collidere* < *com-* together + *laedere* strike]

col·li·sion (kə lizh′ən), *n.* **1** a violent rushing against; hitting or striking violently together; crash. **2** clash; conflict. [< Late Latin *collisionem* < Latin *collidere* collide]

co·logne (kə lōn′), *n.* a fragrant liquid, not so strong as perfume. [< French *(eau de) Cologne* (water of) Cologne]

com·bi·na·tion (kom′bə nā′shən), *n.* **1** a combining or a being combined; union. **2** thing made by combining; set of things combined together. **3** series of numbers or letters dialed in opening or closing a combination lock: *the combination of a safe.* **4** in mathematics: **a** arrangement of individual items in groups so that each group has a certain number of items. **b** the groups thus formed. Possible two-letter combinations of *a, b,* and *c* are *ab, ac,* and *bc.*

com·bine (kəm bīn′) *v.t.* **-bined, -bin·ing.** join together; unite: *combine forces.*

co·me·di·an (kə mē′dē ən), *n.* **1** actor in comedies; actor of comic parts. **2** person who amuses others with funny talk and actions.

com·mem·o·ra·tion (kə mem′ə rā′shən), *n.* **1** act of commemorating. **2** service or celebration in memory of some person or event.

com·mis·sar·y (kom′ə ser′ē), *n., pl.* **-sar·ies. 1** store handling food and supplies in a mining camp, lumber camp, army camp, etc. **2** deputy; representative. [< Medieval Latin *commissarius* < Latin *committere* commit]

com·mit·ment (kə mit′mənt), *n.* **1** a committing. **2** a pledge; promise.

com·mit (kə mit′), *v.t.,* **com·mit·ted, com·mit·ting. 1** do or perform (usually something wrong): *commit a crime.* **2** hand over for safekeeping; deliver. **3** send to prison or an asylum. **4** give over; carry over; transfer: *commit a poem to memory.* **5** reveal (one's opinion). **6** involve; pledge. [< Latin *committere* < *com-* with + *mittere* send, put]

com·mon name (kom′ən nām′), word or words by which a person, animal, place, or thing is ordinarily known. Animals have scientific names and common names.

com·mo·tion (kə mō′shən), *n.* **1** violent movement; agitation; turbulence: *the commotion of the storm.* **2** bustle or stir; confusion.

com·mu·ni·ca·tion (kə myü′nə kā′shən), *n.* **1** a giving or exchanging of information or news by speaking, writing, etc.: *People who are deaf often use sign language as a means of communication.* **2** information or news given in this way. **3** letter, message, etc., which gives information or news.

com·mu·ni·ty (kə myü′nə tē), *n., pl.* **com·mu·ni·ties. 1** all the people living in the same place and subject to the same laws: *The three communities' efforts to combine their recreational activities was very successful.* **2** all of the animals, plants, and other organisms sharing a common environment.

com·mute (kə myüt′), *v.,* **-mut·ed, -mut·ing,** *n.* —*v.t.* **1** exchange; substitute. **2** change (an obligation, penalty, etc.) to a less severe one: *The governor commuted the prisoner's sentence.* —*v.i.* travel regularly to and from work especially between suburb and downtown. —*n.* the distance or trip ordinarily traveled by a commuter: *a long commute.* [< Latin *commutare* < *com-* + *mutare* to change] —**com·mut′a·ble,** *adj.*

commotion (def. 2)
The collapse of the bookshelf caused a **commotion.**

a	hat	**ī**	ice	**u̇**	put	**ə** stands for	
ā	age	**o**	not	**ü**	rule	**a**	in about
ä	far, calm	**ō**	open	**ch**	child	**e**	in taken
âr	care	**ȯ**	saw	**ng**	long	**i**	in pencil
e	let	**ô**	order	**sh**	she	**o**	in lemon
ē	equal	**oi**	oil	**th**	thin	**u**	in circus
ėr	term	**ou**	out	**ᵀH**	then		
i	it	**u**	cup	**zh**	measure		

competition (def. 2)

men racing in a

competition

com·pan·ion (kəm pan′yən), *n.*
1 person who goes along with another; person who shares in what another is doing. **2** person paid to live or travel with another as a friend and helper. **3** anything that matches or goes with another in kind, size, color, etc. [< Old French *compaignon* < Late Latin *companionem* < Latin *com-* together + *panis* bread]

com·pare (kəm pâr′), *v.,* **-pared, -par·ing,** *n.* —*v.t.* **1** find out or point out how persons or things are alike and how they differ: *I compared the two books to see which one had the better pictures.* **2** consider as similar; liken: *The fins of a fish may be compared to the wings of a bird; both are used in moving.* **3** change the form of (an adjective or adverb) to show the comparative, and superlative degrees; name the positive, comparative, and superlative degrees of. —*v.i.* be considered like or equal; be compared: *Canned fruit can't compare with fresh fruit.* —*n.* [< French *comparer* < Latin *comparare* < *com-* with + *par* equal]

com·par·i·son (kəm par′ə sən), *n.*
1 act or process of comparing; finding the likenesses and differences. **2** likeness; similarity.

com·pe·ti·tion (kom′pə tish′ən), *n.*
1 effort to obtain something wanted by others; rivalry: *competition among businesses.* **2** contest.

com·pet·i·tive (kəm pet′ə tiv), *adj.*
of competition; having or based on competition; decided by competition.

com·pile (kəm pīl′), *v.t.,* **-piled, -pil·ing. 1** collect and gather together in one list or account. **2** make (a book, a report, etc.) out of various materials. [< Latin *compilare* pile up < *com-* together + *pilare* press]

com·ple·ment (kom′plə mənt), *n.*
1 something that completes or makes perfect. **2** number required to fill: *The plane had its full complement of passengers; all seats were taken.* **3** word or group of words completing a predicate. In "The man is good," *good* is a complement. **4** amount needed to make an angle or an arc equal to 90 degrees. **5** (in mathematics) those members of a set that do not belong to a subset.

com·ple·men·tar·y (kom′plə men′ tər ē), *adj.* forming a complement; completing: *The four seasons are complementary parts of a year.*

com·plete (kəm plēt′), *adj.,* **1** with all the parts; whole; entire: *a complete set of Dickens's novels.* **2** perfect: thorough: *a complete surprise.* **3** finished: done: *My homework is complete.* —**com·plete′ly,** *adv.*

com·pli·ment (kom′plə mənt), *n.*
1 something good said about one; something said in praise of one's work, etc. **2** a courteous act.

com·pli·men·tar·y (kom′plə men′ tər ē), *adj.* **1** like or containing a compli-ment; praising. **2** given free: *a complimentary ticket.*

com·pro·mise (kom′prə mīz), *v.,* **-mised, -mis·ing,** *n.* —*v.t.* settle (a dispute) by agreeing that each will give up a part of what he or she demands. —*v.i.* make a compromise. —*n.* **1** settlement of a dispute by a partial yielding on both sides. **2** anything halfway between two different things.

con·ceit·ed (kən sē′tid), *adj.* having too high an opinion of oneself or one's ability or importance; vain.

con·cen·trate (kon′sən trāt), *v.,* **-trat·ed, -trat·ing,** —*v.t.* **1** bring together in one place: *A convex lens is used to concentrate rays of light.* **2** make stronger; intensify: *We concentrated the acid solution by adding more acid to it.* **3** re-move rock, sand, etc., from (metal or ore). —*v.i.* **1** come together in one place. **2** pay close attention; focus the mind (on or upon): *She concentrated upon the problem.*

con·cen·tra·tion (kon′sən trā′shən), *n.* **1** a concentrating. **2** a being concentrated. **3** close attention: *He gave the problem his full concentration.* **4** amount of substance contained in a given quantity of a solution or mixture.

con·ces·sion (kən sesh′ən), *n.* **1** a conceding; granting; yielding. **2** anything conceded or yielded; admission; acknowledgment.

con·cord (kon′kôrd, kong′kôrd), *n.* agreement; harmony.

con·di·tion·er (kən dish′ə nər), *n.*
1 device or substance that maintains or improves the quality of something. **2** air conditioner.

con·do·min·i·um (kon′də min′ē əm), *n.* apartment house in which each apartment is purchased as a piece of real estate and separately valued for property tax purposes.

concentrate (*v.i.,* def. 2)

trying to **concentrate**

at his desk

con·duc·tor (kən duk′tər), *n.* **1** person who conducts; leader or guide; director; manager. **2** director of an orchestra, chorus, etc. **3** person in charge of a railroad train, bus, etc.

con·fec·tion·er·y (kən fek′shə ner′ē), *n., pl.* **-er·ies. 1** candies or sweets; confections. **2** business of making or selling confections. **3** place where confections, ice cream, cakes, etc., are made or sold.

con·fet·ti (kən fet′ē), *n.* bits of colored paper thrown about at carnivals, weddings, parades, etc. [< Italian, plural, bonbons, candies, ultimately < Latin *con-* with, together + *facere* made, do]

con·fis·cate (kon′fə skāt), *v.t.*, **-cat·ed, -cat·ing. 1** seize for the public treasury. **2** seize by authority; take and keep: *The teacher confiscated my comic.*

con·fis·ca·tion (kon′fə skā′shən), *n.* a confiscating or a being confiscated.

con·gress (kong′gris), *n. pl.* **con·gress·es.** the lawmaking body of a nation, especially of a republic: *We heard that Congress's decision was to shelve the vote.*

con·gru·ent (kən grü′ənt, kong′grü ənt), *adj.* **1** (in geometry) coinciding exactly when superimposed; having the same size and shape: *congruent triangles.* **2** in harmony; agreeing. [< Latin *congruentem* coming together, agreeing] **—con·gru′ent·ly,** *adv.*

con·jec·ture (kən jek′chər), *n., v.*, **-tured, -tur·ing. —n.** formation of an opinion admittedly without sufficient evidence for proof; guessing. —*v.t., v.i.* guess.

Con·nect·i·cut (kə net′ə kət), *n.* **1** one of the northeastern states of the United States. 3,108,000 pop.; 5000 sq. mi. (13,000 sq. km.) *Capital:* Hartford. *Abbrev.:* Conn. or CT **2** river flowing between New Hampshire and Vermont, through Massachusetts and Connecticut, and into Long Island Sound. 407 mi. (655 km.)

con·quis·ta·dor (kon kwis′tə dôr, kon kē′stə dôr), *n., pl.* **con·quis·ta·dors, con·quis·ta·do·res** (-dôr′ēz). **1** a Spanish conqueror in North or South America during the 1500s. **2** conqueror. [< Spanish]

con·scious (kon′shəs), *adj.* **1** having experience, aware; knowing: *conscious of a sharp pain.* **2** able to feel or perceive; awake: *About five minutes after fainting I became conscious again.*

con·sid·er·a·tion (kən sid′ə rā′shən), *n.* **1** act of thinking about in order to decide; attention; deliberation: *careful consideration given to a question.* **2** thoughtfulness for others and their feelings; regard; respect.

con·sum·a·ble (kən sü′mə bəl), *n.* something that may be used up, such as fuel or food on a spacecraft. *—adj.* capable of being used up: *consumable goods.*

con·sum·er (kən sü′mər), *n. pl.* **con·sum·ers. 1** person who uses food, clothing, or anything grown or made by producers. **2** person or thing that consumes.

con·tam·i·nate (kən tam′ə nāt), *v.t.*, **-nat·ed, -nat·ing.** make impure by contact; defile; pollute: *Drinking water is contaminated when sewage seeps into the water supply.*

con·tam·i·na·tion (kən tam′ə nā′shən), *n.* **1** a contaminating or a being contaminated; pollution. **2** thing that contaminates: impurity.

con·tem·po·rar·y (kən tem′pə rer′ē), *adj., n., pl.* **-rar·ies. —adj. 1** belonging to or living in the same period of time: *Walt Whitman and Emily Dickinson were contemporary poets.* **2** of the same age or date: *contemporary trees.* **3** of or having to do with the present time; modern: *contemporary literature.* —*n.* **1** person living in the same period of time as another or others. **2** person or thing of the same age or date. [< *con-* together + Latin *temporarius* belonging to time < *tempus* time]

contemporary (def. 3)

a **contemporary** building and sculpture in downtown Chicago

a	hat	**ī**	ice	**u̇**	put	**ə** stands for
ā	age	**o**	not	**ü**	rule	**a** in about
ä	far, calm	**ō**	open	**ch**	child	**e** in taken
âr	care	**ȯ**	saw	**ng**	long	**i** in pencil
e	let	**ô**	order	**sh**	she	**o** in lemon
ē	equal	**oi**	oil	**th**	thin	**u** in circus
ėr	term	**ou**	out	**ŦH**	then	
i	it	**u**	cup	**zh**	measure	

crescent

different countries' flags

with **crescent** moons

con·tend (kən tend′), *v.i.* **1** work hard against difficulties; fight; struggle. **2** take part in a contest; compete. **3** argue; dispute. —*v.t.* declare to be a fact; maintain as true. [< Latin *contendere* strain, strive < *com-* + *tendere* stretch] —**con·tend′er,** *n.*

con·ten·tious (kən ten′shəs), *adj.* fond of arguing; given to disputing; quarrelsome.

con·ti·nent (kon′tə nənt), *n.* **1** one of the seven great masses of land on the earth. **2** mainland.

con·tin·u·al (kən tin′yü əl), *adj.* **1** never stopping: *the continual flow of the river.* **2** repeated many times; very frequent.

con·tin·u·ous (kən tin′yü əs), *adj.* without a stop or break; connected; unbroken; uninterrupted: *a continuous line.*

con·tour map (kon′tur map′), map showing heights at regular intervals above sea level by means of contour lines.

con·tra·dict (kon′trə dikt′), *v.t.* **1** say that (a statement, rumor, etc.) is not true; deny. **2** deny the words of (a person); say the opposite of what (a person) has said. **3** be contrary to; disagree with: *His quick anger contradicted his previous statement.*

con·trol (kən trōl′), *v.,* **con·trolled, con·trol·ling,** *n.* —*v.t.* have power or authority over; direct: *The government controls the printing of money.* —*n.* device that regulates a machine. [< Old French *contreroller* < *contrerolle* register < *contre* against + *rolle* roll]

co·or·di·nate (*v.* kō ôrd′n āt; *n.* kō ôrd′n it), *v.,* **-nat·ed, -nat·ing,** *n., pl.* **co·or·di·nates.** —*v.t.* arrange in proper order or relation; harmonize; adjust: *Coordinating the movements of the arms and legs is the hardest part of learning to swim.* —*n.* (in mathematics) any of two or more numbers that define the position of a point, line, or plane by reference to a fixed figure, system of lines, etc.

cor·dial (kôr′jəl), *adj.* warm and friendly in manner; hearty; sincere.

cor·po·ra·tion (kôr′pə rā′shən), *n.* **1** group of persons who obtain a charter that gives them as a group certain legal rights and privileges distinct from those of the individual members of the group. **2** group of persons with authority to act as one.

cor·po·re·al (kôr pôr′ē əl, kôr pōr′ē əl), *adj.* of or for the body; bodily.

cor·re·la·tion (kôr′ə lā′shən, kor′ə lā′shən), *n.* the mutual relation of two or more things: *There is a close correlation between climate and crops.*

cor·rup·tion (kə rup′shən), *n.* **1** bribery; dishonesty. **2** a changing for the worse; making impure or incorrect. **3** a causing (a form, meaning, dialect, etc.) to differ from standard usage.

coun·try (kun′trē), *n., pl.* **coun·tries.** **1** all the land of a nation. **2** land where a person was born or is a citizen: *What is that country's population? All the countries' ambassadors were there.*

cow·ard·ice (kou′ər dis), *n.* lack of courage; being made afraid.

cres·cent (kres′nt), *n.* **1** shape of the moon in its first or last quarter. **2** anything that curves in a similar way. —*adj.* shaped like the moon in its first or last quarter.

crime (krīm), *n.* an act that is against the law.

crim·i·nal (krim′ə nəl), *n.* person guilty of a crime. —*adj.* **1** guilty of wrongdoing. **2** of or having to do with crime or its punishment; wrong.

crim·i·nol·o·gy (krim′ə nol′ə jē), *n.* the scientific study of crime, its prevention and treatment, and criminals.

crit·ic (krit′ik), *n.* **1** person who makes judgments of the merits and faults of books, music, pictures, plays, acting, etc.: *The artist's work was praised by the critics, but was not popular with the public.* **2** person whose profession is writing such judgments for a newspaper, magazine, etc. **3** person who disapproves or finds fault; faultfinder. [< Latin *criticus* < Greek *kritikos* able to decide < *krinein* decide, judge]

cross-ex·am·i·na·tion (krôs′eg zam′ə nā′shən, kros′eg zam′ə nā′shən), *n.* **1** examination to check a previous examination, especially the questioning of a witness by the lawyer for the opposing side to test the truth of the witness's testimony. **2** a close or severe questioning.

cru·el·ty (krü′əl tē), *n., pl.* **-ties. 1** being cruel; readiness to give pain to others or to delight in their suffering. **2** a cruel act or acts.

cur·i·os·i·ty (kyür′ē os′ə tē), *n., pl.* **-ties. 1** an eager desire to know. **2** a being too eager to know. **3** something arousing curiosity; novelty.

cur·i·ous (kyür′ē əs), *adj.* **1** eager to know: *a curious student.* **2** too eager to know; prying: *Being so curious about other people's business might get you in trouble.* **3** strange, odd, or unusual.

cur·ric·u·lum (kə rik′yə ləm), *n., pl.* **cur·ric·u·lums, cur·ric·u·la** (-lə). **1** the whole range of studies offered in a school, college, etc., or in a type of school. **2** program of studies leading to a particular degree, certificate, etc.

cus·to·di·an (ku stō′dē ən), *n.* **1** person in charge; guardian; keeper: *the legal custodian of a child.* **2** person who takes care of a building or offices; janitor.

cy·to·plasm (sī′tə plaz′əm), *n.* the living substance or protoplasm of a nucleus.

D

da·ta (dā′tə, dat′ə), *n.pl.* of **datum.** facts from which conclusions can be drawn; things known or admitted; information. [< Latin, plural of *datum* (thing) given.] → **Data.** When *data* refers to a group of facts as a unit, it is used with a singular verb in informal English: *The data we have collected is convincing.* In formal English *data* is regarded as a plural: *The data we have collected are convincing.*

daz·zling (daz′ling), *adj.* brilliant or splendid. —**daz′zling·ly,** *adv.*

de·caf·fein·at·ed (dē kaf′ə nā′tid), *adj.* having the caffeine extracted.

de·cep·tion (di sep′shən), *n.* **1** a deceiving. **2** trick meant to deceive; fraud. [< Late Latin *deceptionem* < Latin *decipere*]

dec·i·bel (des′ə bəl), *n.* unit for measuring the relative intensity of sounds.

dec·i·gram (des′ə gram), *n.* unit of mass equal to one tenth of a gram.

dec·i·li·ter (des′ə lē′tər), *n.* unit of volume equal to one tenth of a liter.

decimal system (des′ə məl sis′təm), system of numeration which is based on units of 10.

de·ci·sion (di sizh′ən), *n.* **1** a making up of one's mind; resolution. **2** a settling of a question, dispute, etc.; a giving judgment. **3** judgment reached or given; verdict. **4** firmness and determination.

de·cline (di klīn′), *v.t.,* **-clined, -clin·ing, 1** turn away from doing; refuse (to do something). **2** refuse politely.

de·com·po·si·tion (dē′kom pə zish′ən), *n.* **1** act or process of decomposing. **2** decay; rot.

de·crease (*v.* di krēs′; *n.* dē′krēs, di krēs′), *v.,* **-creased, -creas·ing,** *n.* —*v.t., v.i.* make or become less. —*n.* a growing less; lessening.

de·duc·tion (di duk′shən), *n.* a reaching of conclusions by reasoning; inference. A person using deduction reasons from general laws to particular cases. EXAMPLE: All animals die; this cat is an animal; therefore, this cat will die.

de·duc·tive (di duk′tiv), *adj.* reasoning by deduction.

de·fend·ant (di fen′dənt), *n.* person accused or sued in a court of law.

de·fer·ment (di fėr′mənt), *n.* a putting off; postponement; delay.

def·i·nite·ly (def′ə nit lē), *adv.* **1** in a definite manner. **2** certainly.

de·hu·mid·i·fy (dē′hyü mid′ə fī), *v.t.,* **-fied, -fy·ing.** remove moisture from (the air, etc.). —**de′hu·mid′i·fi·er,** *n.*

de·hy·drate (dē hī′drāt), *v.,* **-drat·ed, -drat·ing.** —*v.t.* take water or moisture from. —*v.i.* lose water.

de·ject·ed (di jek′tid), *adj.* in low spirits; sad; discouraged.

dek·a·gram (dek′ə gram), *n.* unit of mass equal to 10 grams.

dek·a·li·ter (dek′ə lē′tər), *n.* unit of volume equal to 10 liters.

Del·a·ware (del′ə wâr), *n.* one of the southeastern states of the United States. 595,000 pop.; 2400 sq. mi. (6220 sq. km.) *Capital:* Dover. *Abbrev.:* Del. or DE

						ə stands for	
a	hat	ī	ice	ů	put		
ā	age	o	not	ü	rule	a	in about
ä	far, calm	ō	open	ch	child	e	in taken
âr	care	ȯ	saw	ng	long	i	in pencil
e	let	ô	order	sh	she	o	in lemon
ē	equal	oi	oil	th	thin	u	in circus
ėr	term	ou	out	ŦH	then		
i	it	u	cup	zh	measure		

diamond (def. 5)

a baseball **diamond**

dingo

A **dingo** can be 2 feet high at the shoulder.

de·moc·ra·cy (di mok′rə sē), *n., pl.* **-cies. 1** government that is run by the people who live under it. **2** country, state, or community having such a government.

de·o·dor·ant (dē ō′dər ənt), *n.* preparation that neutralizes unpleasant odors. —*adj.* that neutralizes unpleasant odors.

de·part (di pärt′), *v.i.* **1** go away; leave: *The flight departs at 6:15.* **2** turn away; change (*from*): *She departed from her usual way of working.*

de·par·ture (di pär′chər), *n.* **1** act of going away; leaving. **2** a turning away; change: *a departure from our old custom.*

de·pend·ent (di pen′dənt), *adj.* **1** relying on another for help, support, etc.: *A child is dependent on its parents.* **2** resulting from another thing; depending: *Good crops are dependent on the right kind of weather.* **3** under the control or rule of another; subject.

dep·ri·va·tion (dep′rə vā′shən), *n.* **1** act of depriving. **2** condition of being deprived; loss; privation.

de·prive (di prīv′), *v.t.,* **-prived, -priv·ing. 1** take away from by force; divest: *deprive a dictator of power.* **2** keep from having or doing: *Worry deprived me of sleep.*

der·ma·tol·o·gy (dėr′mə tol′ə jē), *n.* branch of medicine that deals with the skin, its structure, and its diseases. —**der′ma·tol′o·gist,** *n.*

de·scend·ant (di sen′dənt), *n.* **1** person born of a certain family or group: *a descendant of the Pilgrims.* **2** offspring; child, grandchild, etc. You are a direct descendant of your earlier ancestors. —*adj.* going or coming down; descending.

de·scent (di sent′), *n.* **1** a coming down or going down from a higher to a lower place: *the descent of a balloon.* **2** a downward slope. **3** way or passage down: means of descending. **4** a handing down from parent to child. **5** family line; ancestry: *of Italian descent.*

de·scrip·tion (di skrip′shən), *n.* **1** act of describing. **2** composition or account that describes or gives a picture in words.

de·spise (di spīz′), *v.t.,* **de·spis·es, de·spised, de·spis·ing.** look down on; scorn.

de·spond·ent (di spon′dənt), *adj.* having lost heart, courage, or hope; discouraged; dejected.

de·tect (di tekt′), *v.t.* **1** discover (a person) in the performance of some act: *The child was detected hiding under the bed.* **2** discover the presence, existence, or fact of.

de·tec·tion (di tek′shən), *n.* **1** a finding out; discovery: *the detection of crimes.* **2** a being found out or discovered: *His detection will be a matter of only a few hours.*

dé·tente or **de·tente** (dā tänt′), *n.* the easing of tensions, especially between nations or political groups. [< French *détente,* literally, a loosening, relaxation]

di·a·logue (dī′ə lóg, dī′ə log), *n.* **1** conversation between two or more persons. **2** conversation in a play, novel, story, etc. [< Greek *dialogos* < *dia-* between + *logos* speech]

dia·mond (dī′mənd, dī′ə mənd), *n.* **1** a colorless or tinted precious stone, formed of pure carbon in crystals. Diamond is the hardest natural substance known. **2** a plane figure shaped like this: ◊. **3** a playing card marked with one or more red, diamond-shaped figures. **4** diamonds, *pl.* suit of such playing cards. **5** in baseball: **a** the area bounded by home plate and the three bases; infield. **b** the whole field.

dic·ta·tion (dik tā′shən), *n.* **1** act of saying or reading words aloud to another person who writes them down. **2** words said or read aloud to be written down.

dic·ta·tor (dik′tā tər, dik tā′tər), *n.* **1** person exercising absolute authority, especially a person who seizes control of a government. **2** (in Roman history) an official given absolute authority over the state in times of emergency.

dif·fer·ent (dif′ər ənt), *adj.* **1** not alike; not like; unlike: *A boat is different from an automobile.* **2** not the same; separate; distinct: *I saw her three different times today.* **3** not like others or most others; unusual. —**dif′fer·ent·ly,** *adv.*

di·ges·tion (də jes′chən, dī jes′chən), *n.* **1** the digesting of food. **2** ability to digest food.

din·go (ding′gō), *n., pl.* **-goes.** a wolflike wild dog of Australia. [< native Australian name]

di·rec·tor·y (də rek′tər ē, dī rek′tər ē), *n., pl.* **-tor·ies.** list of names and addresses, usually in alphabetical order. A telephone book is a directory.

dis·a·bil·i·ty (dis′ə bil′ə tē), n., pl. **-ties. 1** lack of ability or power: *The player's disability was a sprained ankle.* **2** something that disables.

dis·ad·van·taged (dis′əd van′tijd), adj. lacking advantages; being in an unfavorable condition.

dis·a·gree·a·ble (dis′ə grē′ə bəl), adj. **1** not to one's liking; unpleasant. **2** not friendly; bad-tempered; cross.

dis·arm (dis ärm′), v.t. **1** take weapons away from: *The police disarmed the robbers.* **2** remove anger or suspicion from; make friendly: *The speaker's honesty disarmed the angry crowd.* **3** make harmless.

dis·as·ter (də zas′tər), n. event that causes much suffering or loss; a sudden or great misfortune, such as a destructive fire or an earthquake. [< Middle French *désastre* unfavorable star, calamity < Latin *dis-* without + *astrum* star < Greek *astron*]

dis·col·or (dis kul′ər), v.t. change or spoil the color of; stain. —v.i. become changed in color.

dis·com·fort (dis kum′fərt), n. **1** lack of comfort; uneasiness. **2** thing that causes discomfort; inconvenience. —v.t. make uncomfortable.

dis·con·tin·ue (dis′kən tin′yü), v.t., **-tin·ued, -tin·u·ing. 1** cause to cease; put a stop to; break off; give up; stop: *The train has been discontinued.* **2** cease from; cease to take, use, etc.

dis·cord (dis′kôrd), n. disagreement of opinions and aims.

dis·cour·age (dis kėr′ij), v.t., **-aged, -ag·ing. 1** lessen the courage or confidence of; dishearten: *Repeated failures discouraged him.* **2** try to prevent by disapproving; dissuade.

dis·crim·i·na·to·ry (dis krim′ə nə tôr′ē, dis krim′ə nə tōr′ē), adj. showing partiality or prejudice.

dis·en·chant (dis′en chant′), v.t. **dis·en·chant·ed, dis·en·chant·ing.** set free from enchantment or illusion.

dis·grace·ful (dis grās′fəl), adj. causing loss of honor or respect; shameful; dishonorable.

dis·gust·ed (dis gus′tid), adj. filled with disgust. —**dis·gust′ed·ly**, adv.

dis·in·ter·est·ed (dis in′tər ə stid, dis in′tər es′tid), adj. **1** free from selfish motives; impartial; fair. **2** uninterested.

dis·miss·al (dis mis′əl), n. **1** condition or fact of being sent away or removed. **2** a written or spoken order removing someone.

dis·re·spect (dis′ri spekt′), n. lack of respect; rudeness; impoliteness.

dis·rup·tive (dis rup′tiv), adj. causing disorder.

dis·sent (di sent′), v.i. **1** think differently; disagree: *Two of the judges dissented from the decision of the other three.* **2** withhold consent. —n. **1** difference of opinion; disagreement. **2** declaration of disagreement of opinion about something.

dis·tend (dis tend′), v.t., v.i. stretch out by pressure from within; swell out; expand: *The balloon was distended almost to the bursting point.* [< Latin *distendere* < *dis-* apart + *tendere* to stretch]

dis·tinct (dis tingkt′), adj. **1** not the same; separate: *She asked me about it three distinct times.* **2** different in quality or kind; distinctive: *Mice are distinct from rats.* **3** easily seen, heard, or understood; clear.

dis·tinc·tion (dis tingk′shən), n. **1** a distinguishing from others; making a difference; discrimination. **2** difference. **3** special quality or feature; point of difference. **4** honor. **5** mark or sign of honor. **6** excellence; superiority: *Everyone agreed that she was a person of distinction.*

dis·tin·guished (dis ting′gwisht), adj. famous; well-known.

dis·tor·tion (dis tôr′shən), n. **1** a twisting out of shape. **2** condition of being distorted. **3** anything distorted: *a story full of distortions.* **4** a distorted form or image.

disaster
the San Francisco earthquake **disaster,** 1906

a	hat	**ī**	ice	**u̇**	put	**ə** stands for	
ā	age	**o**	not	**ü**	rule	**a**	in about
ä	far, calm	**ō**	open	**ch**	child	**e**	in taken
âr	care	**ȯ**	saw	**ng**	long	**i**	in pencil
e	let	**ô**	order	**sh**	she	**o**	in lemon
ē	equal	**oi**	oil	**th**	thin	**u**	in circus
ėr	term	**ou**	out	**ᴛʜ**	then		
i	it	**u**	cup	**zh**	measure		

diversity

the **diversity**

of flowers

di·ver·si·ty (də vėr′sə tē, dī vėr′sə tē), *n., pl.* **-ties. 1** complete difference; unlikeness. **2** variety: *a diversity of food on the table.*

DNA, deoxyribonucleic acid, a nucleic acid in the chromatin of all living cells that carries the genetic code.

does·n't (duz′nt), does not: *She doesn't have a bicycle.*

dog·ged (dȯ′gid, dȯg′id), *adj.* not giving up; stubborn: *She has dogged determination.* [< *dog*]
—**dog′ged·ly,** *adv.*
—**dog′ged·ness,** *n.*

dom·i·nant (dom′ə nənt), *adj.* **1** most powerful or influential; controlling; ruling; governing. **2** rising high above its surroundings; towering over: *Dominant hills sheltered the bay.* **3** (in biology) of, having to do with, or designating a dominant character: *a dominant gene.*

dou·ble bar graph (dub′əl bär′ graf′), *n.* a graph that compares two or more different quantities using rectangles of different lengths.

dow·ry (dou′rē), *n., pl.* **-ries.** money or property that a woman brings to the man she marries.

drown (droun), *v.i.,* **drowned, drown·ing.** die under water or other liquid because of lack of air to breathe: *Grabbing the log saved the swimmer from drowning.*

dur·a·ble (dùr′ə bəl), *adj.* lasting a long time.

dur·a·tion (du rā′tion), *n.* length of time.

dy·na·mo (dī′nə mō), *n., pl.* **dy·na·mos. 1** generator, which turns mechanical energy into electrical energy. **2** motor, which turns electrical energy into mechanical energy. **3** INFORMAL. a dynamic person; live wire. [short for *dynamoelectric machine*]

E

Eas·ter (ē′stər), *n.* the annual Christian festival on the first Sunday after the first full moon on or after March 21, celebrating Jesus' resurrection; Easter Sunday. [Old English *ēastre,* originally, name of dawn goddess < *ēast* east]

e·col·o·gist (ē kol′ə jist), *n.* an expert in ecology.

e·col·o·gy (ē kol′ə jē), *n.* **1** branch of biology that deals with organisms in relation to their environment and to one another. **2** the sum of relationships between organisms and an environment: *a threatened ecology.* **3** branch of sociology that deals with the relations between human beings and their environment. [< German *Ökologie* < Greek *oikos* house + *-logia* study of]

e·co·nom·ics (ē′kə nom′iks, ek′ə nom′iks), *n. pl. in form, sing. in use.* science of the production, distribution, and consumption of goods and services. Economics studies the problems of capital, labor, wages, prices, taxes, etc.

e·con·o·my (i kon′ə mē), *n., pl.* **-mies. 1** management of affairs and resources of a country, area, or business. **2** system of managing the production, distribution, and consumption of goods.

e·co·sys·tem (ē′kō sis′təm, ek′ō sis′təm), *n.* a physical environment with the community of various organisms that inhabits it, considered as an ecological unit. An ecosystem may be a lake, a vacant lot, a desert, etc. [< *eco-* + *system*]

ef·fect (ə fekt′), *n.* something made to happen by a person or thing; result.

ef·fec·tive (ə fek′tiv), *adj.* **1** able to produce an effect: *an effective order.* See synonym study below. **2** producing the desired effect; getting results: *an effective medicine.* **3** striking; impressive.
—**ef·fec′tive·ly,** *adv.*
—**ef·fec′tive·ness,** *n.*
Syn. *adj.* **1 Effective** and **efficient** mean producing an effect. **Effective** applies to anyone or anything that can or does produce an effect: *Several new drugs are effective in treating serious diseases.* **Efficient** implies that the effect is produced without waste of time or energy: *A skilled surgeon is efficient.*

ef·fi·cient (ə fish′ənt), *adj.* able to produce the effect wanted without waste of time, energy, etc.; capable; competent. See **effective** for synonym study. [< Latin *efficientem* < *ex-* + *facere* do, make] —**ef·fi′cient·ly,** *adv.*

ei·der (ī′dər), *n.* any of a genus of large, northern sea ducks, usually black and white, with very soft feathers on their breasts. [< Scandinavian (Old Icelandic) *æthr*]

eighth (ātth), *adj.* **1** next after the seventh; last in a series of 8. **2** being one of 8 equal parts. —*n.* **1** next after the seventh; last in a series of 8. **2** one of 8 equal parts.

e·las·tic (i las′tik), *adj.* having the quality of returning to its original size, shape, or position after being stretched, squeezed, bent, etc.: *Rubber bands, sponges, and steel springs are elastic.* —*n.* tape, cloth, cord, etc., woven partly of rubber.

e·las·tic·i·ty (i las′tis′ə tē, ē′las tis′ə tē), *n.* elastic quality: *Rubber has elasticity.*

e·lec·tric·i·ty (i lek′tris′ə tē, ē′lek tris′ə tē), *n.* **1** form of energy which can produce light, heat, motion, magnetism, and chemical changes, and which can be generated by friction, induction, or chemical changes. **2** electric current.

el·e·men·tar·y (el′ə men′tər ē, el′ə men′trē), *adj.* of or dealing with the simple, necessary parts to be learned first; having to do with first principles; introductory.

el·e·va·tion (el′ə vā′shən), *n., pl.* **el·e·va·tions. 1** a raised place; high place: *A hill is an elevation.* **2** height above the earth's surface. **3** height above sea level.

em·bar·rass (em bar′əs), *v.t.* disturb and confuse; make uneasy and ashamed; make self-conscious; disconcert: *She embarrassed me by asking me if I really liked her.* —**em·bar′rass·ing·ly,** *adv.*

e·mer·gen·cy (i mėr′jən sē), *n., pl.* **-cies. 1** a sudden need for immediate action. **2** situation in which such a need arises.

em·is·sar·y (em′ə ser′ē), *n., pl.* **-sar·ies. 1** person sent on a mission or errand. **2** a secret agent; spy. [< Latin *emissarius* < *emittere.* See EMIT.]

e·mit (i mit′), *v.t.,* **e·mit·ted, e·mit·ting. 1** give off; send out; discharge: *The sun emits light and heat.* **2** put into circulation; issue. [< Latin *emittere* < *ex-* out + *mittere* send] —**e·mit′ter,** *n.*

e·mo·tion (i mō′shən), *n.* a strong feeling of any kind. Joy, grief, fear, hate, love, anger, and excitement are emotions.

em·pha·sis (em′fə sis), *n., pl.* **-ses** (-sēz′). **1** special force; stress; importance: *That school puts much emphasis on athletics.* **2** special force put on particular syllables, words, or phrases: *A speaker puts emphasis on important words.*

em·phat·ic (em fat′ik), *adj.* **1** said or done with force or stress: *Her answer was an emphatic "No!"* **2** speaking with force or stress; expressing oneself strongly: *The emphatic speaker often pounded the table and shouted.*

em·u·late (em′yə lāt), *v.t.,* **-lat·ed, -lat·ing.** copy or imitate in order to equal or excel the achievements or qualities of an admired person.

en·com·pass (en kum′pəs), *v.t.* **1** surround completely; encircle. **2** include; contain.

en·cour·age (en kėr′ij), *v.t.,* **en·cour·ag·es, en·cour·aged, en·cour·ag·ing. 1** give courage, hope, or confidence to; urge on; hearten. **2** stimulate (persons or personal efforts) by helping or showing approval; support. —**en·cour′ag·ing·ly,** *adv.*

en·cy·clo·pe·di·a (en sī′klə pē′dē ə), *n.* book or set of books giving information on all branches of knowledge, usually with its articles arranged alphabetically.

end zone (end′ zōn′), (in football) the part of the field between each goal line and the corresponding end of the field.

en·dan·gered (en dān′jərd), *adj.* liable to become extinct: *an endangered species.*

en·deav·or (en dev′ər), *v.i., v.t.* make an effort; try hard: *A runner endeavors to win a race.*

en·fran·chise (en fran′chīz), *v.t.,* **-chised, -chis·ing.** give the rights of citizenship to, especially the right to vote: *The 19th amendment to the Constitution enfranchised American women.*

emit (def. 1)
stacks **emitting**
billows of smoke

a	hat	**ī**	ice	**u̇**	put	**ə** stands for	
ā	age	**o**	not	**ü**	rule	**a**	in about
ä	far, calm	**ō**	open	**ch**	child	**e**	in taken
âr	care	**ȯ**	saw	**ng**	long	**i**	in pencil
e	let	**ô**	order	**sh**	she	**o**	in lemon
ē	equal	**oi**	oil	**th**	thin	**u**	in circus
ėr	term	**ou**	out	**ᴛʜ**	then		
i	it	**u**	cup	**zh**	measure		

erosion (def. 1)

the **erosion** of Wave

Rock in Australia

eruption (def. 2)

the **eruption** of Mount

St. Helens, 1980

en·ter·prise (en′tər prīz), n. 1 an important, difficult, or dangerous plan to be tried; great or bold undertaking. 2 any undertaking; project; venture: *a business enterprise.* [< Old French *entreprise* < *entre-* between + *prendre* to take]

en·tre·pre·neur (än′trə prə nėr′), n. person who organizes and manages a business or industrial enterprise, attempting to make a profit but taking the risk of a loss. [< French < *entreprendre* undertake] **—en·tre·pre·neur·i·al·ism,** n.

en·vi·ron·ment (en vī′rən mənt), n. 1 all the surrounding things, conditions, and influences affecting the development of living things. A person's character is influenced by the social environment. 2 surroundings: *an environment of poverty.* 3 condition of the air, water, soil, etc.; natural surroundings. **—en·vi·ron·men′tal,** adj.

ep·i·sode (ep′ə sōd), n. 1 an outstanding incident in a person's life, in the history of a country, the world, an institution, etc. 2 an incidental set of events or actions separate from, but essential to, the main plot of a novel, story, etc.

e·rode (i rōd′), v., **e·rod·ed, e·rod·ing.** —v.t. 1 eat or wear away gradually; eat into: *Running water erodes soil and rocks.* 2 form by a gradual eating or wearing away: *The stream eroded a channel in the solid rock.* —v.i. be worn away or eaten out. [< Latin *erodere* < *ex-* away + *rodere* gnaw]

e·ro·sion (i rō′ zhən), n. 1 a gradual eating or wearing away by glaciers, running water, waves, or wind: *Trees help prevent the erosion of soil.* 2 a being eaten or worn away.

er·rand (er′ənd), n., pl. **er·rands.** 1 a trip to do something for someone else. 2 what one is sent to do.

e·rup·tion (i rup′shən), n. 1 a bursting forth; outbreak; outburst. 2 a throwing forth of lava, etc., from a volcano or of hot water from a geyser. 3 a breaking out with many small red spots on the skin; rash. 4 the red spots on the skin.

es·cape (e skāp′), v., **-caped, -cap·ing.** —v.i. 1 get out and away; get free; flee: *escape from prison.* 2 come out or find a way out from a container; leak: *Gas had been escaping from the cylinder all* night. —v.t. 1 get free from: *He thinks he will never escape hard work.* 2 keep free or safe from; avoid: *We all escaped the measles.*

es·cort (n. es′kôrt; v. e skôrt′), n. person or group of persons going with another to give protection, show honor, etc. —v.t. go with as an escort.

e·soph·a·gus (ē sof′ə gəs), n., pl. **-gi** (-jī). passage for food from the pharynx to the stomach; gullet. [< Greek *oisophagos* < *oiso-* carry + *phagein* eat]

es·pe·cial·ly (e spesh′ə lē), adv. more than others; specially; chiefly.

et·y·mol·o·gy (et′ə mol′ə jē), n., pl. **-gies.** 1 the derivation of a word. 2 account or explanation of the origin and history of a word. [< Greek *etymologia* < *etymon* the original sense or form of a word (neuter of *etymos* true, real) + *-logos* treating of]

eu·ca·lyp·tus (yü′kə lip′təs), n., pl. **-tus·es, -ti** (-tī). any of a genus of tall evergreen trees of the myrtle family, found mainly in Australia and neighboring islands; gum tree. It is valued for its timber and for a medicinal oil made from its leaves. [< New Latin < Greek *eu-* well + *kalyptos* covered; with reference to the covering on the bud]

e·val·u·ate (i val′yü āt), v.t., **-at·ed, -at·ing.** find out the value or the amount of; estimate the worth or importance of; appraise. **—e·val′u·a′tor,** n.

e·val·u·a·tion (i val′yü ā′shən), n. 1 an evaluating. 2 an estimated value; valuation. 3 appraisal or estimation as to the quality, importance, value, or progress of one's work: *All students will be given an evaluation at the end of the year.*

eve·ry·day (ev′rē dā′), adj. 1 of every day; daily: *Accidents are everyday occurrences.* 2 for every ordinary day; not for Sundays or holidays: *She wears everyday clothes to work.* 3 not exciting; usual. → **Everyday** is one word when it is an adjective, two words when *day* is a noun modified by *every: This was an everyday occurrence. Every day seemed a year.*

eve·ry·one (ev′rē wun, ev′re wən), pron. each one; everybody: *Everyone in the class is here.*

ex·ag·ge·ra·tion (eg zaj/ə rā/shən), n. 1 an exaggerated statement; overstatement. 2 an exaggerating.

ex·am·i·na·tion (eg zam/ə nā/shən), n. 1 an examining. 2 a being examined. 3 test of knowledge or qualifications; list of questions; test. 4 answers given in such a test.

ex·am·ine (eg zam/ən), v.t., -ined, -in·ing. 1 look at closely and carefully; inspect: The doctor examined the wound. 2 question (a witness) formally; interrogate. [< Latin examinare < examen a weighing < exigere weigh accurately < ex- out + agere weigh] —**ex·am/in·er**, n.

ex·as·pe·rate (eg zas/pə rāt/), v.t., -rat·ed, -rat·ing. irritate very much; annoy extremely; make angry: Their continual lateness exasperated me. [< Latin exasperatum irritated < ex- completely + asper rough] —**ex·as/pe·rat/ing·ly**, adv.

ex·cept (ek sept/), prep. 1 leaving out; other than; but: every day except Sunday. 2 **except for**, a with the exception of; except: Everyone was early for the party except for my cousin. b were it not for: We could have had the picnic today except for the rain. —v.t. take or leave out; exclude: Those who passed the first test were excepted from the second. —v.i. make objection; object. —conj. 1 only; but: I would have had a perfect score except I missed the last question. 2 unless.

ex·cep·tion (ek sep/shən), n. 1 a leaving out; excepting: I like all my studies, with the exception of German. 2 person or thing left out: She praised the pictures, with two exceptions. 3 an unusual instance; case that does not follow the rule. —**ex·cep/tion·less**, adj.

ex·cur·sion (ek skėr/zhən, ek skėr/shən), n. a short journey taken for interest or pleasure, often by a number of people together: Our club went on an excursion to the mountains.

ex·ec·u·tive (eg zek/yə tiv), adj. 1 having to do with carrying out or managing affairs: A principal has an executive position. 2 having the duty and power of putting the laws into effect: The President of the United States is the head of the executive branch of the government. —n. person who carries out or manages affairs.

ex·empt (eg zempt/), v.t. make free (from a duty, obligation, rule, etc., to which others are subject); release: be exempted from the final examination. —adj. freed from a duty, obligation, rule, etc., to which others are subject; released. [< Latin exemptum taken out < ex- out + emere take]

ex·er·tion (eg zėr/shən), n. 1 strenuous action; effort: The exertions of the firefighters kept the fire from spreading. 2 a putting into action; active use; use.

ex·haust·ed (eg zȯ/stid), adj. 1 used up. 2 worn out; very tired.

ex·hib·it (eg zib/it), v.t. 1 let be seen; display: He exhibits interest whenever you talk about dogs. 2 show publicly: She hopes to exhibit her paintings in New York. —n. 1 show; display. 2 thing or things shown publicly. [< Latin exhibitum held out, displayed < ex- out + habere hold]

ex·hil·a·ra·tion (eg zil/ə rā/shən), n. a being or feeling exhilarated; high spirits; lively joy.

ex·ot·ic (eg zot/ik), adj. 1 from a foreign country; not native. 2 fascinating or interesting because strange or different: an exotic tropical island. —n. an exotic person or thing. [< Greek exōtikos < exō outside < ex out of] —**ex·ot/i·cal·ly**, adv.

ex·pand (ek spand/), v.t. make larger; increase in size; enlarge.

ex·pan·sion (ek span/shən), n. 1 an expanding: Heat caused the expansion of the gas. 2 a being expanded; increase in size: the expansion of the factory.

exotic (def. 1)
the **exotic** Galah bird
from Australia

a	hat	**ī**	ice	**u̇**	put	**ə** stands for	
ā	age	**o**	not	**ü**	rule	**a**	in about
ä	far, calm	**ō**	open	**ch**	child	**e**	in taken
âr	care	**ȯ**	saw	**ng**	long	**i**	in pencil
e	let	**ô**	order	**sh**	she	**o**	in lemon
ē	equal	**oi**	oil	**th**	thin	**u**	in circus
ėr	term	**ou**	out	**ŦH**	then		
i	it	**u**	cup	**zh**	measure		

ex·pend·i·ture (ek spen′də chủr, ek spen′də chər), *n.* **1** a using up; spending: *That old house requires the expenditure of much money, time, and effort.* **2** amount of money, etc., spent; expense: *Limit your expenditures to what is necessary.*

ex·per·i·ment (ek sper′ə mənt), *n.* trial or test to find out or discover something unknown, to verify a hypothesis, or to illustrate some known truth.

ex·per·ise (ek′spər tēz′), *n.* expert knowledge or opinion.

ex·plain (ek splān′), *v.t.* **1** make plain or clear; tell how to do. **2** tell the meaning of; interpret.

ex·pla·na·tion (ek′splə nā′shən), *n.* **1** an explaining; clearing up a difficulty or mistake. **2** something that explains.

ex·plan·a·to·ry (ek splan′ə tôr′ē, ek splan′ə tōr′ē), *adj.* that explains; serving or helping to explain: *Read the explanatory part of the lesson before you try to do the problems.*

ex·plode (ek splōd′), *v.i.,* **-plod·ed, -plod·ing. 1** burst with a loud noise; blow up: *The building was destroyed when the defective boiler exploded.* **2** burst or expand violently because of the pressure produced by the sudden generation of one or more gases.

ex·plor·a·to·ry (ek splôr′ə tôr′ē, ek splōr′ə tōr′ē), *adj.* of or having to do with exploration.

ex·tend (ek stend′), *v.t.,* **ex·tends, ex·tend·ed, ex·tend·ing. 1** stretch out: *extend your hand.* **2** continue or prolong in time, space, or direction: *I am extending my vacation another week.* **3** increase, expand, or enlarge: *They plan to extend their research in that field.*

ex·ten·sion (ek sten′shən), *n.* **1** an extending; stretching. **2** a being extended. **3** an addition.

ex·tin·guish (ek sting′gwish), *v.t.* **1** put out; quench: *Water extinguished the fire.* **2** bring to an end; snuff out; destroy: *A government may extinguish liberty but not the love of liberty.* [< Latin *exstinguere* < *ex-* out + *stinguere* quench]

ex·treme (ek strēm′), *adj.,* **-trem·er, -trem·est. 1** of the highest degree; much more than usual; very great; *extreme joy.* **2** going to the greatest possible lengths; very severe; very violent: *extreme measures.* **—ex·treme′ly,** *adv.*

family (def. 1)
a **family** of five

F

fam·i·ly (fam′ə lē), *n., pl.* **-lies,** *adj.* **—n. 1** parents and their children thought of as a group. **2** group of people living in the same house. **3** all of a person's relatives. **4** group of related people; tribe or clan. **5** group of related organisms ranking below an order and above a genus. Lions and leopards belong to the cat family. **—***adj.* having to do with a family. [< Latin *familia* household < *famulus* servant]

fan·ci·ful (fan′sə fəl), *adj.* **1** imaginative. **2** imaginary; unreal. **3** quaint or odd in construction or appearance: *fanciful decoration.*

fan·tas·tic (fan tas′tik), *adj.* **1** very odd; wild and strange in shape or manner: *The firelight cast weird, fantastic shadows on the walls.* **2** very fanciful; eccentric; irrational: *The idea that machines could fly seemed fantastic a hundred years ago.* **3** existing only in the imagination; imaginary; unreal: *Superstition causes fantastic fears.* **4** INFORMAL. unbelievably good, high. **—fan·tas′ti·cal·ly,** *adv.*

farm·er (fär′mər), *n.* person who owns or works on a farm.

fa·tigue (fə tēg′), *n., v.,* **-tigued, -ti·guing,** *adj.* **—n. 1** weariness caused by hard work or effort. **2** a weakening (of metal) caused by long-continued use or strain. **—***v.t.* make weary or tired; cause fatigue in; tire. [< Middle French < *fatiguer* to tire < Latin *fatigare*]

fa·vor·ite (fā′vər it), *adj.* liked better than others. **—n. 1** person or thing preferred above others. **2** person treated with special favor.

feed·back (fēd′bak′), *n.* **1** process by which a system, machine, etc., regulates itself by feeding back to itself part of its output. **2** response, especially one that has an effect on the process that generated the response.

fes·ti·val (fes′tə vəl), *n., pl.* **fes·ti·vals. 1** day or special time of rejoicing or feasting, often in memory of some great happening: *Christmas is a Christian festival; Hanukkah is a Jewish festival.* **2** celebration or entertainment, often at recurring periods: *Every year the city has a music festival.* **—***adj.* of or having to do with a festival. [< Medieval Latin *festivalis,* ultimately < Latin *festum* feast]

fi·brin (fī′brən), *n.* a white, tough, elastic, fibrous protein formed by the action of thrombin on fibringen when blood clots.

field trip (fēld′ trip′), trip away from school to give students an opportunity to learn by seeing closely and at first hand.

fierce (firs), *adj.* **fierc·er, fierc·est.** savagely cruel and wild; ferocious.

fi·nal·ly (fī′nl ē), *adv.* **1** at the end; at last. **2** in such a way as to decide or settle the question.

fire·works (fīr′wėrks′), *n., pl.* a display of colored explosions in the sky.

first com·mun·ion (fėrst′ kə myü′nyən), the first time sharing in or receiving the consecrated bread and wine commemorating the passion and death of Christ.

fixed joint (fikst′ joint′), a joint that does not move.

floss (flȯs, flos), *n.* **1** short, loose, silk fibers. **2** a shiny, untwisted silk thread made from such fibers. Waxed, floss is used for cleaning between the teeth. —*v.i.* use dental floss. —*v.t.* use dental floss on.

flour·ish (flėr′ish), *v.i.,* **flour·ish·es, flour·ished, flour·ish·ing.** grow or develop with vigor; do well; thrive.

flu (flü), *n.* disease caused by a virus, often resembling a very bad cold.

fluo·res·cent (flu res′nt, flü′ə res′nt), *adj.* that gives off light by fluorescence. Fluorescent substances glow in the dark when exposed to X rays.

fluor·ide (flu̇r′īd), *n.* compound of fluorine and another element.

food chain (füd′ chān′), group of organisms so interrelated that each member of the group feeds upon the one below it and is in turn eaten by the organism above it.

foot (fu̇t), *n. pl.* **feet** (or **foot** for 2), *n.* **1** the lowest or underlying part; bottom; base: *the foot of a hill.* **2** unit of length, equal to 12 inches.

fo·reign (fôr′ən, for′ən), *adj.* **1** outside one's own country. **2** coming from outside one's own country.

for·mal (fôr′məl), *adj.* **1** with strict attention to outward forms and ceremonies; not familiar and homelike; stiff: *a formal greeting.* **2** according to set customs or rules: *a formal invitation.* **3** of fancy or elegant design suitable for wear at a dance, party, or other affair: *formal attire, a formal dress.* —**for′mal·ly,** *adv.*

for·mer·ly (fôr′mər lē), *adv.* at an earlier time; some time ago; previously.

fort·night (fôrt′nīt, fôrt′nit), *n.* two weeks. [Middle English *fourtenight* fourteen nights]

frac·ture (frak′chər), *n., v.,* **-tured, -tur·ing.** —*n.* **1** a breaking of a bone or cartilage. **2** a breaking. **3** a being broken. **4** result of breaking; a break; crack. —*v.t.* **1** break; crack. **2** cause a fracture in (a bone, etc.): *I fractured my arm.* —*v.i.* undergo fracture; crack. [< Latin *fractura* < *frangere* to break]

free throw (frē′ thrō′), (in basketball) an unhindered shot from a line (**free-throw line**) about 15 feet (4.5 meters) away from the basket, awarded to a player fouled by a member of the opposing team, and worth one point.

French fries (french′ frīz′), potatoes cut into thin strips and fried in deep fat until crisp on the outside.

fright·ened (frīt′nd), *adj.* filled with fright; afraid.

frol·ic (frol′ik), *n., v.,* **-icked, -ick·ing.** —*n.* **1** a merry prank; play; fun. **2** a joyous game or party. —*v.i.* play about joyously; have fun together; make merry: *The children frolicked with the puppy.* [originally adjective < Dutch *vrolijk* gay < Middle Dutch *vro* glad]

frost·bite (frȯst′bīt′, frost′bīt′), *n., v.,* **-bit** (-bit′), **-bit·ten** (-bit′n), **-bit·ing.** —*n.* damage to or destruction of tissue in a part of the body caused by freezing. —*v.t.* injure (a part of the body) by frostbite.

fireworks

formal (def. 1)
a **formal** ceremony
involving English
royalty

a	hat	**ī**	ice	**u̇**	put	**ə** stands for	
ā	age	**o**	not	**ü**	rule	**a**	in about
ä	far, calm	**ō**	open	**ch**	child	**e**	in taken
âr	care	**ȯ**	saw	**ng**	long	**i**	in pencil
e	let	**ô**	order	**sh**	she	**o**	in lemon
ē	equal	**oi**	oil	**th**	thin	**u**	in circus
ėr	term	**ou**	out	**ᴦн**	then		
i	it	**u**	cup	**zh**	measure		

fu·el (fyü′əl), *n., v.,* **-eled, -el·ing** or **-elled, -el·ling.** —*n.* **1** coal, wood, oil, or any other material that can be burned to produce useful heat or power. **2** atomic matter producing heat by fission or fusion, as in a reactor. —*v.t.* **1** supply with fuel. **2** act as a driving force for; support. —*v.i.* get fuel. [< Old French *feuaile,* ultimately < Latin *focus* hearth]

ful·fill or **ful·fil** (fül fil′), *v.t.,* **-filled, -fill·ing.** **1** carry out (a promise, prophecy, etc.); cause to happen or take place; accomplish; realize. **2** perform or do (a duty); obey (a command, law, etc.); execute; discharge. **3** satisfy (a requirement, condition, etc.); serve (a purpose).

full-length (fül′lengkth′, fül′length′), *adj.* **1** showing the entire human form: *a full-length portrait.* **2** of the full or normal length; not short.

fu·ner·al (fyü′nər əl), *n.* **1** ceremonies performed when a dead person's body is buried or cremated. **2** procession taking a dead person's body to the place where it is buried or cremated.

fun·gi (fun′jī), *n.* a pl. of **fungus.**

fun·gus (fung′gəs), *n., pl.* **fun·gi** or **fun·gus·es.** **1** any living organism that resembles a plant but lacks flowers, leaves, and chlorophyll, getting its nourishment from dead or living organic matter and re- producing by spores and division. Mushrooms are members of the fungus kingdom. **2** something that grows rapidly like mushroom.

fungus (def. 1)
fungi growing on the ground

G

gall blad·der (gôl′ blad′ər), sac attached to the liver, in which bile is stored until needed.

Gan·ges Riv·er (gan′jēz′ riv′ər), river flowing across N India and Bangladesh into the Bay of Bengal. It is regarded as sacred by the Hindus. 1550 mi. (2494 km).

gas (gas), *n., pl.* **gas·es.** **1** substance that is not a solid or a liquid; substance that has no shape or size of its own and can expand without limit. Oxygen and nitrogen are gases at ordinary temperatures. **2** INFORMAL. gasoline.

gas·tric glands (gas′trik glandz′), glands in the stomach that produce digestive juices.

gauge (gāj), *n.* **1** a standard measure or a scale of standard measurements used for the measure of such things as the capacity of a barrel, the thickness of sheet iron. **2** instrument for measuring. A steam gauge measures the pressure of steam.

ga·zelle (gə zel′), *n., pl.* **-zelles** or **-zelle.** any of a genus of small, swift, graceful antelope of Africa and Asia.

gen·e·ros·i·ty (jen′ə ros′ə tē), *n., pl.* **-ties.** a being generous; willingness to share with others; unselfishness.

gen·er·ous (jen′ər əs), *adj.* **1** willing to share with others; unselfish: *a generous giver.* **2** large; plentiful: *A quarter of a pie is a generous piece.*

gene (jēn), *n., pl.* **genes.** a minute part of a chromosome, consisting essentially of DNA, that influences the inheritance and development of some character; factor. The genes inherited from its parents determine what kind of organism will develop from a fertilized egg cell. [< German *Gen,* ultimately < Greek *genea* breed, kind]

ge·net·ic (jə net′ik), *adj.* **1** having to do with origin and natural growth. **2** of or having to do with genetics. **3** of or having to do with genes. —**ge·net′i·cal·ly,** *adv.*

ge·nus (jē′nəs), *n., pl.* **gen·er·a** (jen′ər ə) or **ge·nus·es.** group of related organisms ranking below a family and above a species. The scientific name of an organism consists of the genus written with a capital letter and the species written with a small letter. EXAMPLE: *Homo sapiens.* [< Latin]

ge·ol·o·gy (jē ol′ə jē), *n., pl.* **-gies.** **1** science that deals with the composition of the crust of the earth or of other solid heavenly bodies, the layers of which they are composed, and their history. **2** physical features of the earth or of other bodies in a place or region.

gi·gan·tic (jī gan′tik), *adj.* huge; enormous. [< Greek *gigantos*] —**gi·gan′ti·cal·ly,** *adv.*

glid·ing joint (glī′ding joint′), a joint that allows bones to slide past each other.

god·dess (god′is), *n., pl.* **god·dess·es.** **1** a female god. **2** a very beautiful or charming woman.

God (god), *n.*, *pl.* (for 2) **gods. 1** the Supreme Being worshiped in most religions as the maker and ruler of the world. **2 god,** a being that is thought to have supernatural powers and considered worthy of worship.

go·ril·la (gə ril´ə), *n.* the largest and most powerful anthropoid ape, found in the forests of central Africa. It is chiefly arboreal and vegetarian in diet. [< Greek *gorillas*, plural, < African word]

grad·u·a·tion (graj´ü ā´shən), *n.* **1** a graduating from a school, college, or university. **2** ceremony of graduating; graduating exercises.

graf·fi·ti (grə fē´tē), *n., pl.* of **graf·fi·to** (grə fē´tō) for def. 1, *n.sing.* for def. 2. **1** drawings or writings scratched or scribbled on a wall or other surface. **2** INFORMAL. a single such drawing or writing, [< Italian, ultimately < Greek *graphein* write, draw]

gra·ham crack·er (grā´əm krak´ər), cracker made from whole-wheat flour, including all the bran.

grat·i·tude (grat´ə tüd, grat´ə tyüd), *n.* kindly feeling because of a favor received; thankfulness.

Great Bar·ri·er Reef (grāt´ bar´ē ər rēf´), the longest coral reef in the world, in the S Pacific along the NE coast of Australia. 1250 mi.

great-un·cle (grāt´ung´kəl), *n.* granduncle; uncle of one's father or mother.

greed·y (grē´dē), *adj.,* **greed·i·er, greed·i·est. 1** eager for gain, wealth, and the like. **2** having a desire to possess something.

ground wa·ter (ground´ wȯ´tər), water that flows downward and saturates the soil. The upper level is called the water table. Ground water supplies springs and wells.

gua·ca·mo·le (guä´kə mō´lē), *n.* a spread or dip made of mashed avocado, tomato, onion, seasoning, etc. [< Mexican Spanish < Nahuatl *ahuacamolli* < *ahuacatl* avocado + *molli* sauce]

guer·ril·la (gə ril´ə), *n.* member of a band of fighters who harass the enemy by sudden raids, ambushes, etc. Guerrillas are not part of a regular army.

gun·pow·der (gun´pou´dər), *n.* powder that explodes when brought into contact with fire, used in guns, fireworks, and blasting.

H

hab·i·tat (hab´ə tat), *n.* **1** place where an animal or plant naturally lives or grows: *The jungle is the habitat of monkeys.* **2** dwelling place. [< Latin, it inhabits]

Hal·low·een or **Hal·low·e'en** (hal´ō ēn´, hol´ō ēn´), *n.* evening of October 31, before All Saints' Day. [short for *Allhalloweven*]

ham·mock (ham´ək), *n.* a hanging bed or couch made of canvas, netted cord, etc., suspended by cords or ropes at both ends. [< Spanish *hamaca* < Taino]

hand·cuff (hand´kuf´), *n., pl.* **hand·cuffs. 1** one of a pair of metal rings joined by a short chain and locked around the wrists of a prisoner. **2** a similar device that is made of plastic and is disposable. —*v.t.* put handcuffs on.

har·ass (har´əs, hə ras´), *v.t.* **1** trouble by repeated attacks; harry: *Pirates harassed the villages along the coast.* **2** distress with annoying labor, care, misfortune, etc.; disturb; worry; torment.

hast·y (hā´stē), *adj.,* **hast·i·er, hast·i·est. 1** done or made in a hurry; quick: *a hasty glance.* **2** not well thought out: *a hasty decision.* **3** easily angered. **4** done or uttered in sudden anger or irritation: *hasty words.* —**hast´i·ly,** *adv.* —**hast´i·ness,** *n.*

haz·ard·ous waste (haz´ər dəs wāst´), *n.* any industrial by-product from the manufacture of chemicals that destroys the environment or endangers the health of people and animals.

Great Barrier Reef
the **Great Barrier Reef** along the coast of NE Australia

hammock
Relax in a **hammock** on a lazy day.

a	hat	**ī**	ice	**u̇**	put	**ə** stands for	
ā	age	**o**	not	**ü**	rule	**a**	in about
ä	far, calm	**ō**	open	**ch**	child	**e**	in taken
âr	care	**ȯ**	saw	**ng**	long	**i**	in pencil
e	let	**ô**	order	**sh**	she	**o**	in lemon
ē	equal	**oi**	oil	**th**	thin	**u**	in circus
ėr	term	**ou**	out	**ᵺ**	then		
i	it	**u**	cup	**zh**	measure		

heirloom

This grandfather clock is

an **heirloom.**

homemade

a **homemade**

apple pie

head (hed), *n., pl.* **heads** for 1-7, 9, **head** for 8; *adj., v.* —*n.* **1** the top part of the human body containing the brain, eyes, nose, ears, and mouth. **2** the corresponding part of an animal's body. **3** the top part of anything: *the head of a pin.* **4** the front part of anything: *the head of a procession.* **5** the chief person. **6** position of leadership. **7** person. **8** one or ones; individual or individuals. **9** anything rounded like a head: *a head of cabbage.* **go to one's head, 1** affect one's mind. **2** make one dizzy. **3** make one conceited. **lose one's head,** get excited; lose one's self-control. **make head or tail of,** understand. **over one's head, 1** beyond one's power to understand **2** passing over a person without giving that person a chance to act. **put heads together** or **lay heads together,** plan or plot together.

head·ache (hed/āk/), *n.* **1** pain in the head. **2** INFORMAL. something which causes great bother; annoyance.

heard (hėrd), *v.* pt. and pp. of **hear.**

heart·beat (härt/bēt/), *n.* pulsation of the heart, including one complete contraction and relaxation.

heat·stroke (hēt/strōk/), *n.* collapse or sudden illness with high fever and dry skin caused by exposure to excessive heat.

heir·loom (âr/lüm/), *n.* any piece of personal property that has been handed down from generation to generation. [< *heir + loom,* originally, implement]

he·mo·glo·bin (hē/mə glō/bən, hem/ə glō/bən), *n.* substance in the red corpuscles of the blood of vertebrates made up of iron and protein, that carries oxygen from the lungs to the tissues and carries carbon dioxide from the tissues to the lungs.

he·mo·phil·i·a (hē/mə fil/ē ə, hem/ə fil/ē ə), *n.* an inherited disorder of the blood in which clotting does not occur normally, making it difficult to stop bleeding even after the slightest injury. [< Greek *haima* blood + *philia* affection, tendency]

hem·or·rhage (hem/ər ij), *n.* discharge of blood, especially a heavy discharge from a damaged blood vessel.

herd (hėrd), *n.* group of animals of one kind, especially cows, horses, or elephants. [Old English *heord*]

he·red·i·ty (hə red/ə tē), *n., pl.* **-ties. 1** the transmission of physical or mental characteristics from parent to offspring by means of genes. **2** characteristics of body or mind that have come to offspring from parents. **3** tendency of offspring to be like the parents. [< Latin *hereditatem* < *heredem* heir]

hers (hėrz), *pron.* possessive form of **she.** the one or ones belonging to her.

Him·a·la·yas (him/ə lā/əz, hə mä/lyəz), *n.pl.* mountain system extending about 1600 miles (2600 kilometers) from the Pamirs in Pakistan eastward through India, Nepal, Bhutan, and the southern Chinese border.

Hin·du·ism (hin/dü iz/əm), *n.* the religion and social system of the Hindus. The worship of many gods is part of Hinduism.

hinge joint (hinj joint), a joint in which movement is limited to one plane.

Hok·kai·do (hō kī/dō), *n.* the second largest island in Japan. 5,184,000 pop.; 30,100 sq. mi. (78,000 sq. km.)

home·made (hōm/mād/), *adj.* made at home: *homemade bread.*

hon·cho (hon/chō), *n., pl.* **-chos.** SLANG. person in charge; boss. [< Japanese *hanchō* squad leader]

Hon·shu (hon/shü), *n.* the largest and most important island of Japan. 82,560,000 pop.; 88,900 sq. mi. (230,300 sq. km.) Also, **Hondo.**

ho·ri·zon·tal scale (hôr/ə zon/tl skāl/), the bottom of a chart or graph which shows certain values.

hor·ri·fy (hôr/ə fī), *v.t.,* **hor·ri·fied, hor·ri·fy·ing. 1** cause to feel horror. **2** shock very much.

hos·pi·tal (hos/pi təl), *n.* **1** place where sick or injured people are given medical or surgical treatment. **2** a similar place for animals.

hos·pi·tal·i·ty (hos/pə tal/ə tē), *n., pl.* **-ties.** friendly reception; generous treatment of guests or strangers.

host (hōst), *n.* **1** person who receives another person as a guest. **2** keeper of an inn or hotel. **3** a living organism in or on which a parasite lives. —*v.t.* **1** receive or entertain at as a host does. **2** serve as an emcee of. [< Old French *hoste* guest, host < Latin *hospitem* < *hostis* stranger, enemy]

hos·tel (hos/tl), *n.* a lodging place, especially a supervised lodging place for young people on bicycle trips, hikes, etc.

hos·tile (hos′tl; *sometimes* hos′tīl),
adj. **1** of an enemy or enemies: *the
hostile army.* **2** opposed;
unfriendly; unfavorable.

hos·til·i·ty (ho stil′ə tē), *n., pl.* **-ties.**
1 the feeling that an enemy has;
being an enemy; unfriendliness.
2 state of being at war. **3** hostilities,
pl. acts of war.

hur·ri·cane (hėr′ə kān), *n.* **1** (in
meteorology) a wind having a
velocity of more than 75 miles (121
kilometers) per hour. **2** a tropical
cyclone originating in the West
Indies, usually accompanied by
violent thunderstorms. [< Spanish
huracán < Taino *hurakán*]

hy·po·ther·mi·a (hī′pō thėr′mē ə), *n.*
a subnormal body temperature,
especially one low enough to
cause serious physiological
changes, as produced by exposure
to cold, drugs, etc. [< *hypo-* +
Greek *thermē* heat]

I

ice·berg (īs′bėrg′), *n.* a large mass of
ice, detached from a glacier and
floating in the sea; berg. About 90
percent of its mass is below the
surface of the water. [< Dutch
ijsberg, literally, ice mountain.]

i·ci·cle (ī′si kəl), *n., pl.* **i·ci·cles.** a
pointed, hanging stick of ice
formed by the freezing of dripping
water.

i·den·ti·cal (ī den′tə kəl), *adj.* **1** the
same: *Both events happened on
the identical day.* **2** exactly alike.

i·den·ti·ty (ī den′tə te), *n., pl.* **-ties.**
1 a being oneself or itself, and not
another; who or what one is: *The
writer concealed her identity by
signing her stories with a pen
name.* **2** a being identical; exact
likeness.

i·dle (ī′dl), *adj.,* **i·dler, i·dlest.** **1** doing
nothing; not busy; not working:
idle hands. **2** fond of doing
nothing; not willing to work; lazy.

i·dol (ī′dl), *n.* **1** image or other object
worshiped as a god. **2** (in the Bible)
a false god. **3** person or thing
worshiped or loved very much;
object of extreme devotion.

il·le·gal (i lē′gəl), *adj.* not lawful;
against the law; forbidden by law.
—*n.* person who does something
illegal, especially a person who
enters a country illegally.

il·lu·mi·nat·ed man·u·scripts (i lü′
mə nā tid man′yə skripts), old
books and papers decorated with
gold, colors, pictures, and designs.

i·mag·i·nar·y (i maj′ə ner′ē), *adj.*
existing only in the imagination;
not real: *Ghosts are imaginary.*

im·i·tate (im′ə tāt), *v.t.,* **-tat·ed,
-tat·ing.** **1** try to be like or act like;
follow the example of: *The little
boy imitated his older brother.*
2 make or do something like;
copy: *A parrot imitates the sounds
it hears.* **3** act like: *She amused
the class by imitating a baby
and a bear.*

im·i·ta·tion (im′ə tā′shən), *n.* **1** an
imitating: *We learn many things
by imitation.* **2** thing that imitates
something else: *Give as good an
imitation as you can of a rooster.*
—*adj.* made to look like something
better; not real.

im·mo·bi·lize (i mō′bə līz), *v.t.,* **-lized,
-liz·ing.** make motionless.

im·mov·a·ble (i mü′və bəl), *adj.* that
cannot be moved; firmly fixed.

im·mune sys·tem (i myün′ sis′təm),
system of lymphocytes and antibodies that recognize, attack, and
destroy bacteria, viruses, and other
foreign material that enter the body.

im·mu·nize (im′yə nīz), *v.t.,*
im·mu·nized, im·mu·niz·ing.
give immunity to; make immune:
*Vaccination immunizes people
against smallpox.* —**im′mu·ni·
za′tion,** *n.*

im·par·tial (im pär′shəl), *adj.*
showing no more favor to one
side than to the other; fair; just.

im·pend·ing (im pen′ding), *adj.* likely
to happen soon; threatening.

hurricane

the eye of a **hurricane**

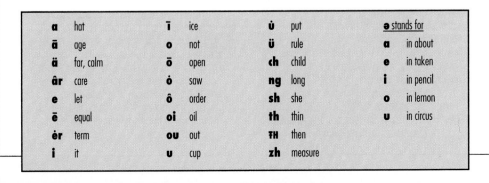

a	hat	**ī**	ice	**u̇**	put	**ə** *stands for*	
ā	age	**o**	not	**ü**	rule	**a**	in about
ä	far, calm	**ō**	open	**ch**	child	**e**	in taken
âr	care	**ȯ**	saw	**ng**	long	**i**	in pencil
e	let	**ô**	order	**sh**	she	**o**	in lemon
ē	equal	**oi**	oil	**th**	thin	**u**	in circus
ėr	term	**ou**	out	**ŦH**	then		
i	it	**u**	cup	**zh**	measure		

indicate (def. 1)

This sign **indicates** several park locations.

inscription

an **inscription** on a grave from the Civil War

im·pli·cate (im′plə kāt), *v.t.,* **-cat·ed, -cat·ing.** show to have a part or to be connected; involve: *The thief's confession implicated two men.*

im·pli·ca·tion (im′plə kā′shən), *n.* **1** an implying. **2** a being implied. **3** something implied; indirect suggestion; hint: *There was no implication of dishonesty.*

im·pro·vise (im′prə vīz), *v.,* **-vised, -vis·ing.** —*v.t.* **1** make up (music, poetry, etc.) on the spur of the moment. **2** make for the occasion: *The stranded motorists improvised a tent out of two blankets and some long poles.* —*v.i.* compose, utter, or do anything without preparation.

im·pul·sive (im pul′siv), *adj.* acting or done upon impulse: *Impulsive buyers often purchase things they don't need.*

in·ap·pro·pri·ate (in′ə prō′prē it), *adj.* not appropriate; not fitting; unsuitable. —**in′ap·pro′pri·ate·ly,** *adv.*

in·at·ten·tive (in′ə ten′tiv), *adj.* not attentive; careless; negligent. —**in′at·ten′tive·ly,** *adv.* —**in′at·ten′tive·ness,** *n.*

in·au·di·ble (in ȯ′də bəl), *adj.* that cannot be heard.

in·ci·den·tal·ly (in′sə den′tl ē), *adv.* **1** in an incidental manner. **2** by the way.

in·cum·bent (in kum′bənt), *adj.* **1** resting on a person as a duty or obligation: *She felt it incumbent upon her to answer the letter at once.* **2** currently holding an office, position. —*n.* person holding an office, position, etc.

in·de·ci·sion (in′di sizh′ən), *n.* lack of decision; tendency to delay or to hesitate.

in·di·cate (in′də kāt), *v.t.,* **-cat·ed, -cat·ing.** **1** point out; point to: *The arrow on the sign indicates the right way to go.* **2** make known; show: *A thermometer indicates temperature.*

in·dic·a·tive (in dik′ə tiv), *adj.* pointing out; showing; being a sign; suggestive: *A headache is sometimes indicative of eyestrain.* —**in·dic′a·tive·ly,** *adv.*

in·dict·ment (in dīt′mənt), *n.* **1** a formal written accusation, especially one presented by a grand jury. **2** accusation.

in·di·vid·u·al·ize (in′də vij′ü ə līz), *v.t.,* **-ized, -iz·ing.** **1** make different for each individual; give a distinctive character to. **2** consider as individuals; list one by one.

in·duc·tion (in duk′shən), *n.* **1** a reasoning from particular facts to general truths or principles. **2** a conclusion reached in this way.

in·fat·u·a·tion (in fach′ü ā′shən), *n.* exaggerated fondness or passion; foolish love.

in·flam·ma·to·ry (in flam′ə tôr′ē, in flam′ə tōr′ē), *adj.* **1** tending to excite or arouse: *an inflammatory speech.* **2** of, causing, or accompanied by inflammation.

in·gre·di·ent (in grē′dē ənt), *n., pl.* **in·gre·di·ents.** one of the parts of a mixture or combination: *the ingredients of a cake.*

i·ni·ti·ate (i nish′ē āt), *v.t.,* **-at·ed, -at·ing.** be the first one to start; set going; begin.

i·ni·ti·a·tive (i nish′ē ə tiv, i nish′ē ā′tiv), *n.* **1** active part in taking the first steps in any undertaking: *A shy person is not likely to take the initiative in making friends.* **2** readiness to start something.

in·jec·tion (in jek′shən), *n.* **1** act or process of injecting: *Drugs are often given by injection.* **2** liquid injected: *an injection of penicillin.*

in·nate be·hav·ior (i nāt′ bi hā′vyər), manner in which a living organism acts that is inborn, or existing from birth.

in·nu·en·do (in′yü en′dō), *n., pl.* **in·nu·en·does.** **1** an indirect hint or reference; insinuation. **2** an indirect suggestion meant to discredit a person: *spread scandal by innuendo.* [< Latin, literally, by nodding to <*innuere* nod to, hint <*in-* + *-nuere* to nod]

in·put (in′pu̇t′), *v.,* **-put, -put·ting,** *n.* —*v.t.* put in; introduce. —*n.* **1** what is put in or taken in. **2** power supplied to a machine. **3** information or instructions put into a computer.

in·scribe (in skrīb′), *v.t.,* **-scribed, -scrib·ing.** **1** write or engrave (words, names, letters, etc.) on stone, paper, metal, etc. **2** mark or engrave (a surface, monument, etc.) with words, names, letters. [< Latin *inscribere* < *in-* on + *scribere* write] —**in·scrib′er.** *n.*

in·scrip·tion (in skrip′shən), *n.* something inscribed; words, names, letters, etc., written or engraved on stone, metal, paper, etc. A monument or a coin has an inscription on it. [< Latin *inscriptionem* < *inscribere.* See INSCRIBE.] —**in·scrip′tion·less,** *adj.*

in·spec·tor (in spek′tər), *n.* **1** person who inspects. **2** officer or official appointed to inspect: *a milk inspector.* **3** a police officer, usually ranking next below a superintendent.

in·spi·ra·tion (in′spə rā′shən), *n.* **1** influence of thought and strong feelings on actions, especially on good actions: *Some people get inspiration from sermons, some from poetry.* **2** any influence that arouses effort to do well: *The teacher was an inspiration to her students.* **3** idea that is inspired; sudden, brilliant idea.

in·spire (in spīr′), *v.t.,* **-spired, -spir·ing. 1** fill with a thought or feeling; influence: *A chance to try again inspired him with hope.* **2** cause (thought or feeling): *The leader's courage inspired confidence in the others.* **3** put thought, feeling, etc., into.

in·stant (in′stənt), *n.* **1** particular moment: *Stop talking this instant!* **2** moment of time: *She paused for an instant.* —*adj.* **1** coming at once; without delay; immediate: *The medicine gave instant relief from pain.* **2** pressing; urgent: *When there is a fire, there is an instant need for action.* **3** prepared beforehand and requiring little or no cooking, mixing, or additional ingredients. [< Latin *instantem* standing near, urgent, insistent < *in-* in + *stare* to stand]

in·stan·ta·ne·ous (in′stən tā′nē əs), *adj.* coming or made in an instant. **—in′stan·ta′ne·ous·ly,** *adv.*

in·stinct (in′stingkt), *n.* **1** a chain of unlearned, coordinated acts characteristic of a particular species or group of animals. *Birds build nests by instinct.* **2** a natural tendency or ability; talent. [< Latin *instinctus* impulse < *instinguere* incite, impel]

in·te·ger (in′tə jər), *n., pl.* **in·te·gers.** any positive or negative whole number, or zero. [< Latin, whole < *in-* not + *tangere* to touch]

in·ten·si·fy (in ten′sə fī), *v.,* **-fied, -fy·ing.** make or become intense or more intense; strengthen; increase. **—in·ten′si·fi·ca′tion,** *n.*

in·ten·tion (in ten′shən), *n.* **1** an intending; purpose; design: *hurt someone's feelings without intention.* **2** meaning; significance: *the intention of the poem.*

in·ter·cede (in′tər sēd′), *v.i.,* **-ced·ed, -ced·ing.** plead for another; ask a favor from one person for another.

in·ter·i·or (in tir′ē ər), *n.* **1** inner surface or part; inside: *The interior of the house was beautifully decorated and furnished.* **2** part of a region or country away from the coast. —*adj.* **1** on or for the inside; inner. **2** away from the coast; inland. [< Latin, inner, comparative of *inter* between]

in·ter·jec·tion (in′tər jek′shən), *n.* **1** an exclamation regarded as a part of speech. *Oh! ah! alas!* and *hurrah!* are interjections. **2** an interjecting. **3** something interjected; remark thrown in; exclamation.

in·ter·mit·tent (in′tər mit′nt), *adj.* stopping for a time and beginning again; pausing at intervals.

in·ter·ro·ga·tion (in ter′ə gā′shən), *n.* an interrogating; a questioning; a formal examination of a witness by asking questions.

in·ter·rup·tion (in′tə rup′shən), *n.* **1** an interrupting. **2** a being interrupted. **3** something that interrupts. **4** intermission.

in·tes·tine (in tes′tən), *n., pl.* **in·tes·tines.** part of the alimentary canal extending from the stomach to the anus; small intestine and large intestine. [< Latin *intestinum* < *intus* within < *in* in]

in·tro·duc·tion (in′trə duk′shən), *n.* **1** an introducing: *The introduction of steel made tall buildings easier to build.* **2** a being introduced: *She was enthusiastic at her introduction to so many new people.* **3** thing that introduces; first part of a book, speech, piece of music.

interior (def. 1)
the **interior** of the
space shuttle Columbia

a	hat	**ī**	ice	**u̇**	put	**ə** stands for
ā	age	**o**	not	**ü**	rule	**a** in about
ä	far, calm	**ō**	open	**ch**	child	**e** in taken
âr	care	**ȯ**	saw	**ng**	long	**i** in pencil
e	let	**ô**	order	**sh**	she	**o** in lemon
ē	equal	**oi**	oil	**th**	thin	**u** in circus
ėr	term	**ou**	out	**ᵀH**	then	
i	it	**u**	cup	**zh**	measure	

in·tro·spec·tion (in′trə spek′shən), *n.* examination of one's own thoughts and feelings.

in·un·da·tion (in′un dā′shən), *n.* an overspreading with a flow of water; flood.

in·vis·i·ble (in viz′ə bəl), *adj.* not visible; not capable of being seen: *Thought is invisible. Germs are invisible to the naked eye.* —**in·vis′i·ble·ness,** *n.* —**in·vis′i·bly,** *adv.*

in·vi·ta·tion (in′və tā′shən), *n.* **1** a polite request to come to some place or to do something. Formal invitations are written or printed. **2** act of inviting.

Is·lam (is′ləm, i släm′), *n.* **1** the religion of the Moslems, based on the teachings of Mohammed as they appear in the Koran. It holds that there is only one God, Allah, and that Mohammed is his prophet. **2** Moslems as a group. **3** the countries inhabited by Moslems or under Moslem rule. [< Arabic *islām* submission (to the will of God)]

i·so·late (*v.* ī′sə lāt, is′ə lāt; *n.* ī′sə lət, ī′sə lāt), *v.,* **i·so·lat·ed, i·so·lat·ing,** *n.* —*v.t.* set apart; separate from others; keep alone: *People with contagious diseases should be isolated.* —*n.* thing, person, or group that is isolated or set apart. [back-formation < *isolated* < French *isolé* < Italian *isolato* < Latin *insulatum* made into an island < *insula* island]

i·tal·ic (i tal′ik, ī tal′ik), *adj.* of or in type whose letters slant to the right: *These words are in italic type.*

i·tin·er·ar·y (ī tin′ə rer′ē, i tin′ə rer′ē), *n., pl.* **-rar·ies,** *adj.* —*n.* **1** route of travel; plan of travel. **2** record of travel. **3** guidebook for travelers. —*adj.* **1** of traveling or routes of travel. **2** itinerant.

its (its), *adj.* possessive form of **it.** of it; belonging to it: *The dog wagged its tail.*

i·vor·y (ī′vər ē), *n., pl.* **i·vor·ies,** *adj.* —*n.* a hard, white substance composing the tusks of elephants, walruses, etc. Ivory is a form of dentin and is used for piano keys, billiard balls, combs, ornaments, etc. —*adj.* made of ivory. [< Anglo-French *ivorie* < Latin *eboreus* of ivory < *ebur* ivory < Egyptian *āb* elephant]

judge (def. 1)
A **judge** is an official who presides over trials.

jag·uar (jag′wär, jag′yü är), *n.* a large, fierce cat of the same genus as the lion, tiger, and leopard; panther. Jaguars live in forests in tropical America. [< Portuguese < Tupi *jaguara*]

ja·la·pe·ño (hä′lä pā′nyō), *n., pl.* **-ños.** a Mexican pepper with a sharp taste. [< Mexican Spanish]

joint (joint), *n., pl.* **joints. 1** the place at which two things or parts are joined. **2** a part in an animal where two bones join, allowing motion, and the immediately surrounding area. **3** one of the parts of which a jointed thing is made up: *the middle joint of the finger.* **4** part of the stem of a plant from which a leaf or branch grows. —*adj.* **1** shared or done by two or more persons. **2** joined with another or others; sharing. [< Old French *jointe,* past participle of *joindre*]

Ju·da·ism (jü′dē iz′əm), *n.* religion of the Jews, based on the teachings of Moses and the prophets as found in the Bible, and on the interpretations of the rabbis. Judaism teaches belief in one God.

judge (juj), *n., v.,* **judged, judg·ing.** —*n.* **1** a public official appointed or elected to hear and decide cases in a court of law. **2** person chosen to settle a dispute or decide who wins a race, contest, etc. —*v.t.* **1** hear and decide (a case) in a court of law. **2** settle (a dispute); decide who wins (a race, contest, etc.). **3** form an opinion or estimate about: *judge the merits of a book.* —*v.i.* **1** act as a judge. **2** form an opinion or estimate. [< Old French *juge* < Latin *judicem* < *jus* law + *dicere* say]

judg·ment (juj′mənt), *n.* **1** result of judging; opinion or estimate. **2** ability to form sound opinions; power to judge well; good sense.

judg·men·tal (juj men′tl), *adj.* having to do with judgment, often a critical judgment.

jun·gle (jung′gəl), *n.* **1** wild land thickly overgrown with bushes, vines, trees, etc. Jungles are hot and humid regions with many kinds of plants and wild animals. **2** a tangled mass. [< Hindustani *jangal* < Sanskrit *jangala* desert]

jus·tice (jus′tis), *n.* **1** just conduct; fair dealing: *have a sense of justice.* **2** a being just; fairness; rightness. **3** well-founded reason; rightfulness; lawfulness. **4** just treatment; deserved reward or punishment.

ju·ve·nile (jü′və nəl, jü′və nīl), *adj.* **1** young; youthful; immature. **2** childish. —*n.* a young person.

K

kan·ga·roo (kang′gə rü′), *n., pl.* **-roos** or **-roo.** any of a family of mammals of Australia and nearby islands who carry their young in a pouch. Kangaroos have a small head, large ears, small forelegs, powerful hind legs, and a heavy tail for balance and support. [probably < native Australian name]

khak·i (kak′ē, kä′kē) *n.* **1** a dull yellowish brown. **2** a heavy twilled wool or cotton cloth of this color, much used for soldiers' uniforms. **3** khakis, *pl.* uniform made of this cloth. —*adj.* dull yellowish-brown. [< Hindi *khākī*, originally, dusty < Persian *khāk* dust]

kick·off (kik′ôf′, kik′of′), *n.* **1** kick that puts a football in play at the beginning of each half and after a field goal or conversion attempt has been made. **2** INFORMAL. any move, etc., made to begin.

kil·o·gram (kil′ə gram), *n.* the basic unit of mass in the metric system, equal to 1000 grams.

kil·o·li·ter (kil′ə lē′tər), *n.* unit of volume equal to 1000 liters.

ki·mo·no (kə mō′nō), *n., pl.* **ki·mo·nos.** a loose outer garment held in place by a wide sash, worn by Japanese men and women. [< Japanese]

king·dom (king′dəm), *n.* **1** nation that is governed by a king or a queen; land or territory ruled by one monarch. **2** one of the primary categories used in classifying organisms. [< Old English *cyningdōm*]

ko·a·la (kō ä′lə), *n., pl.* **ko·a·las.** a gray, furry mammal of Australia that carries its young in a pouch. Koalas have large ears and no tail and look like a small bear. They live in trees and eat eucalyptus leaves. [< native Australian name]

kook·a·bur·ra (kůk′ə bėr′ə), *n.* a large bird of Australia that has a harsh, cackling voice. [< native Australian name]

L

lab·o·ra·to·ry (lab′rə tôr′ē, lab′rə tōr′ē), *n., pl.* **-ries. 1** place where scientific work is done; room or building fitted with apparatus for conducting scientific investigations, experiments, tests, etc. **2** place for manufacturing drugs, chemicals.

la·goon (lə gün′), *n.* **1** pond or small lake connected with a larger body of water. **2** shallow water separated from the sea by low sandbanks. [< Italian *laguna*]

lan·guage (lang′gwij), *n.* **1** human speech, spoken or written. **2** speech of one nation, tribe, or other similar group of people.

lan·tern (lan′tərn), *n.* case to protect a light from wind, rain, etc. It has sides of glass through which the light can shine.

la·zy (lā′zē), *adj.* **-zi·er, -zi·est.** not willing to work or be active.

learned be·hav·ior (lėrnd′ bi hā′vyər), behavior that changes as a result of experiences.

le·gal (lē′gəl), *adj.* **1** of law: *legal knowledge.* **2** of a lawyer or lawyers: *legal advice.* **3** according to law; permitted by law; lawful. [< Latin *legalis* < *lex, legis* law]

le·gal·ize (lē′gə līz), *v.t.,* **-ized, -iz·ing.** make legal; authorize by law; sanction.

leg·is·late (lej′ə slāt), *v.,* **-lat·ed, -lat·ing.** —*v.i.* make or enact laws: *Congress legislates for the United States.* —*v.t.* force by legislation; bring about by legislation. —**leg·is·la·ture,** *n.*

khaki
The **khaki**-colored jeep blends into the surroundings.

kookaburra
Kookaburras nest in tree holes in the forests.

a	hat	**ī**	ice	**ů**	put	**ə** stands for	
ā	age	**o**	not	**ü**	rule	**a**	in about
ä	far, calm	**ō**	open	**ch**	child	**e**	in taken
âr	care	**ò**	saw	**ng**	long	**i**	in pencil
e	let	**ô**	order	**sh**	she	**o**	in lemon
ē	equal	**oi**	oil	**th**	thin	**u**	in circus
ėr	term	**ou**	out	**ŦH**	then		
i	it	**u**	cup	**zh**	measure		

le·git·i·mate (lə jit′ə mit), *adj.*
1 allowed or admitted by law; rightful; lawful: *a legitimate claim.*
2 valid; logical; acceptable. [< Medieval Latin *legitimatum* made lawful < Latin *legitimus* lawful < *lex, legis* law]

leu·ke·mi·a (lü kē′mē ə, lü kē′myə), *n.* form of cancer characterized by an excessive production of white blood cells in the blood. [< New Latin < Greek *leukos* white + *haima* blood] —**leu·ke′·mic,** *adj.*

li·ar (lī′ər), *n.* person who tells lies.

li·cense (lī′sns), *n., v.,* **li·censed, li·cens·ing.** —*n.* **1** permission given by law to do something, as to marry, carry on some business or profession. **2** paper, card, plate, etc., showing such permission. **Poetic license** is the freedom from rules that is permitted in poetry and other arts. **3** too much liberty; disregard of what is right and proper. —*v.t.* give a license to; permit by law. [< Old French *licence* < Latin *licentia* < *licere* be allowed]

lieu·ten·ant (lü ten′ənt; *British, except in the navy,* lef ten′ənt), *n.*
1 person, usually an officer, who acts in the place of someone higher in authority. **2** (in the army, air force, and marines) a first lieutenant or a second lieutenant.

life·guard (līf′gärd′), *n.* person trained in lifesaving who is employed on a beach or at a swimming pool to help in case of accident or danger to swimmers.

life jack·et (līf′ jak′it), a sleeveless jacket filled with a light material, such as kapok, or with compressed air, worn as a life preserver.

lig·a·ment (lig′ə mənt), *n., pl.* **lig·a·ments.** band of strong, flexible, white tissue which connects bones or holds organs of the body in place.

light·ning (līt′ning), *n., adj.,* —*n.* flash of light in the sky caused by a discharge of electricity between clouds, or between one part of a cloud and another part, or between a cloud and the earth's surface. —*adj.* quick as lightning.

lime·light (līm′līt′), *n.* **1** an intense white light produced by heating a piece of lime in a flame, formerly used in a theater to light up certain persons or objects on the stage. **2** center of public attention. —**lime′light′er,** *n.*

lightning
lightning in a
stormy sky

line of sym·me·try (līn′ əv sim′i trē), the real or imaginary line that divides symmetrical objects into equal parts.

lit·er·al (lit′ər əl), *adj.* **1** following the exact words of the original: *a literal translation.* **2** taking words in their usual meaning, without exaggeration or imagination; matter-of-fact. **3** true to fact.

liv·er (liv′ər), *n.* the large, reddish-brown organ in vertebrate animals that secretes bile and is active in the absorption and storage of vitamins, minerals, and sugar (which it changes into glycogen). The liver frees the blood of its waste matter and manufactures blood proteins.

lo·co·mo·tion (lō′kə mō′shən), *n.* act or power of moving from place to place. [< Latin *loco* from a place + English *motion*]

log·i·cal (loj′ə kəl), *adj.* **1** having to do with the principles of logic. **2** reasoning correctly.

long-term mem·or·y (lông′tėrm′ mem′ər ē), information stored in the brain and retrievable over a long period of time.

loot (lüt), *n.* **1** goods taken from an enemy, a captured city, etc., in time of war. **2** anything taken illegally, especially by force or with violence: *burglar's loot.* —*v.t.* **1** plunder, rob, or sack (a city, building, store, etc.). **2** rob or steal, especially by fraud. —*v.i.* plunder; rob. [< Hindustani *lūt*] —**loot′er,** *n.*

loy·al·ty (loi′əl tē), *n., pl.* **-ties.** loyal feeling or behavior; faithfulness.

lu·cra·tive (lü′krə tiv), *adj.* yielding gain or profit; profitable. —**lu′cra·tive·ness,** *n.*

lux·ur·i·ous (lug zhùr′ē əs, luk shùr′ē əs), *adj.* **1** fond of luxury; tending toward luxury; self-indulgent. **2** giving or characterized by luxury; very comfortable.

M

ma·chin·er·y (mə shē′nər ē), *n., pl.* **-er·ies. 1** machines: *construction machinery.* **2** the parts or works of a machine; mechanism: *the machinery of a typewriter.*

mag·net·ic com·pass (mag net′ik kum′pəs), instrument for showing directions, consisting of a needle or compass card that points to the North Magnetic Pole.

mag·ni·fy (mag′nə fī), *v.*, **-fied, -fy·ing.** —*v.t.* **1** cause to look larger than the real size; enlarge. **2** make too much of; go beyond the truth in telling; exaggerate. —*v.i.* increase the apparent size of an object. [< Latin *magnificare* esteem greatly < *magnificus* noble]

main·tain (mān tān′), *v.t.* keep in existence or continuance; carry on; keep up: *maintain a business.*

main·te·nance (mān′tə nəns), *n.* a keeping in good repair.

maize (māz), *n.* **1** corn; Indian corn. **2** the color of ripe corn; yellow. [< Spanish *maíz* < Taino *mahiz*]

make-be·lieve (māk′bi lēv′), *adj.* imaginary: *a make-believe playmate.*

man·da·to·ry (man′də tôr′ē, man′də tōr′ē), *adj.* required by a command or order: *a mandatory sentence for manslaughter.*

ma·neu·ver (mə nü′vər), *n.* **1** a planned movement of troops, ships, etc., especially for tactical purposes. **2** a skillful plan; clever trick: *a series of political maneuvers to get votes.* —*v.i.* **1** perform maneuvers. **2** plan skillfully; use clever tricks; scheme: *maneuver for some advantage.* —*v.t.* move or manipulate skillfully: *maneuver scenery on a stage.*

mar·su·pi·al (mär sü′pē əl), *n., pl.* **mar·su·pi·als.** any of an order of mammals having a pouch covering the mammary glands on the abdomen, in which the female nurses and carries her incompletely developed young. Kangaroos belong to this order.

ma·ter·i·al (mə tir′ē əl), *n.* what a thing is made from; matter from which anything is manufactured or built: *building material.*

math·e·mat·ics (math′ə mat′iks, math mat′iks), *n.* science dealing with the measurement, properties, and relationships of quantities, as expressed in numbers or symbols. Mathematics includes arithmetic, algebra, geometry, calculus, etc.

mat·ter (mat′ər), *n.* **1** what things are made of; material; substance. Matter occupies space, has weight, and can exist in solid, liquid, or gaseous form. **2** thing to do; concern; activity; affair: *business matters.* [< Old French *matiere* < Latin *materia.*]

may·on·naise (mā′ə nāz′), *n.* dressing made of egg yolks, vegetable oil, vinegar or lemon juice, and seasoning, beaten together until thick.

mean (mēn), *adj.* **1** halfway between two extremes. **2** (in mathematics) having a value intermediate between the values of other quantities. —*n.* **1** condition, quality, or course of action halfway between two extremes. **2** (in mathematics) a quantity having a value intermediate between the values of other quantities.

mean·while (mēn′hwīl′), *n., adv.* meantime.

me·chan·i·cal clock (mə kan′ə kəl klok′), a clock that works by means of fixed and moving parts.

med·al·ist or **med·al·list** (med′əl ist), *n.* **1** a designer, engraver, or maker of medals. **2** a recipient of a medal as an award.

me·di·a (mē′dē ə), *n.* **1** a pl. of **medium. 2** medium. **3** mass media. → **media.** The use of *media* instead of *medium* in the sense of "a mass medium, especially journalism or television" has become widespread in informal English. Though originally only a plural form in English, *media* seems established as a singular.

me·di·an (mē′dē ən), *adj.* **1** of, having to do with, or situated in the middle; middle. **2** of a median; having as many above as below a certain number —*n.* the middle number of a sequence arranged in order of size and having an odd number of values. EXAMPLE: The median of 1, 3, 4, 8, 9 is 4. [< Latin *medianus* < *medius* middle.]

maize (def. 1)
maize hanging in a market

marsupial
Tasmanian devils are **marsupials** from an island off SE Australia.

a	hat	**ī**	ice	**u̇**	put	**ə** stands for	
ā	age	**o**	not	**ü**	rule	**a**	in about
ä	far, calm	**ō**	open	**ch**	child	**e**	in taken
âr	care	**ȯ**	saw	**ng**	long	**i**	in pencil
e	let	**ô**	order	**sh**	she	**o**	in lemon
ē	equal	**oi**	oil	**th**	thin	**u**	in circus
ėr	term	**ou**	out	**ᴛн**	then		
i	it	**u**	cup	**zh**	measure		

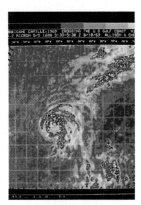

meteorology

studying **meteorology**

from the satellite image

of Hurricane Camille

metronome

a **metronome** for

keeping time in music

med·ic (med′ik), n. INFORMAL.
1 physician. **2** a medical student.
3 member of a medical corps of
the armed forces.

med·i·cate (med′ə kāt), v.t., **-cat·ed,
-cat·ing. 1** treat with medicine:
medicate an infection. **2** put
medicine on or in.

me·dic·i·nal (mə dis′n əl), adj.
having value as medicine;
healing; helping; relieving.
—me·dic′i·nal·ly, adv.

med·i·cine (med′ə sən), n. substance,
such as a drug, used to treat,
prevent, or cure disease.

me·di·o·cre (mē′dē ō′kər, mē′dē
ō′kər), adj. neither good nor bad;
of average or lower than average
quality; ordinary.

mei·o·sis (mī ō′sis), n. (in biology)
the process by which the number
of chromosomes in reproductive
cells of sexually reproducing
organisms is reduced to half the
original number, resulting in the
production of gametes or spores.
[< Greek *meiōsis* a lessening]

mem·o·rize (mem′ə rīz′), v.t., **-rized,
-riz·ing.** commit to memory; learn
by heart: memorize a poem.

mem·o·ry (mem′ər ē), n., pl. **-or·ies.**
ability to remember; capacity to
retain or recall things.

mer·chan·dise (n. mėr′chən dīz,
mėr′chən dīs; v. mėr′chən dīz), n.,
v., **-dised, -dis·ing. —n.** goods for
sale; articles bought and sold;
wares. **—v.t., v.i.** buy and sell.

mer·chant (mėr′chənt), n., pl.
mer·chants. person who buys and
sells items for profit. **—adj.** having
to do with trade; trading;
commercial. [< Old French
marchēant, ultimately < Latin
merx, mercis wares]

me·ringue (mə rang′), n. mixture
made of egg whites and sugar,
beaten stiff. Meringue is often
spread on pies, puddings, etc.

met·a·mor·pho·sis (met′ə môr′fə sis),
n., pl. **-ses** (-sēz′). a marked change
in the form, and usually the habits,
of an animal in its development
after the embryonic stage. Tadpoles
become frogs by metamorphosis.

me·te·or·ol·o·gy (mē′tē ə rol′ə jē), n.
science dealing with the
atmosphere and atmospheric
conditions or phenomena.

me·tic·u·lous (mə tik′yə ləs), adj.
extremely or excessively careful
about details.

met·ro·nome (met′rə nōm), n. device
that can be adjusted to make loud
ticking sounds at different speeds.
Metronomes are used especially to
mark time for persons practicing
on musical instruments. [< Greek
metron measure + *-nomos*
regulating < *nemein* regulate]

me·trop·o·lis (mə trop′ə lis), n.
1 a large city; important center,
especially the center of some
activity: a financial metropolis.
2 most important city of a country
or region. [< Greek *mētropolis*
< *mētēr* mother + *polis* city]

met·ro·pol·i·tan (met′rə pol′ə tən),
adj. of a metropolis; belonging to
a large city or cities.

Mich·i·gan (mish′ə gən), n. **1** one
of the north central states of the
United States. 9,258,000 pop.;
58,200 sq. mi. (150,700 sq. km.)
Capital: Lansing. *Abbrev.:* Mich.
or MI **2 Lake,** one of the five Great
Lakes, the only one entirely in the
United States. 22,400 sq. mi.
(58,000 sq. km.)

mi·crobe (mī′krōb), n. **1** germ;
microorganism. **2** bacterium,
especially one causing diseases or
fermentation. [< French < Greek
mikros small + *bios* life]

mi·cro·bi·ol·o·gy (mī′krō bī ol′ə jē),
n. branch of biology dealing with
microorganisms.

mi·cro·chip (mī′krō chip′), n. a chip
containing thousands of integrated
circuits.

mi·cro·cosm (mī′krō koz′əm), n.
community, etc., regarded as an
epitome of the world; a little world.

mi·cro·film (mī′krō film′), n. film for
making very small photographs
of pages of a book, newspapers,
records, etc., to preserve them in
a very small space.

mi·cro·min·i·a·ture (mī′krō min′ē ə
chŭr, mī′krō min′ə chər), adj.
smaller than a size considered to
be miniature; extremely small.

mi·cro·scope (mī′krə skōp), n. an
optical instrument consisting of a
lens or combination of lenses for
magnifying things that are invisible
or indistinct to the naked eye.

mi·cro·wave (mī′krō wāv′), n. an
electromagnetic radio wave
having a very short wavelength.

mi·gra·to·ry (mī′grə tôr′ē, mī′grə
tōr′ē), adj. moving from one place
to another; migrating.

mil·li·gram (mil′ə gram), n. unit of
mass equal to $1/1000$ of a gram.

mil·li·li·ter (mil′ə lē′tər), *n.* unit of volume equal to ¹/₁₀₀₀ of a liter.

mim·ic (mim′ik), *v.t.*, **mim·icked, mim·ick·ing, 1** make fun of by imitating. **2** copy closely; imitate. *mimic a person's voice.*

min·i·a·ture (min′ē ə chúr, min′ə chər), *n.* anything represented on a very small scale; a reduced image or likeness.

mis·de·mean·or (mis′di mē′nər), *n.* a breaking of the law, not so serious as a felony. Breaking traffic laws are misdemeanors.

mis·pro·nounce (mis′prə nouns′), *v.t., v.i.,* **-nounced, -nounc·ing.** pronounce incorrectly. **—mis′pro·nun′ci·a′tion,** *n.*

mis·sile (mis′əl), *n.* **1** object or weapon that is thrown, hurled, or shot. **2** a self-propelled rocket or bomb, such as a guided missile. [< Latin *missilis* that can be thrown, ultimately < *mittere* send]

mis·sion·ar·y (mish′ə ner′ē), *n., pl.* **-ar·ies.** person sent on a religious mission.

mis·un·der·stand·ing (mis′un′dər stan′ding), *n.* wrong or failure to understand.

mi·to·sis (mī tō′sis, mi tō′sis), *n.* a continuous process in four stages by which a cell having a nucleus divides to form two new cells, each containing the same number of chromosomes as the original cell. [< New Latin < Greek *mitos* thread]

mo·bile (mō′bəl, mō′bīl), *adj.* easy to move.

mode (mōd), *n.* **1** manner or way in which a thing is done; method. **2** (in statistics) the number which occurs most frequently in a set of data. [< Latin *modus* measure, manner]

mon·o·the·is·tic (mon′ə thē is′tik), *adj.* believing in only one God.

mon·soon (mon sün′), *n., pl.* **mon·soons.** a seasonal wind of the Indian Ocean and southern Asia, blowing from the southwest from April to October and from the northeast the rest of the year.

mon·ster (mon′stər), *n., pl.* **mon·sters. 1** any animal or plant that is very unlike those usually found in nature. **2** an imaginary creature of strange and horrible appearance. **—adj.** enormous; huge. [< Old French *monstre* < Latin *monstrum* portent, divine warning]

mo·ral (môr′əl, mor′əl), *n.* lesson, inner meaning, or teaching of a fable, a story, or an event.

mo·rale (mə ral′), *n.* moral or mental condition or attitude of a person or group as regards courage, confidence, enthusiasm.

mo·squi·to (mə skē′tō), *n., pl.* **-toes** or **-tos.** any of a family of small, slender insects with two wings. The females have mouthparts that can pierce the skin of humans and animals and draw blood, causing itching. [< Spanish, diminutive of *mosca* fly]

mo·ti·vate (mō′tə vāt), *v.t.,* **-vat·ed, -vat·ing.** provide with a motive or incentive; induce to act.

mo·ti·va·tion (mō′tə vā′shən), *n.* act or process of furnishing with an incentive or inducement to action. **—mo′ti·va′tion·al,** *adj.*

mo·tive (mō′tiv), *n.* thought or feeling that makes one act; moving consideration or reason; incentive. See **reason** for synonym study.

mo·tor·ist (mō′tər ist), *n.* person who drives or travels in an automobile.

mot·to (mot′ō), *n., pl.* **mot·toes** or **mot·tos.** a brief sentence adopted as a rule of conduct: *"Think before you speak" is a good motto.* [< Italian < Latin *muttum* grunt, word.]

mul·ti·ple (mul′tə pəl), *adj.* of, having, or involving many parts, elements, relations, etc.; manifold.

mum (mum), *n.* INFORMAL. chrysanthemum.

mur·mur (mėr′mər), *n.* **1** a soft, low, indistinct sound that rises and falls a little and goes on without breaks. **2** complaint made under the breath, not aloud. **—v.i. 1** make a soft, low, indistinct sound. **2** speak softly.

a	hat	**ī**	ice	**u̇**	put		**ə** stands for	
ā	age	**o**	not	**ü**	rule	**a**	in about	
ä	far, calm	**ō**	open	**ch**	child	**e**	in taken	
âr	care	**ȯ**	saw	**ng**	long	**i**	in pencil	
e	let	**ô**	order	**sh**	she	**o**	in lemon	
ē	equal	**oi**	oil	**th**	thin	**u**	in circus	
ėr	term	**ou**	out	**ŦH**	then			
i	it	**u**	cup	**zh**	measure			

Mur·phy (mėr′fē), *n.*, *pl.* **-phys** (-fēz). a last name: *Mr. Murphy's car has broken down, so the Murphys can't take a trip.*

mu·si·cian (myü zish′ən), *n.* **1** person skilled in music. **2** person who sings or who plays on a musical instrument, especially as a profession or business.

my·thol·o·gy (mi thol′ə jē), *n.*, *pl.* **-gies.** group of myths relating to a particular country or person: myths.

N

na·bob (nā′bob), *n.* a very rich or important person. [<Hindustani *nabāb, nawwāb*]

nail (nāl), *n.* **hit the nail on the head,** guess or understand correctly; say or do something just right.

nav·i·ga·tor (nav′ə gā′tər), *n.*, *pl.* **nav·i·ga·tors. 1** person who sails the seas. **2** person who has charge of the navigating of a ship or aircraft or who is skilled.

nec·es·sar·y (nes′ə ser′ē), *adj.* that cannot be done without; indispensable; essential.

neg·a·tive (neg′ə tiv), *adj.* in mathematics: **a** less than zero; minus: *−5 is a negative number.* **b** lying on the side of a point, line, or plane opposite to that considered positive.

New Del·hi (nü′ del′ē), capital of India, in the N part, just south of Delhi. 302,000.

news·stand (nüz′stand′,nyüz′ stand′), *n.* place where newspapers and magazines are sold.

ni·a·cin (nī′ə sən), *n.* nicotinic acid. [<*ni(cotinic) ac(id) + -in*]

niche (nich), *n.*, *v.*, **niched, nich·ing.** —*n.* **1** recess or hollow in a wall for a statue, vase, etc.; nook. **2** a suitable place or position; place for which a person is suited. **3** (in biology) a role in an environment or in a community, often occupied by a particular species or organism. —*v.t.* place in a niche or similar recess. [< Middle French, ultimately < Latin *nidus* nest]

niece (nēs), *n.*, *pl.* **niec·es.** daughter of one's brother or sister; daughter of one's brother-in-law or sister-in-law: *I borrowed my niece's coat. I thanked my nieces for the gift. I visited my nieces' apartments.*

musician (def. 1)

young **musicians**

playing violins

night·mare (nīt′mâr′), *n.* **1** a very distressing dream; dream causing great fear or anxiety. **2** a very distressing experience. [Old English *niht* night + *mare* incubus]

no·mad·ic (nō mad′ik), *adj.* of nomads or their life; wandering.

no·mad (nō′mad, nom′ad), *n.*, *pl.* **no·mads. 1** member of a tribe that moves from place to place to have food or pasture for its cattle. **2** wanderer. —*adj.* **1** wandering from place to place to find pasture. **2** wandering. [< Greek *nomados*, ultimately < *nemein* to pasture]

non·break·a·ble (non brāk′ə bəl), *adj.* not able to be broken.

non·cha·lant (non′shə lənt, non′shə länt′), *adj.* without enthusiasm; coolly unconcerned; indifferent.

non·dis·crim·i·na·to·ry (non′dis krim′ə nə tôr ē), *adj.* not showing partiality or prejudice.

non·es·sen·tial (non′ə sen′shəl), *adj.* not essential; not necessary. —*n.* person or thing not essential.

non·ex·ist·ent (non′ig zis′tənt), *adj.* having no existence.

non·fat·ten·ing (non fat′ən ing), *adj.* not producing fat.

non·fic·tion (non fik′shən), *n.* prose literature that deals with real people and events rather than imaginary ones.

non·ne·go·tia·ble (non′ni gō′shə bəl), *adj.* **1** not capable of being sold. **2** not transferable to another.

non·poi·son·ous (non′poi′zn əs), *adj.* not containing poison; not venomous: *a nonpoisonous snake.*

non·prof·it (non prof′it), *adj.* not for profit; without profit.

non·smoker (non smō′ker), *n.* a person who does not smoke tobacco.

non·stop (non′stop′), *adj.*, *adv.* without stopping: *a nonstop flight (adj.). We flew nonstop from New York to Los Angeles (adv.).*

non·tox·ic (non′tok′sik), *adj.* **1** not of poison; not caused by poison. **2** not poisonous.

non·vi·o·lent (non vī′ə lənt), *adj.* not violent; opposing violence.

nor·mal (nôr′məl), *adj.* of the usual standard; regular; usual.

nor·mal·cy (nôr′məl sē), *n.* normal condition.

nor·mal·i·ty (nôr mal′ə tē), *n.* normal condition.

nor·mal·ize (nôr′mə līz), *v.t.*, **-ized, -iz·ing.** make normal: *normalize the relations between two countries.* —**nor′mal·i·za′tion,** *n.*

nos·y (nō′zē), *adj.*, **nos·i·er, nos·i·est.**
INFORMAL. prying or inquisitive.

no·tice (nō′tis), *n.* **1** attention; observation. **2** announcement or warning. **3** a written or printed sign; paper posted in a public place. **4** a warning that one will end an agreement with another at a certain time. **5** a written or printed account, usually brief.

nov·el·ist (nov′ə list), *n.* writer of novels.

nu·cle·ar (nü′klē ər, nyü′klē ər), *adj.* of or having to do with atoms, atomic energy, or atomic weapons; atomic: *the nuclear age.*

nu·cle·us (nü′klē əs, nyü′klē əs), *n.,* *pl.* **nu·cle·i** (-klē ī), **nu·cle·us·es.** **1** a central part or thing around which other parts or things are collected. **2** a beginning to which additions are to be made. **3** the central part of an atom, consisting of a proton, neutrons, and other particles.

num·ber line (num′bər līn′), line divided into equal segments by points corresponding to integers. The points to the right of 0 are positive; those to the left are negative. The set of all the points on the line corresponds to the set of real numbers.

nurs·er·y (nèr′sər ē), *n.,* *pl.* **-er·ies.** **1** room set apart for the care of babies. **2** a place where babies and small children are cared for.

O

o·a·sis (ō ā′sis), *n.,* *pl.* **o·a·ses** (-sēz′). **1** a fertile spot in the desert where there is water and vegetation. **2** any pleasant place where you can relax.

ob·jec·tive (əb jek′tiv), *n.* something aimed at; object; goal.

of·fense (ə fens′ for 1-6; ə fens′, ȯ′fens for 7), *n.* **1** a breaking of the law; crime or sin. **2** cause of wrongdoing. **3** condition of being offended; hurt feelings; anger or resentment: *Try not to cause* offense. **4** hurting someone's feelings: *No offense was meant.* **5** something that offends or causes displeasure. **6** act of attacking; attack: *A gun is a weapon of offense.* **7** an attacking team or force. [< Latin *offense* < *offendere* offend]

of·fice (ȯ′fis, of′is), *n.* place in which the work of a position is done; room or rooms in which to work.

of·fi·cial (ə fish′əl), *adj.* having authority; authoritative: *An official record is kept of the proceedings.*

o·mit (ō mit′), *v.t.,* **o·mit·ted,** **o·mit·ting.** **1** leave out: *omit a letter in a word.* **2** fail to do; neglect. [< Latin *omittere* < *ob-* by + *mittere* let go]

op·e·rate (op′ə rāt′), *v.i.,* **-rat·ed,** **-rat·ing.** do something to the body, usually with instruments, to improve or restore health; perform surgery.

op·e·ra·tion (op′ə rā′shən), *n.* something done to the body, usually with instruments, to improve or restore health: *A tonsillectomy is a common operation.*

op·e·ra·tor (op′ə rā′tər), *n.* **1** person who operates. **2** a skilled worker who operates a machine, telephone switchboard, telegraph. **3** person who runs a factory, mine.

o·pin·ion (ə pin′yən), *n.* **1** what one thinks; belief not so strong as knowledge; judgment. **2** an impression or estimation of quality, character, or value; estimate. **3** a formal judgment by an expert; professional advice. **4** statement by a judge or jury of the reasons for the decision of the court. [< Latin *opinionem* < *opinari* think]

o·pin·ion·at·ed (ə pin′yə nā′tid), *adj.* obstinate or conceited with regard to one's opinions; dogmatic.

o·pos·sum (ə pos′əm), *n.,* *pl.* **-sums** or **-sum.** any of a family of small, omnivorous, marsupial mammals that live mostly in trees and are active chiefly at night; possum. [of Algonquian origin]

oasis (def. 1)
an **oasis** in the desert

office
a business **office** in
a bank

a	hat	**ī**	ice	**u̇**	put	**ə** stands for	
ā	age	**o**	not	**ü**	rule	**a**	in about
ä	far, calm	**ō**	open	**ch**	child	**e**	in taken
âr	care	**ȯ**	saw	**ng**	long	**i**	in pencil
e	let	**ô**	order	**sh**	she	**o**	in lemon
ē	equal	**oi**	oil	**th**	thin	**u**	in circus
ėr	term	**ou**	out	**ᵺ**	then		
i	it	**u**	cup	**zh**	measure		

op·po·site (op′ə zit), *adj.* **1** placed against; as different in direction as can be; face to face; back to back. **2** as different as can be; completely contrary: *Sour is opposite to sweet.* —*n.* thing or person that is opposite: *A brave person is the opposite of a coward.* —*prep.* opposite to: *opposite the church.* —*adv.* in an opposite position or direction; on opposite sides. [< Latin *oppositum* placed against < *ob-* against + *ponere* to place] —**op′po·site·ly,** *adv.*

o·ral (ôr′əl, ōr′əl), *adj.* **1** using speech; spoken: *an oral command.* **2** of the mouth: *oral hygiene. The oral opening in an earthworm is small.* **3** through or by the mouth.

o·rang·u·tan (ô rang′ü tan′), *n.* a large ape of the forests of Borneo and Sumatra, that has very long arms and reddish-brown hair.

or·der (ôr′dər), *n.* **1** the way one thing follows another: *in order of size.* **2** condition in which every part or piece is in its right place. **3** a regular, methodical, or harmonious arrangement. **4** condition; state: *My affairs are in good order.* **5** way things or events happen: *the order of nature.* **6** condition of things in which the law is obeyed and there is no trouble. **7** the principles and rules by which a meeting is run. **8** command: *On a ship the orders of the captain must be obeyed.* **9** a paper saying that money is to be paid, or that something is to be handed over: *a postal money order.* **10** a spoken or written request for goods that one wants to receive: *a grocery order.* **11** the goods so requested. **12** (in biology) a primary group of related organisms ranking below a class and above a family.

or·di·nar·y (ôrd′n er′ē), *adj.* **1** according to habit or custom; usual; regular; normal: *an ordinary day's work.* **2** not special; common; everyday; average: *an ordinary situation.*

or·gan (ôr′gən), *n.* any part of a living organism that is composed of various tissues organized to perform some particular function. The eyes, stomach, heart, and lungs are organs of the body. Stamens and pistils are organs of flowers. [< Latin *organum* < Greek *organon* instrument, related to *ergon* work]

or·gan·ize (ôr′gə nīz), *v.,* **-ized, -iz·ing.** —*v.t.* **1** put into working order; get together and arrange. **2** bring together into a labor union, as the workers of a particular industry: *organize the truckers.* —*v.i.* combine in a company, party, labor union, etc.; form an organization.

o·ri·gin (ôr′ə jin, or′ə jin), *n.* **1** thing from which anything comes; starting point; source; beginning: *the origin of a quarrel, the origin of a disease.* **2** parentage, ancestry, or birth: *a person of Mexican origin.* **3** (in mathematics) the intersection of the horizontal axis and the vertical axis in a coordinate system. [< Latin *originem* < *oriri* to rise]

ours (ourz, ärz), *pron.* possessive form of **we,** the one or ones belonging to us: *This garden is ours.*

o·ver·whelm·ing (ō′vər hwel′ming), *adj.* too many, too great, or too much to be resisted; overpowering.

P

pan·a·ce·a (pan′ə sē′ə), *n.* remedy for all diseases or ills; cure-all. [< Latin < Greek *panakeia* < *pan-* + *akos* cure]

pan·cre·as (pan′krē əs), *n.* a large gland in vertebrates near the stomach that secretes insulin into the blood and **pancreatic juice,** a digestive juice which contains various enzymes, into the small intestine. [< Greek *pankreas* < *pan-* all + *kreas* flesh]

pan·ic (pan′ik), *n., v.,* **pan·icked, pan·ick·ing.** —*n.* sudden unreasoning fear that causes an individual or entire group to lose self-control and take wild flight; demoralizing terror. —*v.i.* be affected with panic.

pants (pants), *n., pl.* **1** trousers. **2** underpants. [short for *pantaloons*]

pa·per (pā′pər), *n.* **1** material in thin sheets made from wood pulp, rags, or other fibrous substances, used for writing, printing, drawing, etc. **2** piece or sheet of paper. [< Old French *papier* < Latin *papyrus* papyrus] —**pa′per·like′,** *adj.*

par·a·chute (par′ə shüt), *n.* apparatus shaped like an umbrella and made of nylon or silk, used in descending gradually through the air from a height.

par·a·dise (par′ə dīs), *n.* **1** heaven.
2 place of great happiness. **3** place
of beauty. **4** Also, **Paradise.** the
garden of Eden.

par·al·lel (par′ə lel), *adj.* **1** (of straight
lines or planes) lying or extending
alongside of one another, always
equidistant. **2** (of curved lines,
surfaces, etc.) always equidistant
at corresponding points.

pa·ral·y·sis (pə ral′ə sis), *n., pl.* **-ses**
(-sēz′). a lessening or loss of the
power of motion or sensation in
any part of the body.

par·tic·i·pant (pär tis′ə pənt), *n.*
person who shares or participates.

par·tic·i·pate (pär tis′ə pāt), *v.i.*,
-pat·ed, -pat·ing. have a share;
take part.

par·tic·i·pa·tion (pär tis′ə pā shən),
n. **1** the act of participating; a
taking part. **2** a sharing.

par·tic·u·late (pär tik′yə lit, pär tik′yə
lāt), *n., pl.* **par·tic·u·lates.** a very
small solid particle, as of dust.

path·o·gen (path′ə jən), *n., pl.*
path·o·gens. any agent capable
of producing disease, especially
a living microorganism or virus.
[< Greek *pathos* disease + English
-gen]

pa·vil·ion (pə vil′yən), *n.* a light
building, usually somewhat open,
used for shelter, pleasure, etc.

peace·ful (pēs′fəl), *adj.* **1** full of
peace; quiet; calm. **2** liking peace;
keeping peace; peaceable. **3** free
from trouble, disturbance, violence.
—peace′ful·ly, *adv.* **—peace′ful·
ness,** *n.*

pe·des·tri·an (pə des′trē ən), *n.*
person who goes on foot; walker.

pe·di·a·tri·cian (pē′dē ə trish′ən), *n.*
doctor who specializes in
pediatrics.

pel·lag·ra (pə lag′rə, pə lā′grə), *n.*
disease marked by inflammation
and scaling of the skin, digestive
disturbances, nervousness, and
sometimes mental disorders. It is
caused by a poor diet. [< Italian
< Latin *pellis* skin]

pend·ant (pen′dənt), *n.* **1** a hanging
ornament, such as a locket.
2 ornament hanging down from
a ceiling or roof.

pen·du·lum (pen′jə ləm, pen′dyə
ləm), *n.* weight so hung from a
fixed point that it is free to swing
to and fro through a regular arc
under the influence of gravity.

pen·guin (pen′gwin, peng′gwin), *n.*
any of an order of web-footed,
short-legged sea birds with black
and white plumage, living in
Antarctica and other cold regions
of the Southern Hemisphere.
Penguins cannot fly but use their
short wings for swimming.

pen·i·cil·lin (pen′ə sil′ən), *n.* any of
a group of antibiotics made from
penicillium molds and used to treat
diseases caused by bacteria.

pen·i·ten·tiar·y (pen′ə ten′chər ē),
n., pl. **-tiar·ies.** prison for criminals,
especially a state or federal prison.

pen·sion plan (pen′shən plan′), a
systematic way to provide a fixed
sum of money by the government,
a company, etc., to a person who
is retired or disabled.

pep·per (pep′ər), *n.* a seasoning with
a hot, spicy taste, made from the
berries of a tropical vine. **Black
pepper** is made from whole berries;
white pepper is made from husked
berries. [Old English *pipor* < Latin
piper < Greek *piperi, peperi*]

pe·ren·ni·al (pə ren′ē əl), *adj.*
1 lasting through the whole year.
2 lasting for a very long time;
enduring. [< Latin *perennis* < *per-*
through + *annus* year]
—pe·ren′ni·al·ly, *adv.*

per·fume (pėr′fyüm, pər fyüm′), *n.* a
sweet-smelling liquid or fragrance
made from natural or synthetic oils.

per·ma·nent (pėr′mə nənt), *adj.*
intended to last; not for a short
time only; lasting. *—n.* INFORMAL.
permanent wave. [< Latin
permanentem staying to the end
< *per-* through + *manere* to stay]
—per′ma·nent·ly, *adv.*

parallel (def. 1)
parallel steel rails
for a train

pepper
red and green **peppers**

a	hat	**ī**	ice	**u̇**	put	**ə** stands for	
ā	age	**o**	not	**ü**	rule	**a**	in about
ä	far, calm	**ō**	open	**ch**	child	**e**	in taken
âr	care	**ȯ**	saw	**ng**	long	**i**	in pencil
e	let	**ô**	order	**sh**	she	**o**	in lemon
ē	equal	**oi**	oil	**th**	thin	**u**	in circus
ėr	term	**ou**	out	**ℸH**	then		
i	it	**u**	cup	**zh**	measure		

per·me·a·ble (pėr′mē ə bəl), *adj.* that can be permeated; allowing the passage or diffusion of liquids or gases through it: *permeable cell walls.* —**per′me·a·bly,** *adv.*

per·mis·sion (pər mish′ən), *n.* a permitting; consent; leave. [< Latin *permissionem* < *permittere* < *per-* through + *mittere* send]

per·mit (pər mit′), *v.t.,* **-mit·ted, -mit·ting.** allow (a person, etc.) to do something: *Permit me to explain.*

per·pen·dic·u·lar (pėr′pən dik′yə lər), *adj.* standing straight up; vertical; upright. —*n.* line or plane at right angles to another line, plane, or surface.

per·se·cu·tion (pėr′sə kyü′shən), *n.* course or period of systematic punishment or oppression.

per·sist·ent (pər sis′tənt, pər zis′tənt), *adj.* **1** not giving up, especially in the face of dislike, disapproval, or difficulties; persisting; persevering. **2** going on; continuing; lasting: *a persistent headache.* —**per·sist′ent·ly,** *adv.*

per·son·al·i·ty (pėr′sə nal′ə te), *n.,* *pl.* **-ties. 1** the personal or individual quality that makes one person be different and act differently from another. **2** pleasing or attractive qualities of a person.

per·suade (pər swād′), *v.t.,* **-suad·ed, -suad·ing.** win over to do or believe; make willing or sure by urging, arguing, etc.; convince. [< Latin *persuadere* < *per-* thoroughly + *suadere* to urge] —**per·suad′er,** *n.*

phar·ma·cist (fär′mə sist), *n.* person licensed to fill prescriptions; druggist.

phone (fōn), *n., v.,* **phoned, phon·ing.** *n.* apparatus, system, or process for transmitting sound or speech to a distant point over wires by means of electrical impulses. —*v.i.* talk through a telephone. —*v.t.* **1** send (a message) by telephone. **2** make a telephone call to.

pho·tog·ra·pher (fə tog′rə fər), *n.* **1** person who takes photographs. **2** person whose business is taking photographs.

phy·lum (fī′ləm), *n., pl.* **-la** (-lə). (in biology) a primary group within a kingdom, ranking above a class. The organisms in a phylum are thought to be related by descent from a common ancestral form. [< New Latin < Greek *phylon* race, stock]

photographer

a **photographer**

posing a young girl

before the camera

phys·i·cal map (fiz′ə kəl map′), a map that shows natural features of the earth's surface, such as landforms, climate, winds, etc.

phy·si·cian (fə zish′ən), *n.* doctor of medicine.

pil·grim·age (pil′grə mij), *n.* **1** a pilgrim's journey; journey to some sacred place as an act of religious devotion. **2** a long journey.

pink (pingk), *n.* color obtained by mixing red with white; a light or pale red, often with a purple tinge. **in the pink,** the highest degree or condition; height.

piv·ot joint (piv′ət joint′), a joint in the body that consists of a bony pivot in a ring of bone and ligament that permits rotatory movement only.

plague (plāg), *n.* **1** highly contagious, epidemic, and often fatal bacterial disease that occurs in several forms. **2** any epidemic disease; pestilence. [< Late Latin *plaga* pestilence < Latin, blow, wound]

plas·ma (plaz′mə), *n.* the clear, almost colorless liquid part of blood or lymph, consisting of water, salts, proteins, and other substances. In the blood, the corpuscles or blood cells float in this liquid. [< Greek, something formed or molded < *plassein* to mold]

plate·let (plāt′lit), *n. pl.* **plate·lets.** any of the colorless, round or oval disks in vertebrate blood, that aid in coagulation.

pneu·mo·nia (nü mō′nyə, nyü mō′nyə), *n.* **1** a bacterial or viral disease in which the lung becomes inflamed, often accompanied by chills, a pain in the chest, a hard, dry cough, and a high fever. **2** inflammation of the lung from irritants. [< Greek < *pneumōn* lung]

po·lite (pə līt′), *adj.* **1** having or showing good manners; characterized by courtesy and consideration; behaving properly. **2** characterized by refined and civilized taste; elegant. —**po·lite′ly,** *adv.*

po·lit·i·cal map (pə lit′ə kəl map′), a map showing governmental, or political, information.

pol·i·ti·cian (pol′ə tish′ən), *n.* **1** person who gives much time to political affairs; person who is experienced in politics. **2** person active in politics chiefly for personal or party profit.

pol·lu·tion (pə lü/shən), n. **1** the dirtying of any part of the environment, especially with waste material. **2** anything that dirties the environment.

pop·u·lar (pop/yə lər), adj. **1** liked or admired by most people or by people generally. **2** liked by acquaintances or associates.

pop·u·la·tion (pop/yə lā/shən), n., pl. **pop·u·la·tions. 1** (in statistics) the entire group of items or individuals from which the samples under consideration are presumed to come. **2** (in biology) the aggregate of organisms which inhabit a particular locality or region.

por·ce·lain (pôr/sə lin, pōr/sə lin), n. **1** a very fine earthenware, usually having a translucent white body and a transparent glaze; china. **2** dish or other object made of this material. [< Middle French *pourcelaine* < Italian *porcellana*]

por·tent (pôr/tent, pōr/tent), n. **1** a warning of coming evil; sign; omen. **2** ominous significance. [< Latin *portentum* indicated beforehand]

port·fo·li·o (pôrt fō/lē ō, pōrt fō/lē ō), n., pl. **port·fo·li·os. 1** a portable case for loose papers, drawings, etc.; briefcase. **2** position and duties of a cabinet member, diplomat, or minister of state.

Por·tu·guese (pôr/chə gēz/, pōr/chə gēz/), n., pl. **-guese. 1** native or inhabitant of Portugal. **2** the Romance language of Portugal. Portuguese is also the chief language of Brazil.

pos·i·tive (poz/ə tiv), adj. counting up from zero; plus: *five above zero.* —n. a positive degree or quantity. [< Latin *positivus*, ultimately < *ponere* to set] **—pos/i·tive·ly,** adv.

pos·i·tive re·in·force·ment (poz/ə tiv rē/in fôrs/mənt), something that reinforces and rewards certain behaviors.

pos·ses·sion (pə zesh/ən), n. **1** a possessing; holding. **2** ownership. **3** thing possessed; property.

post·op·er·a·tive (pōst op/ər ə tiv, pōst op/ə rā/tiv), adj. occurring after a surgical operation. **—post·op/er·a·tive·ly,** adv.

prac·ti·cal·ly (prak/tik lē), adv. **1** so far as the results will be; in effect; really. **2** almost; nearly: *We are practically home.* **3** in a practical way; in a useful way. **4** by actual practice.

pre·cede (prē sēd/), v., **-ced·ed, -ced·ing. —v.t. 1** go or come before in order, place, or time: *A precedes B in the alphabet.* **2** be higher than in rank or importance. —v.i. go or come before.

prec·e·dence (pres/ə dəns, pri sēd/ns), n. **1** act or fact of preceding. **2** higher position or rank; greater importance. **3** right to precede others in ceremonies or social affairs; social superiority.

pre·cip·i·ta·tion (pri sip/ə tā/shən), n. **1** act or state of precipitating; throwing down or falling headlong. **2** a hastening or hurrying. **3** something that is precipitated, such as rain, dew, or snow. **4** amount that is precipitated.

pred·e·ces·sor (pred/ə ses/ər), n. **1** person holding a position or office before another: *John Adams was Jefferson's predecessor as President.* **2** thing that came before another.

pre·dic·tion (pri dik/shən), n. **1** act of predicting. **2** thing predicted; prophecy; forecast.

pre·fer (pri fėr/), v., **-ferred, -fer·ring. —v.t. 1** like better; choose rather: *He prefers golf as a sport, but I prefer swimming to golf. We would prefer that they draw their own conclusions.* **2** put forward or present, especially for consideration in a court of law. *The policeman preferred charges of speeding against the driver.* **3** promote; advance. —v.i. have or express a preference: *I will come later, if you prefer.* [< Latin *praeferre* put before < *prae*- pre- + *ferre* carry]

pollution
It is important to clean up **pollution** in the environment.

a	hat	ī	ice	u̇	put	ə stands for	
ā	age	o	not	ü	rule	a	in about
ä	far, calm	ō	open	ch	child	e	in taken
âr	care	ȯ	saw	ng	long	i	in pencil
e	let	ô	order	sh	she	o	in lemon
ē	equal	oi	oil	th	thin	u	in circus
ėr	term	ou	out	ŦH	then		
i	it	u	cup	zh	measure		

pref·er·a·ble (pref′ər ə bəl), *adj.* to be preferred; more desirable.
—**pref′er·a·bly,** *adv.*

pref·er·ence (pref′ər əns), *n.,* **prefer·enc·es. 1** act or attitude of liking better: *My preference is for beef rather than lamb.* **2** thing preferred; first choice. **3** the favoring of one above another: *A teacher should not show preference for any one student.*

prej·u·dice (prej′ə dis), *n.* opinion formed without taking time and care to judge fairly.

prep·o·si·tion (prep′ə zish′ən), *n.* word that expresses some relation to a noun, pronoun, phrase, or clause which follows it.

preserve (def. 3)
Canning is a way to
preserve food.

pre·serve (pri zėrv′), *v.t.,* **-served, -serv·ing. 1** keep from harm or change; keep safe; protect. **2** keep up; maintain. **3** keep from spoiling: *Ice helps to preserve food.*

pre·tend (pri tend′), *v.i.* **1** make believe: *They weren't really fighting; they were just pretending.* **2** lay claim: *James Stuart pretended to the English throne.* —*v.t.* **1** claim falsely: *She pretended to like the meal so she wouldn't offend the hostess.* **2** claim: *I don't pretend to be a musician.* **3** make believe: *The children pretended that they were grown-up.* [< Latin *praetendere* extend, give as an excuse < *prae-* pre- + *tendere* to stretch]

pre·ten·tious (pri ten′shəs), *adj.* **1** making claims to excellence or importance: *a pretentious person.* **2** doing things for show or to make a fine appearance; showy; ostentatious: *a pretentious style of entertaining guests.*

pret·zel (pret′səl), *n.* a hard biscuit, usually in the form of a knot or stick, glazed and salted on the outside. [< German *brezel*]

prin·ci·pal (prin′sə pəl), *adj.* most important; main; chief: *Chicago is the principal city of Illinois.* —*n.* **1** a chief person; one who gives orders. **2** the head, or one of the heads, of an elementary or secondary school.

prin·ci·ple (prin′sə pəl), *n.* **1** a fundamental, primary, or general truth on which other truths depend: *the principles of democratic government.* **2** a fundamental belief: *religious principles.* **3** an accepted or professed rule of action or conduct.

priv·i·lege (priv′ə lij), *n.* a special right, advantage, or favor.

prob·a·ble (prob′ə bəl), *adj.* **1** likely to happen. **2** likely to be true: *Indigestion is the probable cause of your pain.* [< Latin *probabilis* < *probare* to prove.]
—**prob′a·bly,** *adv.*

pro·ce·dure (prə sē′jər), *n.* **1** way of proceeding; method of doing things: *What is your procedure in making bread?* **2** the customary manners of conducting business.

pro·ceed (prə sēd′), *v.i.* **1** go on after a stop or interruption; move forward; continue: *Please proceed with your story.* **2** be carried on; take place: *The trial may proceed.* **3** carry on any activity: *He proceeded to light his pipe.* **4** begin and carry on an action in a case in a court of law. [< Latin *procedere* < *pro-* forward + *cedere* to move]

pro·ces·sion (prə sesh′ən), *n.* **1** something that moves forward; persons marching or riding. **2** an orderly moving forward.

proc·es·sor (pros′es ər, prō′ses ər), *n.* **1** person or thing that processes. **2** the central processing unit of a computer, especially the part of this unit in which data are examined, compared, changed.

pro·duc·er (prə dü′sər, prə dyü′sər), *n., pl.* **pro·duc·ers.** person or thing that produces, especially one that grows or manufactures things that are used by others.

prod·uct (prod′əkt), *n.* **1** that which is produced; result of work or of growth: *factory products.* **2** number or quantity resulting from multiplying two or more numbers together: *40 is the product of 8×5.*

pro·duc·tive (prə duk′tiv), *adj.* **1** producing abundantly; fertile: *a productive farm.* **2** producing food or other articles of commerce. **3** having good results: *Efforts to resolve the dispute were very productive.* **4** bringing forth; producing: *That field is productive only of weeds.* **5** used in forming new words: *-able is a productive suffix.* —**pro·duc′tive·ly,** *adv.*

pro·duc·tiv·i·ty (prō′duk tiv′ə tē), *n.* power to produce; productiveness.

pro·jec·tion (prə jek′shən), *n.* **1** a sticking out. **2** representation, upon a flat surface, of all or part of the surface of the earth. **3** a forming of projects or plans.

pro·jec·tor (prə jek′tər), *n.*
1 apparatus for projecting an image on a screen. **2** person who forms projects; schemer.

pro·mo·tion·al (prə mō′shə nəl), *adj.* used in promotion.

pro·nounce (prə nouns′), *v.t.*, **-nounced, -nounc·ing.** make the sounds of; speak.

pro·nun·ci·a·tion (prə nun′sē ā′shən), *n.* way of pronouncing. This spelling dictionary gives the pronunciation of each main word.

proph·e·sy (prof′ə sī), *v.*, **proph·e·sied, proph·e·sy·ing.** —*v.i.* **1** tell what will happen. **2** speak when or as if divinely inspired. —*v.t.* foretell; predict.

prop·o·si·tion (prop′ə zish′ən), *n.* what is offered to be considered; proposal: *The corporation made a proposition to buy out the business.*

pros·e·cu·tion (pros′ə kyü′shən), *n.* the carrying on of a lawsuit: *The prosecution will be abandoned if the stolen money is returned.*

pro·spec·tive (prə spek′tiv), *adj.* that is looked forward to as likely or promised; probable; expected.

pros·per·i·ty (pro sper′ə tē), *n., pl.* **-ties.** prosperous condition; good fortune; success.

pro·tec·tion (prə tek′shən), *n.* **1** act of protecting; condition of being kept from harm; defense. **2** thing or person that prevents damage.

pro·tein (prō′tēn′), *n., pl.* **pro·teins.** any of a group of complex organic compounds containing nitrogen that are built up of amino acids. Proteins are essential to the structure and functioning of all animal, plant, and other cells. [< French *protéine* < Greek *prōteios* of the first quality < *prōtos* first]

pro·vi·sion (prə vizh′ən), *n.* statement making a condition; stipulation.

pseu·do·nym (süd′n im), *n.* a fictitious name used by an author instead of his or her real name; pen name. [< Greek *pseudōnymon* < *pseudēs* false + *onyma* name]

psy·chi·a·trist (si ki′ə trist), *n.* doctor who treats mental and emotional disorders; expert in psychiatry.

psy·chol·o·gy (sī kol′ə jē), *n., pl.* **-gies.** **1** science or study of the mind; branch of science dealing with the actions, feelings, thoughts, and other mental or behavioral processes of people and animals. **2** the mental states and processes of a person or persons; mental nature and behavior.

ptar·mi·gan (tär′mə gən), *n., pl.* **-gans** or **-gan.** any of several kinds of grouse which become white in the winter, have feathered feet, and are found in mountainous and cold regions.

pub·lic·i·ty (pu blis′ə tē), *n.* **1** public notice: *the publicity that actors desire.* **2** measures used for getting, or the process of getting, public notice: *I worked on the publicity for the concert.* **3** articles, etc., used in such measures or process.

punc·tu·a·tion (pungk′chü ā′shən), *n.* **1** use of periods, commas, and other marks to help make the meaning clear. Punctuation does for writing and printing what pauses and changes of voice do for speech. **2** punctuation marks.

pun·dit (pun′dit), *n.* a very learned person; expert; authority. [< Hindi *pandit* < Sanskrit *pandita* learned]

punt (punt), *n.* kick given to a football before it touches the ground after dropping it from the hands. —*v.t.* **1** propel (a boat) by pushing with a pole against the bottom of a river, pond, etc. **2** kick (a football) before it touches the ground after dropping it from the hands. —*v.i.* **1** use a punt; travel by punt. **2** punt a football. [< Latin *ponto* pontoon] —**punt′er,** *n.*

pur·suit (pər süt′), *n.* **1** act of pursuing: *the pursuit of game.* **2** that which one engages in, as a profession, business, recreation, etc.; occupation.

pur·vey·or (pər vā′ər), *n.* **1** person who supplies provisions. **2** person who supplies anything.

protein
These foods provide
protein important
in a healthful diet.

a	hat	ī	ice	u̇	put	**ə stands for**
ā	age	o	not	ü	rule	a	in about
ä	far, calm	ō	open	ch	child	e	in taken
âr	care	ȯ	saw	ng	long	i	in pencil
e	let	ô	order	sh	she	o	in lemon
ē	equal	oi	oil	th	thin	u	in circus
ėr	term	ou	out	ᴛʜ	then		
i	it	u	cup	zh	measure		

Q

ravioli

Ravioli is an Italian dish made out of square noodles, a filling, and sauce.

quad·rant (kwod′rent), *n.* (in geometry) one of the four parts into which a plane is divided by two straight lines crossing at right angles. The upper right-hand section is the first quadrant, and, in a counterclockwise direction, the others are the second, third, and fourth quadrants. [< Latin *quadrantem* a fourth]

qua·dru·ple (kwo drü′pəl, kwod′rə pəl), *adj.* **1** consisting of four parts; including four parts or parties; fourfold: *a quadruple agreement.* **2** four times; four times as great.

qual·i·fy (kwol′ə fī), *v.t.,* **qual·i·fied, qual·i·fy·ing. 1** furnish with legal power; make legally capable. **2** make less strong; change somewhat; limit; moderate.

quan·ti·ty (kwon′tə tē), *n., pl.* **-ties. 1** a definite amount or portion: *Use equal quantities of nuts and raisins in the cake.* **2** an indefinite but usually large amount or number: *The baker buys flour in quantity. She owns quantities of books.* **3** the amount of something present: *decrease the quantity of heat in a room.* **4** something that is measurable.

ques·tion·naire (kwes′chə nâr′), *n.* a written or printed list of questions, used to gather informa-tion, obtain a sampling of opinion, etc.

quick (kwik), *adj.* **1** done, happening, or taking place in a very short time: *With a quick turn I avoided hitting the other car.* **2** begun and ended speedily: *a quick visit.* **3** coming soon; prompt; immediate: *a quick answer.* **4** not patient; hasty: *a quick temper.* **5** mentally active or alert: *a quick wit.* —*n.* **1** tender, sensitive flesh: *bite one's nails to the quick.* **2** the tender, sensitive part of one's feelings. —*adv.* quickly.

R

rac·quet·ball (rak′it bȯl′), *n.* game played in a four-walled court with a hollow, rubber ball and a short-handled racket.

rain fo·rest (rān′ fôr′ist), a very dense forest in a region, usually tropical, where rain is very heavy throughout the year.

ran·dom sam·ple (ran′dəm sam′pəl), (in statistics) a sample so drawn from the total group that every item in the group has an equal chance of being chosen.

range (rānj), *n.* **1** in mathematics: **a** the set of all the values a given function may take on. **b** a domain. **2** (in statistics) the difference between the smallest and the greatest values which a variable bears in frequency distribution.

rap·port (ra pôr′, ra pōr′), *n.* **1** relation; connection. **2** agreement; harmony.

rasp·ber·ry (raz′ber′ē, raz′bər ē), *n., pl.* **-ries. 1** any of various small, juicy, edible fruits that grow on bushes. Raspberries are usually red or black. **2** any of the bushes, various species of brambles, that bear raspberries.

rav·i·o·li (rav′ē ō′lē), *n. sing. or pl.* small, square pieces of dough filled with chopped meat, cheese, etc., cooked in boiling water, and served with a tomato sauce.

re·al·i·ty (rē al′ə tē), *n., pl.* **-ties. 1** actual existence; true state of affairs. **2** a real thing; actual fact. **3** in reality, really; actually; in fact; truly: *We thought he was serious, but in reality he was joking.*

re·al·ly (rē′ə lē, rē′lē), *adv.* **1** actually; truly; in fact: *things as they really are.* **2** indeed: *Oh, really?*

rea·son (rē′zn), *n.* **1** cause or motive for an action, feeling, etc.; ground. See synonym study below. **2** justification; explanation. **3** ability or power to think and draw conclusions. —*v.i.* **1** think logically; think things out. **2** draw conclusions or inferences from facts or premises. **3** consider; discuss; argue. —*v.t.* **1** persuade by reasoning. **2** argue; conclude. **Syn.** *n.* **1** Reason, cause, motive mean that which makes something happen. **Reason** applies to a ground or occasion that explains why something has happened: *The reason they went to Arizona was the climate.* **Cause** applies to a person, thing, incident, or condition that directly brings about an action or happening: *The cause of his new diet was his doctor's warning about being overweight.* **Motive** applies to the feeling or desire that makes a person do what he or she does.

rea·son·ing (rē′zn ing), n. **1** the process of drawing conclusions from facts or premises. **2** reasons; logical arguments.

re·cede (ri sēd′), v.i., **re·ced·ed, re·ced·ing. 1** go or move backward. **2** slope backward. **3** withdraw: *recede from an agreement.* [< Latin *recedere* < *re-* back + *cedere* go]

re·ceive (ri sēv′), v.t., **re·ceived, re·ceiv·ing. 1** take (something offered or sent); take into one's hands or possession: *receive gifts.* **2** have (something) bestowed, conferred, etc.: *receive a degree.* **3** be given; get.

re·cep·tor (ri sep′tər), n. cell or group of cells sensitive to stimuli, such as a sense organ.

re·ces·sive (ri ses′iv), adj. **1** likely to go back; receding. **2** (in biology) of or having to do with a recessive character. —n. recessive character. **—re·ces′sive·ly,** adv.

rec·og·ni·tion (rek′əg nish′ən), n. **1** a being recognized: *By a good disguise he escaped recognition.* **2** acknowledgment: *We insisted on complete recognition of our rights.*

rec·og·nize (rek′əg nīz), v.t., **-nized, -niz·ing. 1** be aware of (someone or something) as already known; know again: *recognize an old friend.* **2** identify: *recognize a person from a description.* **3** acknowledge acquaintance with; greet.

rec·ol·lec·tion (rek′ə lek′shən), n. **1** act or power of recalling to mind. **2** memory; remembrance.

rec·om·mend (rek′ə mend′), v.t. **1** speak in favor of; suggest favorably. **2** advise.

re·cord·ing (ri kôr′ding), n. **1** a phonograph record or magnetic tape on which sound has been transcribed. **2** act or process of making records, tapes, videos, etc.

re·cruit (ri krüt′), n. **1** a newly enlisted soldier, sailor, etc. **2** a new member of any group or class.

rec·tan·gle (rek′tang′gəl), n. a four-sided plane figure with four right angles.

rec·ti·tude (rek′tə tüd, rek′tə tyüd), n. **1** upright conduct or character; honesty; righteousness. **2** direction in a straight line; straightness.

red (red), n., adj., **red·der, red·dest.** —n. **1** the color of blood, fire, the ruby, etc. **2** any shade of that color. **3** in the red, in debt; losing money. **4** see red, INFORMAL. become very angry. —adj. **1** having the color of blood, fire, the ruby, etc. **2** being like or suggesting this color.

red blood cells (red′ blud′ selz′), cells in the blood, formed in bone marrow and containing hemoglobin, that carry oxygen from the lungs to various parts of the body.

re·duc·tion (ri duk′shən), n. **1** a reducing. **2** a being reduced. **3** amount by which a thing is reduced: *$5 reduction in cost.*

re·flec·tion (ri flek′shən), n. **1** a reflecting. **2** a being reflected. **3** something reflected. **4** likeness; image. **5** the bending of a part back upon itself. **6** the part bent back. Also, **reflexion. —re·flec′ tion·less,** adj.

re·flex ac·tion (rē′fleks ak′shən), an involuntary action in direct response to a stimulation of some nerve cells.

reg·u·late (reg′yə lāt), v.t., **-lat·ed, -lat·ing. 1** control by rule, principle, or system. **2** put in condition to work properly. **3** keep at some standard.

reg·u·la·tion (reg′yə lā′shən), n. **1** control by rule, principle, or system. **2** rule; law. —adj. according to or required by some rule; standard.

reign (rān), n. period of power of a ruler: *Queen Victoria's reign.*

re·in·car·na·tion (rē′in kär nā′shən), n. **1** rebirth of the soul in a new body. **2** a new incarnation or embodiment.

re·mit (ri mit′), v.i., **-mit·ted, -mit·ting.** send money to a person or place. *Enclosed is our bill; please remit.*

recording (def. 2)
two types of
recording devices

a	hat	**ī**	ice	**u̇**	put	**ə** stands for	
ā	age	**o**	not	**ü**	rule	**a**	in about
ä	far, calm	**ō**	open	**ch**	child	**e**	in taken
âr	care	**ȯ**	saw	**ng**	long	**i**	in pencil
e	let	**ô**	order	**sh**	she	**o**	in lemon
ē	equal	**oi**	oil	**th**	thin	**u**	in circus
ėr	term	**ou**	out	**ŦH**	then		
i	it	**u**	cup	**zh**	measure		

rem·nant (rem'nənt), *n. pl.* **rem·nants.**
1 a small part left; fragment.
2 piece of cloth, ribbon, lace, etc., left after the rest has been used or sold.

re·peat (ri pēt'), *v.t.* **1** do, make, or perform again: *repeat an error.*
2 say again: *repeat a word for emphasis.*

re·peat·ed (ri pē'tid), *adj.* said, done, or made more than once. —**re·peat'ed·ly,** *adv.*

re·peat·er (ri pē'tər), *n.* **1** student who takes a course again or fails to pass on to the next grade. **2** any person or thing that repeats.

rep·e·ti·tion (rep'ə tish'ən), *n.* a repeating; doing or saying again: *Repetition helps learning.*

re·pet·i·tive (ri pet'ə tiv), *adj.* of or characterized by repetition.

re·port·er (ri pôr'tər, ri pōr'tər), *n.*
1 person who reports. **2** person who gathers news for a newspaper, magazine, radio or television station, etc. **3** person who takes down reports of law cases.

rep·re·sent (rep'ri zent'), *v.t.* **1** stand for; be a sign or symbol of: *The 50 stars in our flag represent the 50 states.* **2** act in place of; speak and act for: *People are elected to represent us in the government.*
3 act the part of: *Each child will represent an animal at the party.*
4 show in a picture, statue, carving, etc.; give a likeness of; portray: *This painting represents the end of the world.* **5** be a type of; be an example of: *A raft represents a very simple kind of boat.* [< Latin *repraesentare* < *re-* back + *praesentare* present] —**rep're·sent'a·ble,** *adj.*

re·search (ri sėrch', rē'sėrch'), *n., v.* **re·searched, re·search·ing.** *n.* **1** a careful or systematic hunting for facts or truth about a subject: *the researches of historians.*
2 organized scientific investigation to solve problems, test hypotheses, develop or invent new products, etc.: *atomic research, cancer research.* —*v.i.* make researches; do research. —*v.t.* search into; investigate carefully: *research a topic in history.*

res·er·voir (rez'ər vwär, rez'ər vôr), *n.*
1 place where water is collected and stored for use: *This reservoir supplies the entire city.* **2** anything to hold a liquid: *A fountain pen has an ink reservoir.* [< French *réservoir* < *réserver* to reserve]

rhinoceros

an endangered

rhinoceros

re·source (ri sôrs', ri sōrs'; rē'sôrs, rē'sōrs), *n.* **1** Usually, **resources,** *pl.* any supply that will meet a need; stock or reserve upon which to draw when necessary: *financial resources.* **2** **resources,** *pl.* the actual and potential wealth of a country. [< French *ressource,* ultimately < Latin *re-* again + *surgere* to rise]

re·spect·ful (ri spekt'fəl), *adj.* having or showing respect; considerate and polite. —**re·spect'ful·ly,** *adv.*

re·spec·tive·ly (ri spek'tiv lē), *adv.* as regards each of several persons or things in turn or in the order mentioned: *The three bills were introduced in January, March, and April, respectively.*

res·tau·rant (res'tər ənt, res'tə ränt'), *n.* place to buy and eat a meal.

res·to·ra·tion (res'tə rā'shən), *n.*
1 a restoring; establishing again: *restoration of order.* **2** a bringing back to a former condition: *restoration of an old house.*

re·store (ri stôr', ri stōr'), *v.t.,* **-stored, -stor·ing.** **1** bring back; establish again: *restore order.* **2** bring back to a former condition or to a normal condition: *The old house has been restored.*

re·ten·tion (ri ten'shən), *n.* **1** a retaining. **2** a being retained.
3 power to retain. **4** ability to remember.

re·use (*v.* rē yüz'; *n.* rē yüs'), *v.,* **-used, -us·ing,** *n.* —*v.t.* use again. —*n.* a using again. —**re·us'a·ble,** *adj.*

re·vise (ri vīz'), *v.t.,* **-vised, -vis·ing.** **1** read carefully in order to correct; look over and change; examine and improve: *revise a manuscript.* **2** change; alter: *I revised my opinion.*

rhap·so·dy (rap'sə dē), *n., pl.* **-dies.**
1 extravagant enthusiasm in speech or writing: *go into rhapsodies over a gift.* **2** (in music) an instrumental composition: *Liszt's Hungarian rhapsodies.*

rhine·stone (rīn'stōn'), *n.* an imitation diamond, made of glass or paste. [translation of French *caillou du Rhin,* literally, pebble of the Rhine]

rhi·noc·er·os (rī nos'ər əs), *n., pl.* **-os·es** or **-os.** any of a family of large, thick-skinned mammals of Africa and Asia with one or two upright horns on the snout. Rhinoceroses eat grass and other plants. [< Greek *rhinokerōs* < *rhinos* nose + *keras* horn]

rhyme (rīm), v., **rhymed, rhym·ing,** n.
—v.i. **1** sound alike in the last part:
*"Long" and "song" rhyme. "Go to
bed" rhymes with "sleepyhead."*
2 make rhymes. —v.t. put or make
into rhyme: *rhyme a translation.*

rhythm (riᵀн′əm), n. **1** movement
with a regular repetition of a beat,
accent, rise and fall, or the like: *the
rhythm of the tides, the rhythm of
one's heartbeats.* **2** the measured
recurrence of accented and
unaccented syllables in a foot or
line of verse.

room·mate (rüm′māt′, rùm′māt′), n.
person who shares a room with
another or others.

root (rüt, rùt), n. **1** the part of a plant
that grows downward, usually into
the ground. **2** the essential part,
base. **3** word from which other
words are made.

ro·ta·tion (rō tā′shən), n. **1** act or
process of moving around a center
or axis; turning in a circle;
revolving. **2** one such movement.

run·ner-up (run′ər-up′), n. player or
team that takes second place in a
contest.

rup·ture (rup′chər), n. **1** a breaking.
2 a being broken. **3** a breaking off
of friendly relations, especially a
breaking off of relations between
nations that threatens a war.

S

sa·cred (sā′krid), adj. **1** belonging to
or dedicated to God or a god; holy:
the sacred altar. **2** connected with
religion; religious: *sacred writings,
sacred music.* [originally past
participle of Middle English *sacren*
sanctify < Latin *sacrare* < *sacer*
holy] —**sa′cred·ly,** adv.

sac·ri·fice (sak′rə fīs), n., v., **-ficed,
-fic·ing.** —n. **1** act of offering to a
god. **2** the thing offered: *The
ancient Hebrews killed animals on
the altars as sacrifices to God.* **3** a
giving up of one thing for another.

—v.t. **1** give or offer to a god.
2 give up. **3** permit injury or
disadvantage to, for the sake of
something else. —v.i. offer or make
a sacrifice.

safe·ty (sāf′tē), n., pl. **-ties,** adj. —n.
quality or state of being safe;
freedom from harm or danger;
security. —adj. giving safety;
making harm unlikely.

sales·man (sālz′mən), n., pl. **sales·
men.** person whose work is selling.

sal·i·var·y glands (sal′ə ver′ē
glandz′), various glands that empty
their secretions into the mouth. The
salivary glands of human beings
and certain other vertebrates are
digestive glands that secrete saliva
containing the digestive enzyme
ptyalin, salts, mucus, etc.

sam·u·rai (sam′ù rī′), n., pl. **-rai.**
1 the military class in feudal
Japan, consisting of the retainers
of the great nobles. **2** member of
this class. [< Japanese]

Sap·po·ro (sə pôr′ō, sə pōr′ō), n. a
city on W Hokkaido, in N Japan.

sat·is·fac·tor·y (sat′i sfak′tər ē), adj.
good enough to satisfy; satisfying.

Sat·ur·day (sat′ər dē, sat′ər dā), n.
the seventh day of the week,
following Friday.

sa·van·na or **sa·van·nah** (sə van′ə),
n. **1** a treeless plain in the
southeastern United States or
tropical America. **2** grassland
with scattered trees between the
equatorial forests and the hot
deserts in either hemisphere.
[< Spanish *sabana* < Carib]

scen·er·y (sē′nər ē), n., pl. **-er·ies.**
1 the general appearance of a
place; natural features of a
landscape. **2** the painted
hangings, screens, etc., used in
a theater to represent places.

sci·en·tif·ic name (sī′ən tif′ik nām′), a
name given to plants and animals
to classify them scientifically.

sci·en·tist (sī′ən tist), n. person who
has expert knowledge of some
branch of science, especially a
physical or natural science.

root (def. 1)
tree **roots** above
the ground

a	hat	ī	ice	ù	put	**ə stands for**	
ā	age	o	not	ü	rule	a	in about
ä	far, calm	ō	open	ch	child	e	in taken
âr	care	ò	saw	ng	long	i	in pencil
e	let	ô	order	sh	she	o	in lemon
ē	equal	oi	oil	th	thin	u	in circus
ėr	term	ou	out	ᵀн	then		
i	it	u	cup	zh	measure		

scram (skram), *v.i.,* **scrammed, scram·ming.** SLANG. go at once. [short for *scramble*]

scrib·ble (skrib′əl), *v.,* **-bled, -bling,** *n.* —*v.t.* write or draw carelessly or hastily. —*v.i.* make marks that do not mean anything. —*n.* something scribbled. [< Medieval Latin *scribillare,* ultimately < Latin *scribere* write]

script (skript), *n.* **1** written letters, figures, signs, etc.; handwriting: *German script.* **2** style of printing that looks like handwriting. **3** manuscript of a play, motion picture, radio or television broadcast, etc. —*v.t.* write a script for. [< Latin *scriptum,* originally neuter past participle of *scribere* write]

scroll (skrōl), *n., pl.* **scrolls. 1** roll of parchment or paper, especially one with writing on it. **2** ornament resembling a partly unrolled sheet of paper, or having a spiral or coiled form. —*v.i.* move across a computer screen in a horizontal or vertical direction. [alteration (influenced by *roll*) of Middle English *scrow,* ultimately < Old French *escroe* scrap; of Germanic origin]

scrub·ber (skrub′ər), *n.* **1** person or thing that scrubs. **2** device that removes certain substances, such as pollutants, from gas, smoke, etc.

sec·ond·ar·y (sek′ən der′ē), *adj.* **1** next after the first in order, place, time, etc. **2** not main or chief; having less importance.

sec·re·tar·y (sek′rə ter′ē), *n., pl.* **sec·re·tar·ies.** person who writes letters, keeps records, etc., for a person, company, club, etc.: *Our secretary's job is to keep the minutes of the meeting. Both secretaries' reports are on your desk.*

se·cur·i·ty (si kyùr′ə tē), *n., pl.* **-ties. 1** freedom from danger, care, or fear; feeling or condition of being safe. **2** something that secures or makes safe: *Rubber soles are a security against slipping.*

sem·i·an·nu·al (sem′ē an′yü əl) *adj.* occurring every half year.

sem·i·cir·cle (sem′i sèr′kəl), *n.* half a circle: *We sat in a semicircle.*

sem·i·co·lon (sem′i kō′lən), *n.* mark of punctuation (;) that shows a separation not so complete as that shown by a period but greater than that shown by a comma.

shear

shearing wool from a sheep

sem·i·con·scious (sem′i kon′shəs), *adj.* half-conscious; not fully conscious. —**sem′i·con′scious·ly,** *adv.* —**sem′i·con′scious·ness,** *n.*

sem·i·fi·nal (sem′i fī′nl), *adj.* of or having to do with the two games, matches, or rounds that come before the final one in a tournament. —*n.* Often, **semifinals,** *pl.* one of these two.

sem·i·month·ly (sem′i munth′lē), —*adj.* happening or appearing twice a month. —*adv.* twice a month.

sem·i·of·fi·cial (sem′ē ə fish′əl), *adj.* partly official; having some degree of authority.

sem·i·pre·cious (sem′i presh′əs), *adj.* having some value; somewhat precious. Garnets are semiprecious stones. They are less valuable than diamonds, which are precious stones.

sem·i·pri·vate (sem′i prī′vit), *adj.* partly private: *a semiprivate conference.*

sem·i·pro·fes·sion·al (sem′i prə fesh′ə nəl), *n.* a part-time professional athlete.

sem·i·skilled (sem′i skild′), *adj.* partly skilled: *a semiskilled laborer.*

sem·i·soft (sem′i sȯft′, sem′i soft′), *adj.* of medium softness: *semisoft cheese.*

sem·i·sweet (sem′i swēt′), *adj.* moderately sweet: *semisweet chocolate.*

sen·a·tor (sen′ə tər), *n.* member of a senate.

ser·ies (sir′ēz), *n., pl.* **ser·ies. 1** number of similar things in a row. **2** number of things placed one after another. **3** number of things, events, etc., coming one after the other.

shear (shir), *v.t.,* **sheared, sheared** or **shorn** (shôrn), **shear·ing. 1** cut with shears or scissors: *shear wool from sheep.* **2** cut the wool or fleece from: *shear sheep.* **3** cut close.

sheer (shir), *adj.* **1** very thin; almost transparent: *sheer curtains.* **2** unmixed with anything else; complete: *sheer nonsense, sheer weariness.* —*n.* a thin, fine, almost transparent cloth.

shep·herd (shep′ərd), *n.* person who takes care of sheep.

sher·bet (shèr′bət), *n.* **1** a frozen dessert made of fruit juice, sugar, and water, milk, or whites of eggs. **2** a cooling drink made of fruit juice, sugar, and water.

shock (shok), *n.* condition of physical collapse or depression, accompanied by a sudden drop in blood pressure, often resulting in unconsciousness.

sho·gun (shō′gun, shō′gün), *n.* the former hereditary commander in chief of the Japanese army. The shoguns were the real rulers of Japan for hundreds of years until 1867. [< Japanese *shōgun* < Chinese *chiang chün* army leader]

short-term mem·or·y (shôrt′tėrm′ mem′ər ē), information retained in the brain and retrievable from it over a brief time period.

sickle cell anemia (sik′əl sel′ ə nē′mē ə), a hereditary form of anemia in which the normally round red blood cells become sickle cells, ineffective in carrying oxygen.

silt de·pos·it (silt′ di poz′it), *n., pl.* **silt de·pos·its** (di poz′its), **1** very fine particles of earth, sand, etc., carried by moving water and deposited as sediment: *The harbor is being choked up with silt.* **2** deposit of sediment occurring as a stratum in soil.

si·mul·cast (sī′ məl kast′), *n.,* transmit a program over radio and television simultaneously.

sin·cere (sin sir′), *adj.,* **-cer·er, -cer·est.** free from pretense; genuine; real; honest: *sincere thanks, a sincere person.* [< Latin *sincerus*] **—sin·cere′ly,** *adv.*

skel·e·ton (skel′ə tən), *n.* **1** the framework of bones and cartilage in vertebrates that supports the muscles, organs, etc., and protects the viscera. **2** the hard supporting or covering structure of an invertebrate.

skin (skin), *n.* **1** the outer layer of tissue of the human or animal body, especially when soft and flexible. **2** hide; pelt. **3** any outer covering or surface layer, as the rind of a fruit.

sleigh (slā), *n.* carriage or cart mounted on runners for use on ice or snow. —*v.i.* ride in a sleigh.

smog (smog), *n.* a combination of smoke and fog in the air. [blend of *smoke* and *fog*]

snow·mo·bile (snō′mō bēl′), *n., v.,* **-biled, -bil·ing.** —*n.* a small, automotive vehicle for use in snow, usually with skis or runners in front, and tractor treads in the rear. —*v.i.* travel by snowmobile.

so·cial·ize (sō′shə līz), *v.i.,* **-ized, -iz·ing.** be social or sociable: *He has never learned to socialize with his fellow workers.*

so·ci·e·ty (sə sī′ə tē), *n., pl.* **-ties.** **1** group of persons joined together for a common purpose or by a common interest. **2** all the people; human beings living together as a group: *Drug-control laws are enacted for the good of society.* **3** the people of any particular time or place.

so·ci·ol·o·gy (sō′sē ol′ə jē), *n.* study of the nature, origin, and development of human society and community life; science of social facts.

sol·i·tar·y (sol′ə ter′ē), *adj., n., pl.* **-tar·ies.** —*adj.* **1** alone or single; only: *A solitary rider was seen in the distance.* **2** without companions; away from people; lonely: *lead a solitary life.* —*n.* person living alone, away from people.

so·lo·ist (sō′lō ist), *n.* person who performs without a partner: *The young girl sang as a soloist.*

sol·stice (sol′stis), *n.* either of the two times in the year when the sun is at its greatest distance from the celestial equator and appears to be farthest north or south in the heavens.

some·one (sum′wun, sum′wən), *pron.* some person; somebody: *Someone is at the door.*

some·times (sum′tīmz), *adv.* now and then; at times: *She comes to visit sometimes.*

son-in-law (sun′in lȯ′), *n., pl.* **sons-in-law.** husband of one's daughter.

socialize
socializing at the dinner table

a	hat	**ī**	ice	**u̇**	put	**ə** stands for	
ā	age	**o**	not	**ü**	rule	**a**	in about
ä	far, calm	**ō**	open	**ch**	child	**e**	in taken
âr	care	**ȯ**	saw	**ng**	long	**i**	in pencil
e	let	**ô**	order	**sh**	she	**o**	in lemon
ē	equal	**oi**	oil	**th**	thin	**u**	in circus
ėr	term	**ou**	out	**ᵀᴴ**	then		
i	it	**u**	cup	**zh**	measure		

souvenir

a **souvenir** from a

holiday play

soul (sōl), *n.* **1** the spiritual part of a person as distinct from the physical, and regarded as the source of thought, feeling, and action. Many persons believe that the soul is immortal. **2** energy or power of mind or feelings; spirit: *She puts her whole soul into her work.* [Old English *sāwol*]

sou·ve·nir (sü'və nir', sü'və nir), *n.* something given or kept for remembrance; keepsake. [< French < Latin *subvenire* come to mind < *sub-* up from under + *venire* come]

space shut·tle (spās' shut'l), a reuseable winged spacecraft, designed to be launched into orbit around the earth by a rocket, but to glide back to earth and land like an airplane.

Span·iard (span'yərd), *n., pl.* **Span·iards.** native or inhabitant of Spain.

spe·cial·ist (spesh'ə list), *n.* **1** person who pursues one particular branch of study, business, etc. A heart specialist is a doctor who treats diseases of the heart. **2** (in the U.S. Army) an enlisted man or woman with administrative or technical duties.

spe·cial·ize (spesh'ə līz), *v.,* **-ized, -iz·ing.** —*v.i.* **1** pursue some special branch of study, work, etc. **2** develop in a special way; take on a special form, use, etc. —*v.t.* **1** make special or specific; give a special character, function, etc., to. **2** adapt to a special function or condition: *Lungs and gills are specialized for breathing.*

spe·cial·ty (spesh'əl tē), *n., pl.* **-ties.** **1** a special study, line of work, profession, trade, etc.: *American history is the specialty of my history teacher.* **2** product, article, etc., to which special attention is given.

spe·cies (spē'shēz), *n., pl.* **-cies.** **1** group of related organisms that have certain permanent characteristics in common and are able to interbreed. **2** a distinct kind or sort; kind; sort: *There are many species of advertisements.* **3** the species, the human race. [< Latin, originally, appearance]

spe·cif·ic (spi sif'ik), *adj.* **1** definite; precise; particular: *There was no specific reason for the quarrel.* **2** characteristic (of); peculiar (to); distinctive: *Feathers are a feature specific to birds.* **3** curing some particular disease. **4** produced by some special cause: *a specific disease.* **5** of or having to do with a species. —*n.* **1** any specific statement, quality, etc. **2** a cure for some particular disease: *Vitamin B_{12} is a specific for pernicious anemia.*

spec·ta·cle (spek'tə kəl), *n.* **1** something presented to the view as noteworthy, striking, etc.; thing to look at; sight: *a charming spectacle of children at play.* **2** a public show or display.

spec·tac·u·lar (spek tak'yə lər), *adj.* **1** making a great display or show; very striking or imposing to the eye: *a spectacular storm.* **2** having to do with a spectacle or show. —*n.* a spectacular display.

spec·ta·tor (spek'tā tər, spek tā'tər), *n.* person who looks on without taking part; observer; onlooker. [< Latin < *spectare* to watch < *specere* to view]

spice (spīs), *n., v.,* **spiced, spic·ing.** —*n.* **1** any of various more or less strongly flavored or scented substances obtained from plants and used to season food. Pepper, cinnamon, cloves, ginger, and nutmeg are common spices. **2** a spicy, fragrant odor. **3** something that adds flavor or interest. —*v.t.* **1** put spice in; season. **2** add flavor or interest to. [< Old French *espice*, ultimately < Latin *species* sort]

splint (splint), *n.* **1** arrangement of wood, metal, plaster, etc., to hold a broken or dislocated bone in place. **2** a thin, flexible strip of wood, such as is used in making baskets. **3** a thin metal strip or plate. **4** a hard, bony growth on the splint bone of a horse, mule, etc. **5** DIALECT. a splinter of wood or stone; chip. —*v.t.* **1** secure, hold in position, or support by means of a splint or splints. **2** support as if with splints. [< Middle Dutch or Middle Low German *splinte*]

spon·sor (spon'sər), *n.* **1** person or group that formally endorses or supports something or someone: *the sponsor of a law.* **2** person who stands with the parents at an infant's baptism, agreeing to assist in the child's religious upbringing if necessary; godfather or godmother. **3** business firm or other organization that pays the costs of a radio or television program advertising its products or services. —*v.t.* act as sponsor for. [< Latin < *spondere* to promise]

space shuttle

the **space shuttle**

Discovery landing at

Edwards Air Force Base

spoon (spün), *n.* **1** utensil consisting of a small, shallow bowl at the end of a handle, used to take up or stir food or drink. **2** something shaped like a spoon. **3 born with a silver spoon in one's mouth,** born lucky or rich. —*v.t.* take up with or as if with a spoon. [Old English *spōn* chip, shaving] —**spoon′like′,** *adj.*

sprain (sprān), *v.t.* injure (the ligaments or muscles of a joint) by a sudden twist or wrench. —*n.* injury caused by a sudden twist.

state (stāt), *n., v.,* **stat·ed, stat·ing.** —*n.* **1** situation in which a person or thing is; condition of being: *the state of the weather.* **2** Often, **State.** one of several organized political groups which together form a nation. —*v.t.* **1** tell in speech or writing; express; say: *state one's reasons.* **2** specify: *state a price.* [< Latin *status* condition, position < *stare* to stand; common in Latin phrase *status rei publicae* condition of the republic.]

sta·tion·ar·y (stā′shə ner′ē), *adj.* **1** having a fixed station or place; not movable. **2** standing still; not moving. **3** not changing in size, etc.

sta·tion·er·y (stā′shə ner′ē), *n.* writing materials such as paper, cards, and envelopes.

ster·e·o·phon·ic (ster′ē ə fon′ik, stir′ē ə fon′ik), *adj.* of or having to do with a system of sound reproduction using two or more microphones, recording channels, loudspeakers, etc., in order to give a three-dimensional effect. —**ster′e·o·phon′i·cal·ly,** *adv.*

stin·gy (stin′jē), *adj.,* **-gi·er, -gi·est.** **1** unwilling to spend or give money; not generous. **2** scanty; meager.

stom·ach (stum′ək), *n.* **1** the organ of a vertebrate body that serves as a receptacle for food and in which early stages of digestion occur. In human beings, it is a large, muscular, saclike part of the alimentary canal, occupying the upper part of the left side of the abdomen. **2** the part of the body

containing the stomach; abdomen; belly. **3** appetite. **4** desire; liking: *I have no stomach for killing harmless creatures.* —*v.t.* **1** be able to eat or keep in one's stomach. **2** put up with; bear; endure: *He could not stomach such insults.* [< Greek *stomachos* < *stoma* mouth]

stom·ach·ache (stum′ək āk′), *n.* pain in the stomach.

straight (strāt), *adj.* **1** without a bend or curve; not crooked or irregular: *a straight line.* **2** going in a line; direct: *straight aim.* **3** frank; honest: *a straight answer.* **4** right; correct.

straight·a·way (strāt′ə wā′), *n.* a straight course. —*adj.* in a straight course. —*adv.* straightway.

straight·edge (strāt′ej′), *n.* strip of wood or metal having one edge accurately straight, used in obtaining or testing straight lines and level surfaces.

straight·en (strāt′n), *v.t.* **1** make straight: *Straighten your shoulders.* **2** put in the proper order or condition: *straighten up a room, straighten out a misunderstanding, straighten one's accounts.* **3** Usually, **straighten out.** INFORMAL. reform the behavior of: *A good talking-to should straighten the child out.* —**straight′en·er,** *n.*

straight-faced (strāt′fāst′), *adj.* showing no emotion, humor, etc.

straight·for·ward (strāt′fôr′wərd), *adj.* **1** honest; frank. **2** going straight ahead; direct. —*adv.* directly. —**straight′for′ward·ly,** *adv.* —**straight′for′ward·ness,** *n.*

strait (strāt), *n.* **1** a narrow channel connecting two larger bodies of water. **2** straits, *pl.* difficulty; need; distress: *be in desperate straits.*

strike·out (strīk′out′), *n.* in baseball: **1** an out caused by three strikes. **2** a striking out.

sub·mit (səb mit′), *v.i.,* **-mit·ted, -mit·ting.** yield to the power, control, or authority of another; surrender: *They submitted to the will of the majority.*

spoon (def. 1)

two **spoons** in a formal table setting

a	hat	**ī**	ice	**u̇**	put
ā	age	**o**	not	**ü**	rule
ä	far, calm	**ō**	open	**ch**	child
âr	care	**ȯ**	saw	**ng**	long
e	let	**ô**	order	**sh**	she
ē	equal	**oi**	oil	**th**	thin
ėr	term	**ou**	out	**ₜH**	then
i	it	**u**	cup	**zh**	measure

ə stands for

a in about
e in taken
i in pencil
o in lemon
u in circus

sub·scribe (səb skrīb/), v., **-scribed, -scrib·ing.** —v.t. promise to give or pay (a sum of money): *subscribe $15 to the hospital fund.* —v.i. promise to accept and pay for a number of copies of a newspaper, magazine. [< Latin *subscribere* < *sub-* under + *scribere* write] —**sub·scrib/er,** n.

sub·scrip·tion (səb skrip/shən), n. the right to receive something obtained by paying a certain sum.

sub·sti·tute (sub/stə tüt, sub/stə tyüt), n., v., **-tut·ed, -tut·ing,** adj. —n. thing used instead of another; person taking the place of another: *Margarine is a substitute for butter.* —v.t. **1** put in the place of another: *We substituted brown sugar for molasses in these cookies.* **2** take the place of. —v.i. take the place of another; be a substitute. —adj. put in or taking the place of.

sub·tle·ty (sut/l tē), n., pl. **-ties. 1** subtle quality. **2** something subtle.

sub·ur·ban (sə bėr/bən), adj. **1** of, having to do with, or in a suburb. **2** characteristic of a suburb or its inhabitants.

suc·ceed (sək sēd/), v.i. **1** turn out well; do well; have success. **2** accomplish what is attempted or intended. [< Latin *succedere* < *sub-* up to, near + *cedere* go]

suc·cess·ful (sək ses/fəl), adj. having success; ending in success; prosperous; fortunate. —**suc·cess/ful·ly,** adv.

suc·ces·sion (sək sesh/ən), n. **1** group of persons or things coming one after another; series. **2** the coming of one person or thing after another.

suc·ces·sive (sək ses/iv), adj. coming one after another; following in order. —**suc·ces/sive·ly,** adv. —**suc·ces/sive·ness,** n.

suc·ces·sor (sək ses/ər), n. **1** person who follows or succeeds another in office, position, or ownership of property. **2** person or thing that comes next after another in a series.

sud·den (sud/n), adj. **1** happening without warning or notice; not expected: *a sudden stop, a sudden rise to power.* **2** found or hit upon unexpectedly; abrupt: *a sudden turn in the road.* **3** quick; rapid. [< Old French *sodein* < Latin *subitaneus* < *subitus* sudden] —**sud/den·ly,** adv. —**sud/den·ness,** n.

sul·fur (sul/fər), n. a light-yellow, highly flammable nonmetallic element that exists in several allotropic forms and burns in the air with a blue flame and a stifling odor. Sulfur is found abundantly in volcanic regions, and is also a constituent of proteins. *Symbol:* S; *atomic number* 16.

sun·screen (sun/skrēn/), n. a chemical compound, especially para-aminobenzoic acid, that screens out the ultraviolet rays of the sun, used in skin preparations to prevent sunburn.

su·per·in·tend·ent (sü/pər in ten/dənt), n. person who oversees, directs, or manages.

su·per·i·or (sə pir/ē ər, sù pir/ē ər), adj. **1** above the average; very good; excellent: *superior work in school.* **2** higher in quality; better; greater: *a superior blend of coffee.* **3** higher in position, rank, importance, etc.: *a superior officer.* **4** showing a feeling of being above others; proud.

su·per·vise (sü/pər vīz), v.t., **-vised, -vis·ing.** look after and direct (work or workers, a process, etc.); superintend; manage: *Study halls are supervised by teachers.*

su·per·vi·sion (sü/pər vizh/ən), n. management; direction: *The house was built under the careful supervision of an architect.*

sup·ple·men·tar·y (sup/lə men/tər ē), adj. **1** additional. **2** added to supply what is lacking.

sup·posed (sə pōzd/), adj. accepted as true; considered as possible or probable; assumed: *a supposed fact.* —**sup·pos/ed·ly,** adv.

sur·geon (sėr/jən), n. doctor who performs operations; medical practitioner who specializes in surgery. [< Old French *cirurgien* < *cirurgie*]

sur·ger·y (sėr/jər ē), n., pl. **-ger·ies. 1** the art and science of treating diseases, injuries, deformities, etc., by operations and instruments. **2** operating room or other areas where surgical operations are performed. **3** the work performed by a surgeon; operation.

sur·rep·ti·tious (sėr/əp tish/əs), adj. **1** stealthy; secret: *a surreptitious glance.* **2** secret and unauthorized; clandestine: *surreptitious meetings.*

sus·pect (sus/pekt), n. person suspected. [< Latin *suspectum* looked under < *sub-* under + *specere* to look]

sus·pend (sə spend′), *v.t.* **1** hang down by attaching to something above: *The lamp was suspended from the ceiling.* **2** hold in place as if by hanging: *We saw the smoke suspended in the still air.*

sus·pen·sion bridge (sə spen′shən brij′), *n., pl.* **sus·pen·sion bridg·es** (brij′iz). bridge having its roadway anchored at each end and suspended on cables or chains between towers.

sym·met·ric (si met′rik), *adj.* symmetrical.

sym·met·ri·cal (si met′rə kəl), *adj.* having symmetry; well-proportioned. —**sym·met′ri·cal·ly,** *adv.*

sym·pa·thize (sim′pə thīz), *v.i.,* **-thized, -thiz·ing. 1** feel or show sympathy: *sympathize with a child who is hurt.* **2** share in or agree with a feeling or opinion: *My mother sympathizes with my plan to be a doctor.*

T

ta·ma·le (tə mä′lē), *n.* a Mexican food made of corn meal and minced meat, seasoned with red peppers, wrapped in cornhusks, and roasted or steamed. [< Mexican Spanish < Nahuatl *tamalli*]

Tas·ma·ni·a (taz mā′nē ə, taz mā′nyə), *n.* island off SE Australia. It is a state of Australia. 457,000 pop.; 26,400 sq. mi. (68,400 sq. km.) *Capital:* Hobart. —**Tas·ma′ni·an,** *adj., n.*

tea cer·e·mo·ny (tē′ ser′ə mō′nē), a special set of acts for serving tea.

teach·er (tē′chər), *n.* person who teaches, especially one who teaches in a school.

tech·ni·cal·i·ty (tek′nə kal′ə tē), *n., pl.* **-ties. 1** a technical matter, point, detail, term, expression, etc. **2** technical quality or character.

tech·ni·cian (tek nish′ən), *n.* an expert in the technicalities of a subject.

tech·nol·o·gy (tek nol′ə jē), *n.* **1** the use of scientific knowledge to control physical objects and forces. **2** the entire sum of practical methods for controlling physical objects and forces.

tem·po·rar·y (tem′pə rer′ē), *adj., n., pl.* **-rar·ies.** —*adj.* lasting for a short time only; used for the time being; not permanent. —*n.* person, often a secretary or other office worker, hired for a limited time.

ten·don (ten′dən), *n.* a tough, strong band or cord of fibrous tissue that joins a muscle to a bone or some other part and transmits the force of the muscle to that part; sinew. [< Medieval Latin *tendonem* < Greek *tenōn;* influenced by Latin *tendere* to stretch]

ten·sion (ten′shən), *n.* **1** a stretching. **2** a stretched condition. **3** a strained condition. [< Latin *tensionem* < *tendere* to stretch]

ten·sor (ten′sər, ten′sôr), *n.* muscle that stretches or tightens.

ter·ra cot·ta (ter′ə kot′ə), **1** kind of hard, often unglazed, brownish-red earthenware, used for vases, statuettes, decorations on buildings, etc. **2** a dull brownish red. [< Italian, baked earth]

ter·ra·pin (ter′ə pin), *n.* any of a genus of edible North American turtles that live in fresh water or tidewater. [of Algonquian origin]

tes·sel·late (*v.* tes′ə lāt; *adj.* tes′ə lit, tes′ə lāt), *v.,* **-lat·ed, -lat·ing,** *adj.* —*v.t.* make of small squares or blocks, or in a checkered pattern. —*adj.* made in small squares or blocks or in a checkered pattern. [< Latin *tessellatus,* ultimately < *tessera.*] —**tes′sel·la′tion,** *n.*

their (ᴛͪâr), *adj.* possessive form of **they.** of them; belonging to them: *I like their house.*

theirs (ᴛͪârz), *pron.* possessive form of **they.** the one or ones belonging to them: *Our house is white; theirs is brown.*

the·mat·ic map (thē mat′ik map′), a map that has one special topic.

tamale

A **tamale** is a Mexican food made of corn meal, corn husks, and a filling.

terra cotta

a **terra cotta** pot for a plant

a	hat	**ī**	ice	** u̇**	put	**ə** *stands for*	
ā	age	**o**	not	**ü**	rule	**a**	in about
ä	far, calm	**ō**	open	**ch**	child	**e**	in taken
âr	care	**ȯ**	saw	**ng**	long	**i**	in pencil
e	let	**ô**	order	**sh**	she	**o**	in lemon
ē	equal	**oi**	oil	**th**	thin	**u**	in circus
ėr	term	**ou**	out	**ᴛͪ**	then		
i	it	**u**	cup	**zh**	measure		

there (ᴛʜâr; *unstressed* ᴛʜər), *adv.*
1 in or at that place: *Sit there.*
2 to or into that place: *How did that get there? Go there at once.*
3 *There* is also used in sentences in which the verb comes before its subject. *There are three new houses on our street. Is there a drugstore here?*

thir·ti·eth (thér′tē ith), *adj., n.* next after the 29th; last in a series of 30.

threat·en (thret′n), *v.t.* **1** make a threat against; say what will be done to hurt or punish. **2** be a sign or warning of (possible evil or harm): *Black clouds threaten rain.* **3** be a cause of possible evil or harm to: *A flood threatened the city.* —*v.i.* **1** be a threat. **2** utter a threat.

through (thrü), *prep.* **1** from end to end of; from side to side of; between the parts of; from beginning to end of. **2** because of; by reason of.

thug (thug), *n.* ruffian; hoodlum. [< Hindi *thag* < Sanskrit *sthaga* rogue]

time-out (tīm′out′), *n.* period when play is suspended during a game, at the request of one team, a player, an umpire, etc.

tis·sue (tish′ü), *n.* **1** in biology: **a** substance forming the parts of living organisms. **b** mass of similar cells which performs a particular function. **2** a thin, light or delicate cloth. **3** tissue paper. [< Old French *tissu*, originally past participle of *tistre* to weave < Latin *texere*]

To·ky·o (tō′kē ō, tō′kyō), *n.* capital of Japan, in the central part, on SE Honshu. 8,592,000.

top·o·graph·ic map (top′ə graf′ik map′), a map showing accurate and detailed description of surface features such as mountains, rivers.

tor·na·do (tôr nā′dō), *n., pl.* **-does** or **-dos.** an extremely violent and destructive whirlwind extending down from a mass of dark clouds as a twisting funnel and moving over the land in a narrow path. [alteration of Spanish *tronada* < *tronar* to thunder]

tor·pe·do (tôr pē′dō), *n., pl.* **-does.** a large, cigarshaped missile that contains explosives and travels under water by its own power, launched from submarines.

tour·na·ment (tér′nə mənt, túr′nə mənt), *n.* contest in any game

of skill in which a number of competitors play a series of games.

tox·in (tok′sən), *n.* any poison formed by an organism as a result of its metabolism. Toxins formed by bacteria cause diseases such as diphtheria and scarlet fever.

trag·e·dy (traj′ə dē), *n., pl.* **-dies.** a very sad or terrible happening.

trait (trāt), *n.* a distinguishing feature or quality of mind, character, etc.; characteristic: *Courage and truthfulness are desirable traits.* [< Middle French < Latin *tractus* a drawing < *trahere* to draw]

tra·jec·tor·y (trə jek′tər ē), *n., pl.* **-tor·ies.** the curved path of a projectile, comet, planet, etc. [< Medieval Latin *trajectorius* throwing across, ultimately < Latin *trans-* across + *jacere* to throw]

tran·scribe (tran skrīb′), *v.t.,* **-scribed, -scrib·ing. 1** copy in writing or in typewriting. **2** set down in writing or print: *a speech transcribed in the newspapers, word for word.* [< Latin *transcribere* < *trans-* over + *scribere* write] —**tran·scrib′er,** *n.*

trans·fer (tran sfér′, tran′sfér′), *v.,* **-ferred, -fer·ring.** —*v.t.* convey or remove from one person or place to another; hand over: *The clerk was transferred to another department.* —*v.i.* **1** change from one public vehicle, such as a bus, train, etc., to another. **2** change from one place to another: *I transferred from the state university to a college nearer home.*

trans·for·ma·tion (tran′sfər mā′shən), *n.* **1** a transforming. **2** a being transformed. **3** (in mathematics) the changing of the form of an expression into another form.

trans·la·tion (tran slā′shən, tranz lā′shən), *n.* (in mathematics) a sliding of a figure from one location to another without turning it.

trans·mit (tran smit′, tranz mit′), *v.t.,* **-mit·ted, -mit·ting.** send over; pass on; pass along; let through: *I will transmit the money by special messenger.*

trav·el (trav′əl), *v.i.,* **-eled, -el·ing** or **-elled, -el·ling. 1** go from one place to another; journey: *travel across the country.* **2** go from place to place selling things: *travel for a large firm.* **3** move; pass; proceed: *Light and sound travel in waves.*

time-out

calling a **time-out**

treas·ure (trezh′ər, trā′zhər), n., v., **-ured, -ur·ing.** —n. **1** wealth or riches stored up; valuable things: *The pirates buried their treasure along the coast.* **2** any thing or person that is much loved or valued. —v.t. **1** value highly; cherish; prize. **2** put away for future use; store up; hoard.

tri·al (trī′əl), n. **1** the examining and deciding of a civil or criminal case in a court of law. **2** process of trying or testing the fitness, truth, strength, or other quality of something: *The mechanic gave the motor another trial to see if it would start.* —adj. **1** made, done, used, or taken as a trial: *a trial model, a trial run.* **2** of or having to do with a trial in a court of law: *trial testimony.* [< Anglo-French < *trier* to try]

trial-and-error learning (trī′əl ənd er′ər lėr′ning), a method of learning by trying out different responses to a new situation until one response is successful.

tri·an·gle (trī′ang′gəl), n. **1** a plane figure having three sides and three angles. **2** something shaped like a triangle.

trig·o·nom·e·try (trig′ə nom′ə trē), n. branch of mathematics that deals with the relations between the sides and angles of triangles and the calculations based on these. [ultimately < Greek *tri-* three + *gōnia* angle + *metron* measure]

tril·lion (tril′yən), n., adj. **1** (in the United States, Canada, and France) 1 followed by 12 zeros. **2** (in Great Britain and Germany) 1 followed by 18 zeros. [< *tri-* + (m)*illion*]

tri·ple (trip′əl), adj., n., v., **-pled, -pling.** —adj. **1** three times as much, as many, as large, as strong, etc. **2** having three parts; threefold. —n. **1** number or amount that is three times as much. **2** (in baseball) hit by which a batter gets to third base. —v.t. make three times as much or as many: *triple one's income.*

tri·plet (trip′lit), n. **1** one of three children born at the same time to the same mother. **2** group of three.

tri·pod (trī′pod), n. a three-legged support for a camera, etc. [< Latin < Greek *tripodos* < *tri-* three + *podos* foot]

tru·ly (trü′lē), adv. **1** in a true manner; exactly; rightly; faithfully: *Tell me truly what you think.* **2** in fact; really; genuinely: *It was truly a beautiful day.*

tun·dra (tun′drə, tun′drə), n. a vast, level, treeless plain in the arctic regions. The ground beneath the surface of the tundras is frozen even in summer. Much of Alaska and northern Canada is tundra. [< Russian]

Turk·ish (tėr′kish), adj. of, having to do with, or belonging to Turkey, its people, or their language. —n. the Turkic language of the Turks.

twen·ty-one (twen′tē wun′), n. three times seven; 21.

ty·coon (tī kün′), n. **1** businessman having great wealth and power. **2** title given by foreigners to the former hereditary commanders in chief of the Japanese army; shogun. [< Japanese *taikun* < Chinese *tai* great + *kiun* lord]

ty·phoon (tī fün′), n. **1** a violent storm or tempest occurring in India. **2** a violent cyclone or hurricane occurring in the western Pacific, chiefly during the period from July to October. [< Chinese *tai fung* big wind]

tripod

a **tripod** for a camera

U

ug·ly (ug′lē), adj., **-li·er, -li·est.** **1** very unpleasant to look at: *an ugly house, an ugly face.* **2** bad; disagreeable; offensive: *ugly language.* **3** threatening: *ugly clouds.* **4** ill-natured; bad-tempered: *an ugly mood, an ugly disposition.* [< Scandinavian (Old Icelandic) *uggligr* dreadful < *uggr* fear] —**ug′li·ness,** n.

a	hat	ī	ice	ů	put	ə stands for	
ā	age	o	not	ü	rule	a	in about
ä	far, calm	ō	open	ch	child	e	in taken
âr	care	ȯ	saw	ng	long	i	in pencil
e	let	ô	order	sh	she	o	in lemon
ē	equal	oi	oil	th	thin	u	in circus
ėr	term	ou	out	ŦH	then		
i	it	u	cup	zh	measure		

umbrella (def. 1)

bamboo **umbrellas**

on the beach

um·brel·la (um brel′ə), *n., pl.*
um·brel·las. 1 a light, portable,
circular cover for protection against
rain or sun, consisting of a fabric
held on a folding frame of thin ribs,
which slide on a rod or stick. **2** any
protective covering or shelter.
—*adj.* like an umbrella. [< Italian
ombrella, ultimately < Latin *umbra*
shade] —**um·brel′la·like′,** *adj.*

un·be·liev·a·ble (un′bi lē′və bəl),
adj. not believable; incredible.

un·break·a·ble (un brā′kə bəl), *adj.*
not breakable; not easily broken.

un·busi·ness·like (un biz′nis līk′), *adj.*
without system and method; not
efficient.

un·con·scious (un kon′shəs), *adj.* not
conscious; not able to feel or think.

un·con·trol·la·ble (un′kən trō′lə bəl),
adj. not having power or authority
over; not able to restrain or check.

un·de·feat·ed (un′di fē′tid), *n.* a not
being defeated; not being
overcome in a contest or conflict.

un·em·ploy·ment (un′em ploi′mənt),
n. **1** lack of employment; being
out of work. **2** INFORMAL. number
or percentage of workers that are
unemployed.

un·ex·pect·ed (un′ek spek′tid), *adj.*
not expected: *an unexpected
difficulty.* —**un′ex·pect′ed·ly,** *adv.*

un·for·tu·nate·ly (un fôr′chə nit lē),
adv. **1** in an unfortunate way or
manner. **2** INFORMAL. it is
unfortunate that.

un·gu·late (ung′gyə lit), *adj.* having
hoofs.

u·ni·cy·cle (yü′nə sī′kəl), *n.* a vehicle
consisting of a frame mounted on
a single wheel, propelled by
pedaling, used especially by
acrobats, etc.

u·ni·form·i·ty (yü′nə fôr′mə tē), *n.,
pl.* **-ties.** uniform condition or
character; sameness throughout.

u·ni·fy (yü′nə fī), *v.t., v.i.,* **-fied,
-fy·ing.** make or form into one;
unite.

un·in·ter·est·ed (un in′tər ə stid, un
in′tə res′tid), *adj.* not interested;
paying no attention.

un′in·tim·i·dat·ed (un′in tim′ə
dā tid), *v.t.,* not intimidated; not
frightened; not influenced or
forced by fear.

u·nique (yü nēk′), *adj.* **1** having no
like or equal; being the only one
of its kind: *a unique specimen of
rock.* **2** INFORMAL. very uncommon
or unusual. [< Middle French <
Latin *unicus* < *unus* one]

u·ni·son (yü′nə sən, yü′nə zən), *n.*
harmonious combination or union;
agreement: *The feet of marching
soldiers move in unison.*

u·ni·ver·sal (yü′nə vėr′səl), *adj.*
1 of or for all; belonging to all;
concerning all: *Food is a universal
need.* **2** existing everywhere: *The
law of gravity is universal.*
3 covering a whole group of
persons, things, cases, etc.

u·ni·ver·si·ty (yü′nə vėr′sə tē), *n., pl.*
-ties. 1 institution of learning of the
highest grade, usually including
schools of law, medicine, teaching,
business, etc., as well as (in the
United States) a college of liberal
arts and a graduate school.
2 buildings that constitute a
university.

un·mo·ti·vat·ed (un′mō′tə vā tid),
v.t., not provided with a motive
or incentive; not having an
inducement to act.

un·pleas·ant·ness (un plez′nt nis), *n.*
1 unpleasant quality. **2** something
unpleasant. **3** quarrel.

un·pre·dict·a·ble (un′pri dik′tə bəl),
adj. that cannot be predicted;
uncertain or changeable.

un·suc·cess·ful (un′sək ses′fəl), *adj.*
not successful; without success.
—**un′suc·cess′ful·ly,** *adv.*

un·ti·dy (un tī′dē), *adj.* not in order;
not neat: *an untidy house.*
—**un·ti′di·ness,** *n.*

un·trust·wor·thy (un′trust′wėr ᵺē),
adj. that cannot be depended
on or trusted; not deserving
confidence; not reliable.

un·yield·ing (un′yēld′ing), *adj.*
1 not producing; not bearing.
2 not giving, not granting.

up-to-date (up′tə dāt′), *adj.*
1 extending to the present time:
an up-to-date record of sales.
2 keeping up with the times in
style, ideas, etc.; modern.

up·ris·ing (up′rī′zing, up rī′zing), *n.*
1 revolt; rebellion. **2** a rising up.
3 an upward slope; ascent.

up·roar (up′rôr′, up′rōr′), *n.* a loud
or confused noise.

ur·ban·ize (ėr′bə nīz), *v.,* **ur·ban·ized,
ur·ban·iz·ing.** make or become
urban: *urbanize a district.*
—**ur′ban·i·za′tion,** *n.*

u·su·al (yü′zhü əl), *adj.* **1** commonly
seen, found, or happening;
ordinary; customary. **2** as usual, in
the usual manner; as is customary.
[< Late Latin *usualis* < Latin *usus*
use, custom < *uti* to use]
—**u′su·al·ness,** *n.*

u·su·al·ly (yü′zhü ə lē), *adv.*
according to what is usual;
commonly; ordinarily; customarily.

u·surp (yü zėrp′, yü sėrp′), *v.t.,*
u·surps, u·surped, u·surp·ing.
seize and hold (power, position,
authority, etc.) by force or without
right. —*v.i.* commit usurpation.
[< Latin *usurpare* < *usu* through
use + *rapere* seize] —**u·surp′er,** *n.*

u·ti·lize (yü′tl īz), *v.t.,* **-lized, -liz·ing.**
make use of; put to practical use.
—**u′ti·liz′a·ble,** *adj.* —**u′ti·li·za′tion,** *n.* —**u′ti·liz′er.** *n.*

V

vac·cine (vak′sēn′, vak sēn′), *n.*
1 preparation of weakened or killed
bacteria or viruses of a particular
disease, used to inoculate a person
in order to prevent or lessen the
effects of that disease. Vaccines
work by causing the body to
develop antibodies. **2** the virus
causing cowpox, prepared for use
in preventive inoculation against
smallpox. [< Latin *vaccinus* of
cows < *vacca* cow]

vac·u·um (vak′yü əm, vak′yùm), *n.,*
pl. **vac·u·ums, vac·u·a** (vak′yü ə).
1 an empty space without even air
in it. **2** an enclosed space from
which almost all air or other matter
has been removed. **3** an empty
space; void.

val·e·dic·to·ri·an (val′ə dik tôr′ē ən,
val′ə dik tōr′ē ən), *n.* student who
gives the farewell address at the
graduating exercises. The student
usually ranks highest.

van (van), *n.* **1** a large enclosed truck
or wagon for moving furniture or
household goods. **2** a small,
enclosed truck designed for light
hauling or for recreational use.

ve·hi·cle (vē′ə kəl), *n.* **1** any means
of carrying, conveying, or
transporting: *a space vehicle.*
2 carriage, cart, wagon,
automobile, sled, or any other
conveyance used on land.

ve·ran·da or **ve·ran·dah** (və ran′də),
n. a large porch or gallery along
one or more sides of a house.
[< Hindustani *varandā*]

ver·dict (vėr′dikt), *n.* **1** the decision of
a jury. **2** any decision or judgment.
[< Anglo-French *verdit* < Old
French *ver* true + *dit* spoken]

ver·ti·cal (vėr′tə kəl), *adj.* straight
up and down; perpendicular to
a level surface; upright. A person
standing up straight is in a vertical
position. —*n.* a vertical line, plane,
direction, position, part, etc.

ver·ti·cal scale (vėr′tə kəl skāl′), the
left side of a chart or graph which
shows certain values.

vic·tim (vik′təm), *n.* **1** person, animal,
or thing sacrificed, injured, or
destroyed. **2** person badly treated
or taken advantage of; dupe.

vi·rus (vī′rəs), *n.* **1** any of a group
of disease-producing agents
composed of protein and nucleic
acid, smaller than any known
bacteria and dependent upon
the living tissue of hosts for their
reproduction and growth. **2** a
poison produced in a person or
animal suffering from an infectious
disease. [< Latin, poison]

vis·i·bil·i·ty (viz′ə bil′ə tē), *n., pl.*
-ties. **1** condition or quality of
being visible. **2** condition of light,
atmosphere, etc., with reference to
the distance at which things can
be clearly seen.

vis·i·ble (viz′ə bəl), *adj.* **1** that can be
seen: *The shore was barely visible
through the fog.* **2** readily evident;
apparent; obvious. [< Latin *visibilis*
< *videre* to see]

vi·sion (vizh′ən), *n.* **1** power of seeing;
sense of sight. **2** act or fact of
seeing; sight.

vi·ta·min or **vi·ta·mine** (vī′tə mən), *n.*
any of certain organic substances
required for the normal growth and
nourishment of the body. Lack of
essential vitamins causes such
diseases as rickets and scurvy, as
well as general poor health. —*adj.*
of, having to do with, or containing
vitamins.

veranda Take a
walk around the
veranda.

vertical
The walls of Ayer Rock
are nearly **vertical.**

a	hat	**ī**	ice	**ù**	put	**ə** stands for	
ā	age	**o**	not	**ü**	rule	**a**	in about
ä	far, calm	**ō**	open	**ch**	child	**e**	in taken
âr	care	**ȯ**	saw	**ng**	long	**i**	in pencil
e	let	**ô**	order	**sh**	she	**o**	in lemon
ē	equal	**oi**	oil	**th**	thin	**u**	in circus
ėr	term	**ou**	out	**ŦH**	then		
i	it	**u**	cup	**zh**	measure		

vo·cab·u·lar·y (vō kab′yə ler′ē), *n.,
pl.* **-lar·ies. 1** stock of words used
by a person, group of people,
profession, etc.: *Reading will
increase your vocabulary.*
2 collection or list of words, usually
in alphabetical order, with their
translations or meanings.

vol·can·ic (vol kan′ik), *adj.* **1** of or
caused by a volcano; having to
do with volcanoes: *a volcanic
eruption.* **2** like a volcano; liable to
break out violently: *a volcanic
temper.* **—vol·can′i·cal·ly,** *adv.*

vol·ca·no (vol kā′nō), *n., pl.* **-noes** or
-nos. 1 an opening in the earth's
crust through which steam, ashes,
and lava are expelled in periods
of activity. **2** a cone-shaped hill
or mountain around this opening,
built up of the material thus
expelled. [< Italian < Latin
Vulcanus Vulcan]

warm-up

various **warm-ups** for
the legs

W

warm-up (wôrm′up′), *n.* practice or
exercise taken for a few minutes
before entering a game, etc.

war·ri·or (wôr′ē ər, wor′ē ər), *n.*
person experienced in fighting
battles. [< Old North French
werreieor <werreier wage war
<werre war]

wash-and-wear (wäsh′ən wâr′,
wȯsh′ən wâr′), *adj.* specially
treated to require little or no ironing
after washing and drying: *wash-
and-wear fabrics.*

Wash·ing·ton (wäsh′ing tən,
wȯ′shing tən), *n.* capital of the
United States, covering the entire
District of Columbia. Washington is
situated along the Potomac River
between Maryland and Virginia.
638,000.

wed·ding (wed′ing), *n.* **1** a marriage
ceremony. **2** a close union or
association.

weird (wird), *adj.,* **weird·er, weird·est.
1** unearthly or mysterious: *They
were awakened by a weird shriek.
The creaking planks made the
weirdest sound of all.* **2** odd;
fantastic; queer: *The shadows
made weird figures on the wall.*

wheel·bar·row (hwēl′bar′ō), *n.* a
small vehicle with a wheel at one
end and two handles at the other,
used for carrying loads.

whim·si·cal (hwim′zə kəl), *adj.* odd;
fanciful: *a whimsical expression.*
—whim′si·cal·ly, *adv.*

whirl·pool (hwėrl′pül′), *n.* current of
water whirling round and round
rapidly; eddy or vortex of water.

white blood cells (hwīt′ blud′ selz′),
any colorless blood cells with a
nucleus, that destroy germs.

wig (wig), *n.* an artificial covering of
natural or false hair for the head.
[< *periwig*]

wil·de·beest (wil′də bēst′), *n.* gnu.
[< obsolete Afrikaans, wild beast]

wit·ness (wit′nis), *n., pl.* **wit·ness·es.
1** person who saw something
happen; spectator; eyewitness.
2 person who gives evidence or
testifies under oath in a court of
law: *The witness's testimony was
brief. Both witnesses' testified
against the defendant.*

word proc·es·sor (wėrd′ pros′es ər),
1 computer or other complex
machine used to edit, store, and
reproduce words. **2** person who
uses such a machine.

worn (wôrn, wōrn), *v.* pp. of **wear.**
—adj. 1 damaged by long or hard
wear or use: *worn rugs.* **2** tired;
wearied: *a worn face.*

writ·er (rī′tər), *n.* **1** person who writes.
2 person whose profession or
business is writing; author.

Y

yo·gurt (yō′gərt), *n.* a kind of
thickened, slightly fermented liquid
food made from milk acted upon
by bacteria. [< Turkish]

your·self (yu̇r self′, yər self′), *pron., pl.*
your·selves. 1 the emphatic form of
you. *You yourself know the story is
not true.* **2** the reflexive form of **you.**
You will hurt yourself. **3** your real
or true self: *You aren't yourself
today.*

Z

zer·o (zir′ō), *n., pl.* **zer·os** or **zer·oes,**
adj. —n. the figure or digit 0;
naught. **—adj. 1** of or at zero.
2 not any; none at all: *a zero
probability.*

zoological garden (zō′ə loj′ə kəl
gärd′n), place where animals
are kept and shown; zoo.

zo·ol·o·gist (zō ol′ə jist), *n.* an expert
in zoology.

zo·ol·o·gy (zō ol′ə jē), *n.* branch of
biology that deals with animals
and animal life; study of the
structure, physiology, development,
classification, etc., of animals.

Writer's Thesaurus

Introduction

Many of your spelling words have synonyms, words with similar meanings. This thesaurus lists those spelling words alphabetically, defines them, and provides synonyms. For many words, you can also look up antonyms, words with opposite meanings. This thesaurus can even introduce you to new words.

Understand a Thesaurus Entry

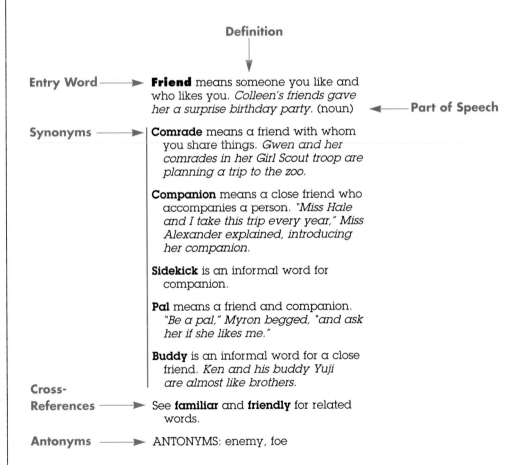

Definition

Entry Word ——▸ **Friend** means someone you like and who likes you. *Colleen's friends gave her a surprise birthday party.* (noun) ◂—— **Part of Speech**

Synonyms ——▸ **Comrade** means a friend with whom you share things. *Gwen and her comrades in her Girl Scout troop are planning a trip to the zoo.*

Companion means a close friend who accompanies a person. *"Miss Hale and I take this trip every year," Miss Alexander explained, introducing her companion.*

Sidekick is an informal word for companion.

Pal means a friend and companion. *"Be a pal," Myron begged, "and ask her if she likes me."*

Buddy is an informal word for a close friend. *Ken and his buddy Yuji are almost like brothers.*

Cross-References ——▸ See **familiar** and **friendly** for related words.

Antonyms ——▸ ANTONYMS: enemy, foe

313

A a

About means somewhere near in number, size, or time. *Jaime is about six feet tall. The school bus usually gets to the corner at about 7:45.* (adverb)

Around can mean about. *I usually wake up around 6:30. Around thirty people live in Julia's building.*

Approximately means as nearly as you can estimate. *On a clear night, a person can see approximately 3,000 stars without using a telescope.*

More or less means about. It emphasizes that the estimate could be too large or too small. *The house costs eighty-five thousand dollars, more or less.*

SEE **estimate** for related words.

Adapt means to change something or someone so as to suit a need. *Bill had to adapt to sharing his room when baby Albert was born.* (verb)

Adjust means to change something to a better position or fit. *You can adjust the seat of the car if you are cramped.*

Conform means to act so as to suit rules or standards. *I don't want to be friends with Becky if that means conforming to her ideas of how to dress.*

Argue means to disagree strongly and give reasons for your opinion. *Sandy argued with the umpire who called her out at second base.* (verb)

Dispute can mean to argue loudly or at length. *The neighbors are disputing about how late it's OK to play music.*

Squabble means to dispute over something seemingly unimportant. *The children squabbled about who should be first in line.*

Quarrel means to dispute angrily. *We heard Dave and Chuck quarrel and then saw them wrestle on the ground.*

Feud means to quarrel fiercely for a long time, especially one group with another. *Ranchers feuded with farmers about land uses.*

SEE **fight** for related words.

WORD POOL

There are many words for the quality shown by someone who is brave.

bravery	gallantry
nerve	boldness
guts	pluck
courage	heart
spunk	daring
heroism	valor

B b

Belief means an idea that someone holds to be true. *It is Joanna's belief that Willard sent her that valentine.* (noun)

Trust means belief that someone or something will do what is expected. It suggests expecting good things. *"And this be our motto," wrote Francis Key, "'In God is our trust.'"*

Faith means a very strong, unquestioning belief. *Rev. Martin Luther King, Jr., spoke of his faith in freedom and justice.*

SEE **idea** and **opinion** for related words.

Brave means showing no fear in a dangerous or difficult situation. *Sheila is brave enough to tell her friends that smoking is stupid.* (adjective)

Courageous means brave and strong in spirit. A courageous person chooses to do what is right even when it is difficult or dangerous. *Two courageous boys rescued my brother when he fell through the ice.*

Fearless means having no fear. *That fearless cat plays with a huge dog.*

Unafraid means having no fear. *On the day of the big test, Ellen was unafraid because she had studied hard.*

Daring means willing and eager to face danger and take risks. *The daring pilots thrilled the crowd with their stunts at the air show.*

ANTONYMS: cowardly, fearful

C c

Common means happening often or often met with. *"It's just a common cold," Dr. Wu told Jerome.* (adjective)

Ordinary means like most others. *Since the note was written on ordinary paper, the police concentrated on tracing its rare purple ink.*

Normal means like most others. It suggests that this is a good way to be. *It is normal for people to want to be liked and respected.*

Popular can mean widespread and done, had, or known by many people. *Grandpa and Grandma like to do popular dances from years ago.*

SEE **usual** for related words.

Consider means to think carefully about something before making a decision. *Sal's mother is considering a second job to help pay for the house.* (verb)

Contemplate means to consider something for a long time. *If Ray is seriously contemplating a career in the Navy, he should talk to a recruiter.*

Take into account and **keep in mind** mean to include something particular in your thinking. *Ralph tries to take into account that his grandparents grew up without TV, but it is hard to keep in mind how much life has changed for them.*

SEE **decide** for related words.

ANTONYMS: disregard, ignore

Continue means to go on. *World War II continued from 1939 until the defeat of Germany and Japan in 1945.* (verb)

Last means to continue. *The parade lasted for an hour and a half.*

Remain and **linger** can mean to continue. *Lisbet remains in poor health, with a cough that has been lingering for weeks now.*

Persist can mean to last for a long time. *The weather service expects the drought to persist all summer.*

Control means the ability to direct or guide people or events. *The governor announced that the forest fires are now under control.* (noun)

Power can mean control. *Marilynn has the power to make my day with one smile.*

Authority means control, often of a particular sort. *A police officer has the authority to arrest people.*

Mastery means control, especially complete control. *With total mastery, the tightrope artist rode his bicycle on the high wire.*

Crime means an act that breaks a law. *Why are television shows so full of crimes?* (noun)

Offense means an act that breaks a law, or an act that many people think is bad. *Driving a car with a broken rear light is a minor offense, so the police officer wrote a warning ticket.*

Wrong can mean an offense. *I think Peter has done me a wrong, but he refuses to apologize.*

Misdeed is a formal word that means an offense. *The prosecutor urged the jury not to let the criminal's misdeeds go unpunished.*

Sin means an act that breaks a religious law. *The Ten Commandments forbid sins such as killing, stealing, and lying.*

Criminal means a person who breaks the law. It suggests a person who breaks many laws. *The judge sentenced the criminal to five years in prison for stealing cars.* (noun)

Crook can mean a person who breaks the law often. This meaning is informal. *The police recovered the money from the robbery, but the crooks got away.*

Outlaw means a criminal. It suggests a criminal of old times. *Robin Hood, the legendary outlaw, robbed the rich and gave to the poor.*

Desperado means a bold, reckless criminal, especially of old times. *A band of desperadoes invaded the little Western town.*

Hoodlum means a criminal, especially one who is likely to hurt people. *A group of hoodlums is responsible for the series of assaults on subway passengers.*

A band of **desperadoes** invaded the little western town.

Cruel means willing to give or see pain. *Even before the Civil War, some Southerners believed keeping people in slavery was cruel.* (adjective)

Vicious can mean deliberately cruel. *Black Beauty was badly treated by his vicious owner.*

Merciless means completely lacking in mercy. *The king's tax collectors went about their business in merciless fashion.*

Ruthless means merciless and brutal. *Josef Stalin was a ruthless dictator who had millions of people killed.*

SEE **fierce** for related words.

ANTONYMS: kind, merciful

Curious means eager to know more. *The bear is curious about the possibility of getting honey from the beehive.* (adjective)

Inquiring means interested in many subjects and eager to learn about them. *The ancient Greeks were famous for their inquiring minds.*

Inquisitive means extremely curious, especially about other people's lives. *Norma is quite inquisitive; she always asks where I went and who was with me.*

Prying means inquisitive in an unpleasant way. *"Would it be a prying question if I asked how you got that black eye?" Tim asked Jackie.*

Nosy is an informal word that means prying. *The nosy neighbor always comes past when we get the mail.*

ANTONYM: uninterested

D d

Decide means to make up your mind. *It was such a hot day that we decided to go to the city swimming pool.* (verb)

Determine means to decide firmly, often from several choices. *Jolene is still trying to determine which hairdo looks best on her.*

Conclude can mean to decide after thinking it over. *The police concluded that the driver who caused the accident had been drinking.*

Settle means to decide finally. *Bella thinks Sally should settle on a ponytail.*

Decrease means to make or become less. *Gabriel's mother suggested he decrease the salt in the meat loaf next time.* (verb)

Lessen means to decrease. *As she spoke, Sachie's anxiety about her report began to lessen.*

Reduce means to make less. *A nutritionist gave a lecture to the sixth and seventh graders about reducing fat and sugar in their diets.*

Cut back means to reduce. *Dahlia rattled her piggy bank and figured she'd have to cut back her spending on movies.*

ANTONYMS: add, increase

Definite means clear and exact. *"Molly needs a definite answer: Will you buy her guitar or not?" asked Jim.* (adjective)

Clear-cut can mean definite. *Daley has a clear-cut choice—he can apologize, or he can forget about coming to my party.*

Distinct can mean definite and unmistakable. *Since Jonah had played the game before, he had a distinct advantage over me.*

Decided means definite and unquestionable. *Georgia's smile faded, and her eyes took on a look of decided annoyance.*

Explicit means clearly and fully stated. *Sonya gave us explicit directions for getting to her house.*

Sonya gave us **explicit** directions for getting to her house.

Descend means to come down. *Rob can descend the hill in his wheelchair faster than we can walk down.* (verb)

Drop can mean to go down suddenly. *Salina rushed back to get her jacket because the temperature had dropped 20 degrees during the night.*

Land can mean to descend from the sky. *The plane had to land suddenly when a passenger became ill during the flight.*

Sink means to descend slowly or gradually. *Christy's chin sank onto her chest as she learned the disappointing news.*

Dive can mean to go down suddenly. *We saw the falcon dive at its prey.*

ANTONYMS: ascend, rise

Describe means to tell about someone or something. *In her report, Ramona described the natural beauty of the Grand Canyon.* (verb)

Portray can mean to describe. *In Uncle Tom's Cabin, Harriet Beecher Stowe portrayed life under slavery.*

Characterize means to describe the special qualities of someone or something. *Dachshunds are characterized by short legs and a long body.*

Represent can mean to describe, often in an untruthful way. *The man at the door represented himself as a fire inspector, but he left quickly when Mrs. Luna asked him for identification.*

Detail means to describe something fully, telling even the smallest facts. *Mr. Moravcik will detail for us what math work is due this week.*

Different means not alike. *Edgar and Edwin try hard to be different, because they don't want to be known as "the twins."* (adjective)

Various means different. It is used when there are many different things. *Every morning, Babur opens his family's shop and sets out the thirty baskets of various spices.*

Miscellaneous means of many sorts, not all the same. It may suggest no effort to choose. *My sister collects only clear marbles, but she keeps some miscellaneous ones to trade.*

Varied means of many sorts. It suggests that the differences are planned. *Good nutrition means eating varied wholesome foods, not just your favorites.*

Mixed means of many kinds combined together. *Connie thinks "Mixed Nuts" would be a good name for our comedy act.*

Assorted means mixed. *I always choose assorted jellybean flavors because I can never decide on just one flavor.*

ANTONYMS: alike, identical, same, similar

Disaster means something very bad that happens suddenly. *Disasters such as the 1989 San Francisco earthquake remind us of nature's awesome power.* (noun)

Catastrophe means a huge disaster with terribly destructive effects. *It will be years before the city recovers from the catastrophe of the hurricane.*

Tragedy can mean an event that causes great sadness. *The long war in Vietnam was a tragedy for millions of people.*

Shock can mean a sudden event that causes fear or grief. *The shock of waking up in a burning house caused Enrique to have nightmares for months.*

Discouraged means having lost courage, confidence, or enthusiasm. *Sharon became discouraged when she found that all the tapes she wanted were sold.* (adjective)

Downhearted means discouraged. *We were downhearted when our dog, Mugsy, didn't come home for the third night in a row.*

Dismayed means discouraged and afraid. *The candidate was dismayed when the polls showed her far behind.*

Down in the dumps is an idiom that means downhearted. *Ray has been down in the dumps since Dana broke up with him.*

ANTONYMS: encouraged, heartened

WATCH IT!

Various and **varied** look alike, but they have different meanings. Consider the sentence: "This restaurant offers a *varied* menu." This sentence emphasizes that the differences are planned. But the sentence "The leaves turn *various* colors in the fall" emphasizes the many different kinds of colors.

Dismiss can mean to get rid of a worker. *After ten years with the company, the bus driver was dismissed.* (verb)

Discharge can mean to dismiss a worker, usually for a good reason. *Maureen was afraid to tell her parents she'd been discharged from her job for being late too often.*

Fire can mean to dismiss a worker suddenly. This meaning is informal. *Late Friday afternoon, six people in the print shop were fired.*

Lay off means to dismiss a worker, often for a specific period of time. *Mrs. Turner was laid off from her job last month, but she hopes to be rehired soon.*

ANTONYMS: employ, hire

E e

Effect means something that happens because of something else. *One effect of the very cold weather was a great increase in the amount of heating fuel consumed.* (noun)

Result means an effect, especially a particular event. *As a result of the newspaper's support for her, Mrs. Estevez won the mayoral election.*

Outcome means an effect, especially one that happens at the end of many events. *The outcome of the trial is still in doubt.*

Consequence means an effect, especially one that has several causes or happens awhile after the cause. *As a consequence of walking in the woods wearing shorts, Mario got poison ivy on his legs.*

ANTONYM: cause

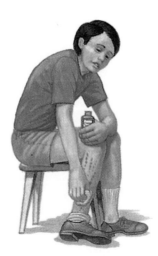

As a **consequence** of walking in the woods wearing shorts, Mario got poison ivy on his legs.

Elementary means first and simplest. *Rona is learning how to use tools in her elementary carpentry class.* (adjective)

Basic means first and necessary for everything that follows. *A basic part of judo is learning how to fall.*

Introductory means said or done first, to help with what follows. *Marlon's first day of work began with an introductory film about the company.*

Preliminary means said or done first. *Before the trial began, Judge Carver made preliminary remarks to the jury.*

ANTONYM: advanced

Embarrassed means uneasy, self-conscious, and insecure. *Midge was terribly embarrassed when Jeff told everyone at the party that she didn't want to be there.* (adjective)

Abashed means embarrassed, especially when the feeling comes suddenly. *Hillary was more abashed than hurt when she walked into the glass door.*

Fazed means confused and disturbed. It is an informal word, mostly used with "not." *Luisa is not fazed by having lost the election, and she will run again.*

Flustered means confused and nervous. *Boos from the fans got the pitcher flustered, and he walked the next two batters.*

Emergency means a sudden and dangerous situation that calls for quick action. *The Kims had an emergency last night—Myung had an asthma attack and had to go to the hospital.* (noun)

Crisis can mean a dangerous situation, especially the most dangerous part of a story or set of events. *The crisis in the movie came when all six of the explorers fell into the river.*

Predicament means a difficult or dangerous situation that is hard to get out of. *Trapped in a burning building, the hero is in a terrible predicament.*

Crunch and **pinch** can mean an emergency. These meanings are informal. *"We're in a severe financial crunch," said Mr. Charles, pacing the office floor, "and we have to pay the bills soon." "We've gotten out of similar pinches in the past," responded his partner. "Something will turn up before the end of the month."*

Encourage means to help someone gain courage or confidence. *The basketball coach's praise encouraged Rafael to try out for the team.* (verb)

Inspire means to fill someone with courage or confidence. *Mrs. Chernoff's success in night school inspired her husband to learn English there too.*

Cheer on means to encourage someone by yelling. *The scout troop cheered on their team in the tug-of-war.*

Root for means to cheer on. *"If I have to root for anybody," Lucy said, "I'm rooting for the guys who lost the last time."*

SEE **urge** for related words.

Escape means to get away or to get out. *Thanks to the smoke alarm, all the residents of the apartment escaped the fire. The canary escaped from its cage and has been flying around the house all afternoon.* (verb)

Elude means to escape in a clever way. *The rebels eluded government troops by dressing as wealthy tourists.*

Break out can mean to escape from being locked up, often by using force. *Taking several guards as hostages, six prisoners broke out of the state penitentiary.*

Fly the coop is an idiom that means to escape from being or feeling locked up. *"Gracious!" Mrs. Tingle exclaimed at the open cage door. "Our hamster appears to have flown the coop!"*

SEE **evade** for related words.

Especially means more than others or in a special way. *Luis likes to eat fruit, especially papaya. Mary Ann was especially glad to see Philip, since he had been away all summer.* (adverb)

Particularly means especially. *"I hate getting out of bed," Minh yawned, "particularly on dark, rainy days like this."*

Specifically means with attention to a single item or detail. *Isabel wants to be a nurse, specifically to help old people.*

Primarily means more than others or mainly. *Hilary's mother is primarily a children's doctor, but she sees grownups on occasion.*

Estimate means to form an opinion about the size, weight, amount, or value of something. *Evan estimates that he has about 125 marbles in the jar.* (verb)

Value means to estimate the worth of something in money. *The store values this baseball card at twenty dollars, but I got it at a show for sixteen.*

Evaluate means to judge the value or quality of something. *The coach will evaluate our skills before deciding who may join the wrestling team.*

Rate means to evaluate. *The Azteca is rated as one of the best restaurants in town.*

Evade means to get away from someone or something by trickery or cleverness. *By changing her name, her clothes, and her car, Ms. Craig managed to evade the private investigator.* (verb)

Dodge can mean to evade. It suggests twisting aside to get out of the way. *The quarterback dodged questions after the game by staying in the shower until the reporters left.*

Duck can mean to dodge. *The candidate ducked all requests for a debate, claiming to be too busy.*

Sidestep can mean to get away from something, as if by stepping out of the way. *Fabian managed to sidestep questions about his filthy jeans by going in the back door.*

SEE **escape** for related words.

Examine means to look at something carefully in order to find out about it. *The dentist will examine Sari's teeth for cavities.* (verb)

Scan can mean to look something over closely. *Jinella scanned the footprints with a magnifying glass.*

Study can mean to examine thoroughly. *Gregory studied the bus schedule again, wondering if his grandmother had missed a connection somewhere.*

Check can mean to look at something in order to see if it is all right. *Kay needs a ride tomorrow because her mom has to have their car's brakes checked.*

WATCH IT!

Some words can mean contradictory things. *Scan* can mean to look over closely. *The programmer will have to scan the computer printout line by line in order to figure out what has gone wrong.* Or *scan* can mean to look over quickly. *Toni scanned the morning headlines, hoping to find some good news.*

Expand means to become larger. *The United States expanded greatly with the Louisiana Purchase.* (verb)

Swell means to become larger by puffing up. *Nelson sprained his wrist, and it's swelling rapidly.*

Bulge means to swell out. *See the hamster's cheeks bulge with food.*

Mushroom means to become larger quickly. *The number of robberies in the neighborhood has mushroomed since the police foot patrol stopped.*

Snowball can mean to expand faster and faster. It suggests something out of control. *Shortages of food and snowballing popular discontent contributed to the breakup of the Soviet Union in 1991.*

Explain means to make something easier to understand by talking or writing about it. *This book explains the background of the war in Vietnam.* (verb)

Interpret means to explain the meaning of something. *Rob interprets the movie as a comedy, but Tara thinks it was serious.*

Clarify means to make something clearer and easier to understand. *Celia could not understand the diagram and asked the teacher to clarify it.*

Spell out means to give a careful, detailed, and easy-to-understand explanation. *Roger had trouble setting the VCR until Marissa spelled out the process, one step at a time.*

ANTONYMS: confuse, misinterpret

Explode means to break into bits suddenly with a loud noise. *The fuel tank exploded and destroyed the space shuttle.* (verb)

Burst can mean to explode. *The kitten was so startled when the balloon burst that she climbed up the curtains.*

Blast can mean to make something explode. *Many rocks had to be blasted to build this tunnel.*

Blow up means to explode. *Prick the potatoes with a fork so that they don't blow up in the microwave.*

Go off means to explode. *Uncle Ted lost a finger as a boy because a firecracker went off in his hand.*

HAVE YOU HEARD...?

You may have heard people say that someone has "shed light on the question." This means to provide information about a subject, especially a subject in doubt—as if shining a light into darkness. "My next witness," said Ms. Ortega, "can shed some light on the question of the defendant's whereabouts at that time."

F f

Fierce means ready and willing to fight. It suggests anger and desire to cause injury. *The Vikings were fierce warriors.* (adjective)

Ferocious means very fierce. It is used mostly about animals. *The grizzly bear became ferocious when she saw someone too close to her cubs.*

Savage means fierce, uncontrolled, and uncivilized. *Drawing his cutlass, the savage pirate demanded the ship's treasure.*

Vicious can mean fierce by nature, without reason. *The vicious little dog ran onto the sidewalk barking loudly.*

SEE **cruel** for related words.

Fight means to oppose someone or something with actions or words. *My grandfather fought in the Second World War. Our congresswoman is fighting the plan to dump chemicals outside town.* (verb)

Struggle means to fight with difficulty. *African Americans have long struggled against injustice and hatred.*

Battle means to fight for a long period of time. *To cross the bay, the swimmers battled the waves and tide.*

Combat means to fight something strongly. *The nurse explained to Joshua that shots are very important in combating disease.*

SEE **argue** for related words.

Formal means according to accepted ideas of public good manners. *The principal sent each graduate a formal letter of congratulations.* (adjective)

Courtly means having manners suitable for a royal court. *The peasant boy made such a courtly speech to the queen that she made him her page.*

Refined means extremely polite and in no way coarse or unpleasant. *Mr. Garcia is so very refined that he always stands up when a woman enters the room.*

Well-bred means taught good manners in childhood. *Charmayne got the job because she's smart and well-bred.*

SEE **polite** for related words.

ANTONYMS: casual, informal

G g

Generous means willing and eager to share. *Mr. Peterson's students like him because he is generous with his time and attention.* (adjective)

Charitable means generous to those in need. *Mr. and Mrs. Wu do a lot of charitable work at the hospital.*

Liberal means generous. It suggests giving freely and in large amounts. *All the Rodriguez kids get liberal weekly allowances.*

Lavish means extremely liberal. *Every year the whole family gets together for a lavish holiday dinner.*

ANTONYMS: miserly, stingy

H h

Hostile means being an enemy and fighting or ready to fight. *I don't like to play tennis with her because she gets hostile.* (adjective)

Quarrelsome means quick to quarrel. *When we complained about his junk-filled yard, the man next door became rude and quarrelsome.*

Aggressive means likely to attack and begin a fight. *At night, the used car lot is guarded by aggressive dogs who rush at the fence when anybody comes near.*

On bad terms is an idiom that means hostile. It suggests that fighting is very possible but not happening. *Uncle Jonas has been on bad terms with the family since he refused to let them sell the farm.*

SEE **argue** and **fight** for related words.

ANTONYMS: agreeable, friendly

I i

Idea means a mental picture or plan. *In the empty apartment, Pauline was forming an idea of where to put the furniture and all her plants.* (noun)

Notion means an idea. *"I'm not sure why," Ina said, "but I have a notion the new secretary won't stay long."*

Thought means an idea about something. *Reporters asked for Senator Lopez's thoughts on how to prevent more bank failures.*

Inspiration can mean a sudden, very good idea. *"I don't know what to do for the science fair," Jerry told his father, "but I'm hoping for an inspiration."*

Brainstorm means inspiration. *The advertising department has had a brainstorm: a new way of packaging!*

Concept means a general idea of something. *This drawing shows an architect's concept of the new office building.*

SEE **belief** and **opinion** for related words.

Imaginary means existing only in the imagination. *Dad had to apologize after he sat on my little brother's imaginary friend.* (adjective)

Unreal means imaginary. *The things that happen in dreams are unreal but interesting.*

Fictitious means made up. *Tarzan isn't a real person; he's purely fictitious.*

Fanciful can mean showing much imagination. *Ramona's fanciful illustrations are the best thing in our school paper.*

SEE **pretend** for related words.

ANTONYMS: actual, real

Imitate means to try to be, look, or sound like something or someone else. *Monica can imitate the calls of the birds in the forest near her home.* (verb)

Copy can mean to imitate. *After her sister's friends went home, Regina tried to copy their style of dancing.*

Impersonate can mean to imitate a person's voice, style, and appearance, pretending to be that person. *That actor can impersonate the President perfectly.*

Mimic means to make fun of someone or something by imitating. *Boys on the team often mimic the coach's high voice, but only when he's not around.*

Mock can mean to mimic. It implies ridicule or cruelty. *The clown stood behind the ringmaster, mocking his gestures.*

SEE **pretend** for related words.

Ramona's **fanciful** illustrations are the best thing in our school paper.

Intention means what a person has in mind to do or get by doing. *Automobile companies do research with the intention of increasing fuel efficiency.* (noun)

Purpose means a strong intention. It suggests choosing to act in particular ways. *"My purpose in letting the students run the school for a week," said Mrs. Peebles, "is to let them find out how much work it really takes."*

Goal can mean something for which a person works, usually with effort. *"We have a goal," Coach Bryant yelled, "and it is to win this game!"*

Point can mean a purpose. *"Right now the point is to clean up this mess, not to blame each other," Lori told her sister.*

Object can mean a purpose. *The object of this film is to alert people to the destruction of the rain forests.*

WORD STORY

Vital comes from the Latin word meaning "life." When something is truly vital, people call it "a matter of life and death."

L l

Language means the speech or writing of a group of people who understand each other. It includes vocabulary and grammar. *The airport announcer repeats all messages in several languages.* (noun)

Tongue can mean a language. It is used mostly in books. *The armies of Islam carried the Arabic tongue to many countries.*

Speech can mean spoken language. *Words often are common in speech before being accepted in writing.*

Dialect means a local form of a language. *Spanish is a language with a number of different dialects that are spoken in different countries or in different areas of the same country.*

Legal means permitted by law or according to law. *Calvin said he would do anything to help his older brother— so long as it was legal.* (adjective)

Lawful means legal. *Since Mr. Torres made no will, his only cousin is his lawful heir.*

Rightful means according to law. *A military government has imprisoned the rightful president.*

Legitimate means rightful. *Ms. Littledog's insurance company ruled that her claim was legitimate and paid her $2,000.*

N n

Necessary means needed. *Iron, coal, and limestone are necessary to make steel.* (adjective)

Essential means completely necessary. *The keyboard is an essential part of a computer.*

Vital can mean essential. *Lt. Privac returned from her mission with the vital supplies.*

Indispensable means too necessary to do without. *A dictionary and a thesaurus are indispensable tools for a writer.*

ANTONYM: unnecessary

New means recently made, become known, or come into existence. *Jorge's family is moving into a new house that was finished just last month.* (adjective)

Novel means new or of a new kind. *The judges of the kite contest said Colin's five-sided design was a novel idea.*

Original can mean novel. *The prime minister is seeking original approaches to solving the country's economic problems.*

Contemporary can mean modern. *Miles's grandparents plan to sell their antiques and buy contemporary furniture.*

ANTONYMS: ancient, antique, old

O o

Opinion means what someone thinks about something. Opinions may be supported by facts, but they can still be questioned. *Do you share Roger's opinion that Chinese food is the best food?* (noun)

View can mean a very personal opinion. *In Ms. Luchesi's view, Einstein had the wisest eyes she's ever seen.*

Judgment can mean an opinion based on carefully considering and deciding. *In Mrs. Delany's judgment, Tina is ready for music school.*

Conclusion can mean an opinion reached by reasonable thinking. *After passing the same buildings three times, the driver came to the conclusion that she was lost.*

SEE **belief** and **idea** for related words.

Opponent means a person on the opposite side in a game, argument, or fight. *Pablo is my favorite opponent, because he's so good at the game.* (noun)

Antagonist means an opponent, especially an unfriendly one. *Captain Corcoran's antagonist in the struggle for control of the starship was a creature from Planet Omicron.*

Rival means an opponent who wants the same things as another person. *Kelly and Iona are rivals for a single opening on the softball team.*

Opposition can mean a group of opponents, especially in politics. *Mr. Khodai led the opposition to the plan to cut social services.*

SEE **argue** and **fight** for related words.

ANTONYM: ally

Opposite means completely different from each other. *The ships are headed in opposite directions through the canal.* (adjective)

Contrary means opposite. *The Sedlacek sisters hold contrary opinions about which of them started the fight.*

Reverse means exactly opposite, especially in direction or position. *How fast can you say the alphabet in reverse order?*

Contradictory means saying something opposite to what was said before. *The candidate has made several contradictory statements about raising or not raising taxes.*

ANTONYMS: alike, same

Origin means the thing or place that something comes from. It often suggests the reasons for the new thing. *This huge traffic jam had its origin in one flat tire.* (noun)

Source means the person or place where something comes from. It often suggests a steady supply. *Rachel's new cat is a constant source of amusement.*

Root can mean a source or a cause. *The root of Lamar's interest in trains is that his grandfather was a railroad engineer.*

Derivation can mean an origin, especially of words. *The derivation of "Halloween" is two words meaning "holy evening."*

ANTONYMS: end, finish

Overwhelm means to overpower completely. *The U.S. basketball team overwhelmed its opponents.* (verb)

Flood can mean to overwhelm, as if by covering with water. *Shoppers flood the malls during the holiday season.*

Swamp can mean to overwhelm and make helpless, as if by filling with water. *Mr. Evans says that part of teaching is feeling swamped by paperwork.*

Drown can mean to overwhelm finally, as if by keeping under water. *The crowd roared its agreement, drowning a few scattered protests.*

P p

Participate means to be one of the people who do something, especially together. *Mr. Hurkel encouraged everyone to participate in the singing.* (verb)

Engage means to participate. It emphasizes the activity more than the group. *Scott and Sue, engaged in conversation, didn't notice that the bus was leaving.*

Cooperate means to work together, especially in order to make the work easier. *Officer Redwing told the crowd, "If everyone cooperates, we can all go home soon."*

Take part means to participate. *Everyone at the picnic took part in the tug-of-war at the end of the day.*

Get into the act is an idiom that means to participate. *Rennie and Miguel had almost settled their argument when Nora got into the act and made it worse.*

Everyone **took part** in the tug-of-war at the end of the day.

Permission means agreement that it is all right for someone to do something. *"Who gave you permission to keep your bikes in the basement?" the janitor asked sternly.* (noun)

Consent and **leave** mean permission. *"Do I have your consent to go on the field trip, Dad?" asked Mike. "The teacher says we need to get our parents' leave."*

Authorization can mean official permission. *Only a laboratory with special authorization can experiment with these deadly germs.*

Go-ahead is an informal word that means permission to begin or proceed. *Mr. Marcum gave our recycling program the go-ahead.*

Persuade means to make someone agree with you by giving reasons. *"What will it take to persuade you to give up one of those cookies?" asked Tasha with a smile.* (verb)

Convince means to make someone believe that something is true. *Irina convinced Jacob that it wasn't she who told his secret.*

Talk into means to persuade someone by speaking. *Latisha tried to talk her mother into letting her bleach her hair.*

Sell on means to convince someone of an idea as if you were selling it. *Vicky hopes to sell her parents on the idea of an after-school job at Burger Barn.*

SEE **urge** for related words.

Polite means having or showing good manners. *You may not like what Ebony says, but she's always polite in the way she says it.* (adjective)

Courteous means polite and thoughtful. *"How courteous!" Mrs. Taylor exclaimed, when the bus driver got out to help her lift the stroller.*

Gracious means courteous, pleasant, and kind. *Even with the nine unexpected guests, Ms. Nuñez remained calm and gracious.*

Tactful means able to say and do the things that are best suited to other people's feelings. *Richard wondered if there was a tactful way to tell John he should wash his hair more often.*

ANTONYMS: ill-mannered, impolite, rude

Pollute means to make something filthy and unfit for human use. It is used mostly about the environment. *Aunt Alma says the city air is so polluted that the birds should wear gas masks.* (verb)

Contaminate means to pollute, especially by contact with something unclean. *"Once a needle has been used, it's contaminated, so we use a new needle for every shot," the nurse explained.*

Soil means to make something dirty. *Before automobiles, dirt from thousands of horses soiled the streets of every city.*

Foul means to make something extremely dirty. *The Riveras' cabin was fouled by raccoons who spent the winter there.*

Prejudice means an unfair and usually bad opinion formed because of personal feeling. *George grew up with a prejudice against anyone from other countries.* (noun)

Intolerance means unwillingness to let other people think or act differently from you. *Abby is getting over her intolerance of people who disagree with her.*

Bias can mean a tendency to favor some people over others because of prejudice. *For decades, a bias toward immigrants from northwest Europe was shown in United States law.*

Discrimination can mean an unfair difference in the treatment of someone or some group, compared to others. *The newspaper says that discrimination against hiring older people is still common.*

Pretend means to make yourself seem to be doing something that you are not really doing. *Gerry knew that Grandpa was only pretending to be asleep.* (verb)

Make believe means to pretend to be someone or something else. *"OK, now we'll make believe I'm the movie star and you're the TV reporter," said Stephen.*

Suppose can mean to pretend something, in order to play with the idea. *"Suppose you owned a big ranch," Hank said to Joan. "Would you let wolves live there?"*

SEE **imaginary** and **imitate** for related words.

R r

Rotate means to turn around a central point. *The gas station has a tall rotating sign so that drivers will notice it.* (verb)

Revolve means to go in a curve around some place. *The moon revolves around the Earth once about every 27 ⅓ days.*

Turn means to go around like a wheel. *The turning fan blades sent a cool breeze through Jared's room.*

Circle means to move in a circle. *The wolves circle the elk, waiting for a sign of weakness.*

Wheel means to turn quickly and gracefully. *Bharati wheeled and shot the ball right into the basket.*

Rule means to have political power over others. *Mexico's ruling party, founded in 1929, has had two different names.* (verb)

Govern means to rule. It is often used about the work done by people with political power. *Many American cities are governed by a council and a city manager, without a mayor.*

Reign means to be a queen, king, or other monarch. *Queen Liliuokalani reigned in Hawaii from 1891 to 1893.*

Tyrannize means to use political power cruelly and unjustly. *A military government tyrannizes that unfortunate country.*

S s

Series means several things one after another. It suggests that the things are similar. *After a series of robberies, shopowners are nervous.* (noun)

Sequence can mean a series. It suggests a clear pattern, in which each thing leads to or causes the next. *For the spacecraft to have the right orbit, its engines must fire in the proper sequence.*

Succession means several things or people that happen in order. It emphasizes that they are all parts of one process in time. *A succession of great African American artists has enriched this country's culture.*

Round can mean a familiar series of events or activities. *Grandma's day is a round of visits with her friends in the neighborhood.*

Special means of a kind different from others. *Today is a special day for Ray because he starts competing in the national spelling bee.* (adjective)

Individual can mean of or for a single person or thing. *Every box of this pudding holds twelve individual servings in plastic containers.*

Particular can mean belonging to one person or thing. *There are many Spanish-speaking countries, each with its own particular culture.*

Specific can mean belonging to some particular thing or group of things, as a characteristic. *Each chemical element has a specific number of protons in the nucleus of an atom.*

ANTONYMS: common, general, ordinary

Substitute means to put someone or something in another's place, or to take another's place. *The recipe says you can substitute honey for sugar when making these cookies.* (verb)

Replace means to take another's place. *Han will replace Gil in left field next inning.*

Displace means to replace. *In the experiment, neon is pumped into the glass tube and displaces the oxygen that was in there originally.*

Relieve can mean to replace someone on duty. *The guards at the Tomb of the Unknown Soldier are relieved frequently.*

The guards at the Tomb of the Unknown Soldier are **relieved** frequently.

T t

Threatening means giving a warning that something bad is about to happen. *The little dog let out a threatening snarl and looked as fierce as it could.* (adjective)

Menacing means threatening. *The two boxers stared at each other in a menacing way.*

Sinister means threatening in a way that suggests wicked power. *The villain gave a sinister laugh.*

Ominous is a formal word that means threatening. It often suggests that the particular danger is not clear or not known. *An ominous quiet hung over the battlefield, and the soldiers grew tense and watchful.*

U u

Urge means to try to get someone to do something by saying to do it. *Highway police are urging people not to drive during this blizzard.* (verb)

Press can mean to urge by asking strongly several times. *Since it was so late, the Douglasses pressed us to stay for supper.*

Incite means to urge, especially by arousing emotion. *The army officer incited his men to attack the fort.*

Coax means to urge in gentle, pleasant ways. *"Just a little chicken soup,"* Mr. Greer coaxed his sick daughter.*

Egg on means to urge or encourage. *If Donna is too nervous to try out for cheerleading with us, we'll have to egg her on.*

SEE **encourage** and **persuade** for related words.

Usual means most commonly seen, found, or happening. *In Chicago some snow is usual in winter. We'll meet for lunch at the usual time.* (adjective)

Customary means usual or according to custom or habit. *For the Bedouins of Saudi Arabia, the customary way to travel is by camel.*

Traditional means customary because it has been handed down from generation to generation. *Acupuncture, which relieves pain by inserting needles into certain parts of the body, is a traditional Chinese medical treatment.*

WORD STORY

Egg on does not mean to urge someone by using eggs. This *egg* is another word, spelled the same way, that comes from an old Icelandic word meaning "edge." If you "egg someone on," it is as if you sharpen that person's will and put an edge on it.

Regular means usual and according to custom or rule. *Sarah was late and missed her regular bus.*

Habitual can mean usual or customary. *"All right, let's get to business!" is our teacher's habitual way of starting class.*

SEE **common** for related words.

ANTONYMS: peculiar, rare, unusual

V v

Very means more than usually. *A very tall boy like Hank may have trouble buying clothes.* (adverb)

Extremely means much more than usual. *It has been extremely hot this week.*

Exceedingly means extremely. *In the past, it was often exceedingly difficult for people with disabilities to enter buildings and vehicles.*

Highly means fully and actively. *Parents in this neighborhood are highly involved with school activities.*

W w

Weird means very strange and mysterious. *From deep in the forest, She Walks Away heard a weird croaking rumble.* (adjective)

Uncanny means weird. *In "The Hound of the Baskervilles," Sherlock Holmes pursues an uncanny giant dog.*

Creepy can mean weird and frightening. *The heroine of the movie has to save her friend from some creepy villains.*

Supernatural means beyond the power of science to explain. *Tales of supernatural beings and powers are found in every culture, all over the world.*

The heroine of the movie has to save her friend from some **creepy** villians.

The Word List in English and Spanish

A

abandon (13) — abandonar
abbreviation (3) — abreviatura
abduction (20) — secuestro
absolute value (CC) — valor absoluto
academic (8) — académico, académica
academy (8) — academia
acceptable (13) — aceptable
accidentally (23) — accidentalmente
accommodate (3) — acomodar
accomplishment (3) — logro
accountant (21) — contador, contadora
acid rain (CC) — lluvia ácida
acne (CC) — acné
adapt (22) — adaptarse
adolescent (35) — adolescente
adopt (22) — adoptar
advertise (16) — anunciar
advice (22) — consejo
advise (22) — aconsejar
advisory (19) — asesor, asesora
affect (22) — afectar
afghan (35) — manta
agrarian (CC) — agrario, agraria
aircraft (10) — avión; aviones
algebra (29) — álgebra
all-around (17) — general; comprensivo
alternate (26) — alterno, alterna
alternative (26) — alternativa
alumni (10) — ex alumnos
amasses (CC) — acumular
amino acids (CC) — aminoácidos
ancestor (13) — antepasado
ancestors (CC) — antepasados
anemia (CC) — anemia
animism (CC) — animismo
anniversary (19) — aniversario
anorexia nervosa (CC) — anorexia nerviosa
antibiotic (CC) — antibiótico
antibodies (CC) — anticuerpos
appendix (20) — apéndice
appreciate (29) — apreciar
apprehensive (CC) — temeroso, temerosa
apprentice (16) — aprendiz

approximately (3) — aproximadamente
Arabic (CC) — árabe
argued (5) — discutir (pasado)
arguing (5) — discutiendo
arid (CC) — árido, árida
arthritis (29) — artritis
artist (CC) — artista
asterisk (15) — asterisco
asteroid (15) — asteroide
asthma (35) — asma
astrology (15) — astrología
astronaut (15) — astronauta
astronomer (15) — astrónomo, astrónoma
astronomy (15) — astronomía
attendant (21) — asistente, asistenta
audible (28) — audible
audience (7) — audiencia
audio-visual (28) — audiovisual
audit (28) — revisar
audition (28) — audición
auditorium (28) — auditorio
authority (9) — autoridad
avocados (10) — aguacates
axes (CC) — ejes

B

bachelor (29) — soltero
bacteria (10, CC) — bacterias
bagel (25) — rosca de pan
ball-and-socket joint (CC) — articulación
bankrupt (20) — insolvente
batik (CC) — batik
bayou (25) — riachuelo
beige (1) — beige
believe (1) — creer
bicentennial (27) — bicentenario
biceps (27) — bíceps
bicycle (27) — bicicleta
bifocals (27) — lentes bifocales
bile (CC) — bilis
binoculars (14) — binoculares
biology (15, CC) — biología
biosphere (CC) — biosfera
biscuit (1) — bizcocho
biweekly (27) — bisemanal

bizarre | consideration

bizarre (CC)	raro, rara
bone (CC)	hueso
bookshelves (10)	estantes
boomerangs (CC)	bumerangs
boundaries (CC)	límites
boundary (23)	límite
bravery (19)	valentía
bribery (19)	soborno
briefcase (1)	portafolio
brochure (2)	folleto
bronze (CC)	bronce
brothers-in-law (10)	cuñados
Buddhism (CC)	budismo
bulimia (CC)	bulimia
bulletin (14)	anuncio, comunicado

C

calculator (31)	calculadora
Calcutta (CC)	Calcuta
calligraphy (CC)	caligrafía
calories (CC)	calorías
calves (10)	becerros
camaraderie (CC)	camaradería
Canberra (CC)	Canberra
candidate (23)	candidato, candidata
capital (4)	capital
capitol (4)	capitolio
caravans (CC)	caravanas
carbon monoxide (CC)	monóxido de carbono
cardigan (13)	chaqueta de punto
career (CC)	profesión
cargoes (10)	cargamentos
caribou (25)	caribú
cartilage (CC)	cartílago
cartographers (CC)	cartógrafos
caste (CC)	casta
category (7)	categoría
cell (CC)	célula
cell membrane (CC)	membrana celular
cemetery (14)	cementerio
centigram (CC)	centigramo
centiliter (CC)	centilitro
certainty (9)	certeza
challenges (CC)	desafíos
chandelier (2)	araña de luces
chauffeur (2)	chofer
chefs (10)	cocineros
chemist (21)	químico, química

chimpanzee (25)	chimpancé
Christianity (CC)	cristianidad
Christmas (23)	Navidad
cinnamon (3, CC)	canela
circumnavigate (CC)	circumnavegar
civilize (16)	civilizar
class (CC)	clase
classification (CC)	clasificación
cocoa (25)	cacao
coffee (25)	café
collide (32)	chocar
collision (32)	choque
cologne (35)	colonia
combination (8)	combinación
combine (8)	combinar
comedian (21)	comediante
commitment (3)	compromiso
committed (5)	comprometer *(pasado)*
committing (5)	comprometiendo
common name (CC)	nombre común
commotion (33)	alboroto
communication (31)	comunicación
community (CC)	comunidad
commute (CC)	viajar
companion (13)	compañero, compañera
compare (CC)	comparar
comparison (13)	comparación
competition (14)	competencia
competitive (31)	competitivo, competitiva
complement (4)	complementar
complementary (CC)	complementario
completely (1)	completamente
compliment (4)	cumplido; cumplimentar
compromise (16)	comprometer
concentrate (26)	concentrarse
concentration (26)	concentración
concession (33)	concesión
conditioner (CC)	acondicionador de pelo
condominium (31)	apartamento en condominio
conductor (20)	director
confetti (3)	confeti
congruent (CC)	congruente
conjecture (20)	conjetura
Connecticut (3)	Connecticut
conquistadors (CC)	conquistadores
conscious (35)	consciente
consideration (31)	consideración

consumer (CC)	consumidor, consumidora
consumers (CC)	consumidores
contemporary (CC)	contemporáneo
continent (14)	continente
continual (22)	incesante
continuous (22)	continuo
contour map (CC)	mapa topográfico
contradict (28)	contradecir
controlled (5)	controlar *(pasado)*
controlling (5)	controlando
coordinates (CC)	coordenadas
corruption (20)	corrupción
countries (11)	países
countries' (11)	de los países
country's (11)	del país
cowardice (16)	cobardía
crescent (35)	creciente
crime (8)	crimen
criminal (8)	criminal
cruelty (9)	crueldad
curiosity (32)	curiosidad
curious (32)	curioso, curiosa
custodian (21)	custodio
cytoplasm (CC)	citoplasma

D

data (10)	datos
dazzling (CC)	deslumbrante
decaffeinated (31)	descafeínado
decibel (CC)	decibel
decigram (CC)	decigramo
deciliter (CC)	decilitro
decimal system (CC)	sistema decimal
decision (1)	decisión
decline (34)	negarse
decomposition (CC)	descomposición
decrease (34)	disminución
deductive (20)	deductivo, deductiva
defendant (21)	acusado, acusada
definitely (23)	definitivamente
dehydrate (34)	deshidratarse
dejected (20)	desanimado, desanimada
dekagram (CC)	decagramo
dekaliter (CC)	decalitro
Delaware (7)	Delaware
deodorant (34, CC)	desodorante
depart (8)	partir

departure (8)	partida; salida
dependent (21)	dependiente
dermatologist (CC)	dermatólogo, dermatóloga
descent (22)	descenso
description (9)	descripción
despises (CC)	despreciar
detect (26)	detectar
detection (26)	detección
dialogue (CC)	diálogo
diamond (7)	diamante; diamante de béisbol
dictation (28)	dictado
dictator (28)	dictador
different (3)	diferente
digestion (CC)	digestión
dingo (CC)	dingo
directory (19)	directorio
disability (34)	incapacidad
disagreeable (31)	desagradable
disaster (15)	desastre
discontinue (34)	discontinuar
discourage (34)	desanimar
disgraceful (34)	vergonzoso, vergonzosa
disgusted (7)	repugnado, repugnada
disinterested (22)	desinteresado, desinteresada
dismissal (33)	salida
disrespect (34)	descortesía
disruptive (20)	perturbador, perturbadora
dissent (22)	disentir
distinguished (2)	distinguido, distinguida
distortion (CC)	distorsión
diversity (CC)	diversidad
DNA (CC)	ADN
doesn't (1)	no *(+ verb)*
dominant (CC)	dominante
double bar graph (CC)	gráfica de barra doble
dowry (CC)	dote
drowning (29)	ahogarse

E

Easter (23)	Pascua
ecologist (CC)	ecólogo, ecóloga
ecology (15)	ecología
economics (26)	economía
economy (26)	economía
ecosystem (CC)	ecosistema
effect (22)	efecto

efficient (CC)	eficiente
eighth (23)	octavo, octava
elastic (26)	elástico, elástica
elasticity (26)	elasticidad
electricity (9)	electricidad
elementary (7)	primario, primaria
elevations (CC)	elevaciones
embarrass (3)	avergonzar
emergency (31)	emergencia
emotion (33)	emoción
encourages (CC)	alentar
encyclopedia (31)	enciclopedia
end zone (17)	zona de anotación
enterprise (16)	empresa
environment (CC)	medio ambiente
episode (14)	episodio
errands (23)	mandados
eruption (20)	erupción
escape (29)	escape
escort (29)	acompañar
esophagus (CC)	esófago
especially (29)	especialmente
etymology (15)	etimología
eucalyptus (CC)	eucalipto
evaluate (26, CC)	evaluar
evaluation (26)	evaluación
everyone (17)	todos
exaggeration (31, CC)	exageración
examination (2)	examen
except (8)	excepto
exception (8)	excepción
executive (2)	ejecutivo, ejecutiva
exempt (2)	exento, exenta
exertion (2)	esfuerzo
exhausted (2)	exhausto, exhausta
exhibit (2)	exposición
exotic (2)	exótico, exótica
expand (32)	expandir
expansion (32)	expansión
experiment (1)	experimento
explain (32)	explicar
explanation (32)	explicación
explanatory (19)	explicativo, explicativa
explode (29)	explotar
exploratory (19)	exploratorio, exploratoria
extend (32)	extender
extends (CC)	extender
extension (32)	extensión
extinguish (2)	extinguir
extremely (23)	extremadamente

F

family (CC)	familia
farmer (CC)	granjero, granjera
fatigue (CC)	fatiga
favorite (7)	favorito, favorita
festivals (CC)	festivales
fibrin (CC)	fibrín
field trip (17)	excursión
fierce (1)	feroz
finally (14)	finalmente
fireworks (CC)	fuegos artificiales
fixed joint (CC)	articulación fija
floss (CC)	seda dental
flourishes (CC)	prosperar
fluorescent (35)	fluorescente
fluoride (CC)	fluoruro
food chain (CC)	cadena alimenticia
foreign (35)	extranjero, extranjera
formally (22)	formalmente
formerly (22)	anteriormente
fracture (CC)	fractura
free throw (17)	tiro libre
French fries (17)	papas fritas
frightened (23)	asustó; asustado, asustada
frostbite (CC)	congelación
fuel (CC)	combustible
fulfill (29)	cumplir
full-length (17)	de cuerpo entero
funeral (23)	funeral

G

gall bladder (CC)	vesícula biliar
Ganges River (CC)	río Ganges
gastric glands (CC)	glándulas gástricas
gauge (1)	indicador
generosity (32)	generosidad
generous (32)	generoso, generosa
genes (CC)	genes
genetic (CC)	genético, genética
genus (CC)	género
geology (15)	geología
gigantic (CC)	gigantesco, gigantesca
gliding joint (CC)	articulación
goddesses (CC)	diosas
gods (CC)	dioses
graffiti (3)	grafiti

gratitude (7)	gratitud
Great Barrier Reef (CC)	Gran Barrera de Arrecifes
great-uncles (10)	tíos abuelos
ground water (CC)	agua subterránea
guacamole (2)	guacamole
gunpowder (CC)	pólvora

H

habitat (CC)	hábitat
Halloween (3)	día de brujas
handcuffs (10)	esposas
harass (3)	hostigar
hazardous waste (CC)	desperdicio tóxico
headache (23)	dolor de cabeza
heard (4)	escuchar, oir (pasado)
heatstroke (CC)	insolación
heirloom (35)	herencia de familia
hemoglobin (CC)	hemoglobina
hemophilia (CC)	hemofilia
herd (4)	rebaño
heredity (CC)	herencia
hers (11)	de ella
Himalayas (CC)	Himalayas
Hinduism (CC)	hinduísmo
hinge joint (CC)	articulación
Hokkaido (CC)	Hokkaido
homemade (17)	hecho en casa
Honshu (CC)	Honshu
horizontal scale (CC)	escala horizontal
horrified (5)	horrorizar (pasado)
horrifying (5)	horrorizando
hospital (13)	hospital
host (CC)	huésped
hostel (4)	hostería
hostile (4)	hostil
hurricane (25)	huracán
hypothermia (CC)	hipotermia

I

iceberg (25)	témpano de hielo
icicles (29)	carámbanos
identical (13)	idéntico, idéntica
identity (23)	identidad
idle (4)	ocioso, ociosa
idol (4)	ídolo
illuminated manuscripts (CC)	manuscritos iluminados
imaginary (19)	imaginario, imaginaria
imitate (8)	imitar
imitation (8)	imitación

immobilize (33)	inmovilizar
immovable (33)	inamovible
immune system (CC)	sistema inmunológico
immunized (CC)	inmunizado, inmunizada
impartial (13)	imparcial
impending (20)	inminente
improvise (16)	improvisar
incumbent (21)	titular
induction (20)	inducción
infatuation (CC)	enamoramiento
ingredients (14)	ingredientes
initiate (26)	iniciar
initiative (26)	iniciativa
injection (20)	inyección
innate behavior (CC)	comportamiento innato
inspector (28)	inspector, inspectora
inspiration (8)	inspiración
inspire (8)	inspirar
instantaneously (31)	instantáneomente
instinct (CC)	instinto
integers (CC)	números enteros
intention (9)	intención
intercede (33)	interceder
interior (13)	interior
intermittent (33)	intermitente
interruption (3)	interrupción
intestines (CC)	intestinos
introduction (9)	presentación
invisible (CC)	invisible
invitation (14)	invitación
Islam (CC)	islam
isolated (CC)	aislado, aislada
its (11)	su
ivory (CC)	marfil

J

jaguar (25)	jaguar
joints (CC)	articulaciones
Judaism (CC)	judaismo
judge (CC)	juez
justice (16)	justicia
juvenile (7)	infantil

K

kangaroos (CC)	canguros
kilogram (CC)	kilogramo
kiloliter (CC)	kilolitro
kimonos (CC)	kimonos
kingdom (CC)	reino

koalas (CC)	koalas
kookaburra (CC)	kookaburra

L

laboratory (23)	laboratorio
lagoon (25)	laguna
language (2)	lenguaje
lantern (29)	linterna
learned behavior (CC)	comportamiento aprendido
legalize (16)	legalizar
leukemia (CC)	leucemia
lieutenant (1)	teniente
lifeguard (CC)	salvavidas
life jacket (CC)	chaqueta salvavidas
ligaments (CC)	ligamentos
lightning (CC)	relámpago
limelight (CC)	a vista del público
line of symmetry (CC)	línea de simetría
literal (14)	literal
liver (CC)	hígado
locomotion (33)	locomoción
logical (13)	lógico, lógica
long-term memory (CC)	memoria a largo plazo
loyalty (9)	lealtad
lucrative (CC)	lucrativo, lucrativa

M

machinery (19)	maquinaria
magnetic compass (CC)	brújula magnética
maintain (32)	mantener
maintenance (32)	mantenimiento
make-believe (17)	fingido, fingida
mandatory (19)	obligatorio
maneuver (1)	maniobrar
marsupials (CC)	marsupiales
material (14)	material
mathematics (7)	matemáticas
mayonnaise (3)	mayonesa
mean (CC)	medio, media
meanwhile (2)	mientras tanto
mechanical clock (CC)	reloj mecánico
media (10)	medios
median (CC)	mediana
medicine (14)	medicina
meiosis (CC)	meiosis, meyosis
memorize (16)	memorizar
memory (7, CC)	memoria
merchandise (16)	mercancía

merchants (CC)	comerciantes
metropolis (CC)	metrópolis
metropolitan (13)	metropolitano, metropolitana
Michigan (2)	Michigan
microbe (15)	microbio
microchip (15)	microchip
microcosm (15)	microcosmo
microfilm (15)	microfilm
microscope (15)	microscopio
microwave (15)	microonda
migratory (19)	migratorio, migratoria
milligram (CC)	miligramo
milliliter (CC)	mililitro
mimicked (5)	imitar (pasado)
mimicking (5)	imitando
miniature (7)	miniatura
missile (33)	cohete
misunderstanding (31)	malentendido
mitosis (CC)	mitosis
mobile (33)	móvil
mode (CC)	modo
monotheistic (CC)	monoteísta
monsoon (25)	monzón
monsoons (CC)	monzones
monsters (CC)	monstruos
moral (22)	moraleja
morale (22)	moral
mosquito (25)	zancudo
motivate (33)	motivar
motive (33)	motivo
motorist (21)	motorista
mottoes (10)	lemas
Mr. Murphy's (11)	del señor Murphy
multiple (13)	múltiple
murmur (13)	murmullo
Murphys (11)	los Murphy
musician (21)	músico, música
mythology (15)	mitología

N

navigators (CC)	navegantes
necessary (3)	necesario, necesaria
negative (CC)	negativo
New Delhi (CC)	Nueva Delhi
newsstand (17)	puesto de periódicos
niacin (CC)	niacina
niche (CC)	nicho
niece's (11)	de la sobrina

nieces (11)	sobrinas
nieces' (11)	de las sobrinas
nightmare (CC)	pesadilla
nomadic (CC)	nomádico, nomádica
nomads (CC)	nómadas
nonexistent (34)	inexistente
nonfiction (34)	no ficción
nonpoisonous (34)	no venenoso, no venenosa
nonprofit (34)	no lucrativo, no lucrativa
nonstop (34)	sin parar
nonviolent (34)	no violento, no violenta
normal (26)	normal
normality (26)	normalidad
notice (16)	notar
novelist (21)	novelista
nuclear (29)	nuclear
nucleus (CC)	núcleo
number line (CC)	línea de números
nursery (19)	guardería

O

oases (10)	oasis
oasis (CC)	oasis
objective (20)	objetivo
office (26)	oficina; despacho
official (26)	oficial
operate (8)	operar
operation (8)	operación
opinion (14)	opinión
opossum (25)	zarigüeya
opposite (CC)	opuesto
order (CC)	orden
ordinary (19)	común
organ (CC)	órgano
organize (16)	organizar
origin (CC)	origen
ours (11)	nuestro, nuestra
overwhelming (2)	abrumador, abrumadora

P

pancreas (CC)	páncreas
panicked (5)	aterrar (pasado)
panicking (5)	aterrando
paper (CC)	papel
parachute (2)	paracaídas
paradise (16)	paraíso
parallel (3)	paralelo, paralela
participant (21)	participante

participate (8)	participar
participation (8)	participación
particulates (CC)	partículas
pathogens (CC)	patógenos
pedestrian (21)	peatón
pellagra (CC)	pelagra
pendant (20)	pendiente
pendulum (20)	péndulo
penguin (2)	pingüino
pension plan (CC)	plan de pensión
pepper (CC)	pimienta
perfume (1)	perfume
permeable (CC)	permeable
permission (32)	permiso
permit (32)	permitir
personality (9)	personalidad
persuade (CC)	persuadir
pharmacist (21)	farmacéutico, farmacéutica
photographer (CC)	fotógrafo, fotógrafa
phylum (CC)	tipo
physical map (CC)	mapa físico
physician (21)	doctor, doctora
pilgrimage (CC)	peregrinaje
pivot joint (CC)	articulación de pivote
plague (CC)	plaga
plasma (CC)	plasma
platelets (CC)	plaquetas
pneumonia (35)	neumonía
politely (1)	cortésmente
political map (CC)	mapa político
politician (21)	político, política
pollution (CC)	contaminación
popular (14)	popular
populations (CC)	poblaciones
porcelain (CC)	porcelana
portfolios (10)	portafolios
Portuguese (CC)	portugueses
positive (CC)	positivo
positive reinforcement (CC)	refuerzo positivo
possession (3)	posesión
practically (23)	casi
precede (22)	preceder
predecessor (33)	predecesor, predecesora
prediction (28)	pronóstico
prejudice (16)	prejuicio
preserve (1)	preservar

pretzel (25)	bizcocho salado en forma de lazo
principal (4)	rector, rectora
principle (4)	principio
privilege (29)	privilegio
probably (14)	probablemente
procedure (33)	procedimiento
proceed (22)	proceder
procession (33)	procesión
producers (CC)	productores
productivity (20)	productividad
projection (CC)	proyección
projector (20)	proyector
pronounce (32)	pronunciar
pronunciation (32)	pronunciación
prosperity (CC)	prosperidad
protection (CC)	protección
proteins (CC)	proteínas
provision (28)	disposición; provisión
psychiatrist (35)	psiquiatra
psychology (35)	psicología
publicity (9)	publicidad
punctuation (31)	puntuación
pursuit (CC)	búsqueda

Q

quadrant (CC)	cuadrante
qualified (5)	calificar (pasado)
qualifying (5)	calificando
quantity (23)	cantidad

R

racquetball (17)	raquetbol
rain forest (17)	selva tropical
random sample (CC)	muestra aleatoria
range (CC)	rango, límites
raspberry (35)	frambuesa
ravioli (31)	ravioles
reality (9)	realidad
really (7)	realmente; verdaderamente
reasoning (CC)	razonamiento
receding (33)	que retrocede; retrocediendo
received (5)	recibir (pasado)
receiving (5)	recibiendo
receptor (CC)	receptor
recessive (CC)	recesivo, recesiva
recognition (9)	reconocimiento
recognize (7)	reconocer

recommend (3)	recomendar
recruit (1)	reclutar
rectangle (13)	rectángulo
red blood cells (CC)	células rojas
reduction (9)	rebaja
reflection (CC)	reflexión
reflex action (CC)	acción reflexiva; reflejos
regulate (8)	regular
regulation (8)	regulación
reign (35)	reino
reincarnation (CC)	reencarnación
remit (33)	remitir; remesar
remnants (29)	retales
repeat (32)	repetir
repetition (32)	repetición
reporter (CC)	reportero, reportera
represent (CC)	representar
researched (5)	investigar (pasado)
researching (5)	investigando
reservoir (25)	represa
resources (CC)	recursos
respectfully (22)	respetuosamente
respectively (22)	respectivamente
restaurant (7)	restaurante
restoration (26)	restauración
restore (26)	devolver
retention (9)	retención
reusable (31)	de uso repetido
revise (28)	revisar
rhinestone (35)	imitación de diamante
rhinoceros (35)	rinoceronte
rhyme (35)	rimar
rhythm (35)	ritmo
roommate (17)	compañero de cuarto, compañera de cuarto
rotation (CC)	rotación
runner-up (17)	en segundo lugar
rupture (20)	rotura

S

sacred (CC)	sagrado, sagrada
sacrifice (16)	sacrificar
safety (9)	seguridad
salesman's (11)	del vendedor
salesmen's (11)	de los vendedores
salivary glands (CC)	glándulas salivares
samurai (CC)	samurai
Sapporo (CC)	Sapporo
satisfactory (19)	satisfactorio, satisfactoria

Saturday (14)	sábado
scenery (19)	decorado; paisaje
scientific name (CC)	nombre científico
scientist (CC)	científico, científica
scrolls (CC)	pergaminos
scrubber (CC)	depurador
secondary (19)	secundario, secundaria
secretaries (11)	secretarios, secretarias
secretaries' (11)	de los secretarios, de las secretarias
secretary (7)	secretario, secretaria
secretary's (11)	del secretario, de la secretaria
security (9)	de seguridad
semicircle (27)	semicírculo
semicolon (27)	punto y coma
semifinals (27)	semifinales
semiprivate (27)	semipúblico
semisweet (27)	semidulce
senator (14)	senador, senadora
series (10)	serie
shear (4)	cortar con tijeras
sheer (4)	puro, pura
shepherd (35)	pastor
sherbet (29)	sorbete
shock (CC)	choque
short-term memory (CC)	memoria a corto plazo
sickle cell anemia (CC)	anemia producida por la ruptura de las células rojas
silt deposits (CC)	depósitos de sedimento
sincerely (23)	sinceramente
skeleton (CC)	esqueleto
skin (CC)	piel
sleigh (1)	trineo
smog (CC)	smog
snowmobile (17)	trineo motorizado
socialize (16)	socializar
society (9)	sociedad
sociology (15)	sociología
solitary (19)	solitario, solitaria
soloist (21)	solista
someone (17)	alguien
sometimes (17)	algunas veces
son-in-law (17)	yerno
soul (CC)	alma
souvenir (29)	recuerdo
space shuttle (CC)	transbordador espacial
Spaniards (CC)	españoles

specialist (21)	especialista
specialize (16)	especializar
specialty (9)	especialidad
species (CC)	especie
specific (23)	específico, específica
spectacle (28)	espectáculo
spectacular (28)	espectacular
spectator (28)	espectador, espectadora
spices (CC)	especias
splint (CC)	tablilla
sponsor (13)	patrocinador, patrocinadora
sprain (CC)	torcedura
stationary (4)	estacionario, estacionaria
stationery (4)	papel y sobres de carta
stomach (CC)	estómago
stomachache (17)	dolor de estómago
straight (4)	recto, recta
strait (4)	estrecho
submit (33)	someter
subscription (9)	subscripción
substitute (14)	substituto
suburban (13)	suburbano, suburbana
successfully (3)	con éxito
sulfur (13)	sulfuro
sunscreen (CC)	crema protectora del sol
superintendent (21)	superintendente
superior (13)	superior, superiora
supervise (16)	supervisar
supervision (28)	supervisión
supplementary (CC)	suplementario, suplementaria
supposedly (23)	supuestamente
surgeon (CC)	cirujano, cirujana
surgery (19)	cirugía
suspect (28)	sospechoso, sospechosa
suspended (20)	colgado, colgada
suspension bridges (CC)	puentes colgantes
symmetric (CC)	simétrico, simétrica
sympathize (16)	compadecerse

T

Tasmania (CC)	Tasmania
tea ceremony (CC)	ceremonia del té
teacher (CC)	maestro, maestra
technician (21)	técnico, técnica
technology (15)	tecnología
temporary (19)	provisional

terra cotta (CC)	terracota
tessellation (CC)	teselado
their (4)	su, sus
theirs (11)	suyo, suya
thematic map (CC)	mapa temático
there (4)	allí; ahí; allá
thirtieth (1)	trigésimo, trigésima
threatening (23)	amenazador, amenazadora
through (1)	por; a través de
tissue (CC)	tejido
Tokyo (CC)	Tokio
topographic map (CC)	mapa topográfico
tornado (25)	tornado
torpedoes (10)	torpedos
tournament (7)	torneo
toxin (CC)	toxina
tragedy (29)	tragedia
traits (CC)	rasgos, características
transformation (CC)	transformación
translation (CC)	traducción
transmitted (33)	transmitido, transmitida
traveled (5)	viajar (pasado)
traveling (5)	viajando
treasure (14)	tesoro
trial-and-error learning (CC)	aprendizaje por tanteo
triangle (27)	triángulo
trillion (27)	billón
triple (27)	triple
triplets (27)	trillizos, trillizas
tripod (27)	trípode
truly (29)	su seguro servidor, su segura servidora; realmente
tundra (25)	tundra
Turkish (CC)	turco
twenty-one (17)	veintiuno
typhoon (25)	tifón

U

umbrellas (CC)	sombrillas
unbelievable (31)	increíble
unbreakable (34)	irrompible
unconscious (34)	sin conocimiento
uncontrollable (31)	incontrolable
undefeated (34)	invicto, invicta
unemployment (34)	desempleo
unfortunately (34)	desafortunadamente

unicycle (27)	monociclo
unify (27)	unificar
uninterested (22)	apático, apática
unique (27)	único, única; sin igual
unison (27)	unísono
universal (27)	universal
university (9)	universidad
unpleasantness (31)	lo desagradable
untidiness (31)	desorden
untrustworthy (31)	desconfiado, desconfiada
urbanized (CC)	urbanizado, urbanizada
usually (7)	usualmente
usurps (CC)	usurpar

V

vaccine (CC)	vacuna
vacuum (7)	vacío
vehicle (35)	vehículo
verdict (28)	veredicto
vertical (13)	vertical
vertical scale (CC)	escala vertical
victim (7)	víctima
virus (CC)	virus
visible (28)	visible
vision (28)	visión
vitamin (14)	vitamina
vocabulary (19)	vocabulario
volcanic (CC)	volcánico, volcánica
volcano (25)	volcán

W

Washington (29)	Washington
weirdest (1)	el más raro, la más rara
wheelbarrow (CC)	carretilla
whirlpool (2)	remolino de agua
white blood cells (CC)	células blancas
witness's (11)	del testigo
witnesses (11)	testigos
witnesses' (11)	de los testigos
word processor (CC)	procesador de palabras
writer (CC)	escritor, escritora

Y

yogurt (25)	yogurt
yourselves (10)	ustedes mismos

Z

zeros (10)	ceros